THE McCLELLANDS
OF CLOUGHENRAMER

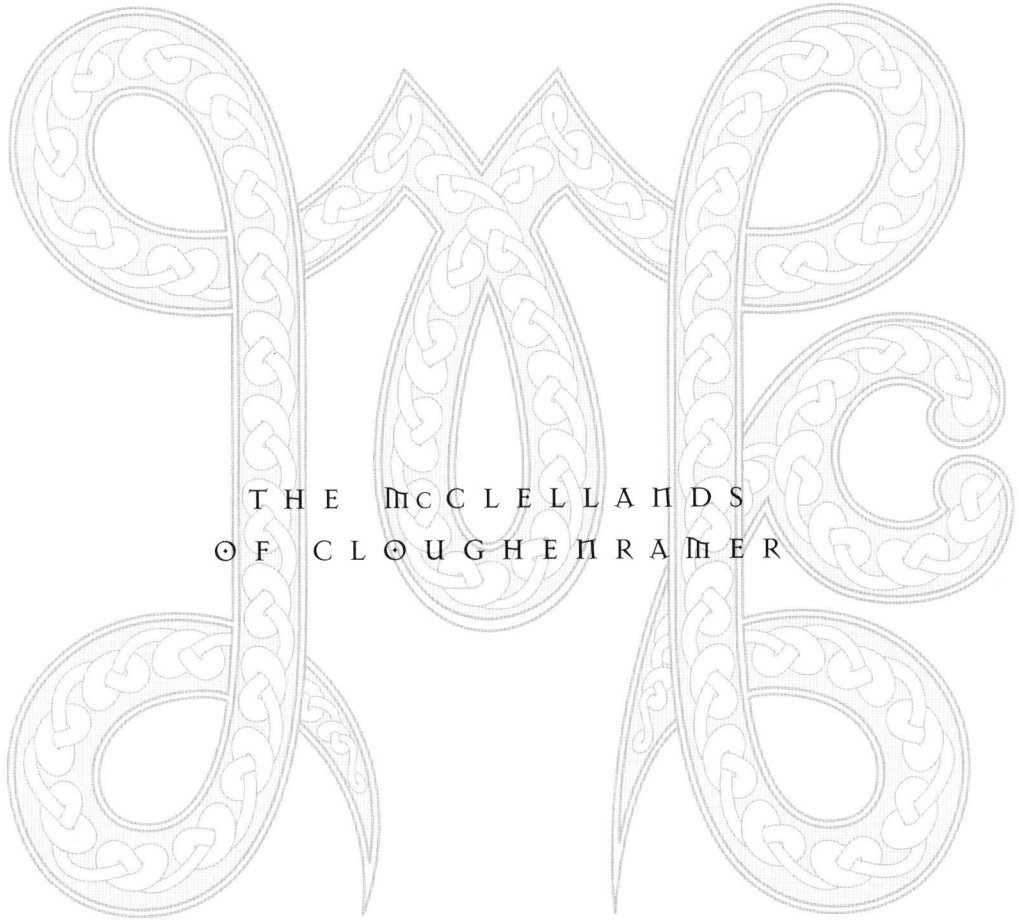

THE McCLELLANDS OF CLOUGHENRAMER

By Norman P. McClelland

Library of Congress Catalog Card Number:
2002092674

ISBN: 978-0-9721169-2-3

The McClellands Of Cloughenramer

Published by Norman P. McClelland
Phoenix, Arizona
U.S.A.

Printed in the U.S.A.

Last digit is print number: 10 9 8 7 6 5 4 3 2 1

CONTENTS

Norman & Barbara
McClelland

2007

Private Collection

THE McCLELLANDS OF CLOUGHENRAMER

FOREWORD

This book, The McClellands of Cloughenramer,
is a companion volume to
The Parkers of Ballykeel, *published in 2002,*
and The Wrights of Finnard, *published in 2004.*

I have long known and deeply respected our Irish past, but the detailed knowledge of who made up that ancestry and what gave meaning to their lives was missing.

This book provides tangible links to places, events, and, most importantly, people with whom I share not only a common lineage, but also, as I have discovered, an empathy and warm understanding.

I am grateful to the Ulster Historical Foundation, which did a search for information concerning the McClelland family in 1983.

My cousin Samuel David (Uel) Wright, long recognized as the family historian, has made available to me research material built up over our many years, and supplemented it with more recent research that brings our family story up to the present time. Additionally, Uel is co-author, and much of the credit is due to him for this publication.

I am also indebted to Peggy Magee, a professional genealogist from Prescott, Arizona; her attention to detail and discovery of documentation has been invaluable. With her help, we have rediscovered McClelland family members in America.

A political or economic history of Ireland will tell of a people who in the 17th century made the short but hazardous trip from Scotland to the northeastern part of Ireland. It will also record that many of those people in the 18th and 19th centuries made further and equally hazardous journeys to various parts of the New World, Australia, and South Africa, and yet others who chose to remain in Ireland. What is not recorded is who the people were, where they lived, and what gave purpose to their lives. That is the subject of this book.

As you turn these pages, you will find characteristics that occur again and again, such as the love for education, a dynamic individualism that always seeks what is best, and a sense of humor which tempers both.

But above all, you will find family units solidly underpinned by a religious faith that over the generations has aided each one as it faced the challenges of life and strove to fulfill its dreams and destiny.

Norman P. McClelland
Phoenix, Arizona
November 2006

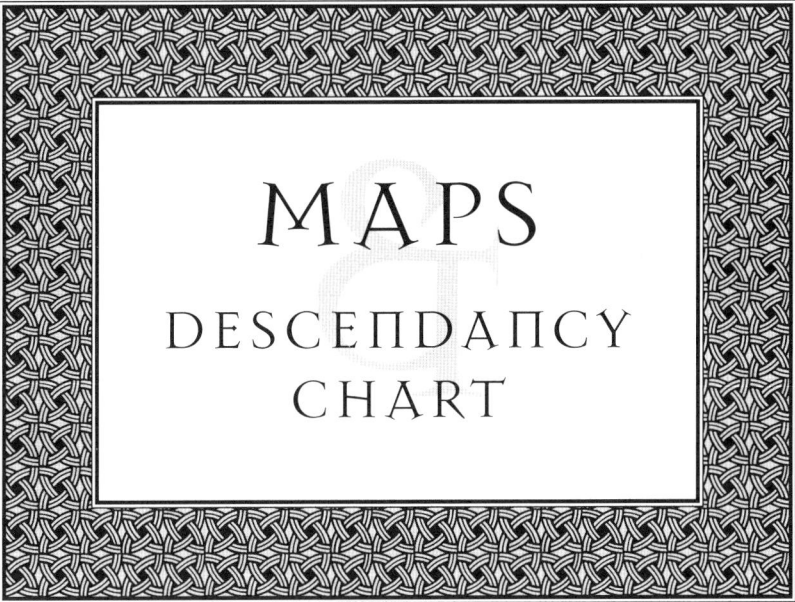

MAPS

DESCENDANCY CHART

John McClelland 1757-1832

Thomas McClelland 1801-1866
Susan Henning 1814-1864

Elmer Edward McClelland 1861-1933
Mary Salome Settlemyer 1863-1946

Matilda McClelland 1863-
Levi W. Hastings

Elmer Edward Ellsworth McClelland 1902-1963
Ruth La Verne Tuttle 1905-1977

Shirley Stella Turner 1914-

William Dennis McClelland 1932-
Ann Wainwright 1933-

Paul Joseph McClelland 1941-
Francine Jane Schaaf 1941-

Stephen Edward McClelland 1945-2006
Patricia Jacqueline Short 1947-

Damien Karl McClelland 1979-
Caitlin Jane McClelland 1982-

Janette Marie McClelland 1955-
Dean Newton

Mary Jordana McClelland 1961-
Lindsay Alfred Gertson 1962-

Mark Dennis McClelland 1963

Paul Daniel McClelland 1963-
Sherry Laverne Akers

Shawn Patrick McClelland 1966-
Janette Denise Woods

Susan Renee McClelland 1967-
Charles William Mize

Tyrel Dean Newton 1981-

Megan Marie Gertson 1983-
Chelsa Lynn Gertson 1988-

Megan Alysia McClelland 1989-
Kelsey Ann McClelland 1992-
Zackery Ryan McClelland 2000-

Eileen May Irwin 1919-2002
John Cochrane 1911-1995

David Wiley Irwin 1957-
Catherine Lindsay Swinscoe

John Dunlop Irwin 1957-

Kenneth John Cochrane 1948-
Neisha Merydeth Alford 1951-

Hazel Margaretta Cochrane 1951-
John Copeland

Harold Robert Cochrane 1951-
Robyn Lees 1949-

Johanne Elizabeth Cochrane 196

Matthew David Irwin 1990-
Benjamin Peter Irwin 1993-
Jonathan Robert Irwin 1993

Renee Marie Cochrane 1980-
Ben Michael Cochrane 1982-
Matthew Cameron Cochrane 1984-

Johanna Nicola Copeland 1981-
Niall Samuel John Copeland 1985-

Maya Lees 1976-

Nari Lees 1978-
Leigh Harris

Marlu Harris 2001-
Sen Harris 2005-

N

Lough Neagh

Belfast Lough

Bangor

Holywood

LOWER CASTLEREAGH

Belfast

Newtownards

ARDS

Comber

Greyabbey

Lisburn

Carryduff

UPPER CASTLEREAGH

Kircubbin

LOWER IVEAGH

Hillsborough

Saintfield

Porta Vogie

Lurgan

Dromore

Strangford Lough

Crossgar

Gilford

Ballynahinch

Killyleagh

Portaferry

KINELARTY

Banbridge

UPPER IVEAGH

Downpatrick

Strangford

LECALE

Ballyroney

Castlewellan

Dundrum

Ardglas

Rathfriland

NEWRY

Newcastle

Finnard

Dundrum Bay

Newry

Drumgath

MOURNE

Warrenpoint

Annalong

Kilkeel

COUNTY DOWN

McClelland Ancestral Home

County Boundary

Parish Boundary

Large City

Small City

Road

0   8   15 KM

0   4   8 Miles   15 Miles

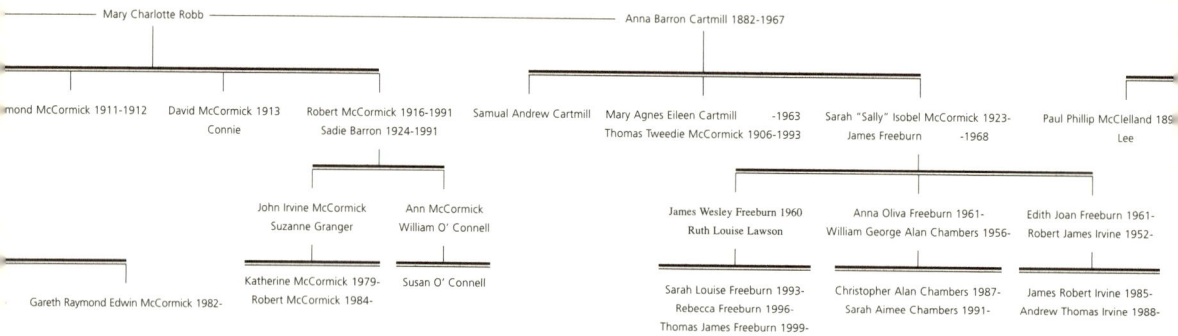

Mary Charlotte Robb — Anna Barron Cartmill 1882-1967

mond McCormick 1911-1912 | David McCormick 1913 Connie | Robert McCormick 1916-1991 Sadie Barron 1924-1991 | Samual Andrew Cartmill | Mary Agnes Eileen Cartmill -1963 Thomas Tweedie McCormick 1906-1993 | Sarah "Sally" Isobel McCormick 1923- -1968 James Freeburn | Paul Phillip McClelland 189 Lee

John Irvine McCormick Suzanne Granger | Ann McCormick William O' Connell | James Wesley Freeburn 1960 Ruth Louise Lawson | Anna Oliva Freeburn 1961- William George Alan Chambers 1956- | Edith Joan Freeburn 1961- Robert James Irvine 1952-

Gareth Raymond Edwin McCormick 1982- | Katherine McCormick 1979- Robert McCormick 1984- | Susan O' Connell | Sarah Louise Freeburn 1993- Rebecca Freeburn 1996- Thomas James Freeburn 1999- | Christopher Alan Chambers 1987- Sarah Aimee Chambers 1991- | James Robert Irvine 1985- Andrew Thomas Irvine 1988-

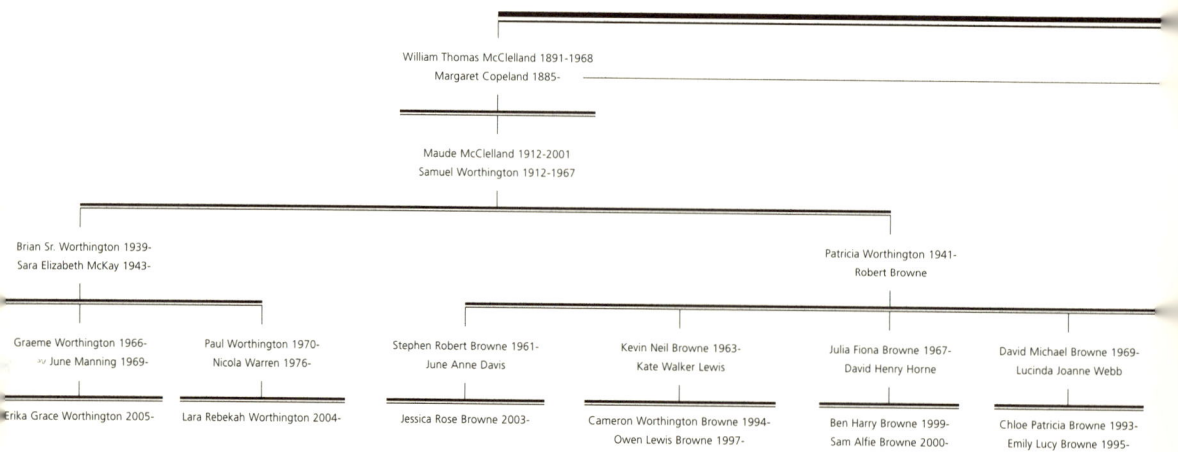

William Thomas McClelland 1891-1968
Margaret Copeland 1885-

Maude McClelland 1912-2001
Samuel Worthington 1912-1967

Brian Sr. Worthington 1939-
Sara Elizabeth McKay 1943-

Patricia Worthington 1941-
Robert Browne

Graeme Worthington 1966- June Manning 1969- | Paul Worthington 1970- Nicola Warren 1976- | Stephen Robert Browne 1961- June Anne Davis | Kevin Neil Browne 1963- Kate Walker Lewis | Julia Fiona Browne 1967- David Henry Horne | David Michael Browne 1969- Lucinda Joanne Webb

Erika Grace Worthington 2005- | Lara Rebekah Worthington 2004- | Jessica Rose Browne 2003- | Cameron Worthington Browne 1994- Owen Lewis Browne 1997- | Ben Harry Browne 1999- Sam Alfie Browne 2000- | Chloe Patricia Browne 1993- Emily Lucy Browne 1995-

Anna Lucinda Tweedie 1870-1906
John Alexander McCormick 1902-1944

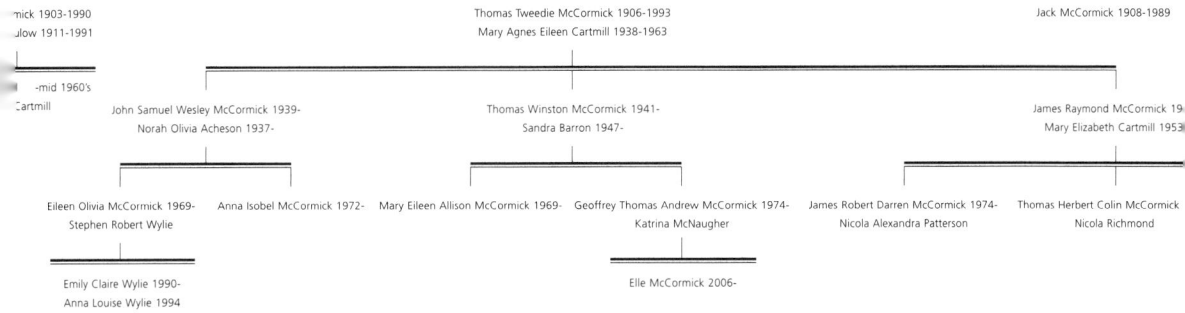

...mick 1903-1990
...ulow 1911-1991

Thomas Tweedie McCormick 1906-1993
Mary Agnes Eileen Cartmill 1938-1963

Jack McCormick 1908-1989

...-mid 1960's
...Cartmill

John Samuel Wesley McCormick 1939-
Norah Olivia Acheson 1937-

Thomas Winston McCormick 1941-
Sandra Barron 1947-

James Raymond McCormick 19...
Mary Elizabeth Cartmill 1953...

Eileen Olivia McCormick 1969-
Stephen Robert Wylie

Anna Isobel McCormick 1972-

Mary Eileen Allison McCormick 1969-

Geoffrey Thomas Andrew McCormick 1974-
Katrina McNaugher

James Robert Darren McCormick 1974-
Nicola Alexandra Patterson

Thomas Herbert Colin McCormick
Nicola Richmond

Emily Claire Wylie 1990-
Anna Louise Wylie 1994

Elle McCormick 2006-

(continued)

Sarah Maud McClelland 1883-1927
Albert George Hawthorn 1880-1960

William Mc Clelland 1885-1886

William Robert Hawthorn 1907-1979
Molly Agnew 1944- 2004

Dora Lucinda Hawthorn 1913-1954

Maud Elizabeth Hawthorn 1919-
Robert Climie Vallance 1922-

...55-
...60-

Daphne Florence Wright 1959-
Ian McCulla 1960-

Robin Hawthorn 1942-

Maurine Jane Hawthorn 1944-
Jeffrey Louis Jay

Anita Frances Vallance 1955-
Gary Gibson

Pauline Mary Vallance 1958-
Nick McElhill

...
...

Amy Louise McCulla 1987-
David McCulla 1989-

David Dalyrimple Jay 1975-
Lucy Miranda Jay 1978-

Alexander James Gibson 1993-

Breandan Vallance McElhill 1991-
Niamh Hawthorn McElhill 1991-

...34-

Brian Jr. Worthington 1965-
Susanne Violet Jordan ...

Lois Susanne Worthington 1998-
Rhys Henry Worthington 2003-

N

McClelland
Ancestral Home

Tormore Villa

Rockvale School

Townland of
Cloughenramer

Newry City

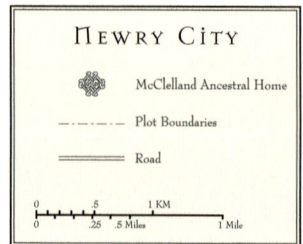

Newry City

McClelland Ancestral Home

Plot Boundaries

Road

McCLELLAND FAMILY DESCENDANCY

Margaret Peggy McClelland 1835-1872
Thomas Tweedie 1832-1907

William John Tweedie 1868-1938
Anne Elizabeth Hooke 1871-1929

Margaret Lucy Tweedy 1900-1982
William Joseph McWilliams 1894-1967

Annie Tweedie 1901-1977
Joseph Enos Dunlop 1899-1990

Margaret Annie Dunlop 1933-
William Henry Harry McGaffin 1922-

William Tweedie Dunlop 1934-2004
Joan Harriet Hood 1934-

John Dunlop 1939-
Edna Rosemary Willis

Hugh Richard Dunlop 1940-
Linda

Anne Dunlop
Ruth Dunlop

Gary Dunlop McGaffin 1960-
Anne Elizabeth Henning 1955-

Ivor Bradford McGaffin 1962-

Alan Henry McGaffin 1966-
Ann Jobson 1966-

Karen Patricia Dunlop 1967-
Allan Wilson

Keith Willis Dunlop 1968-
Jennifer Lesley McCullough

Shelly Margaret Claire McGaffin 1984-
Neal William McGaffin 1986-
Joanne McGaffin 1991-

Jennifer ruth Wilson 1998-
Euan James Wilson 2002-

Kristen Emily Dunlop 2000-
Romy Hannah Dunlop 2002-

William McClella
Sarah Donnell

Mary Minnie McClelland 1881-1960
Robert Samuel Wright 1869-1956   (continued)

Samuel Joseph Wright 1920-1996
Mary Elizabeth Molly Campbell 1926-1983   (continued)

David Wright 1925-1995
Mary Elizabeth (Elsie) Glenny 1927

Clive Samuel Wright 1954-
Janet Price Baldwin 1955-

Jane Elizabeth Wright 1962-
David Searle 1957-

Emma Margaret Wright 1963-
John Macleod 1963-

Margaret Mary Wright 1950-
Rahmatool "Robert" Somauroo 1945-

Pauline Elizabeth Wright 1954-
Mohammad Yousuf Jeetoo 1952-

Brenda N
William P

Sheila Wright 1985-1985
Michael Edward Wright 1987-
Andrew Donald Wright 1988-
Philip James Wright 1996-

Lydia Catherine Searle 1988-
Emily Louise Searle 1992-

Rebecca Mary Macleod 1992-
Callum Samuel Macleod 1994-

Kahlil David Somauroo 1980-
Adam Hossen Somauroo 1982-

Rebecca Elizabeth Jeetoo 1991

Gary
Helen Ma

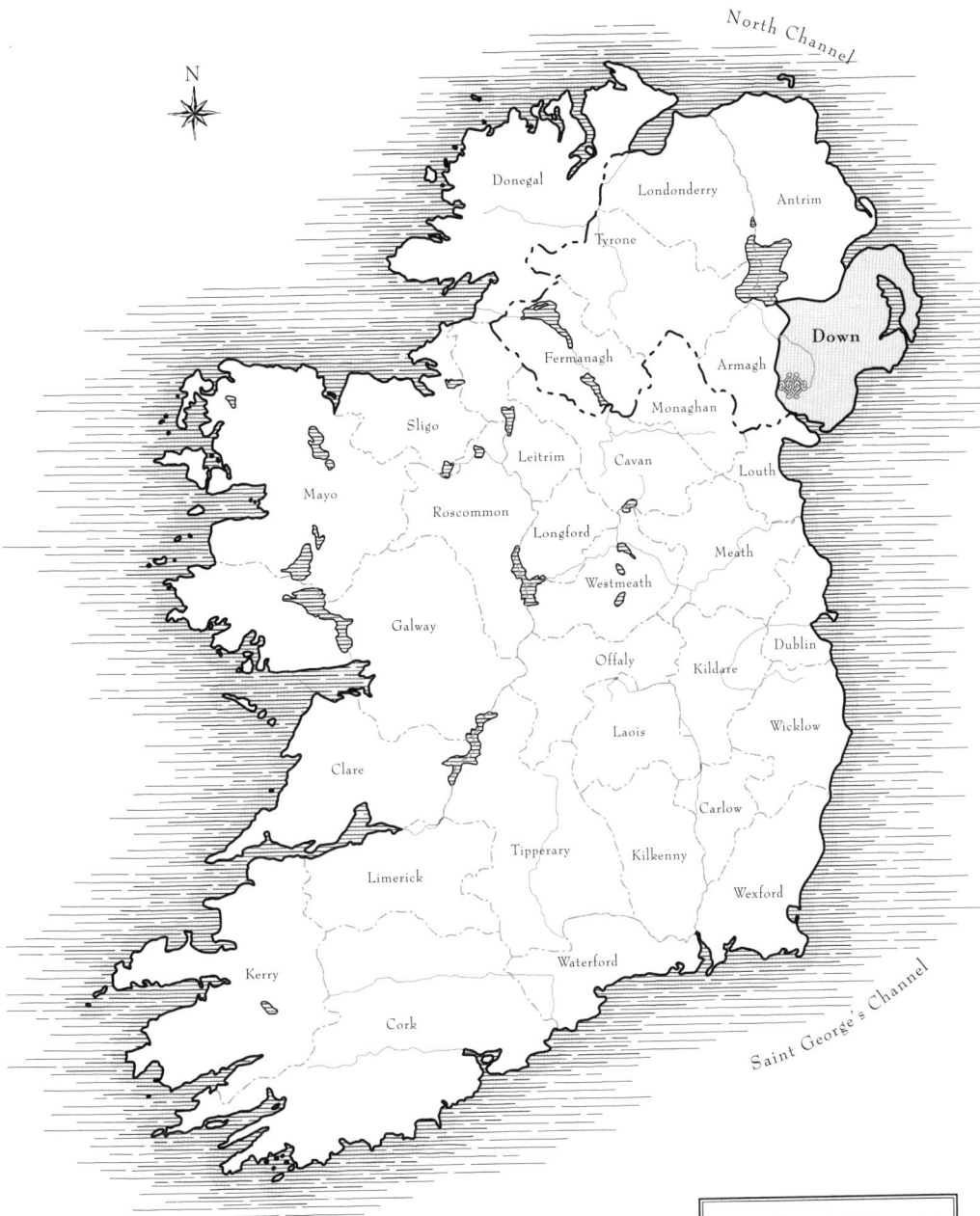

N

North Channel

Donegal
Londonderry
Antrim
Tyrone
Down
Fermanagh
Armagh
Monaghan
Sligo
Leitrim
Cavan
Louth
Mayo
Roscommon
Longford
Meath
Westmeath
Galway
Offaly
Kildare
Dublin
Laois
Wicklow
Clare
Carlow
Tipperary
Kilkenny
Limerick
Wexford
Kerry
Waterford
Cork

Saint George's Channel

IRELAND

McClelland Ancestral Home

------- International Boundary

---·--- County Boundary

0   25   50 KM
0   25   25 50 KM   50 Miles

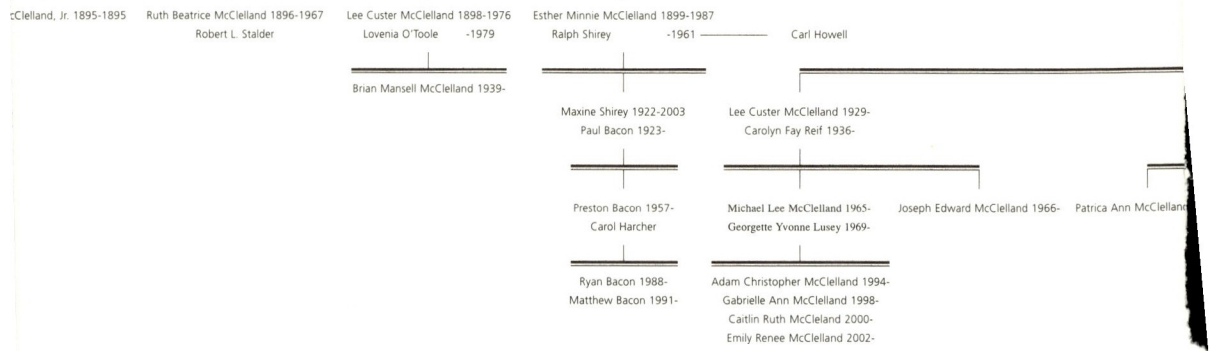

:Clelland, Jr. 1895-1895   Ruth Beatrice McClelland 1896-1967   Lee Custer McClelland 1898-1976   Esther Minnie McClelland 1899-1987
Robert L. Stalder   Lovenia O'Toole   -1979   Ralph Shirey   -1961   ————   Carl Howell

Brian Mansell McClelland 1939-

Maxine Shirey 1922-2003   Lee Custer McClelland 1929-
Paul Bacon 1923-   Carolyn Fay Reif 1936-

Preston Bacon 1957-   Michael Lee McClelland 1965-   Joseph Edward McClelland 1966-   Patrica Ann McClelland
Carol Harcher   Georgette Yvonne Lusey 1969-

Ryan Bacon 1988-   Adam Christopher McClelland 1994-
Matthew Bacon 1991-   Gabrielle Ann McClelland 1998-
Caitlin Ruth McCleland 2000-
Emily Renee McClelland 2002-

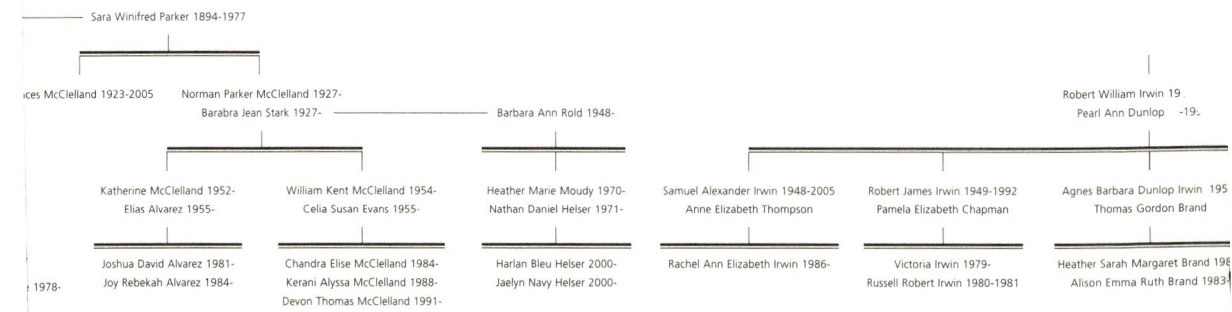

Sara Winifred Parker 1894-1977

:ces McClelland 1923-2005   Norman Parker McClelland 1927-   Robert William Irwin 19
Barabra Jean Stark 1927-   ————   Barbara Ann Rold 1948-   Pearl Ann Dunlop   -19:

Katherine McClelland 1952-   William Kent McClelland 1954-   Heather Marie Moudy 1970-   Samuel Alexander Irwin 1948-2005   Robert James Irwin 1949-1992   Agnes Barbara Dunlop Irwin 195
Elias Alvarez 1955-   Celia Susan Evans 1955-   Nathan Daniel Helser 1971-   Anne Elizabeth Thompson   Pamela Elizabeth Chapman   Thomas Gordon Brand

Joshua David Alvarez 1981-   Chandra Elise McClelland 1984-   Harlan Bleu Helser 2000-   Rachel Ann Elizabeth Irwin 1986-   Victoria Irwin 1979-   Heather Sarah Margaret Brand 198
1978-   Joy Rebekah Alvarez 1984-   Kerani Alyssa McClelland 1988-   Jaelyn Navy Helser 2000-   Russell Robert Irwin 1980-1981   Alison Emma Ruth Brand 1983-
Devon Thomas McClelland 1991-

Lucy McClelland 1879-1923
Robert Hawthorn 1876-1928

1907-1980   Sarah Roberta Wright 1909-1964   Mary Lucinda (Mollie) Wright 1911-2000
-1989   James Alexander Adams   -1975

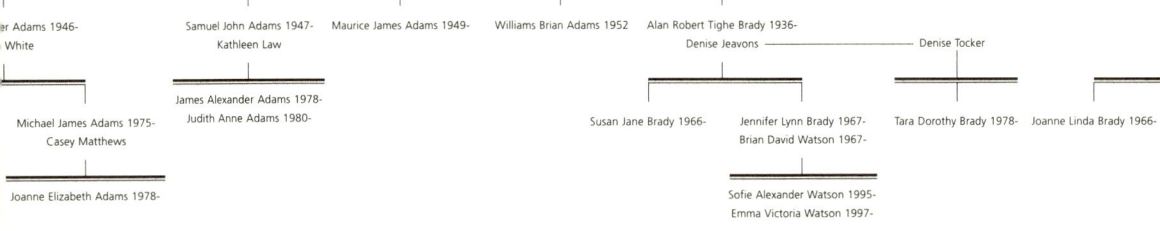

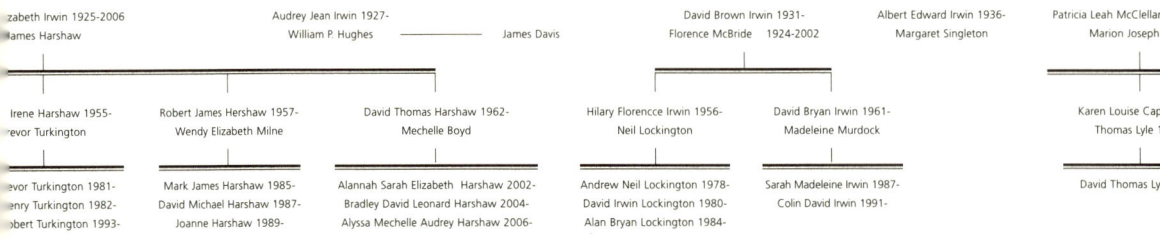

er Adams 1946-   Samuel John Adams 1947-   Maurice James Adams 1949-   Williams Brian Adams 1952   Alan Robert Tighe Brady 1936-
White   Kathleen Law   Denise Jeavons ——————— Denise Tocker

Michael James Adams 1975-   James Alexander Adams 1978-   Susan Jane Brady 1966-   Jennifer Lynn Brady 1967-   Tara Dorothy Brady 1978-   Joanne Linda Brady 1966-
Casey Matthews   Judith Anne Adams 1980-   Brian David Watson 1967-

Joanne Elizabeth Adams 1978-   Sofie Alexander Watson 1995-
                                                                               Emma Victoria Watson 1997-

izabeth Irwin 1925-2006   Audrey Jean Irwin 1927-   David Brown Irwin 1931-   Albert Edward Irwin 1936-   Patricia Leah McClelland
ames Harshaw   William P. Hughes ——————— James Davis   Florence McBride   1924-2002   Margaret Singleton   Marion Joseph C

Irene Harshaw 1955-   Robert James Hershaw 1957-   David Thomas Harshaw 1962-   Hilary Florencce Irwin 1956-   David Bryan Irwin 1961-   Karen Louise Caple
evor Turkington   Wendy Elizabeth Milne   Mechelle Boyd   Neil Lockington   Madeleine Murdock   Thomas Lyle 19

evor Turkington 1981-   Mark James Harshaw 1985-   Alannah Sarah Elizabeth Harshaw 2002-   Andrew Neil Lockington 1978-   Sarah Madeleine Irwin 1987-   David Thomas Lyle
enry Turkington 1982-   David Michael Harshaw 1987-   Bradley David Leonard Harshaw 2004-   David Irwin Lockington 1980-   Colin David Irwin 1991-
obert Turkington 1993-   Joanne Harshaw 1989-   Alyssa Mechelle Audrey Harshaw 2006-   Alan Bryan Lockington 1984-

William McClelland 1839-1909
Sarah Donnelly 1845-1885

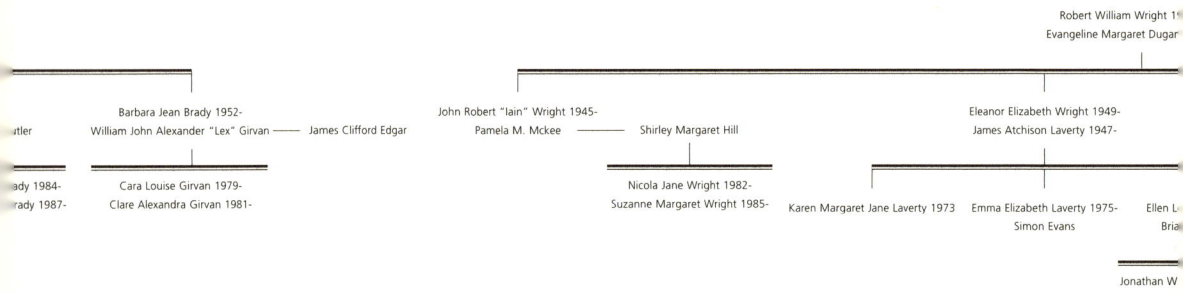

Robert William Wright 1█
Evangeline Margaret Dugar

...tler

Barbara Jean Brady 1952-
William John Alexander "Lex" Girvan ———— James Clifford Edgar

John Robert "Iain" Wright 1945-
Pamela M. Mckee ———— Shirley Margaret Hill

Eleanor Elizabeth Wright 1949-
James Atchison Laverty 1947-

...ady 1984-
...rady 1987-

Cara Louise Girvan 1979-
Clare Alexandra Girvan 1981-

Nicola Jane Wright 1982-
Suzanne Margaret Wright 1985-

Karen Margaret Jane Laverty 1973

Emma Elizabeth Laverty 1975-
Simon Evans

Ellen L█
Bria█

Jonathan W

George McClelland 1846-1927
Adeline L. Johnson 1856-1931

Alice McClelland 1883-1969
Eugene J. Johnson 1881-

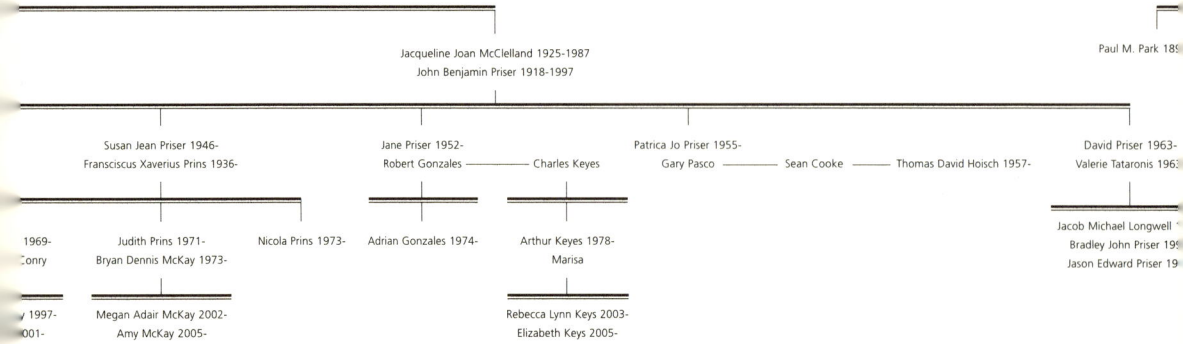

Jacqueline Joan McClelland 1925-1987
John Benjamin Priser 1918-1997

Paul M. Park 189█

Susan Jean Priser 1946-
Fransciscus Xaverius Prins 1936-

Jane Priser 1952-
Robert Gonzales ———— Charles Keyes

Patrica Jo Priser 1955-
Gary Pasco ———— Sean Cooke ———— Thomas David Hoisch 1957-

David Priser 1963-
Valerie Tataronis 1963

...1969-
...onry

Judith Prins 1971-
Bryan Dennis McKay 1973-

Nicola Prins 1973-

Adrian Gonzales 1974-

Arthur Keyes 1978-
Marisa

Jacob Michael Longwell
Bradley John Priser 199█
Jason Edward Priser 19█

...y 1997-
...001-

Megan Adair McKay 2002-
Amy McKay 2005-

Rebecca Lynn Keyes 2003-
Elizabeth Keyes 2005-

Samuel Joseph Wright 1920-1996
Mary Elizabeth Molly Campbell 1926-1983

Samuel David "Uel" Wright 1952-
Ellen June Groves 1951-

Helen Anne Wright 1949-
Gordon McConville 1951-

Roberta Mary Wright 1951-

Joanne Wright 1980-
Sarah Ellen Margaret Wright 1982-

81-

Alistair Gordon McConville 1975-
Joanne Griffiths

Carys Elizabeth McConville 1976-
Ben Thompson

Andrew Samuel Walter McConville 1980-
Stephanie Ruth Dyke 1981-

Claire Alexandra McConville 1983-
Nick John Widdows

ry 2006-

Louisa Kate "lulu" McConville 1998-
Ewan Patrick McConville 2002-

Rosie Grace Thompson 2003-
Alice Elizabeth Thompson 2005-

Alex McClelland 1848-1912
Mary Virginia Koplin 1851-1936

Lucy McClelland 1850-1872

Matilda McClelland 1852-1929

Esther McClelland 1855-1866

David McClelland 1858-1887

Mary Eva McClelland 1874-1946
George H. Park 1872-1947

Margaret K. McClelland 1877-1902

Ellie Grace McClelland 1879-1949

Margaret Park 1898-1959
Christian Schultz 1872-1934

Virginia Park 1906-1997
Marion Swager 1906-1989

George Park Schultz
Althea L. Leonhart

CHAPTER KEY

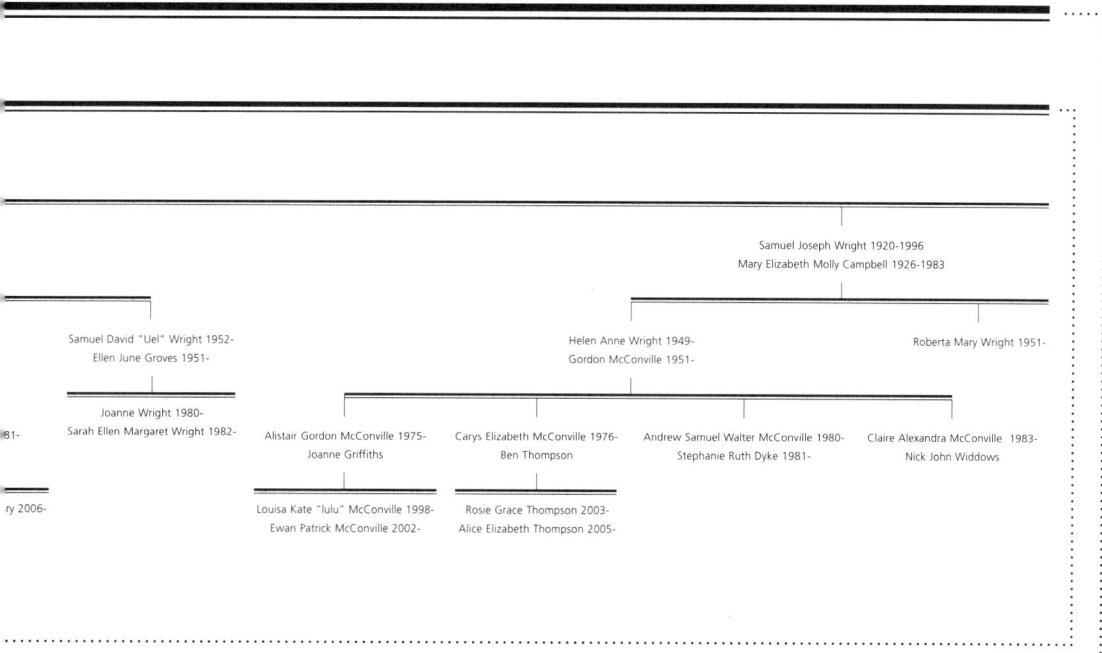

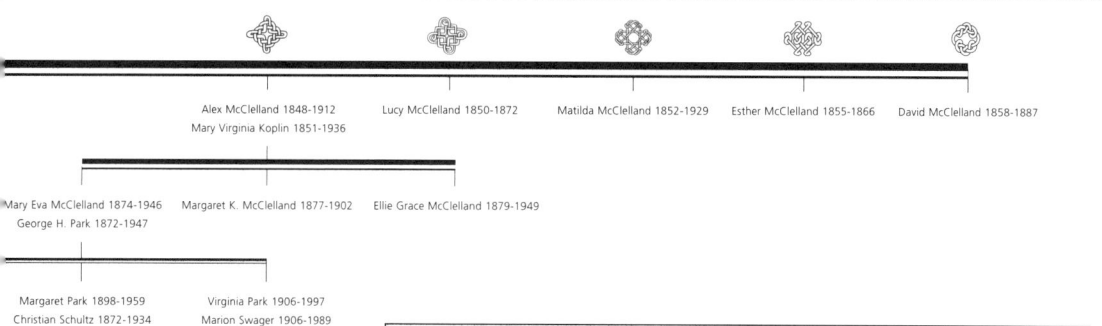

I.		Margaret Peggy McClelland
II.		John McClelland
III.		William McClelland
IV.		Susan McClelland
V.		George McClelland

VI.		Alex McClelland
VII.		Lucy McClelland
VIII.		Matilda McClelland
IX.		Esther McClelland
X.		David McClelland

Mary Minnie McClelland 1881-1
Robert Samuel Wright 1869-19

thy Jean Wright 1912-1979
ard Tighe Brady 1911-1986

d Brady 1939-
ith Ferguson

Rosemary Muriel Brady 1944-
Michael Wilson

Samuel Denis Brady 1949-
Ruth Meeke

Brady 1967-
urner

Alison Grace Brady 1975-
Stephen Webb

Stephen Edward Wilson 1967-
Jo Fenton

Jonathan Michael Wilson 1968-
Cristina Delgado Puig

Paul Singleton Wilson 1970-
Jill Brown

Peter James McMahon Wilson 1974-
Joanne Prior

Richard William Tighe Brady 1974-
Katheryn Clare Brady 1976-

Ol
And

rady 1997-
Brady 1999-

Holly Rebekah Webb 2005-
Max Daniel Brady 2006 -

Rory Edward McMahon Wilson 1996-
Angus Robert Ramsey Wilson 1998-
Annabel Emily Rose Wilson 2001-

Carla Tighe Wilson 2005

Rebecca Jennifer Wilson 2000-
Joshua Paul Wilson 2003-

Ellie Rose Wilson 1997-
Isaac Michael Wilson 2002-

Susan McClelland 1841-1919
James Bradford 1856-1920

David Livingston McClelland 1899-1967
Myrtle Wilhelmina Haller 1899-1986

Robert Coleman Stephens

Robert Coleman Stephens, Jr. 1951-
Jeanette LaValle 1973-

Ann Elizabeth Stephens 1954-
Richard Raymond Willert 1946-

David Thomas Stephens 1962-
Ana Morales 1960

Michael John Priser 1945-
Nancy Joanne Travers 1945-

Jill Dion Stephens 1977-
Robert Coleman III Stephens 1979-

Keeley Crystal Willert 1978-
William Scovel Shear 1975-

Kent Christian Willert 1981-
Emily Ingham 1982-

Alissa Beth Willert 1991(adopted 1994)-

Catalina (Cali) Stephens 1999-

Sean Michael Priser 1986-
Naomi Alison Priser 1988-
Sara Elizabeth Priser 1990-

Jac
Pe

Dar
T

John McClelland 1837-1910
Elizabeth McCauley 1841-1899

Susan McClelland 1865-1944
Sandy Kane

Harriet (Hattie) McClelland 1868-1942
Earnest Reynolds 1878-

Minnie May McClelland 1872-1947
William Turner 1859-1927

Samuel Francis McClelland McClel|

Harriet Rose McClelland 1904-1991
George William Reber 1902-1967

Harriet Pauline Turner 1893-1964

Robert M. Turner 1895-1976
Margaret Fuller   -1973

William Wallace Turner 1911-1995
Leona Cook Schweer 1907- 1989

Mau
L

Barbara Ruth Reber 1929-

George William Reber, Jr. 1932-
Norma Spicer 1937-

Suzanne Lee Reber 1939-
Edgar Foster ————— Charles Chuck Brasher 1938-

Carol Schweer 1930-1970

Nancy Claire Turner 1944-
Lon Foster

George M. Reber 1959-
Eva   1961-

Daryl N. Reber 1961-
Irene

Marla L. Reber 1967-

Eileen Marie Brasher 1970-
Richard Allen Baucum

Jennifer Cathe
Edward Fr

Leticia Mireya Baucum 1992-
Romario Charles Baucum 1994-
Ximena Baucum 2002-
Elizabeth Baucum 2004-

Alison Mae

Sarah Ann Henning 1867-1908

Margaret McClelland 1894-1937
Robert J. Irwin 1889-1971

Emma Margaret Irwin 1921-
Henry R. Clarke   -1971

Thomas Alexander Irwin 1922-1992
Mary McGraph 1924-2006

Alan Robert Clarke 1951-

Thomas Henry Clarke 1954-1999

Margaret Isobel Clarke 1955-
Robert (Robin) Owen Convery 1954-1998

Daphne Elizabeth Harshaw 1954-
Robert Acheson

David Andrew Convery 1981-
Stephen Robert Convery 1984-
Kathryn Helen Convery 1990-
Michael Thomas Convery 1992-

Lynn Elizabeth Acheson 1976-
Marc Montgomery

Neill Robert Acheson 1979-

Jill Emma Acheson 1982-

Amy Mavis Acheson 19

THE McCLELLANDS OF CLOUGHENRAMER

PREFACE

Each generation considers a record of its place in the contemporary to be of little interest or value. Yet within a few years what was considered mundane to one generation becomes
priceless to the next. We have all looked despairingly at people in old photographs—their
identity lost for ever—who were so familiar to our late relatives, but that no one considered
necessary to name on the back of the photograph.

While not claiming to be definitive, the aim of this book, *The McClellands of
Cloughenramer*, is to trace and place for posterity the family and descendants of Thomas
McClelland, who married Susan Henning on the 30th of August 1833.

The McClelland family is known to have been living in the Co. Down townland of
Cloughenramer over 200 years ago. While we know something of the generations before
Thomas, the picture is far from complete. A lot more research may yield a little more
knowledge, and the desire to hold out for yet one more piece of information before publication is always a difficult though necessary temptation to resist.

Hopefully in days to come the record of people and events contained in this book will
become the block upon which others can build.

It was not the intention to chronicle the views, attitudes, or opinions of the people found
on these pages; interpretation such as that is the territory of the biographer. This book is
about family, and the aim is to show how and where the descendents of Thomas McClelland
and Susan Henning fit together.

And yet this project is about more than the mere mechanics of constructing a family tree. As you turn these pages, you will find examples of the highs and lows, the joys and
sorrows that are part and parcel—yes, the very heartbeat—of family life. Common threads
between generations there certainly are, but they are for you the reader to tease out, and
future family historians to comment upon.

Following an opening chapter that provides a summary of what is currently known of the ancestors of Thomas McClelland, the book is organized into ten chapters, one for each child of Thomas McClelland and Susan Henning. In each chapter, descendants are listed by generation to the present, or to whenever that particular branch of the family died out.

My interest in family history dates back over thirty years. In the mid 90s, I had the good fortune to meet with my cousin Norman McClelland, who, shared a passion for family history and had the ambition to embark on a published account of the lives and descendants of each of his four grandparents. This book is the third of four intended volumes.

Had a book such as this been published a century ago, it would today be spoken of in hushed tones and held in the reserve section of major libraries. That you can place it on your bookshelf today and hand it to descendents tomorrow is due to the vision, energy and commitment of Norman P. McClelland.

Posterity in general and future generations of this family in particular will indeed be grateful.

Uel Wright
Finnard, Co. Down
November 2006

THE ANCESTORS OF JOHN McCLELLAND

A census of Ireland was carried out by Sir William Petty on behalf of the government between 1654-1659, in which the population of townlands was recorded as English, Scots, or Irish. The names of people were not recorded. The town of Newry had a recorded population of 174 people, 66 of whom were English, the remainder, Irish. The townland of Cloughenramer (spelled Cloghanrawer in the survey and shown jointly with the neighbouring townland of Toremore) is recorded as having 22 people, all of whom were Irish.

To understand the physical setting of the town where the McClelland family was destined to settle in Ireland, we pause to consider Newry then and now:

NEWRY THEN AND NOW

Newry lies in the furthest southeastern part of both Ulster and Northern Ireland. Approximately half of the city falls in County Down, the other half in County Armagh. The city sits in a valley, nestled between the Mourne Mountains to the east and the Ring of Gullion to the southwest, both of which are designated Areas of Outstanding Natural Beauty. The Clanrye River runs through the town parallel to the canal, forming part of the border between County Down and County Armagh. The city also stands at the northernmost end of Carlingford Lough, where the canal enters the sea. The

THE TOWN HALL IN NEWRY (CENTER) UNDER WHICH FLOWS THE CLANRYE RIVER – CIRCA 1900 (FROM THE PRIVATE COLLECTION OF MR. I. MAJOR)

2001 census showed Newry to have a population of 27, 433, almost 90% of which were from a Catholic background.

The name Newry comes from the original Irish "Iur Chinn Tra," which translates as "the yew at the head of the strand"—a reference to an apocryphal story that St. Patrick planted a yew tree there in the fifth century. In modern Irish, the full name of the town is rarely used; instead, it is abbreviated to "An Iúr."

POTATO DRILLING ON THE HILLS AROUND NEWRY – CIRCA 1920s (FROM THE PRIVATE COLLECTION OF MR. I. MAJOR)

MERCHANTS QUAY IN NEWRY, WHERE SHIPS USING THE CANAL WERE ABLE TO STEAM INTO THE HEART OF THE TOWN. CIRCA 1900 (FROM THE PRIVATE COLLECTION OF MR. I. MAJOR)

The town was established in 1144 with the building of a monastery, which was burnt down in 1162 to be replaced by a Cistercian monastery. This monastery was converted to a collegiate church in 1543, before being surrendered to the crown in 1548.

Sir Nicholas Bagenal, Marshal of the army in Ireland, took over the site around 1550, later building a castle, the remains of which can still be seen on Castle Street.

The commercial health of Newry has always been closely linked to contemporary transport systems. As the first major town en route from Dublin to Belfast, its location has always been of strategic importance. As transport developed over the years, so did the significance of the town. Newry's population peak in 1881 had much to do with the popularity of the inland canal, the mills, the tram, and the railways. However, the turn of the century saw the beginning of a decline in these industries. By the 1960s the railways, trams, and canal transport industry had all closed down.

TAKING CORN TO NEWRY: A SCENE WHICH WOULD HAVE BEEN FAMILIAR TO
FARMERS SUCH AS THE MCCLELLANDS. CIRCA 1900S (FROM THE PRIVATE
COLLECTION OF MR. I. MAJOR)

The political unrest which became known as "The Troubles" further depressed the town
for the next thirty-odd years.

Happily, Newry has turned itself around and is now a vibrant commercial centre. An
injection of public capital in the 1970s greatly improved communications and sowed the
seeds which have now come to fruition, making Newry a positive and exciting place to live.

MIGRATION OF PEOPLE FROM SCOTLAND
AND NORTHERN ENGLAND

At the end of the 17th century, a large migration of people from Scotland and northern
England was underway, and the counties of Antrim and Down were being peopled by the
ancestors of many who still live there today. Among these migrants were the ancestors of
Thomas McClelland.

One of the significant factors driving these people to migrate was the desire for freedom
to worship God in a manner dictated by their conscience and not by any civil or military
administration. Successive English monarchs from James I (1603 – 1625) to Charles
II (1660 – 1685), and even Oliver Cromwell during the period of the Commonwealth
(1649 – 1660) tried to impose religious uniformity on the prickly, independent Scottish
Presbyterians. Yet despite savage repression, these "stiff-necked" people would not bend to
anything that smacked of Episcopacy.

It is, therefore, little wonder that by the end of the 17th century Ulster—which had been enjoying a period of relative peace, held the promise of good and plentiful land, and offered a measure of religious tolerance not enjoyed at home—began to look very attractive, and many chose to make the short sea journey between the two countries.

In those days, a migrant people did not have the formal system of state back-up enjoyed today. As such, formal records containing personal details which would be so valuable to family historians did not begin to accumulate for at least one or two generations. So it is not until the end of the 18th century that records showing individual family names begin to appear.

The earliest information about the family McClelland at Cloughenramer is in two memorials dated 1751 and 1761. Nicholas McClelland is shown living or owning property at Cloughenramer. A memorial dated 1807 places John McClelland in Cloughenramer, and suggests that John is the father of Thomas McClelland. John was 44 years old at the time of Thomas's birth in 1801.

A livestock survey dated 1803 indicates that John McClelland, Newry Parish, D654/ A2/29, Cloughenramer, owned the following:

oxen	cows	young cattle	sheep goats	pigs	riding horses	wagons	carts	cars
0	5	3	5	3	0	0	0	1

barrels wheat	oats	barley	loads hay	straw	cwt. potatoes	flour	oatmeal
0	20	0	12	0	25	0	3

A *Newry Commercial Telegraph* article reports that John McClelland, age 75, died November 20th, 1832. No doubt this is the John McClelland on the livestock list in 1803. John was born circa 1767. He was buried in Newry.

GRANDPARENTS, PARENTS, UNCLES AND
AUNTS OF THOMAS MCCLELLAND

Who were the uncles and aunts of Thomas McClelland? There are McClellands shown living in the Newy area as early as 1715. Thomas, William, James, and John are all possibilities.

Did Thomas have siblings? There are McClellands who would fit the bill, including Andrew in Lisnaree. John was baptized in 1797, along with William and James.

What is known is that the McClellands called their farm Rockfield, as frequently referenced in the newspapers.

THOMAS MCCLELLAND

First Generation

Thomas McClelland was born about 1801 at Cloughenramer on "Rockfield Farm" near Newry, County Down, Ireland.

THE ROADSIDE NAME WHICH IDENTIFIES THE
TOWNLAND OF CLOUGHENRAMER.

Thomas McClelland and Susan Henning McClelland were married on August 30th, 1833 in Newry, County Down, Ireland. Susan Henning was born about 1814, in Ireland.

HARRY AND MARGARET McGAFFIN AT THE McCLELLAND ANCESTRAL
HOME – CLOUGHENRAMER, NEWRY, COUNTY DOWN

Thomas and Susan had ten children, five girls and five boys: Margaret Peggy McClelland, born February 10, 1835; John McClelland, born March 17, 1837; William McClelland, born July 20, 1839; Susan McClelland, born August 4, 1841; George McClelland, born July 28, 1846; Alex McClelland, born June 1848; Lucy McClelland, born November 8, 1850; Matilda McClelland, born October 4, 1852; Esther McClelland, born January 8, 1855; and David McClelland, born April 29, 1858.

FIRST NEWRY (SANDY'S STREET) PRESBYTERIAN CHURCH WHERE
GENERATIONS OF McCLELLANDS WORSHIPPED

Memorial No. 26 – 65 shows Thomas McClelland purchasing eighteen acres and thirty-four perches from Mercy Glenny on July 8, 1861.

MEMORIAL No. 26-65
JULY 8, 1861

Memorial No. 26-65:

"A Memorial of an indenture lease in fee form bearing date the eighth day of July in the year of our Lord one thousand eight hundred and sixty-one made between Mercy Glenny of Newry in the county of Down Spinster of the one part and Thomas McClelland of Cloughenramer in the said county of Down farmer of the other part whereby the said Mercy

Glenny did for the considerations therein mentioned demise grant set release and confirm unto the said Thomas McClelland (in his actual possession then being as therein mentioned) and to his heirs and assigns all that part and those that part and parcel of the town and lands of Cloughenramer then in the tenure and occupation of him the said Thomas McClelland and Robert Hutton containing eighteen acres and thirty-four perches Irish Plantation measure of thereabouts and marked numbers 1, 2, and 3 on the Map annexed to a certain deed of partition bearing date the Eighth day of March one thousand eight hundred and fifty eight and colored red on said Map situate being and being in the Parish of Barony of Newry and County of Down. To hold unto the said Thomas McClelland his heirs and assign forever He the said Thomas McClelland his heirs and assigns yielding and paying unto the said Mercy Glenny her heirs and assigns the clear? yearly rent or sum of Thirty Seven pounds three shillings starting? to be paid by two equal payments in the year viz on every first day of May and first day of November in every year and which said indenture of lease contains covenant for payment of rent and distress and reenter in nonpayment and the observance & performance by the said Thomas McClelland his heirs and assigns of the ____ _____ provinces, conditions and agreements of save and except the covenant or proviso for payment of rent Mentioned _____ contained in a certain indenture of fee form lease bearing date the twenty-second day of March one thousand seven hundred and thirty-one and made between Robert Nedham Junior of the one part and Robert Gordon, James Gordon and George Gordon of the other part and which on the part and behalf of the said Mercy Glenny her heirs and assigns are or ought to be observed performed fulfilled and kept and also convenants for Quid enjoyment and further assurance and the said indenture of lease as to the execution thereof by the said Mercy Glenny is witness by John Andrews Junior and Thomas Andrews both of Comber in the County of Down Gentlemen and the said indenture of lease as to the execution thereof by the said Thomas McClelland witnessed by Thomas Carey and Matthew Glenny both of Newry in the County of Down solicitors."

The Thomas McClelland homestead included leases from Robert Glenny, Mercy Glenny, and Robert G. Atkinson.

McClelland Homestead 1864

No. and Letters of Reference to Map.	Names.		Description of Tenement.	Area.	Rateable Annual Valuation.		Total Annual Valuation of Rateable Property.
	Townlands and Occupiers.	Immediate Lessors.			Land.	Buildings.	

VALUATION OF TENEMENTS.
PARISH OF NEWRY.

No.		Townlands and Occupiers.	Immediate Lessors.	Description of Tenement.	Area.			Land.			Buildings.			Total.		
		CLOGHANRAMER. (Ord. S. 46 & 47.)														
1		Thomas Clarke,	Robert Glenny,	House, offices, and land.	32	0	30	36	0	0	2	5	0	38	5	0
2		John Rourke,	Same,	House, offices, and land.	14	2	5	16	10	0	2	10	0	19	0	0
3		John Byrne,	Same,	House, offices, and land.	15	2	20	14	10	0	2	0	0	16	10	0
4		Daniel Curren,	Same,	House, offices, and land.	14	3	0	14	0	0	2	5	0	16	5	0
5	a	Andrew Clarke,	Same,	House, offices, and land.	17	0	21	17	10	0	2	10	0	20	0	0
–	b	National School-house and land,	(See Exemptions.)													
6		Hugh O'Neill,	Robert Glenny,	House, offices, and land.	21	0	20	28	10	0	2	10	0	31	0	0
7		Thomas M'Clelland,	Same,	Office and land.	16	0	25	21	0	0	1	10	0	22	10	0
8		Thomas M'Clelland,	Mercy Glenny,	House, offices, and land	21	0	10	18	10	0	3	10	0	22	0	0
9		Thomas M'Clelland,	Rev. Robt. G. Atkinson,	Land,	0	0	0	5	5	0	—			5	5	0
–	a	Unoccupied,	Thomas M'Clelland,	House,							0	15	0	0	15	0
10		Isaac W. Dickinson,	In fee.	Bog,	6	1	0	0	15	0	—			0	15	0
11		Robert Tottenham,	Thomas M'Clelland,	House, office, and land.	9	2	20	8	5	0	0	5	0	8	10	0
12	a	John Copeland,	Robert Glenny,	House, offices, and land.	7	2	20	6	0	0	1	5	0	7	5	0
–	b	James Copeland,	Same,	House, offices, & garden,	0	1	5	0	5	0	1	10	0	11	5	0
13				Land,	12	0	10	9	10	0						
14		Charles Campbell,	Jane Morgan,	House, offices, and land.	8	2	15	6	10	0	1	5	0	7	15	0
15		Bernard O'Neill,	Same,	House, office, and land.	5	0	30	4	0	0	0	15	0	4	15	0
16		James M'Canley,	Same,	House, office, and land.	5	2	20	4	10	0	0	15	0	5	5	0
17		Alexander Bamber,	Same,	House, office, and land.	5	3	5	4	10	0	0	15	0	5	5	0
18		Patrick Campbell,	Same,	House, office, and land.	5	2	30	4	5	0	0	10	0	4	15	0
19		Samuel Wier, jun.,	Rev. Robt. G Atkinson,	Herd's ho., off., & land,	23	0	20	20	10	0	1	15	0	22	5	0
20		Samuel Wier. jun.,	In fee.	Land,	17	1	20	18	0	0	—			18	0	0
–	a	John M'Alinden,	Samuel Wier, jun.,	House and sm. garden,	—			—			1	0	0	1	0	0
21		Samuel Wier,	Isaac W. Dickinson,	House, offices, and land.	4	0	30	3	15	0	7	10	0	11	5	0
22		Michael Rice,	Same,	Land,	5	0	10	4	10	0	—			4	10	0
23		Patrick Kerr,	Same,	Herd's ho., off, & land,	2	2	5	3	0	0	1	0	0	4	0	0
24	a	Peter Meehan,	Same,	Herd's ho., off., & land,	3	3	0	4	0	0	0	5	0	4	5	0

1864

Valuation of Tenements Parish of Newry 1864

Thomas McClelland died June 17th, 1866 at Cloughenramer, Newry, County Down, Ireland.

* * *

Obituary - Thomas McClelland

"McClelland – On the 16th inst., at his residence, Rockfield, Newry, Mr. Thomas McClelland, aged sixty-five years, whose guileless character, and unaffected piety, had won him the esteem of all who knew him."

CHAPTER I
Margaret Peggy McClelland

SECOND GENERATION

Margaret Peggy McClelland, John McClelland, William McClelland,
Susan McClelland, George McClelland, Alex McClelland, Lucy McClelland,
Matilda McClelland, Esther McClelland, David McClelland

Margaret Peggy McClelland – Second Generation

Margaret Peggy McClelland, the eldest daughter of Thomas McClelland and Susan Henning, was born on February 10th, 1835 and baptized February 15th, 1835. She was brought up in the family home at Rockfield, a few miles from the ancient port town of Newry, County Down. Little is known of her early years, but as the eldest in a family of ten living on a farm, she would have been busy helping her mother in the home and her father on the farm when extra hands were needed to harvest crops.

The family was Presbyterian and, in keeping with the ethos of that denomination, placed great store on education. Margaret was clearly an able child, and would have attended Rockvale National School, which was only a few hundred yards from the family home in the townland of Cloughenramer.

In those days, able pupils with an interest in teaching became paid monitors in their local school. After three or four years of study and practical teaching, they would undergo a public examination, and, if successful, would be sent for six months to a Model School, founded by the government to demonstrate good teaching practice. This would be followed by a further and final period of training at Marlborough Street Training College in Dublin.

We know from details on her marriage certificate that Margaret was a school teacher still living at the family home of Rockfield in 1866. Given that she was 31 at the time of her marriage, it seems likely that she was a career teacher, with at least ten years post-training experience. She was married to Thomas Tweedie on September 25th, 1866 in the Presbyterian Church at Rostrevor, County Down.

MARGARET PEGGY McCLELLAND AND THOMAS TWEEDIE
MARRIAGE CERTIFICATE – SEPTEMBER 25, 1866

The following letter from Rev. Arthur J.E. Curry was received by Margaret McGaffin on November 4th, 1988. It includes a marriage record of Thomas Tweedie and Margaret McClelland.

LETTER FROM REV. ARTHUR J. E. CURRY TO MARGARET MCGAFFIN, 1988

Thomas Tweedie, a near neighbor living at Tormore, would have known her at an early age and in all likelihood attended the same school. Both families were members of the Downshire Road Presbyterian Church.

Margaret and Thomas set up home on the farm at Tormore, where the Tweedies had had a presence since 1834. Given her upbringing, the role of a farmer's wife would not have been unfamiliar to the new Mrs. Tweedie.

THOMAS TWEEDIE CIRCA 1870

The couple had two children: William John, born March 18, 1868, and Anna Lucinda, born September 10, 1870. Their third child, a boy, was stillborn April 3, 1872. A day later, Margaret died with Thomas at her bedside. She was 37 years old. Her death certificate records that she died of "smallpox four days certified." In an age when many died young, this was nevertheless a particularly poignant death. To have reached the final stage of her pregnancy only to discover that she had contracted a fatal disease must have been devastating, a blow perhaps only softened by the knowledge that her unborn child would survive her. To then deliver a son, stillborn, must have been the final straw. Margaret was buried in the Tweedie family burial ground at St. Patrick's Church in Newry.

TORMORE VILLA
THE HOME OF MARGARET McCLELLAND TWEEDIE AND HER HUSBAND, THOMAS. NOTE: THE BARN BETWEEN THE DWELLING HOUSE AND GLASS HOUSE IS WHERE THOMAS CARRIED OUT ALL OF HIS JOINERY WORK.

THOMAS TWEEDIE FAMILY CENSUS OF 1901
THOMAS TWEEDIE, AGE 67, AND CHILDREN WILLIAM JOHN, AGE 33, ANNA LUCINDA, AGE 30, ANNIE
E. HOOKE TWEEDIE, DAUGHTER-IN-LAW, AGE 30, AND GRANDDAUGHTER, MARGARET LUCY, 10 MONTHS

In addition to farming, Thomas was an accomplished cabinet-maker, and examples of his work survive to this day. A grandfather clock and chair are still to be found in the family home at Tormore. The most public example of his work is the pulpit in Kingsmills Presbyterian Church, County Armagh, constructed when the building was being renovated in the 1880s. It is still in use each Sunday.

GRANDFATHER CLOCK
MADE BY THOMAS
TWEEDIE. THE CLOCK
IS STILL WORKING AND
STANDS IN THE TORMORE
HOME OF MARGARET AND
HARRY McGAFFIN.

PULPIT IN KINGSMILLS PRESBYTERIAN CHURCH, COUNTY ARMAGH, MADE
BY THOMAS TWEEDIE DURING RENOVATIONS OF THE CHURCH IN THE
1880S. THE PULPIT IS STILL IN USE.

Thomas was to live as a widower for the next 15 years, dying on December 13th, 1907. He was laid to rest beside his wife at St. Patrick's Church in Newry, County Down.

Obituary – Thomas Tweedie

"The remains this highly respected old gentleman were removed from his late residence, Tormore, yesterday at 11 o'clock for interment in St. Patrick's Church Burying ground, and the extent of the funeral cortege showed the general sympathy of the people for a wide district round. The deceased, who had reached the advanced age of 75 years, was well known for his honesty of purpose during a long life. An ardent and unflinching supporter of the Unionist cause, his conduct was such that his views were respected even by the bitterest political opponents. Stern and unrelenting in the pursuance of public life, he was known socially as a man of many good parts. In religion he was a Presbyterian, and was for years a staunch member of Downshire Road Presbyterian Church. The attendance at the funeral was large and respectable, and a long line of vehicles followed the hearse.

The chief mourners were – William Tweedie, Dublin Road, Newry (brother); W. J. Tweedie, North Street, Newry (son); Alfred Tweedie, King Street, Newry (nephew); and John McCormack, Kingsmills (son-in-law). The attendance of the general public included Messrs. J.A. Newell, manager, Northern Bank, Newry; Robert Kerr, Newry; Robert Ledlie; W. D. Watt, Newry Model School; Jos. Lawson, John McGladdery, James McKeown, Wm. Pollock, Wm. Rainey, James McGaffin, Hugh Murphy, George Weir, J. McCracken, W. McGladdery, R. Cooper, J. O'Neill, Newry, D. McAnuff, G. Henry, Joseph McCullagh, Samuel Hooks, Joseph Rainey, Joseph Henning, Charles Cunningham, Andrew Bradford, Wm. Gordon, Robert McGladdery, T. A. Wilson, J. H. Dillon, Wm. Dillon, Jos. McMinn, G. Copeland, Wm. Copeland, Andrew McMinn, Joseph Davidson, D. Torley, James O'Hare. Daniel O'Hare, R. Henry, James McGladdery. James Thompson, Samuel Fleming, Samuel Armstrong, Arthur Morgan, James McKinstrey, Wm. McClelland, Samuel Wright, Samuel Hegan, David Hegan, Samuel Weir, David Preston, James Glenny, John Ryan, James

Chapman, J. McKinley, M. Murdock, and many others. The burial service at the graveside was conducted by the Rev. William Wylie, senior minister of Downshire Road Presbyterian Church, who, previous to the removal from the house, conducted

a short service."

THOMAS AND MARGARET TWEEDIE GRAVE,
ST. PATRICK'S CHURCH OF IRELAND, NEWRY,
COUNTY DOWN

THIRD GENERATION

William John Tweedie, Anna Lucinda Tweedie

William John Tweedie – Third Generation

William John Tweedie, first child of Margaret McClelland and Thomas Tweedie, was born on March 18th, 1868 in Newry, County Down, Ireland. During his lifetime, he told family members that he was born at his mother's family home at Cloughenramer. This would not have been unusual, as many mothers in those days returned to their family homes to give birth.

WILLIAM JOHN TWEEDIE
OF TORMORE, NEWRY

ANNIE ELIZABETH HOOKE
WIFE OF WILLIAM JOHN TWEEDIE

He married Annie Elizabeth Hooke on April 20th, 1898 in Agnes Street Church, Belfast, Ireland. Annie Elizabeth Hooke was born on August 1st, 1871 in Newry, County Down, Ireland.

WILLIAM JOHN TWEEDIE AND ANNIE ELIZABETH HOOKE MARRIAGE
CERTIFICATE – APRIL 20, 1898

WEDDING OF WILLIAM JOHN TWEEDIE & ANNIE ELIZABETH HOOKE
BACK ROW: UNKNOWN, WILLIAM J. TWEEDIE, ALEXANDER CROWE;
FRONT ROW: SARAH HOOKE, ANNIE E. HOOKE & MINNIE HOOKE

They had two daughters: Margaret Lucy, born May 25, 1900 in Newry, County Down, Ireland and Annie, born September 29, 1901 in Newry, County Down, Ireland.

LEFT TO RIGHT: ANNIE TWEEDIE & MARGARET
LUCY TWEEDIE
ABOUT 1902

LEFT TO RIGHT: MARGARET LUCY TWEEDIE
AND ANNIE TWEEDIE
AUGUST 12, 1905

CERTIFICATE OF MEMBERSHIP, THE PRESBYTERIAN CHURCH IN IRELAND – 1908

William John was a jeweler and pawnbroker with a shop in North Street, Newry. He had also inherited his father's skills in joinery and woodwork. He and Annie renovated Tormore Villa, completing the project in 1897. All of the windows, doors, and woodwork were made in a small workshop in the farmyard. It may be of interest to note that when the windows were replaced in 1993, the contractors found that all similar windows were exactly the same size, despite the fact that the house is built of stone. The family lived in the house as the renovations were in progress. The house today is largely as William John left it.

THOMAS TWEEDIE FAMILY CENSUS OF 1911.
WILLIAM JOHN, AGE 43, ANNIE ELIZABETH, AGE 40, MARGARET ELIZABETH, AGE 10, ANNIE, AGE 9, MARY JANE HOOKE, VISITOR, AGE 42, AND SAMUEL HOOKE, VISITOR, AGE 51

William John had a reputation for being very impatient and stubborn. He was interested in horticulture and loved music. His daughter Annie realized his musical ambitions by obtaining her degree from the Royal Academy of Music in London in 1929. William John himself, however, was to establish his own appreciation for music more publicly when he founded and presented a Perpetual Challenge Cup for Senior Pianoforte Solo in 1929. The first winner was Margaret K. Browne. The award continues to be conferred today—the 2006 winner was seventeen-year-old Donna Magee from Mayobridge. Her brother Darren won the cup in 2005 and is now studying music in Dublin.

MISS DONNA MAGEE, 2006 WINNER OF THE W. J. TWEEDIE PERPETUAL CHALLENGE TROPHY

Annie Elizabeth died March 27th, 1929 in Newry, County Down, Northern Ireland.

Obituary – Annie Elizabeth Tweedie

"The death of Mrs. W. J. Tweedie, which sad event took place on Wednesday morning at the family residence, Tormore, Newry has evoked sincere sorrow throughout the district, and the deepest sympathy is extended to her sorrowing husband and daughters and other relatives in their sad bereavement.

The remains were removed on Friday afternoon to the family burying ground, St. Patrick's Churchyard, Newry, and the esteem in which deceased was held and the sympathy extended to the bereaved husband and relatives was amply evidenced by the very large concourse of mourners that followed the remains to their last resting.

The chief mourners were Messrs. W. J. Tweedie (husband), Samuel Hooke (brother), John McCormick and A. L. Crowe (brothers-in-law), James H. Crowe, Samuel Hooke, Robert Hooke, George McCormick, Thomas McCormick (nephews), John W. Dillon, Alex Dillon, R. W. Henry, J. P. (cousins), Dr. Tweedie, Harold Tweedie, John Elliott, Jas. McDonald, James King, Fred Wilson, Wm. Fagan, Samuel Wright (relatives).

Rev. W. G. Strahan, D. D., conducted the service at the house and at the graveside. Messrs. Gordon & Co., Sugar Island, Newry, carried out the funeral arrangements."

William John died October 1st, 1938, in Ardmaine Nursing Home, in Newry.

Obituary – William John Tweedie

"Funeral of Well Known Newry Man
Mr. W. J. Tweedie, Tormore

Amid many manifestations of deep sorrow the funeral of Mr. Wm. J. Tweedie, Tormore, who died in Ardmaine Nursing Home, Newry, early on Saturday morning last, took place to St. Patrick's Churchyard, Newry on Monday.

The cortege, which was large and representative, testified to the high regard and esteem in which the deceased was held by all sections of the community.

Deceased, who was an extensive farmer, was the proprietor of a pawnbroker establishment in North St., Newry.

He was a former member of Newry No. 1 Rural District Council and the Newry Board of Guardians.

Deceased's daughter is the wife of Mr. Joseph Dunlop, agricultural inspector in the Newry district.

The funeral services were conducted by Rev. P. McKee, B.A., Downshire Road Presbyterian Church, do., and Rev. James Mulligan, B.A., Jerretspass Presbyterian Church.

The chief mourners were: Geo. McCormick, Thos. McCormick, James H. Crowe, Robert Hooke, and Samuel Hooke (nephews); J. E. Dunlop (son-in-law); A. Crowe, Samuel Hooke, John McCormick (brothers-in-law), Harold Tweedie, Frank Tweedie and Fred Wilson (cousins); John W. Dillon, Robert Harper, Wm. Dillon, D. McClelland, John Elliott, Samuel Wright (relatives).

Messrs. Gordon and Co., Sugar Island, Newry, carried out the funeral arrangements."

Annie Elizabeth and William Thomas Tweedie are both buried in the family plot, St. Patrick's Church of Ireland, Newry, County Down.

FOURTH GENERATION

Margaret Lucy Tweedie, Annie Tweedie

Margaret Lucy Tweedie - Fourth Generation
Margaret Lucy Tweedie, first child of William John Tweedie and Annie Elizabeth Hooke, was born on May 25th, 1900 at Tormore Villa in Newry, County Down, Ireland.

Margaret married William Joseph McWilliams on August 18th, 1925 in 1st Newry Presbyterian Church, Newry, County Down, Northern Ireland. William Joseph was born on March 20th, 1894 in Glasgow, Scotland and was an engineer by profession.

MARGARET LUCY TWEEDIE AND WILLIAM JOSEPH McWILLIAMS
MARRIAGE CERTIFICATE – AUGUST 18, 1925

MARGARET LUCY TWEEDIE McWILLIAMS & HER HUSBAND, WILLIAM
JOSEPH McWILLIAMS CIRCA 1925

Margaret and her new husband sailed for New York on January 9th, 1926 on the S.S.
California from Moville, County Londonderry, Northern Ireland.

```
MARGARET L.McWILLIAM
MARGARET LUCY McWILLIAM (Nee Margaret Lucy Tweedie)
                                        DIES KILKEEL 25.2.82
Born May 25,1900 at Tormore, Newry, Northern Ireland.CREMARED ROSELAWN 2.3.82
Married August 18,1925 to William J.McWilliam at Sandys Street.Presbyterian
     Church, Newry, Northern Ireland.
Sailed for New York, U.S.A. on Jan.9,1926 via S.S."CALIFORNIA"(Anchor Line)
(Or "Caledonia") from Moville, County Londonderry, Northern Ireland.
Arrived New York Jan.19,1926.
Left New York May 12,1928 via SS"Adriatic"(Cunard Line) or White Star Line.
Returned to N.Y. July 29,1928 via SS"Adriatic".
Left New York on Aug.9,1930 Via SS"Arabic"(Cunard or White Star Line)
Returned to New York June 22,1931 Via SS"Cedric"(Cunard or White Star Line)
Left New York on May 31,1947 via Trans World Airlines.
Returned to New York Aug.1,1947 via Trans World Airlines.
Left New York on June 15,1956 Via British Overseas Airways.
Returned to New York July 15,1956 via British Overseas Airways.
Left New York April 30,1960 via British Overseas Airways.
Returned to New York July 3, 1960 via British Overseas  Airways.
Left New York April 29,1961 via British Overseas Airways
Returned to New York July 8,1961 via British Overseas Airways.
Left New York May 14,1965 via B.O.A.C.
Returned to New York July 16,1965 Via B.O.A.C.                Mr.McRoberts of
Left New York May 6,1966 via Irish Intl.Airlines             has second of
Returned to New York July 15,1966 via Irish Intl.Airlines.   my trips 1969
Left New York Aug.14,1967 via Irish Intl.Airways             to 1975
Returned to New York Sept.20,1967 via Irish Intl.Airways.
Left N.Y.April 17,1968 via Irish Intl.Airways
Returned to New York May 8,1968 via Irish Intl.Airways.
                    Re; Margaret L McWilliam
Became Naturalized American Citizen on April 9,1940 a District Court
of U.S. Brooklyn, N.Y.   U.S.Citizenship Certificate p.4392531.

Father's name: William John Tweedie. Deceased 1938 (As about 70)
Mother's maiden name:Annie Elizabeth Hooke. Deceased Mar,1929 (Age about 58).
Sister's name:Annie Tweedie (Mrs. Joseph E.Dunlop) One sister -no brothers.
     Sister - Annie (Tweedie) Dunlop died July 4,1977.
     Mother's date of Birth: Aug 1, 1871 Born at Greggans Whitecross
                                              Co. Armagh, No. Ireland.
     Father's date of Birth: Mar 13, 1868 Born at Tormore: Newry
                                              Co. Down, No. Ireland.
     Husbands' date of Birth March 20, 1894 Born at Glasgow, Scotland
```

EMIGRATION/TRAVEL RECORDS OF MARGARET LUCY
TWEEDIE McWILLIAMS 1926 – 1968

The couple set up house at 104-50, 102nd Street, Ozone Park, New York. They had no children. Margaret worked as a bookkeeper at Windsor & Newton's, a paint and artwork outlet in New York. William Joseph continued work as an engineer.

William Joseph died in New York on April 25th, 1967. Margaret returned home. She died in Slieve Roe House Nursing Home, Kilkeel, County Down on February 25th, 1982. She was cremated and her ashes scattered in Roselawn Cemetery, Belfast.

Annie Tweedie – Fourth Generation

Annie Tweedie, second child of William John Tweedie and Annie Elizabeth Hooke, was born on September 29th, 1901 in Newry, County Down, Ireland. Annie was brought up in the family home at Tormore with her sister, Margaret.

Annie inherited her father's love for music and was an accomplished pianist. She became a Licentiate of the Royal Academy of Music in 1929 and passed her sole and final examination on the first attempt. She was known to have cycled to Belfast to take piano lessons.

Annie married Joseph Enos Dunlop on September 14th, 1932 in Ryan's Presbyterian Church.

ANNIE TWEEDIE AND JOSEPH ENOS DUNLOP, MARRIAGE CERTIFICATE – SEPTEMBER 14, 1932

ANNIE TWEEDIE AND JOSEPH ENOS DUNLOP WEDDING DAY – SEPTEMBER 14, 1932

Joseph was born on November 21st, 1899 in the townland of Craigs, Finvoy, County Antrim. The fifth child in a family of nine, he also had an older half-brother and two half-sisters. When Joseph was four, the family moved to a 100-acre farm at Ballybrakes, County Antrim, which Joseph helped run until his father's death in 1919. The family farm was then inherited by his brother Hugh, so Joseph had to seek alternative work. He ended up joining the Ministry of Agriculture, training in flax production. With the decline of the flax industry,

WEDNING DAY – SEPTEMBER 14, 1932
BRIDESMAIDS: MARGARET PEGGY FULLERTON TWEEDIE, KATHLEEN DUNLOP;
BRIDE & GROOM: JOSEPH ENOS DUNLOP & ANNIE TWEEDIE
BEST MAN: THOMAS HENRY AGNEW

Joseph was transferred to Newry and joined the potato inspectorate. His early training in flax production was not wasted, however, as the advent of World War II saw a new demand for linen. Joseph traveled extensively over Northern Ireland advising production.

Joseph and Annie had four children: Margaret Annie, born July 1, 1933, William Tweedie, born July 7, 1934, John born September 19, 1939, and Hugh Richard, born in 1940.

Following their marriage, the couple lived in the family home at Tormore with Annie's father until his death in 1938. Joseph then succeeded his father-in-law as sub-district commandant in the Ulster Special Constabulary, but resigned his post two years later on grounds of ill health.

In 1952 Joseph was transferred to the Department of Agriculture head office in Belfast, where he subsequently became Deputy Head of the Potato Section for Northern Ireland. Upon retirement in 1965, he left Belfast and built a retirement bungalow opposite Tormore Villa.

Upon marrying, Joseph, originally a member of Finvoy Presbyterian Church and then St. James Presbyterian Church, Ballymoney, joined First Newry (Sandy's Street) Presbyterian Church where Annie had worshipped since childhood. The couple took an active part in the life of the congregation—Joseph sang in the choir and served on the Church Committee, and was eventually elected as a church elder.

Joseph and Annie were members of the Newry Rowing Club and traveled to various regattas in the 1920s and early 1930s. They also took pleasure in driving the first motor cars and motorbikes. Annie, after gaining early distinction on the piano, taught music for a short time after her marriage but seldom played later in life, when her energies were transferred to raising her four children. She was generous, kind and caring, with a great interest in people.

Annie died at Tormore on July 4, 1977, leaving Joseph on his own for a further thirteen years until his death on July 20th, 1990. Both she and Joseph were cremated and their ashes scattered at Roseland Cemetery, Belfast.

The Book of Remembrance held at the Crematorium

Dunlop, Annie
(nee Tweedie)

Born 29.9.1901. Died 4.7.1977.
Loved and remembered by
Her husband, Joseph Enos
And children, Margaret, Billy, John
and Richard

Dunlop, Joseph Enos McCaughern

Born 21.11.1899 at Craigs, Ballymoney
Died 20.7.1990 at Tormore, Newry where
Annie Tweedie his beloved wife was born
29.9.1901 and died 4.7.1977. He gave
thanks for God's wonderful goodness and
mercy. Loved and remembered by Margaret,
Billy, John and Richard.

AT TORMORE – JULY 1947
BACK ROW: MARGARET TWEEDIE MCWILLIAMS, MARGARET DUNLOP, SARAH CROWE,
MARGARET (PEGGY) TWEEDIE, WM. T. DUNLOP; FRONT ROW: ANNIE TWEEDIE DUNLOP,
RICHARD DUNLOP, J.E. DUNLOP & JOHN DUNLOP. NOTE: SARAH CROWE WAS A SISTER OF
MRS. WM. J. TWEEDIE.

AT TORMORE – JULY 1947
BACK ROW: WM. MCWILLIAMS, MARGARET DUNLOP, SARAH CROWE,
MARGARET (PEGGY) TWEEDIE, WM. TWEEDIE DUNLOP; FRONT ROW:
MARGARET MCWILLIAMS, RICHARD DUNLOP, J. E. DUNLOP & JOHN
DUNLOP

JOSEPH ENOS DUNLOP'S 90TH BIRTHDAY NOVEMBER 21, 1989 (KNOWN IN THE FAMILY AS GRANDPA JOE)
BACK ROW: IVOR MCGAFFIN, KEITH DUNLOP, GARY MCGAFFIN, ALAN MCGAFFIN, HARRY MCGAFFIN;
MIDDLE ROW: JOAN DUNLOP, ROSEMARY DUNLOP, ANNE MCGAFFIN, KAREN DUNLOP, LINDA DUNLOP,
RODNEY HAMILTON; FRONT ROW: SAMUEL HAMILTON, WM. TWEEDIE DUNLOP, MARGARET MCGAFFIN, J.
E. DUNLOP, JOHN DUNLOP, RICHARD DUNLOP; CHILDREN: NEAL MCGAFFIN, SHELLEY MCGAFFIN, ANNE &
RUTH DUNLOP

FIFTH GENERATION

Margaret Annie Dunlop, William Tweedie Dunlop, John Dunlop,
Hugh Richard Dunlop.

Margaret Annie Dunlop – Fifth Generation

Margaret Annie Dunlop, first child of Joseph Enos Dunlop and Annie Tweedie, was born on July 1st, 1933 in Tormore Villa, Newry. Brought up with her three brothers—William Tweedie Dunlop, John Dunlop, and Hugh Richard Dunlop—Margaret was educated at Rockfield P.E. School, Newry Intermediate School, and Victoria College, Belfast.

On leaving school, Margaret worked in the civil service. After her marriage to William Henry McGaffin on March 16th, 1957, she and her husband went to live in Glengormley, County Antrim. Harry, the only son of George Bradford McGaffin (architect, soldier, and farmer, in that order) and Sarah Fleming McGaffin, was born at Sheeptown, Newry on November 26th, 1922. Harry received his early education at Crowreagh Public Elementary

School and Newry Technical College, later graduating from the University of London (Extern). He was brought up on the family farm and commissioned in the Home Guard at the age of nineteen, later serving for a period as sub-district commandant in the Ulster Special Constabulary.

Harry's career with the Ministry of Agriculture (N.I.) commenced in 1953 when he was appointed to the Milk Division (Quality Control Section) based in Londonderry. He was associated with the four main dairy enterprises in the northwest region: Leckpatrick Dairies and the Old City Dairy in Londonderry, Leckpatrick Dairies, Artigarfin, County Tyrone, and Nestles Milk Factory, Omagh, County Tyrone. On the formation of the Northern Ireland Milk Marketing Board, he was seconded for a period of two years, and remained in Londonderry.

Upon his return to the Ministry of Agriculture, Harry was transferred to Antrim County Staff and posted to Ballycastle, where he had the unique and pleasurable experience of working in the beautiful nine glens of Antrim.

Around this time, Harry received a transfer to the South Antrim Office, with responsibility for the greater Belfast area.

At this stage of his career, Harry became deeply involved in the work of the Civil Service Professional Officers Association, serving as representative of the Agricultural Inspectorate Branch on the Central Executive Committee as well as the staff side of the Whitley Council. In 1960 he was appointed chairman of the Agricultural Inspectorate Branch—the largest branch in the Association—after having served as Secretary and Vice-Chairman.

After another transfer to Newry, County Down in 1962, Margaret and Harry were delighted to take over Tormore Villa.

MARGARET ANNIE DUNLOP
& HARRY McGAFFIN
WEDDING DAY –
MARCH 16, 1957

Harry and Margaret's sons Gary Dunlop McGaffin and Ivor Bradford McGaffin were born in Belfast. Alan Henry McGaffin was born in Tormore Villa following Harry's transfer.

Margaret took up a post with the Northern Ireland Housing Executive in 1973. She was based in the Newry District Office and rose to the rank of Senior Housing Officer before retirement in 1993.

As a senior officer with the Ministry of Agriculture, Harry was responsible for the administration of all farm development grants in the widespread Newry agricultural area, which was later expanded to take in Rathfriland.

After retiring from the Department in 1984, Harry now finds the care and maintenance of three family farms in addition to duties as unpaid groundsman at Tormore Villa a full-time occupation which he enjoys very much.

Records show that the McGaffin family have been members of First Newry Presbyterian Church since 1812. Harry followed in the steps of his great-grandfather and father when he was ordained to the Eldership in 1969. He was a member of the committee and a Sunday school teacher for many years. Margaret and Harry are still very active in the congregation.

Harry served for a number of years on the Board of Governors of three local primary schools, and Margaret has a long association with the Scout and Guide Movement in the Newry area. In recent years, Margaret has become heavily involved with the work of Altnaveigh House Cultural Society based in Newry, particularly Altnaveigh House Women's Group, where she serves as a director. This group was formed to promote and broaden women's interests through friendship, interaction with other groups, and cultural, educational and social activities.

LEFT TO RIGHT: MARGARET MCGAFFIN, HARRY MCGAFFIN, NORMAN MCCLELLAND & DAISY MAGOWAN
FAMILY REUNION 1997

SIXTH GENERATION

Gary Dunlop McGaffin, Ivor Bradford McGaffin, Alan Henry McGaffin

Gary Dunlop McGaffin – Sixth Generation

Gary Dunlop McGaffin, first child of Margaret Annie Dunlop and William Henry McGaffin, was born on February 22nd, 1960 in the St. George's District, Belfast. Gary attended Windsor Hill Primary School and Newry High School, where he was a member of the First Eleven hockey team.

Always a keen motor-sport enthusiast, Gary built and rallied cars for a number of years. He chose a career in banking and is currently manager of the Markethill branch of the Northern Bank.

Gary married Anne Elizabeth Henning on October 15th, 1983.

ANNE ELIZABETH HENNING & GARY DUNLOP McGAFFIN WEDDING DAY – OCTOBER 15, 1983
BACK ROW, LEFT TO RIGHT: DR. RICHARD DUNLOP, ALAN McGAFFIN, IVOR McGAFFIN, REV. JOHN DUNLOP, JIM McKIMMON, GWYNETH McKIMMON, LINDA DUNLOP, WM. TWEEDIE (BILL) DUNLOP; FRONT ROW, LEFT TO RIGHT: KEITH DUNLOP, J.E. DUNLOP, MARGARET McGAFFIN, GARY & ANNE McGAFFIN, HARRY McGAFFIN, KAREN DUNLOP, ROSEMARY DUNLOP & JOAN DUNLOP

Anne, also a keen hockey player, received her early education at Rockvale Primary School and Newry High School. She worked for a time in the Agricultural Research unit based in Hillsborough.

The couple live on Gosford Road, Markethill, County Armagh. They have three children: Shelley Margaret Claire, born April 17, 1984, Neal William, born September 1, 1986, and Joanne, born June 18, 1991.

GARY AND ANNE McGAFFIN

THE McGAFFIN FAMILY
LEFT TO RIGHT: JOANNE, GARY, SHELLEY, ANNE,
AND NEAL McGAFFIN

SEVENTH GENERATION

Shelley Margaret Claire McGaffin, Neal William McGaffin, Joanne McGaffin

Shelley Margaret Claire McGaffin – Seventh Generation

Shelley Margaret Claire McGaffin, first child of Gary Dunlop McGaffin and Anne Elizabeth McGaffin, was born on April 17th, 1984 in Newry, County Down.

Shelley received her early education at Markethill Primary and Markethill High School. She also attended Armagh Technical College. She has recently completed a nursing degree from The Queen's University of Belfast.

Shelley was involved in amateur dramatics and the Duke of Edinburgh Award scheme. A talented musician, she has also attained grade 8 in music examinations.

Neal William McGaffin – Seventh Generation

Neal William McGaffin, second child of Gary Dunlop McGaffin and Anne Elizabeth McGaffin, was born on September 1st, 1986 in Banbridge, County Down.

Neal received his early education at Markethill Primary and Markethill Secondary School. He then attended Armagh Technical College. Having recently completed his apprenticeship in the building industry, Neal is considering setting up his own building firm.

An avid supporter of Blackburn Rovers Football Club, Neal frequently makes the cross to England to watch his favorites compete in the Premiership League.

Joanne McGaffin – Seventh Generation

Joanne McGaffin, third child of Gary Dunlop McGaffin and Anne Elizabeth McGaffin, was born on June 18th, 1991 in Newry, County Down.

Like her brother and sister, Joanne received her early education at Markethill Primary and is currently a pupil at Markethill Secondary School.

Joanne plays the piano and enjoys hockey. She is also involved in the Duke of Edinburgh Award Scheme.

Ivor Bradford McGaffin – Sixth Generation

Ivor Bradford McGaffin, second child of Margaret Annie Dunlop and William Henry McGaffin, was born on February 23rd, 1962 in the St George's District, Belfast. Ivor attended Windsor Hill Primary School and Newry High School, later entering catering college. He worked in the food industry for a number of years, eventually leaving the catering industry to attend a course on Environmental Health at the University of Glasgow.

He is currently living in Paisley, Scotland and works for Rolls Royce.

THE McGAFFIN BOYS
LEFT TO RIGHT: IVOR, ALAN, AND GARY

Alan Henry McGaffin – Sixth Generation

Alan Henry McGaffin, third child of Margaret Annie Dunlop and William Henry McGaffin, was born on June 10th, 1966 in Newry, County Down. Alan attended Windsor Hill Primary School, Newry High School, and the University of Ulster Jordanstown Campus, where he received a degree in Environmental Health. He is currently principal environmental health officer with the Greenock Council in Scotland

Alan, a gifted sportsman, played hockey at school, provincial, and international levels, captaining Ireland at the under-21 level.

Alan married Ann Jobson on August 31st, 1996, in Scotland. Ann was born on June 30th, 1966. The couple are keen hill walkers and live in Renfrew, Scotland. Ann also works as an environmental health officer.

ALAN HENRY McGAFFIN AND ANN JOBSON
WEDDING DAY – AUGUST 31, 1996

William Tweedie Dunlop – Fifth Generation

William Tweedie Dunlop, second child of Annie Tweedie and Joseph Enos Dunlop, was born on July 8th, 1934 in Newry, County Down, Northern Ireland.

Bill Dunlop was born and brought up at Tormore Villa, a few miles from what is now the city of Newry in County Down. He grew up in a strong Christian family which worshipped in First Newry Presbyterian Church where his father was an elder.

His early education was at Rockvale Public Elementary School; he occasionally had to travel the two miles to and from school by pony and trap. One of his vivid memories from the time involved killing a duck by accidentally riding over it while cycling furiously home one day. The incident was not reported to his parents or the owner of the duck!

Bill later attended Newry Model School and, at age 13, became a boarder at Armagh Royal School, where, among other achievements, he received a Special Prize for Music

Appreciation and the Morean Shield of Honor, a trophy which was awarded to a pupil based on votes by teaching staff and 5th- and 6th-year students.

He graduated from The Queen's University of Belfast in 1956 with a B.Sc. in Civil Engineering.

Bill married Joan Harriet Hood on September 14th, 1957 in The Church of Christ the Redeemer, Bessbrook, County Armagh. The date, by coincidence, was his parents' Silver Wedding anniversary. Joan, the daughter of Sam and Ettie Hood, was the first girl in a family of two boys and two girls and grew up in Bessbrook, where her father was manager of the Bessbrook Spinning and Weaving Company. Linen made in Bessbrook actually gained a measure of fame world-wide, as some of their product was used on the Cunard's Queen Mary and in the Savoy Hotel in London.

Bill had a natural ability for sports. While a strong competitor who loved to win, he could also be very gracious in defeat. At the Royal School in Armagh he held the record for the mile and was selected to play cricket for Ulster Schools. He went on to play senior league cricket in Armagh. He particularly enjoyed playing cricket in Bessbrook, and met Joan on holiday during a match—the result of which he doesn't particularly remember!

Beyond cricket, Bill was renowned for his determination not to be beaten at squash. Rugby, however, was probably his greatest sporting love, and he played for Queen's University's First Fifteen and for Ulster at Junior Provincial level. He was for some years on the committee of the Ulster branch of the Irish Rugby Football Union, and chairman of the grounds committee at Ravenhill for three years. He was also a member of the Dunmurry Golf Club, where he watched his handicap rise over the years from 7 to 16.

Bill's great love for classical music was shared by Joan, and together they attended concerts as often as they could.

In addition to working in Ireland, Bill's profession took him "over the water" to Scotland and overseas to Libya and the United Arab Emirates where, in association with Consarc, he opened an office in the Emirate of Sharjah. In total, he and Joan spent some ten years in these countries, and Bill often wondered whether they could be classed as economic migrants to the UAE. Some of his projects during this time included building a seventy-thousand-seat football/athletic stadium in Tripoli, subways, a cement factory, motor-ways, and bridges. In the U.K, he was engaged on two earth dams: Seaghan in Northern Ireland and Black Esk in Scotland.

From 1973 until his semi-retirement in 1997, Bill was a partner in William J. McDowell and Partners, a firm of Consulting Civil and Structural Engineers based in Belfast. Bill retired fully in 1999.

On their return home from the Middle East, Bill and Joan renewed their association with the Presbyterian church when they joined the Dunmurry congregation, where Bill was ordained an elder in 1991. In 1996, Bill and Joan moved house from Belfast to Aghalee but remained active members of Dunmurry Presbyterian Church.

On September 11, 1997, a family party was held at Tormore Villa to celebrate the Ruby Wedding Anniversary of Bill and Joan Dunlop. It was also the 100th Birthday of "Tormore Villa," which had been completed in 1897.

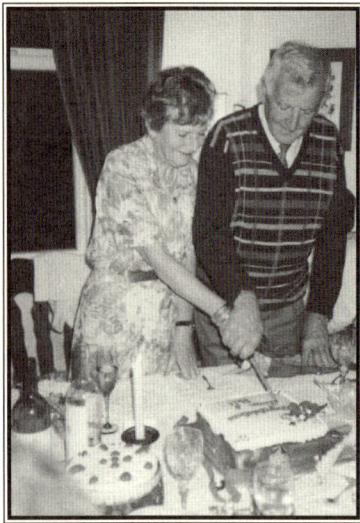

BILL AND JOAN DUNLOP
40TH WEDDING ANNIVERSARY
TORMORE VILLA
SEPTEMBER 11, 1997

Bill took a keen interest in and was Vice Chairman of Aghalee and District Development Association until his illness.

Bill died on July 30th, 2004. As with his parents, Bill was cremated and his ashes scattered in Roselawn Cemetery, Belfast.

John Dunlop – Fifth Generation

The Very Rev. Dr. John Dunlop, third child of Annie Tweedie and Joseph Enos Dunlop, was born on September 19th, 1939 at Tormore, near Newry, County Down. He was brought up in connection with 1st Newry Presbyterian Church. John received his primary education from Newry Model School and Newry Grammar School, moving on to the Royal Belfast Academical Institution. He is a graduate of The Queen's University of Belfast and New College, University of Edinburgh.

He was the assistant minister in Fitzroy Avenue Presbyterian Church, Belfast from 1965-68. He then worked with the United Church in Jamaica for ten years, the first three with the Mount Hermon Charge of four churches in Westmoreland, the rest with Webster Memorial United Church in Kingston.

On his return from Jamaica, John was appointed minister of Rosemary Presbyterian Church in North Belfast, a charge he held until his retirement from the active ministry in 2004. In 1992-93 John was elected Moderator of the General Assembly of The Presbyterian Church in Ireland. He was awarded the CBE in the New Year's Honors list January 2004 "for services to the community," an Honorary DD from the Presbyterian Theological Faculty of Ireland and Trinity College Dublin, and an Honorary LLD degrees from the University of Ulster and The Queen's University of Belfast. He was also a member of the Senate at

The Queen's University of Belfast from 1987-1999. In 1985-86 he delivered the Warrack Lectures on "Preaching in the Midst of Conflict" to the Theological faculties of the Universities of Edinburgh, Aberdeen, Glasgow, and St. Andrew's. He was an Eisenhower Fellow in 1989.

John married Edna Rosemary Willis, the sixth child of Fredrick and Margaret Willis, on August 10th, 1965, in her home congregation of Second Comber Presbyterian Church. Rosemary attended Belfast High School and is a graduate of The Queen's University of Belfast, where she was the Vice-President of the Christian Union.

Rosemary taught for two years in Fane Street School in Belfast until Karen Patricia Dunlop was born on August 31st, 1967. When the family moved to Jamaica in 1968, Rosemary worked as a counselor in the newly formed Family Court and as part of the family counseling service based at Webster Memorial Church. The couple's second child Keith Willis Dunlop was born in Montego Bay, Jamaica on December 19, 1968.

EDNA ROSEMARY WILLIS DUNLOP AND
REV. DR. JOHN DUNLOP

Rosemary, an accredited counselor/therapist with the British Association for Counseling and Psychotherapy, has wide experience in the field of couples counseling. In addition, Rosemary, like John, has a deep interest in cross-community conflict resolution. She was a founding member of the Corrymeela Community and has been a member of the Cultural Heritage and Education for Mutual Understanding Working Groups. One-time chair of the Belfast YMCA and a member of the boards of Stanmillis University College and St. Mary's University College, Rosemary at time of writing is a non-executive director on the board of the Mater Hospital, Belfast.

In June 1993, John received the Cultural Traditions Award in recognition of his "established and continuing contribution to debate on cultural diversity within Northern Ireland." In 2002 he received the E.H. Johnston Memorial Trust award from the Presbyterian Church in Canada. His book *A Precarious Belonging: Presbyterians and the Conflict in Ireland* was published by Blackstaff Press in May 1995.

John has written and presented a number of programs for RTE and Ulster Television, where he was the Presbyterian Religious Advisor from 1993-2002. He is a regular contributor to BBC Radio Ulster's and BBC Radio 4's "Thought for the Day," Sunday Worship, and current affairs programs. In 2005, John and Rosemary traveled with Imagine Media Productions Ltd. to the USA, Japan, and China to make six television programs commissioned by BBC Northern Ireland.

In 1996-97 John, with Dr. Peter North, vice-chancellor of Oxford University, and Fr. Oliver Crilly from Strabane, sat as a member of the Independent Review of Parades and Marches.

From December 2001-May 2002, John chaired the North Belfast Action Project with Msgr. Tom Toner and Mr. Roy Adams, which produced a report for the First and Deputy First Ministers and the Minister for Social Development in the Northern Ireland Executive.

John has spoken at many inter-church services, and given numerous lectures at events organized by a wide cross-section of groups, exploring both the importance of understanding different cultures, histories, and religions, and the difficulties involved in the church's identification with particular communities in its responsibility to be agent and facilitator of reconciliation. He has visited the United States on several occasions at the invitation of the Presbyterian Church USA and the US Catholic Conference. In May 1995 he attended and spoke at President Clinton's White House conference on investment with Cardinal Daly.

John was co-convener of the Presbyterian Church's Church and Government Committee for many years, and is secretary of the Joint Independent Group for Study and Action [JIGSA]. He is also a member of the Irish Inter-Church Meeting and the Irish/USA Inter-Church Committee on Northern Ireland, and sits on the Board of Governors of Cavehill Primary School. He is a patron of Wave Trauma Centre, the Northern Ireland Council for Integrated Education, and Habitat for Humanity, and a director of the Northern Ireland Memorial Fund. Until recently, he was also a member of the Board of (British-Irish) Encounter.

John and Rosemary have four grandchildren and live in Newtownabby, County Antrim.

THE DUNLOP FAMILY OUTSIDE THE GATES OF BUCKINGHAM PALACE, LONDON IN 2004
BACK ROW, LEFT TO RIGHT: JENNIFER AND KEITH DUNLOP, ROSEMARY AND JOHN DUNLOP, KAREN AND
ALLAN WILSON; FRONT ROW, LEFT TO RIGHT: ROMY DUNLOP, JENNIFER WILSON, KRISTEN DUNLOP, AND
EUAN WILSON

SIXTH GENERATION

Karen Patricia Dunlop, Keith Willis Dunlop

Karen Patricia Dunlop – Sixth Generation

Karen Patricia Dunlop, first child of John Dunlop and Edna Rosemary Willis, was born on August 31st, 1967 in Belfast. Before she was one year old, she moved with her parents to Lamb's River, Westmoreland, Jamaica, where her father was a minister with the United Church of Jamaica and Grand Cayman.

When the family moved to Kingston, Jamaica in 1971, Karen attended St. Andrew's Preparatory School and, later, when the family moved back to Belfast in 1978, Cavehill Primary School and Belfast Royal Academy. In school she sang in the choir and participated in two choir trips to Edinburgh. She was an active member of the youth programmes in Rosemary Presbyterian Church, including the Girl Guides.

On leaving school, Karen became a student nurse in the Royal Victoria Hospital, Belfast, where she later became a registered general nurse. She later completed her midwifery training in Rankin Memorial Hospital in Greenock. From there she moved as a staff midwife to Law Hospital, which was incorporated into the new Wishaw General Hospital in 2001. She graduated from Glasgow Caledonian University with a B.Sc degree in Midwifery Studies. While working in Law Hospital, she did three months voluntary nursing in a hospital in Zimbabwe with the Elim Church.

Karen joined Kirkton Parish Church in Carluke, South Lanarkshire, Scotland. She has been an active member of the congregation, participating in the singing group, the JIGSAW House Group, a prayer group, and the local Christian Aid Committee.

Karen met Allan Wilson in Kirkton Church, and the couple married on April 5th, 1997 in Rosemary Presbyterian Church, Belfast.

Allan is the youngest child of Jim and Irene Wilson from Glasgow, Scotland. After graduating from the University of Glasgow, Allan worked with the Church of Scotland as a teacher in Kihumbuini Secondary School in Thika, Kenya. From 1991-92 he taught physics and math in the high school on the Scottish island of Islay. In 1993 he was appointed principal teacher of physics in Caldervale High School in North Lanarkshire. In 2003, Allan was accepted as a candidate for the ministry of the Church of Scotland and resigned his position at the school. Allan graduated in 2006 from Glasgow University with a B.D. degree. He is currently an assistant Minister in the Church of Scotland.

The couple has two children: Jennifer Ruth Wilson, born July 14, 1998 in Carluke South Lanarkshire, Scotland, and Euan James Wilson, born September 12, 2002 in Wishaw, North Lanarkshire, Scotland.

THE WILSON FAMILY
LEFT TO RIGHT: ALLAN, JENNIFER, EUAN, AND KAREN

Seventh Generation

Jennifer Ruth Wilson, Euan James Wilson

Jennifer Ruth Wilson – Seventh Generation

Jennifer Ruth Wilson, first child of Karen Patricia Dunlop and Allan John Wilson, was born on July 14th, 1998 in Carluke, South Lanarkshire, Scotland.

Euan James Wilson – Seventh Generation

Euan James Wilson, second child of Karen Patricia Wilson and Allan John Wilson, was born on September 12th, 2002 in Wishaw, North Lanarkshire, Scotland.

Keith Willis Dunlop – Sixth Generation

Keith Willis Dunlop, second child of John Dunlop and Edna Rosemary Willis, was born on December 19th, 1968 in Montego Bay, Jamaica where his father was working in Lamb's River, Westmoreland as a minister with the United Church of Jamaica and Grand Cayman.

When the family moved to Kingston, Jamaica in 1971, Keith attended St. Andrew's Preparatory School. When the family moved back to Belfast in 1978, he attended Belfast Royal Academy.

Keith took full advantage of the sporting facilities offered at school: swimming, playing hockey, cricket, tennis, and water polo. He was also an active member of the Youth Programmes in Rosemary Presbyterian Church, including the Boys' Brigade.

Keith graduated from the University of Ulster at Jordanstown in 1992 with an honors degree in Mechanical Engineering. An enthusiastic hockey player, Keith won a British Universities Sports Federation silver medal with the Northern Ireland Universities team. He also played hockey for the Irish Universities Hockey Team and Senior League hockey with Cliftonville Hockey Club.

Upon graduating, Keith worked for the University of Ulster and Bombardier Aerospace before moving to England to work for MSC Software, which has headquarters in Los Angeles.

On September 20th, 1996, Keith married Jennifer Lesley McCullough in Rosemary Presbyterian Church, Belfast. Jenny was born in Lisburn, the third child of William and Marlene (nee Black—now Finch) McCullough. A pupil of Finaghy Primary School and Victoria College, Belfast, Jenny graduated from the University of Ulster in 1994 with an honors degree in Fashion and Textile Design. As a young person, Jenny had the opportunity to travel extensively, spending summers with her father in Singapore, Australia, and Papua

New Guinea. Jenny was a store manager with Sofa Workshop and currently works as an artist.

The couple is living in the beautiful small town of West Kirby on the Wirral Peninsula in England, where both of their daughters were born. Kristen Emily Dunlop was born May 21, 2000, and Romy Hannah Dunlop March 13, 2002.

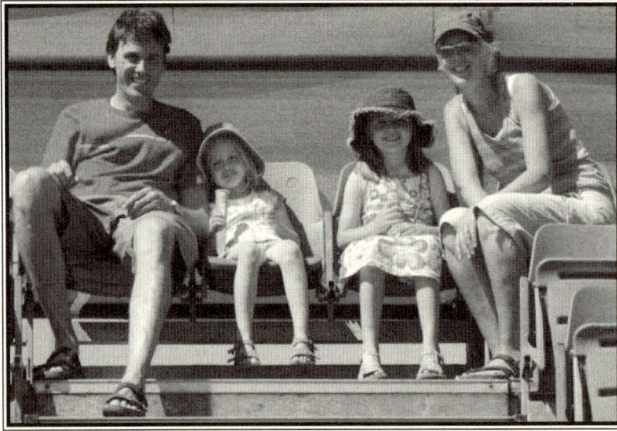

THE DUNLOP FAMILY AT THE BRITISH OPEN GOLF CHAMPIONSHIP AT HOYLAKE, LIVERPOOL
LEFT TO RIGHT: KEITH, ROMY, KRISTEN, AND JENNY
JULY 2006

SEVENTH GENERATION

Kristen Emily Dunlop, Romy Hannah Dunlop

Kristen Emily Dunlop – Seventh Generation

Kristen Emily Dunlop, first daughter of Keith Willis Dunlop and Jennifer Lesley McCullough, was born on May 21st, 2000 in West Kirby on the Wirral Peninsula, England.

Romy Hannah Dunlop – Seventh Generation

Romy Hannah Dunlop, second daughter of Keith Willis Dunlop and Jennifer Lesley McCullough, was born on March 13th, 2002 in West Kirby on the Wirral Peninsula in England.

Hugh Richard Dunlop – Fifth Generation

Hugh Richard Dunlop, fourth child of Annie Tweedie and Joseph Enos Dunlop, was born on September 29th, 1940. He was brought up in the family home at Tormore, Newry and attended Newry Grammar School. He continued his education at The Queen's University of Belfast, where he studied medicine.

After serving as a medical missionary in Malawi, he has for thirty years been a family doctor in Belfast.

Richard is married to a doctor and has two daughters, both of whom are pursuing non-medical careers outside Northern Ireland.

Anna Lucinda Tweedie – Third Generation

Anna Lucinda Tweedie, second child of Margaret Peggy McClelland and Thomas Tweedie, was born on September 10th, 1870 in Newry, County Down, Ireland. It is likely that, in keeping with the times, Anna's mother returned home to Cloughenramer for the birth.

Anna and her brother were brought up at Tormore and attended the local Rockvale Primary School where her mother was formerly a teacher. Given her mother's influence, it is not surprising that Anna decided to make teaching her career as well. While no early records of where she taught survive, we do know that in 1891 she was appointed as principal teacher at Kingsmills National School in County Armagh.

The history of education at this time suggests that Anna would have begun as a paid monitor in her local school of Rockvale, moving on to undertake a three- or four-year course of study combined with practical teaching that culminated with a public examination. A final year would have seen her training at a model school and Marlborough Street Training College in Dublin.

Her predecessor at Kingsmills School was a Mr. Whiteside, who gained a reputation as a strict disciplinarian through his liberal use of the cane. After sixteen years, he and his wife were dismissed from the school for intemperance. Clearly the school management wanted a change of direction, and the newly qualified twenty-one-year-old Anna was their choice. It proved an inspired one.

After a few years, teachers whose work was favorably reported upon were allowed to sit for an examination known as Second of First Class, with those with the highest marks granted permission to sit for First of First Class. This latter examination with a pass mark of 65% was equal to a university degree. Anna was a First Class teacher.

ANNA LUCINDA TWEEDIE McCORMICK (EXTREME RIGHT)
KINGSMILL SCHOOL WITH HER PUPILS CIRCA 1900

Field	Value
Type	Civil Marriages
Date Of Marriage	05/09/1902
Husband Firstname	JOHN A
Husband Surname	MCCORMICK
Husband Townland / Street	DIVERNAGH
Husband Occupation	CARMAN
Husband Age	FA
Husband Denomination	Presbyterian
Husband Marital Status	Bachelor (Previously unmarried)
Husband Father Firstname	JOHN
Husband Father Surname	MCCORMICK
Husband Father Occupation	FARMER
Husband Mother Firstname	
Husband Mother Surname	
Husband Witness Firstname	THOMAS
Husband Witness Surname	MCCORMICK
Wife Firstname	ANNA L
Wife Surname	TWEEDIE
Wife Townland / Street	LISADIAN
Wife Occupation	N S TEACHER
Wife Age	FA
Wife Denomination	Presbyterian
Wife Marital Status	Spinster (Previously unmarried)
Wife Father Firstname	THOMAS
Wife Father Surname	TWEEDIE
Wife Father Occupation	CABINET MAKER
Wife Mother Firstname	
Wife Mother Surname	
Wife Witness Firstname	LUCY
Wife Witness Surname	MCCLELLAND
Denomination	
Comment	BY LICENCE REV J MEEKE
Street	KINGSMILL Presbyterian
Town	NEWRY & MOURNE
Area	LOUGHGILLY
County	CO DOWN

MARRIAGE REFERENCE
ANNA LUCINDA TWEEDIE AND
JOHN McCORMICK
SEPTEMBER 5, 1902

KINGSMILL OLD SCHOOL, WHERE ANNA LUCINDA TWEEDIE
McCORMICK TAUGHT FOR 15 YEARS. THE SCHOOL HAS
BEEN DEMOLISHED.

During her time at Kingsmills, Anna met John Alexander McCormick, a carman from the townland of Divernagh, County Armagh. The couple married in Kingsmills Presbyterian Church on September 5th, 1902.

They had two sons: George, born August 13, 1903, and Thomas, born September 29, 1906.

FAMILY HOME (NOW DEMOLISHED) WHERE JOHN ALEXANDER MCCORMICK AND EACH OF HIS WIVES LIVED, AND WHERE ALL OF HIS CHILDREN WERE BORN. THE PHOTOGRAPH SHOWS SALLY ISOBEL MCCORMICK AND HER HALF-BROTHER ROBERT MCCORMICK MIXING CEMENT.

Anna continued to teach following the birth of her first son, and was still teaching while carrying her second child. Tragically, Anna contracted acute meningitis five days after the birth of Thomas and died suddenly on October 4th, 1906 in Divernagh, County Armagh, Ireland. She was buried in the graveyard adjoining Kingsmills Presbyterian Church, in the McCormick family grave.

KINGSMILLS PRESBYTERIAN CHURCH AND ADJOINING GRAVEYARD WHERE
ANNA LUCINDA TWEEDIE McCORMICK IS BURIED

The high esteem in which she was held was reflected in her obituary, which appeared in the *Newry Reporter* on October 9th, 1906, as well as the poem written in her memory by a local person and addressed to the pupils at Kingsmills School.

Obituary – Anna Lucinda McCormick

"On Saturday last, at 1:30 p.m., the remains of the late Mrs. McCormick, wife of Mr. John A. McCormick, of Divernagh, Bessbrook, and only daughter of Mr. Thomas Tweedie, of Tormore, Newry, were interred in the family burying ground attached to the Kingsmills Presbyterian Church. The deceased lady was 15 years the respected teacher of the Kingsmills National School, and by all who knew her she was held in the highest esteem. Her death on the 4th inst. evoked feelings of the deepest regret throughout the district in which she lived, where she was justly beloved for her many estimable qualities and good works. The funeral was of a very large and representative character. The public of all creeds and classes in the district, including a goodly contingent from Newry, attended to pay their last tribute of respect to her memory, and the mournful cortege included no less than fifty vehicles.

The chief mourners were: Messrs. John A. McCormick (husband), Thomas Tweedie, Tormore (father); W. J. Tweedie (brother-in-law), and Thomas McCormick (brother-in-law).

The Rev. James Meeke, M.A., Presbyterian Minister, Kingsmills, officiated at the graveside."

Pulpit Reference

"On Sabbath morning, at the close of his sermon, which was upon the Christian's death as a 'falling asleep,' the Rev. Mr. Meeke referred in feeling terms to the death of the deceased lady. As the teacher of their day school for 15 years, and as a teacher in the Sabbath school she had a very important part in moulding the lines of a large number of the young and fitting them for positions of usefulness. She fully realized the position of great influence which the Providence of God opened for her, and she realized it not as some do, by growing self important and boastful, but by directing her self with great earnestness to her work. As the leader of the Psalmody in that congregation, she came into close touch with their congregational worship, leading in that part of their service with a devoutness and expressiveness which did good to them all. In the school her gentle and winning way made her beloved by the children, while her firmness and fairness conduced greatly to the order and success of her work. One seldom found a mind so well balanced, so gentle, and just, and temperate. She procured the confidence of the inspectors to a great degree; they frequently spoke to him of the solid and useful work she was doing. Under the old arrangement, she occupied the rank of a first-class teacher, and under the new arrangement, by which increase of salary was given for good service, it was his privilege to pass on to her a substantial increase last year. She did not confine herself to the intellectual training of the children. She was greatly interested in their moral welfare. She taught to ground them in sound temperance principles, and formed a Band of Hope for her children. He had the pleasure of getting the membership cards for her and being present at the signing of the first names on the roll. She never advertised herself, never descended to the tricks which some people adopted to make themselves popular. She had too sacred a sense of duty, too strong a sense of self-respect, and too high an ideal of what she wished to reach in the minds of the children. Suddenly, very suddenly, in the midst of her strength, in the midst of her work, God's finger touched her, and slept. She rests from her labour; she has entered her reward –

> Servant of God, well done! Rest from thy loved employ;
> The battle's fought, the victory's won, enter the Master's joy.

Mr. John A. McCormick and Mr. Thomas Tweedie – the deceased lady's husband and father – desire to take this opportunity of tendering their heartfelt thanks to the numerous friends who sympathized with them, personally and by letter, in their sad bereavement."

In Loving Memory
OF
MRS M'CORMACK,
Who Died on 4th October, 1906.

TO THE CHILDREN OF KINGSMILL SCHOOL.

No more her soothing voice is heard
In Sabbath School or pew,
No more the children gather round
Their teacher kind and true.

She has fought for King and country,
By faith was bravely led,
Till she by death was conquered
And numbered with the dead.

The King, He is Immanuel,
A mighty King is He,
By whom all Christians conquer,
If led by Him they be.

The country, it is Heaven,
That bright and better land,
Where all is peace and concord
And joy at God's right hand.

The foe is sin and satan,
With all incarnal lust,
But she through faith has conquered,
In Jesus placing trust.

T. M'CALDEN.

A poem written in memory of Mrs. John McCormack, Divernagh (mother of Mr. Thomas McCormick). She was a teacher in both the day school and the Sabbath school at Kingsmills.

FOURTH GENERATION

George McCormick, Thomas Tweedie McCormick

George McCormick – Fourth Generation

George McCormick, first child of John Alexander McCormick and Anna Lucinda Tweedie, was born on August 13th, 1903 in the townland of Divernagh, close to the village of Bessbrook in County Armagh, Ireland. His mother, Anna, a schoolteacher in Kingsmills Primary, died when he was three years old, and George went to live with a farmer uncle. It was the land that would provide George with his livelihood when he left the local Eshwary School. He did, however, also inherit the Tweedie ability to work skillfully with his hands as a gardener and a craftsman, a fact to which family members still refer.

George married Mary Cartmill, a widow. Minnie, as she was known, was born Mary Clulow on July 8th, 1911 at Clarkhill, Castlewellan. She and George were married on October 15th, 1947 in Downshire Presbyterian Church, Newry, County Down.

GEORGE MCCORMICK AND MARY CLULOW CARTMILL MARRIAGE CERTIFICATE – OCTOBER 15, 1947

LEFT TO RIGHT: JIM MCCULLAN, MINNIE MCCORMICK (BRIDE), GEORGE MCCORMICK (GROOM), AND SALLY MCCORMICK, WEDDING DAY – OCTOBER 15, 1947

George and Minnie lived at Divernagh, later moving to the seaside town of Rostrevor, County Down. Minnie and her first husband William Cartmill had two sons: William, who was tragically killed in a motorbike accident in the mid 1960s, and James, who was living in Rathfriland at the time of his mother's death.

George died May 2nd, 1990. He was cremated and his ashes interred in Bessbrook Presbyterian Church graveyard thirteen days later. Minnie survived him by just over one year, dying on June 3rd, 1991. The couple is buried in Row 2 Plot 36 with the single word Cartmill on the headstone.

THE BURIAL PLOT OF GEORGE AND MINNIE McCORMICK IN BESSBROOK PRESBYTERIAN CHURCH GRAVEYARD. NOTE: MINNIE'S FIRST HUSBAND WAS CARTMILL

FIFTH GENERATION

William Cartmill, James Cartmill

William Cartmill – Fifth Generation

William Cartmill, first child of Mary Minnie Clulow Cartmill and William Cartmill, was tragically killed in a motorbike accident in the mid 1960s.

James Cartmill – Fifth Generation

James Cartmill, second child of Mary Minnie Clulow Cartmill and William Cartmill, was living in Rathfriland at the time of his mother's death.

Thomas Tweedie McCormick – Fourth Generation

Thomas Tweedie McCormick, second child of John Alexander McCormick and Anna Lucinda Tweedie, was born on September 29th, 1906 in the townland of Divernagh near Bessbrook, County Armagh, Ireland. His mother Anna, a schoolteacher at Kingsmills Primary School, died of acute meningitis five days after Thomas was born.

Thomas attended the local Eshwary Primary School, subsequently returning to the family farm, which was to be his lifelong home and chosen career.

On January 12th, 1938, Thomas Tweedie McCormick married Mary Agnes Eileen Cartmill in Rostrevor Presbyterian Church.

THOMAS TWEEDIE MCCORMICK AND MARY AGNES EILEEN CARTMILL WEDDING DAY – JANUARY 12, 1938
BACK ROW, LEFT TO RIGHT: DAVID MCCORMICK, REV. H.S.CARSER, MRS. ANNA MCCORMICK (THIRD WIFE OF JOHN ALEXANDER MCCORMICK), SADIE RANTON, JONNY RANTON, ROBERT MCCORMICK; FRONT ROW, LEFT TO RIGHT: MAY EDGAR, SALLY ISOBEL MCCORMICK, THOMAS TWEEDIE MCCORMICK (GROOM), MARY AGNES EILEEN MCCORMICK (BRIDE), GEORGE MCCORMICK, AND SAMMY CARTMILL

The couple set up house on the family farm at Divernagh. They had three children: John Samuel Wesley, born January 4, 1939, Thomas Winston, born August 9, 1941, and James Raymond, born August 10, 1943.

Mary Agnes Eileen McCormick died March 14th, 1963 and is buried in Kingsmills Presbyterian Church graveyard.

Thomas was a lifelong member of Kingsmills Presbyterian Church. He was elected to both the Congregational Committee and the Eldership, where he served as Clerk of Session for a number of years before his death on November 22nd, 1993.

Thomas is buried beside his wife Mary Agnes Eileen in the Kingsmills Presbyterian Church graveyard.

FIFTH GENERATION

John Samuel Wesley McCormick, Thomas Winston McCormick, James Raymond McCormick

John Samuel Wesley McCormick – Fifth Generation

John Samuel Wesley McCormick, first child of Thomas Tweedie McCormick and Mary Agnes Eileen Cartmill, was born on January 4th, 1939 in the townland of Divernagh near the village of Bessbrook, County Armagh, Northern Ireland.

JOHN SAMUEL WESLEY McCORMICK AND
NORAH OLIVIA ACHESON
WEDDING DAY – SEPTEMBER 5, 1967

Wesley attended Kingsmills Primary School for a short time (where his grandmother, Anna Lucinda Tweedie McCormick, had taught until her untimely death in 1906). An able pupil, Wesley progressed to Newry Grammar School, where he passed both the Junior and Senior Certificate Examinations.

Following his school days, Wesley was employed in both the retail and wholesale grocery business in Newry. He later worked for the Roads Division of Department of Environment based in Craigavon, County Armagh, taking early retirement from his employment in 1997.

Wesley married Norah Olivia Acheson on September 5th, 1967 in Tullyallen Presbyterian Church.

Norah was born on January 21st, 1937. The couple live in Divernagh, in the home built by Anna McCormick, third wife of John Alexander McCormick, by whom Wesley was brought up.

The couple, : have two children: Eileen Olivia, born February 3, 1969, and Anna Isobel, born February 17, 1972.

Wesley and Norah are kept busy by their two grandchildren, who live next door. They also find time for a little home decorating, tending the garden, and attending activities at Kingsmills Presbyterian Church, where Wesley serves on the Congregational Committee.

SIXTH GENERATION

Eileen Olivia McCormick, Anna Isobel McCormick

Eileen Olivia McCormick – Sixth Generation

Eileen Olivia McCormick, first child of John Samuel Wesley McCormick and Norah Olivia Acheson, was born on February 3rd, 1969. Olive was brought up in the townland of

Divernagh and attended Mountnorris Primary School and Markethill High School. She later attended Newry Technical College, where she obtained a B.Tec in Business Studies. Olive then worked in the Veterinary Office in Armagh City, and later in the Southern Education and Library Board offices, also in Armagh City.

THE WYLIE FAMILY
BACK ROW, LEFT TO RIGHT: WESLEY McCORMICK, ROBERT WYLIE; MIDDLE ROW, LEFT TO RIGHT: NORAH McCORMICK, OLIVE WYLIE, EMILY WYLIE; FRONT ROW: ANNA LOUISE WYLIE

She married Stephen Robert Wylie on September 7th, 1990 in Kingsmills Presbyterian Church. They have two children: Emily Claire, born October 22, 1990, and Anna Louise, born August 8, 1994. While the children were small Olive took time out from work, but has since returned to work in a school canteen in Newry City.

SEVENTH GENERATION

Emily Claire Wylie, Anna Louise Wylie

Emily Claire Wylie – Seventh Generation

Emily Claire Wylie, first child of Eileen Olivia (Olive) McCormick and Stephen Robert Wylie, was born on October 22nd, 1990. She was brought up in the townland of Divernagh, close to the village of Bessbrook in County Armagh, Northern Ireland.

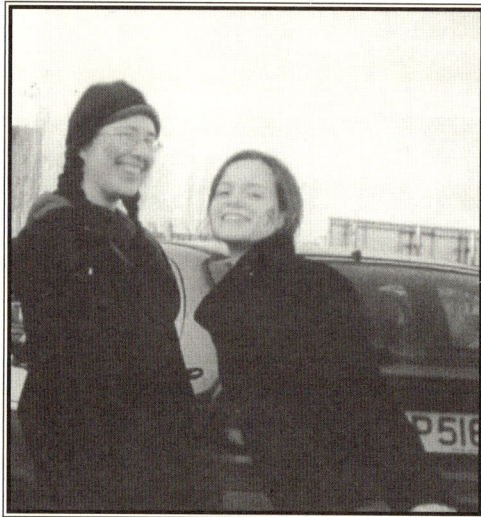

CLAIRE AND FAMILY FRIEND SHARON ATTENDING
THE RUGBY FOOTBALL INTERNATIONAL
IN SCOTLAND

Claire is currently attending Markethill High School. She enjoys art, cooking and watching TV.

Anna Louise Wylie – Seventh Generation

Anna Louise Wylie, second child of Eileen Olivia (Olive) McCormick and Stephen Robert Wylie, was born on August 8th, 1994. Like her sister, she was brought up in the townland of Divernagh close to the village of Bessbrook in County Armagh, Northern Ireland.

Anna is in her final year at Kingsmills Primary School, where her great-great-grand-mother, Anna Lucinda Tweedie McCormick, was principal teacher in the opening years of the 20th century.

ANNA WYLIE WITH HER FAVORITE CALF

Anna likes drawing, painting, and all sorts of animals. She also likes to help her grandfather, who lives next door, with his garden.

Anna Isobel McCormick – Sixth Generation

Anna Isobel McCormick, second child of John Samuel Wesley McCormick and Norah Olivia Acheson, was born on February 17th, 1972. Brought up in the townland of Divernagh in County Armagh, Northern Ireland, Isobel attended Mountnorris and Kingsmills Primary Schools and Newry High School. She then obtained a B.Sc Hons Degree from the University of Ulster and continued her education at Herriot Watt University in Edinburgh, where she received an M.Sc.

Currently working as an environmental health officer in South Lanarkshire Council, Scotland, Isobel is a keen traveler and has visited many parts of the world. She also enjoys hill-walking and traditional music.

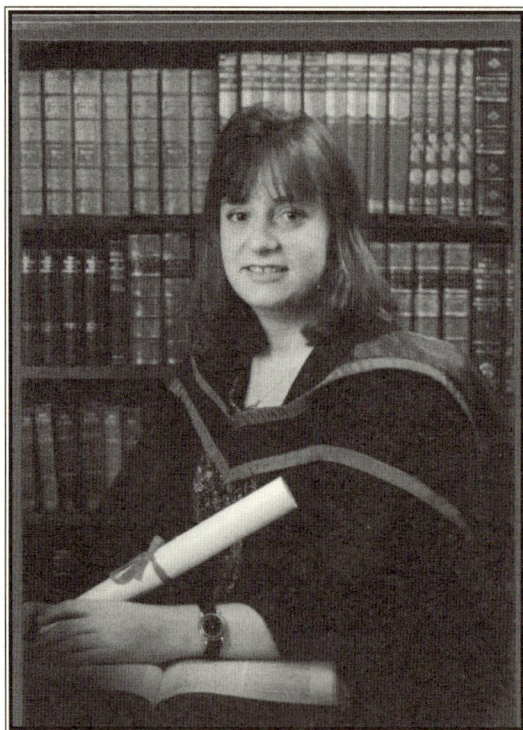

ANNA ISOBEL McCORMICK

Thomas Winston McCormick – Fifth Generation

Thomas Winston McCormick, second child of Thomas Tweedie McCormick and Mary Agnes Eileen Cartmill, was born on August 9th, 1941 in the townland of Divernagh near Bessbrook, County Armagh, Northern Ireland.

Winston attended Bessbrook Primary School and Newry Technical College. He later went to Belfast Technical College, where he obtained an H.N.C. in Civil Engineering. He was employed by the Department of Environment in the Roads Section based in Craigavon until 1995, when he took early retirement.

Winston married Sandra Barron in Rostrevor Presbyterian Church on June 3rd, 1969. Sandra was born on September 1st, 1947.

THE McCORMICK FAMILY
LEFT TO RIGHT: KATRINA McCORMICK, GEOFFREY McCORMICK,
SANDRA AND WINSTON McCORMICK, AND ALLISON McCORMICK

Winston and Sandra have a family of two: Margaret Eileen Allison, born September 7, 1969, and Geoffery Thomas Andrew, born October 25, 1974.

Sandra is a member of the Tandragee Presbyterian Church choir, and Winston serves on the Church Committee.

SIXTH GENERATION

Margaret Eileen Allison McCormick, Geoffrey Thomas Andrew McCormick

Margaret Eileen Allison McCormick – Sixth Generation

Margaret Eileen Allison McCormick, first child of Thomas Winston McCormick and Sandra Barron, was born on September 7th, 1969. Allison was brought up in the townland of Divernagh near the village of Bessbrook in County Armagh, Northern Ireland.

She attended Tandragee Primary School and later Tandragee High School and Portadown College.

Allison is currently employed by the Southern Health and Social Services Board in Armagh City. In her spare time, Allison is a leader with the Anchor Boys in the Tandragee Scout Troop.

LEFT TO RIGHT: GEOFFREY, SANDRA, ALLISON AND WINSTON McCORMICK

Geoffrey Thomas Andrew McCormick – Sixth Generation

Geoffrey Thomas Andrew McCormick, second child of Thomas Winston McCormick and Sandra Barron, was born on October 25th, 1974 in the townland of Lisnalea, County Armagh, Northern Ireland.

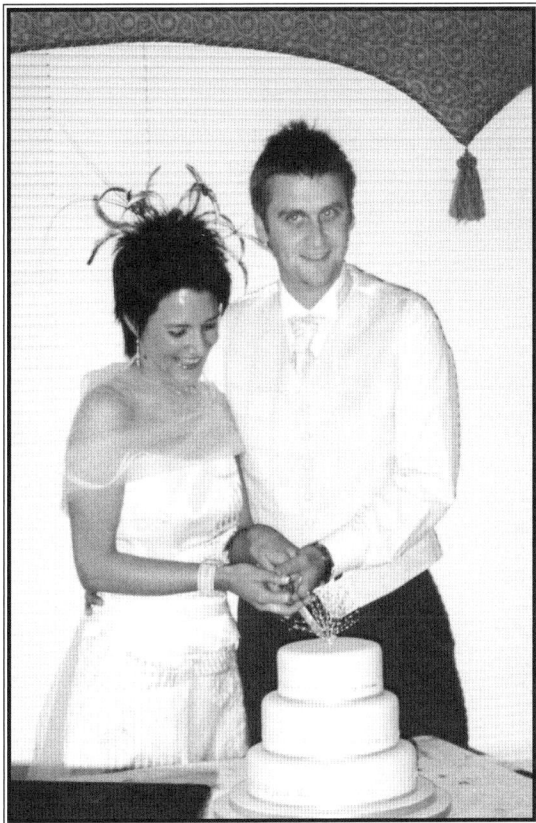

KATRINA MCNAUGHER AND GEOFFREY MCCORMICK
WEDDING DAY – MAY 27, 2005

Geoffrey attended Tandragee Primary and High School. He also studied at Portadown College and The Queen's University of Belfast, where he obtained a B.Sc degree in Geography. He completed a post-graduate course at the University of Ulster, Coleraine and received a diploma in Environmental Management. Geoffrey is currently working with Ballymoney Council.

Geoffrey married Katrina McNaugher on May 27th, 2005 in a civil ceremony at the beautiful National Trust property of Mussenden Temple near Castlerock, County Londonderry. Tina is a cardiac-care nurse. They now live in the village of Moneydig, close to the town of Garvagh.

Geoffrey and Katrina have one child, Ellé McCormick, born November 7th, 2006.

SEVENTH GENERATION

Ellé McCormick – Seventh Generation

Ellé McCormick, first child of Geoffrey Thomas Andrew McCormick and Katrina McNaugher McCormick, was born on Tuesday, November 7th, 2006 in Coleraine General Hospital, County Antrim, North Ireland.

James Raymond McCormick – Fifth Generation

James Raymond McCormick, third child of Thomas Tweedie McCormick and Mary Agnes Eileen Cartmill, was born on August 10th, 1943 in the townland of Divernagh near Bessbrook, County Armagh, Northern Ireland.

Raymond was a pupil at the nearby Bessbrook Primary School. Following the completion of his secondary education, Raymond went to Canada for four years—two years in an Asbestos mine in British Columbia followed by two further years in the Yukon Territory. He then felt the call of home and returned to Divernagh to farm.

Raymond married Mary Elizabeth Cartmill on October 28th, 1972 in Kingsmills Presbyterian Church. Elizabeth was born on May 18th, 1953.

Raymond and Elizabeth have three children: James Robert Darren, born June 20, 1974, Thomas Herbert Colin, born March 19, 1977, and Gareth Raymond Edwin, born April 13, 1982.

Raymond owns a vintage Fordson tractor and attends local vintage rallies when time permits. Elizabeth is a housewife and a member of the Kingsmills Presbyterian Church choir. She enjoys gardening, baking, and playing badminton.

RAYMOND AND ELIZABETH McCORMICK

SIXTH GENERATION

James Robert Darren McCormick, Thomas Herbert Colin McCormick,
Gareth Raymond Edwin McCormick

James Robert Darren McCormick – Sixth Generation

James Robert Darren McCormick, first child of James Raymond McCormick and Mary Elizabeth Cartmill, was born on June 20th, 1974. Darren was brought up in the townland of Divernagh near Bessbrook in County Armagh, Northern Ireland.

Darren attended Newry Model School, Newry High School, and The Queen's University of Belfast, where he obtained a B.Sc degree in Agriculture. Darren then returned to work on the family farm.

He married Nicola Alexandra Patterson in Kingsmills Presbyterian Church on December 17th, 2004. Nicola teaches in Craigavon Junior High School. The couple live on Derrymulligan Road, close to the family farm.

DARREN McCORMICK AND NICOLA PATTERSON
WEDDING DAY – DECEMBER 17, 2004

Thomas Herbert Colin McCormick – Sixth Generation

Thomas Herbert Colin McCormick, second child of James Raymond McCormick and Mary Elizabeth Cartmill, was born on March 19th, 1977. Colin was brought up in the townland of Divernagh near the village of Bessbrook in County Armagh, Northern Ireland.

Colin attended Newry Model School and Newry High School. He then furthered his education at Loughrey Agriculture College and Oakbridge College, Scotland where he was certified as a farrier. Afterwards, he came home and established his own farrier business in the Bessbrook area.

Colin married Nicola Richmond on March 24th, 2001 in Kingsmills Presbyterian Church.

NICOLA RICHMOND AND COLIN McCORMICK
WEDDING DAY – MARCH 24, 2001

Nicola, like Colin, has a keen interest in animals, and both are currently expanding the farrier business to include kennels, a cattery, and an animal grooming business.

Gareth Raymond Edwin McCormick – Sixth Generation

Gareth Raymond Edwin McCormick, third child of James Raymond McCormick and Mary Elizabeth Cartmill, was born on April 13th, 1982 and brought up in the townland of Divernagh near Bessbrook, County Armagh, Northern Ireland.

Gareth attended Newry Model School, Newry High School, Armagh Technical College, and the University of Ulster Jordanstown Campus, where he obtained an H.N.D. in Electrical Engineering. He is currently working at Warrentpoint Harbor as an electrical engineer.

GARETH McCORMICK

On September 25th, 1907, John Alexander McCormick married Mary Charlotte Robb. This, his second marriage, produced four boys: Jack, born September 27, 1908, Edmond, born October 7, 1911, David, born June 13, 1913, and Robert, born April 20, 1916.

FOURTH GENERATION

Jack McCormick, Edmond McCormick, David McCormick, Robert McCormick

Jack McCormick – Fourth Generation

Jack McCormick, first child of John Alexander McCormick and Mary Charlotte Robb, was born on September 27th, 1908 and remained unmarried. He worked for the PYE Radio Company in Dublin.

Jack died on April 29th, 1989 and is buried in the Armagh Road Cemetery in Newry City.

Edmond McCormick – Fourth Generation

Edmond McCormick, second child of John Alexander McCormick and Mary Charlotte Robb, was born on October 7th, 1911 and died six months later on April 6th, 1912. He was buried in the Kingsmills Presbyterian Church graveyard.

David McCormick – Fourth Generation

David McCormick, third child of John Alexander McCormick and Mary Charlotte Robb, was born on June 13th, 1913.

David went to England and during the war married an English girl named Connie. He later developed throat cancer and died. The couple had no family.

Robert McCormick – Fourth Generation

Robert McCormick, fourth child of John Alexander McCormick and Mary Charlotte Robb, was born on April 20th, 1916.

He married Sarah (Sadie) Barron on December 26th, 1945 in Kingsmills Presbyterian Church, County Armagh.

They had two children, John Irvine McCormick and Ann McCormick.

Robert McCormick (senior) died April 25th, 1991. His wife Sadie died on August 4th of the same year. They are buried in the Armagh Road Cemetery, Newry City.

FIFTH GENERATION

John Irvine McCormick, Ann McCormick

John Irvine McCormick – Fifth Generation

John Irvine McCormick, first child of Robert McCormick and Sarah (Sadie) Barron, married Suzanne Granger in 1977. The couple live in Montreal, Canada and have two children: Katherine McCormick, born in 1979, and Robert McCormick, born in 1984.

SIXTH GENERATION

Katherine McCormick, Robert McCormick

Katherine McCormick – Sixth Generation

Katherine McCormick, first child of John Irvine McCormick and Suzanne Granger, was born in 1979.

Robert McCormick – Sixth Generation

Robert McCormick, second child of John Irvine McCormick and Suzanne Granger, was born in 1984.

Ann McCormick – Fifth Generation

Ann McCormick, second child of Robert McCormick and Sarah (Sadie) Barron, married William O'Connell. The couple live near Ballinahinch, County Down, and have a daughter, Susan.

SIXTH GENERATION

Susan O'Connell – Sixth Generation

Susan O'Connell, daughter of Ann McCormick and William O'Connell.

On July 5th, 1922 John Alexander McCormick married Anna Barron Cartmill in First Newry Presbyterian Church, County Down.

Anna was born on August 20th, 1882 and was the widow of Samuel Cartmill. They had two children: Samuel Andrew Cartmill and Mary Agnes Eileen Cartmill.

John and Anna had one child, Sarah Isobel McCormick, known as Sally, who was born on May 22nd, 1923.

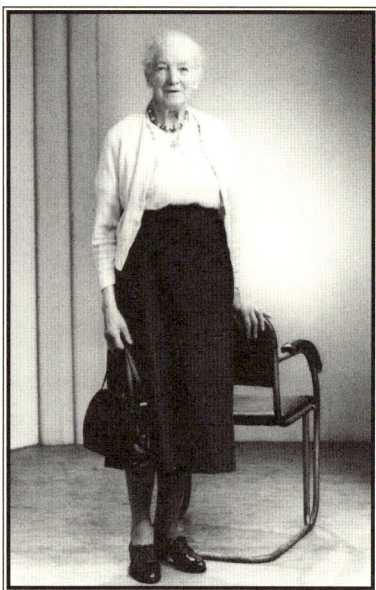

ANNA BARRON CARTMILL MCCORMICK

THE BURIAL PLACE OF JOHN ALEXANDER MCCORMICK AND HIS THIRD WIFE, ANNA MCCORMICK

John Alexander McCormick died on May 30th, 1944, his wife Anna on August 6th, 1967. They are buried in the Kingsmills Presbyterian Church graveyard, County Armagh.

FOURTH GENERATION

Samuel Andrew Cartmill, Mary Agnes Eileen Cartmill

Samuel Andrew Cartmill – Fourth Generation

Samuel Andrew Cartmill was the first child of Samuel Cartmill and Anna Cartmill McCormick.

Mary Agnes Eileen Cartmill – Fourth Generation

Mary Agnes Eileen Cartmill, second child of Samuel Cartmill and Anna Cartmill McCormick, married Thomas Tweedie McCormick on January 12th, 1938.

FOURTH GENERATION

Sarah Sally Isobel McCormick – Fourth Generation

Sarah Sally Isobel McCormick, firstborn of John Alexander McCormick and Anna Cartmill McCormick, was born on May 22nd, 1923.

She married James Freeburn on September 15th, 1959 in First Newry Presbyterian Church, County Down. James was a farmer, but died on June 17th, 1968, leaving Sally to bring up their family of three: James Wesley, born October 13, 1960, and twin girls, Anna Olivia and Edith Joan, born September 8, 1961.

LEFT TO RIGHT: EDITH IRVINE, SALLY McCORMICK, JAMES FREEBURN, ANN CHAMBERS

FIFTH GENERATION

James Wesley Freeburn, Anna Olivia Freeburn,
Edith Joan Freeburn

James Wesley Freeburn – Fifth Generation

James Wesley Freeburn, first child of James Freeburn and Sarah Isobel McCormick, was born on October 13th, 1960.

James married Ruth Louise Lawson on August 3rd, 1989 in Seagoe Parish Church, Portadown, County Armagh.

James and Ruth have three children: Sarah Louise, born September 11, 1993, Rebecca, born February 12, 1996, and Thomas James, born April 24, 1999.

FREEBURN FAMILY
BACK, LEFT TO RIGHT: JAMES AND LOUISE
FREEBURN; FRONT, LEFT TO RIGHT: REBECCA,
SARAH, AND TOM

SIXTH GENERATION

James Robert Irvine, Andrew Thomas Irvine

James Robert Irvine – Sixth Generation
James Robert Irvine, first child of Edith Joan Freeburn and Robert James Irvine, was born on September 13th, 1985.

Andrew Thomas Irvine – Sixth Generation
Andrew Thomas Irvine, second child of Edith Joan Freeburn and Robert James Irvine, was born on July 19th, 1988.

CHAPTER II
John McClelland

SECOND GENERATION

John McClelland – Second Generation

John McClelland, second child of Thomas McClelland and Susan Henning, was born on March 17th, 1837, and baptized March 24th, 1837 in Cloughenramer, Ireland.

John sailed to America by Steamship Jason from Galloway, Scotland, arriving September 5th, 1859.

JOHN MCCLELLAND'S ARRIVAL SEPTEMBER 5, 1859 ON
STEAMSHIP JASON FROM GALLOWAY, SCOTLAND

1860 CENSUS, PITTSBURGH, PENNSYLVANIA
JOHN MCCLELLAND RESIDING IN SAME HOME AS SAMUEL MCCAULEY

John married Elizabeth McCauley prior to 1861, in Pennsylvania. Elizabeth McCauley was born circa 1841 in Londonderry, Ireland. She had at least one sibling, Samuel Francis McCauley. Her parents were Robert McCauley and Martha Jenkins.

John is found in the 1860 census living in a house with Samuel. Elizabeth is found in another residence as a domestic.

John McClelland sold his interest in the family farm, Cloughenramer, in County Down, Ireland to William McClelland on February 8th, 1867.

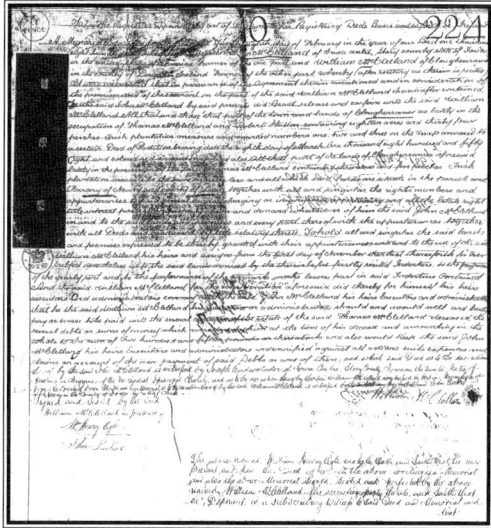

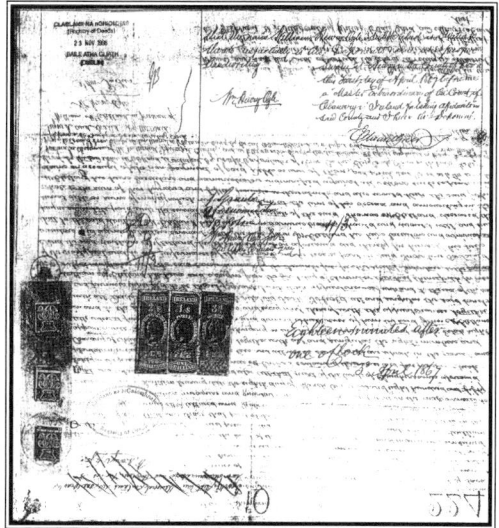

MEMORIAL DEED – JOHN McCLELLAND TO WILLIAM McCLELLAND, FEBRUARY 8, 1867

"Memorial No. 10 - 224.

A Memorial of a Deed bearing date the Twenty eighth day of February in the year of our Lord one thousand eight hundred and sixty seven between John McClelland of Iowa Centre, Story County, State of Iowa in the United States of America, farmer of the one part and William McClelland of Cloughenramer in the County of Down in Ireland, farmer of the other part whereby (after reciting as therein recited). It was witnessed that in pursuance of the Agreement therein mentioned and in consideration of the premises and of the covenant on the part of said William McClelland therein after contained He the said John McClelland by said presents did grant release and confirm unto the said William McClelland all that and those that part of the town and lands of Cloughenramer as lately in the occupation of Thomas McClelland and Robert Hutton containing eighteen acres and thirty four perches Irish plantation measure and marked number one two and three on the map annexed to a certain Deed of Partition bearing the date the eighth day of March one thousand eight hundred and fifty eight and colored red on said map and also all that part of the land of Cloughenramer aforesaid lately in the possession of the said Thomas McClelland containing three acres and five perches Irish plantation measure be the same more or less and all which said lands are suitable in the parish and Barony of Newry and County of Down together with all and singular the rights members and appurtenances to said several lands belonging or in anywise appertaining and all the Estate right title interest possession property claim and

69

demand whatsoever of him the said John McClelland in and to the said lands and premises and every part thereof with appurtenances together with all Deeds and environments? of title relating thereto. To hold all and singular the said lands and premises expressed to be thereby granted with their appurtenances unto and to the use of the said William McClelland his heirs and assigns from the first day of November then last thenceforth forever subject nevertheless as to the said lands demised by the thereinbefore firstly recited Indenture to the payment of the yearly rent and to the performance of the covenants on the lessees part in said Indenture contained. And the said William McClelland for the consideration aforesaid did thereby for himself his heirs executors and administrators covenant with the said John McClelland his heirs executors and administrators that he the said William McClelland his executors or administrators should and would well and truly pay or cause to be paid unto the several creditors of the estate of Thomas McClelland deceased the several debts or sums of money which were due by him at the time of his decease and amounting in the whole to the sum of Two hundred and fifteen pounds or thereabouts and also would the said John McClelland his heirs executors and administrators indemnified against all action suits expenses and claims on account of non-payment of said debts or any of them, and which said Deed as to the execution by the said John McClelland is witnessed by Joseph Cadwalader of Iowa Centre, Story County, Iowa in the United States of America, a clergyman of the Methodist Episcopal Church, and as to the execution thereof by the said William McClelland is witnessed by William Henry Ogle of Newry in the County of Down Solicitor and therein Memorial is the execution thereof by the said William McClelland is witness by the said William Henry Ogle and John Parker of Newry in the County of Down writing clerk."

JOHN McCLELLAND'S NATURALIZATION PAPERS
– CERTIFICATE NO. 11-363 DATED MARCH 4, 1868

John and Elizabeth had six children: Elmer Edward, born June 25, 1861, Matilda, born July 1863, Susan, born November 26, 1865, Harriet (Hattie), born circa 1870, Mary A. (Minnie) McClelland, born May 4, 1872, and Samuel Francis, born June 7, 1876.

Elizabeth McCauley McClelland died October 7th, 1899 in Lead City, South Dakota.

Obituary - Elizabeth McCauley McClelland

"Died at Terry. Mrs. Elizabeth, wife of John McClelland, died Saturday evening at 7:30 after a brief illness with pneumonia at the age of 58 years.

Mrs. McClelland was born in Ireland and came to this country when 15 years of age, locating first in Pennsylvania, where she married, and then went with her husband to Iowa, where she resided 33 years. She only came to Terry four weeks ago to join her husband, who has been in the Hills most of the time for four years. She possessed a most lovable, kindly disposition and made many friends in her new home. The deceased leaves besides her husband, two sons, Dr. E. E. McClelland of La Crosse, Wis., who arrived at her bedside Friday, and Francis McClelland, of Victor, Colorado. She also leaves four daughters, Mrs. L. W. Hastings, of Des Moines, Iowa; Mrs. William Turner, Kewanee, Ills.; Mrs. S.M. Kane, and Miss Hattie McClelland of Deadwood.

The funeral took place at 2 o'clock yesterday afternoon from the M. E. Church at Terry. Interment in Masonic cemetery. Lead Rev. Marten Thomas, officiating."

The 1900 Census shows John McClelland and Susan Kane living in Deadwood, South Dakota.

1900 CENSUS – DEADWOOD, SOUTH DAKOTA
JOHN McCLELLAND & SUSAN KANE

John died October 10, 1910 in Bellefonte, Arkansas.

THIRD GENERATION

Elmer Edward McClelland, Matilda McClelland, Susan McClelland, Harriet (Hattie) McClelland, Mary A. (Minnie) McClelland, Samuel McClelland

Elmer Edward McClelland – Third Generation

Elmer Edward McClelland, first child of John McClelland and Elizabeth McCauley, was born on June 25th, 1861 in Pittsburgh, Pennsylvania. He married Mary Salome Settlemyer on December 4th, 1893 in Polk County, Iowa. Mary was born in May 1863, in Pennsylvania.

Elmer was a medical examiner for the railroad and enjoyed a large patronage in LaCrosse.

**CITY DIRECTORY
DES MOINES, IOWA
1892**

Settlemyer Mary S, Physician,
Grand ave, se cor 7th, res 1811 Clark.

City Directory, Des Moines, Iowa, 1892

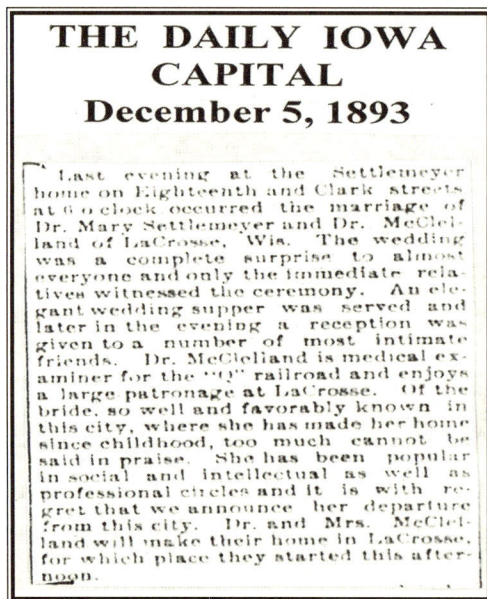

**THE DAILY IOWA
CAPITAL
December 5, 1893**

Last evening at the Settlemyer home on Eighteenth and Clark streets at 6 o'clock occurred the marriage of Dr. Mary Settlemyer and Dr. McClelland of LaCrosse, Wis. The wedding was a complete surprise to almost everyone and only the immediate relatives witnessed the ceremony. An elegant wedding supper was served and later in the evening a reception was given to a number of most intimate friends. Dr. McClelland is medical examiner for the "Q" railroad and enjoys a large patronage at LaCrosse. Of the bride, so well and favorably known in this city, where she has made her home since childhood, too much cannot be said in praise. She has been popular in social and intellectual as well as professional circles and it is with regret that we announce her departure from this city. Dr. and Mrs. McClelland will make their home in LaCrosse, for which place they started this afternoon.

THE DAILY IOWA CAPITAL,
DECEMBER 5, 1893
WEDDING ANNOUNCEMENT ELMER EDWARD
MCCLELLAND & MARY SETTLEMYER

```
                    MARRIAGES..POLK COUNTY, IOWA        PAGE      29
                              BOOK 7
       COPIED BY: PIONEER SONS AND DAUGHTERS, P O BOX 2103, DES MOINES, IOWA 50310



    GROOM                        BRIDE                    DATE         PAGE
    MC CARL FRANK H              CLAY ADA D               11 02 93     177
    MC CAULEY WM H               BALLANTYNE BELLE G       05 18 93     175
    MC CLELLAND ELMER E E        SETTLEMYER MARY SALOME   12 04 93     178
    MC CLELLAND JOSEPH           MORGAN ANNA M            10 08 95     190
    MC CLUNG LEWIS E             DOUBLEDAY MARY A         08 15 95     189
```

POLK COUNTY, IOWA MARRIAGE REGISTRATION
DECEMBER 4, 1893 ELMER E. McCLELLAND AND MARY SALOME SETTLEMYER

Elmer and Mary were both physicians, having graduated from medical school at Drake University in Des Moines, Iowa. Mary Salome also earned a PhD degree. Mary was one of the first women physicians in the area and had a very successful practice, while Elmer turned to pharmacy. The Settlemyer family was of German ancestry and were believed to have migrated to Ireland, and then to America.

ELMER EDWARD AND
MARY SETTLEMYER McCLELLAND, 1890s

The 1930 census shows that Elmer and Mary had migrated to Box Butte, Nebraska.

1930 CENSUS, BOX BUTTE, NEBRASKA LISTS ELMER MCCLELLAND, PHYSICIAN

The couple had seven children: Paul Phillip, born November 4, 1894; Elmer E., born September 19, 1895; Ruth Beatrice, born July 23, 1896; Lee Custer, born June 2, 1898; Esther Minnie, born November 17, 1899; Elmer Edward Ellsworth, born August 18, 1902; and Harriett Rose, born July 10, 1904.

Elmer, Mary, and all of the children ended up migrating to southern California. Elmer died July 24th, 1933 in Los Angeles, California.

On February 7th, 1942, Mary S. McClelland appeared before a notary public in the County of Los Angeles to certify as follows:

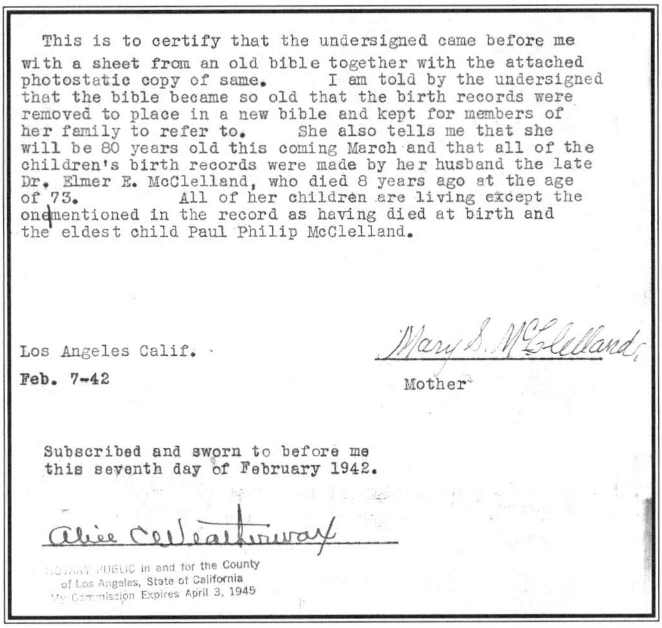

This is to certify that the undersigned came before me with a sheet from an old bible together with the attached photostatic copy of same. I am told by the undersigned that the bible became so old that the birth records were removed to place in a new bible and kept for members of her family to refer to. She also tells me that she will be 80 years old this coming March and that all of the children's birth records were made by her husband the late Dr. Elmer E. McClelland, who died 8 years ago at the age of 73. All of her children are living except the one mentioned in the record as having died at birth and the eldest child Paul Philip McClelland.

Los Angeles Calif.

Feb. 7-42

Mary S. McClelland,

Mother

Subscribed and sworn to before me this seventh day of February 1942.

Alice C. Weatherway

NOTARY PUBLIC in and for the County of Los Angeles, State of California My Commission Expires April 3, 1945

CERTIFICATION BEFORE A NOTARY PUBLIC, FEBRUARY 7, 1942

Family Register.

Births.

Our dear ones God has given us

Elmer Edward Ellsworth McClelland

Mary Salome Settlemyer McClelland

1st Paul Philipp McClelland born in LaCrosse Wisc Sunday morning at 10 oclock Nov 4th 1894

2nd Elmer E. E. McClelland Jr. born Sept 1895 died same day buried in Oak Grove Cemetery LaCrosse Wisc

3rd Ruth Beatrice McClelland born in Des Moines, Iowa, on Thursday morning at 9.00 oclock July 23rd 1896

4th Lee Custer McClelland Born in LaCrosse Wisc Jan 9th 1898 Sunday evening 7.30

5th Esther Minnie McClelland Born in LaCrosse Wisconsin Nov 17th 1899 at 11 oclock

6th Elmer Edward McClelland Born in North LaCrosse Friday morning at 10.00 oclock Aug 13th 190

7th Harriet Rose McClelland Born at Des Moines Iowa July 10th 1904

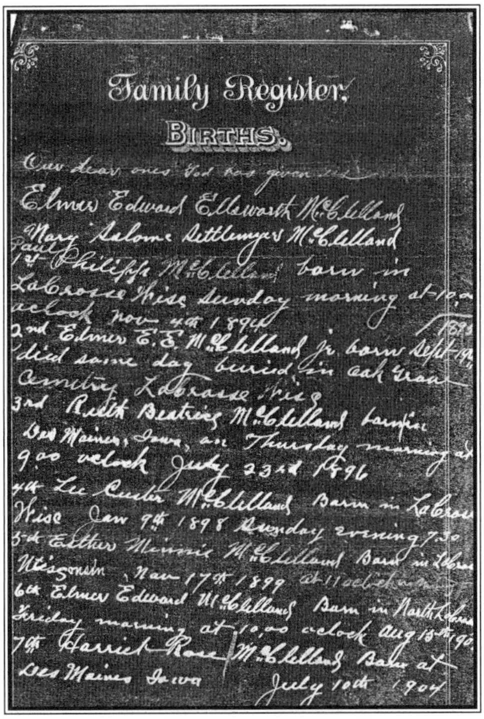

FAMILY REGISTER OF BIRTHS FROM FAMILY BIBLE OF ELMER E. AND MARY SALOME SETTLEMYER MCCLELLAND

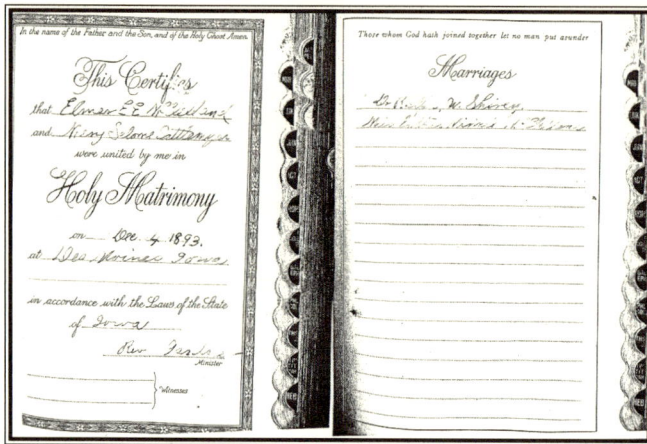

MARY SETTLEMYER'S FAMILY BIBLE – DEC. 4, 1893

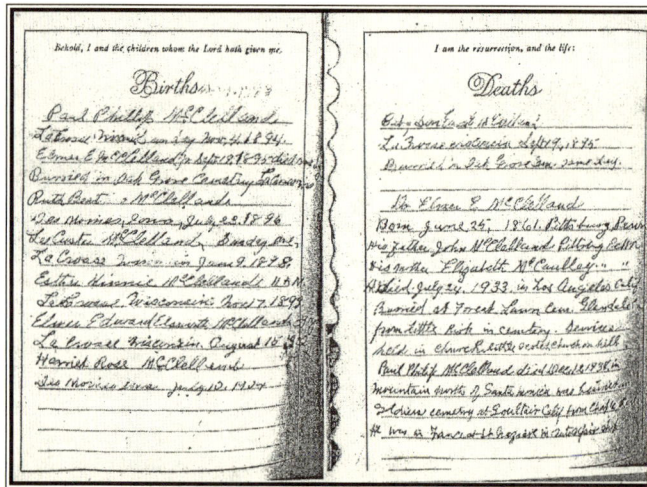

MARY SETTLEMYER'S FAMILY BIBLE – DEC. 4, 1893

Dr. Elmer Edward McClelland died July 24th, 1933 in Sepulveda, California.

Obituary – Dr. Elmer McClelland

"McCLELLAND, July 24, Dr. Elmer Edward of Sepulveda, beloved husband of Mary McClelland, father of Mrs. George W. Reber and Ruth B. McClelland of this city, Paul P. McClelland of West Los Angeles, Lee C. McClelland of Anaheim, Cal., Mrs. R. W. Shirey of Yakima Wash., and Dr. Elmer Edward McClelland, Jr. of Elgin, Neb.; brother of Mrs. Ernest Reynolds of Bothell, Wash., Mrs. Minnie Turner and Mrs. Tillie Hastings of Kewanee, Ill., and Mrs. Sue Kane of Seattle, Wash.

Services Wednesday, July 26 at 10 a.m. from the Wee Kirk o' the Heather, in Forest Lawn Cemetery, Pierce Brothers, directors."

Mary died on October 4th, 1946 in Los Angeles, California.

Obituary – Mary S. McClelland

"McCLELLAND, Mary S., loving mother of Maj. Elmer E. McClelland of Olive, Cal., Esther M. Shirey & Ruth B. McClelland of Los Angeles & Mrs. George W. Reber of Van Nuys, sister of Mrs. Ernest McLaughlin of Tacoma, Wash., Mrs. William P. Stubbs of Des Moines, Ia., & Sam Settlemeyer of Hollywood. Services 9:30 a.m., Tues. in the Wee Kirk o' the Heather, Forest Lawn, Pierce Brothers' Hollywood, directors."

FRONT ROW, LEFT TO RIGHT: ELMER, RUTH; BACK ROW, LEFT TO RIGHT: ESTHER, LEE AND HARRIET McCLELLAND CIRCA 1920s

Left to right: Lee, Esther, Harriet, Elmer, and Ruth McClelland
Circa 1940s – 1950s

Loving brothers and sisters
Left to right: Lee, Ruth, Esther, Harriet and Elmer (Mac) McClelland
Circa 1960s

FOURTH GENERATION

Paul Phillip McClelland, Elmer E. McClelland, Jr., Ruth Beatrice McClelland, Lee Custer McClelland, Esther Minnie McClelland, Elmer Edward Ellsworth McClelland, Harriet Rose McClelland

Paul Phillip McClelland – Fourth Generation

Paul Phillip McClelland, first child of Elmer Edward McClelland and Mary Settlemyer, was born on November 4th, 1894, in Wisconsin. Paul registered for the draft June 5th, 1917. At that time he was working as an auto repairman in Woodward, Iowa. In the 1920 census he is single, rooming in a house in Des Moines, Iowa, and employed as an auto repairman. He married a lady by the name of Lee.

Paul died December 13th, 1938 in Santa Paula, California.

Obituary – Paul Phillip McClelland

"McCLELLAND. At West Los Angeles, Paul McClelland, husband of Mrs. Lee McClelland; son of Mrs. Mary McClelland; brother of Ruth B., Lee and Dr. Elmer E. McClelland, Jr., Mrs. Esther Shirey and Mrs. George Reber.

Services today, 9 a.m., at National Military Home. Todd & Leslie, directors."

Obituary – Paul Phillip McClelland

"Gigantic Bolder Kills Quarry Man

Santa Paula, December 13th. Mashed to death when a gigantic boulder rolled over his body in a Grimes Canyon rock quarry, the body of Paul McClelland, 44, was awaiting funeral arrangements today in the Copeland Ballard Mortuary at Fillmore.

McClelland, who quarried and hauled Grimes Canyon rock to Los Angeles under contract, was attempting to dislodge a chunk of stone which weighed more than a ton. He and his assistant were unable to budge it and McClelland started off after some gun powder to blast it loose.

When the man walked in front of the boulder, it came loose and rolled over him. Taken to a nearby ranch home, McClelland died 30 minutes later."

Elmer E. McClelland, Jr. – Fourth Generation
Elmer E. McClelland, Jr., second child of Elmer Edward McClelland and Mary Settlemyer, was born on September 19th, 1895 in La Crosse, Wisconsin.
Elmer died September 19th, 1895.

Ruth Beatrice McClelland – Fourth Generation
Ruth Beatrice McClelland, third child of Elmer Edward McClelland and Mary Settlemyer, was born on July 23rd, 1896 in Iowa. She married Robert L. Stalder. Ruth moved to California in 1926 and was employed by Western Union as a clerk for 43 years. She moved to San Bernardino County in 1965.
Ruth died May 21st, 1967 in Joshua Tree, San Bernardino, California.

Obituary – Ruth McClelland Stalder

"STALDER, Ruth (McClelland), beloved wife of Robert L. Stalder, sister of Lee McClelland, Mrs. Harriet Reber and Mrs. Esther Howell, sister-in-law of Mrs. Edna Sampson. Services at 2 p.m. Friday, Wee Kirk o' the Heather, Forest Lawn Cemetery."

Lee Custer McClelland – Fourth Generation
Lee Custer McClelland, fourth child of Elmer Edward McClelland and Mary Settlemyer, was born on June 2nd, 1898 in La Crosse, Wisconsin. Lee Custer McClelland registered for the WWI draft on September 12th, 1918. At the time, he was residing in Antioch, Nebraska and employed as a drug clerk in his father's store.

LEE C. MCCLELLAND'S WWI REGISTRATION NO. 26-1-53-C
ANTIOCH, NEBRASKA, SEPTEMBER 12, 1918

He married Lovenia O'Toole on October 24th, 1929 in Anaheim, California. Lovenia was born in South Dakota. She was the daughter of Charles O'Toole and his wife Blanche Mansell.

LEE C. MCCLELLAND & LOVENIA O'TOOLE
MARRIAGE CERTIFICATE

They had one child, Brian Mansell McClelland, born in Orange County, California.

LEE C. McCLELLAND

THE OLIVE DRUG STORE, OLIVE, CALIFORNIA

MODERN WEAPON—This German machine pistol in Olive Druggist Lee McClelland's collection is similar to a burp gun and is a souvenir of World War II.

FOREIGN MAKE—This set of French dueling pistols is part of the collection. They were made by Paris firm still in the business of manufacturing guns.

Los Angeles Times, Nov. 4, 1956

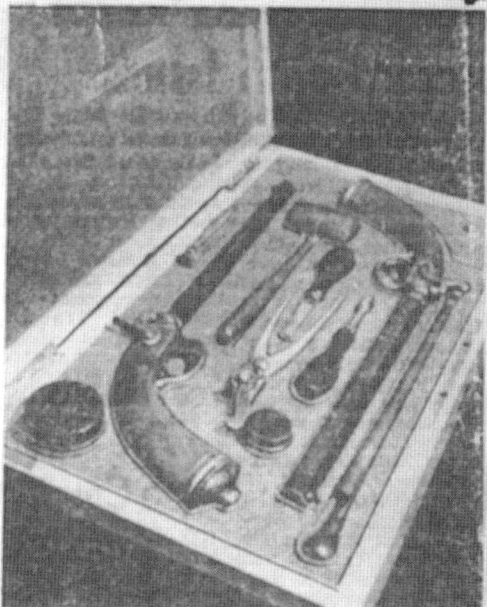

Los Angeles Times 9
SUN., NOV. 4, 1956-R-Part VIII

Olive Druggist Decorates Shop With Firearms

OLIVE — A stranger visiting the community of Olive will be in for a big surprise when he steps into the corner drugstore and finds the shelves are lined with guns.

It's not that Olive is a dangerous place to live but only because Druggist Lee C. McClelland has been collecting guns for 26 years.

The collection contains about 200 antique pistols, 25 rifles and several World War II machine guns.

Specialization Cited

McClelland says he specializes in early American and military firearms in order to limit the size of his collection.

The most prominent display of guns is a case which contains more than 75 Colt revolvers dating from 1849 to 1900. One model, a frontier single-action, has a menacing-looking skull carved on its grip and is the Colt which the cowboys made famous.

The smallest gun in his possession is barely two and one-half inches long. It is said to be one of the smallest automatic pistols ever made.

Tiny Model

Another gun is a seven-shot pistol which fits in the palm of the hand with the barrel protruding between the fingers.

On the rear walls of the store are three rifles which trace three steps in the evolution of firearms.

The first is a matchlock Asiatic rifle used around 1650. The others are a flintlock Kentucky squirrel rifle and a cap-and-ball rifle used during the Civil War.

Potent Weapon

One of the most impressive weapons of the collection is a 4-gauge shotgun. According to McClelland, the large gun is capable of killing from 75 to 100 birds with one shot.

For the rugged individualist McClelland has a combination knife, gun and corkscrew. The corkscrew is the trigger.

Medal Winner

McClelland shoots a few of his guns at meets and has many medals that prove he has a good eye.

He is a life member of the National Rifle Association and the National Muzzle Loading Rifle Association.

Twice a year he participates in the shooting matches held by the Southern California Arms Collectors Association.

"Now I discover that the goal of Communism is to be achieved not by bullets, but by ballots; not by illegal, but by legal means; not by a few evil persons, but by a vote of the majority."
—Admiral Ben Moreell

The Register
ORANGE COUNTY'S OWN NEWSPAPER

CENTRAL ORANGE COUNTY EDITION

57th YEAR—NUMBER 11   10 CENTS   Printed in   SANTA ANA, ORANGE CO., CALIF., MONDAY, DEC. 11, 1961   TWO SECTIONS—32 PAGES ★★★

Olive Business Area Hit; $200,000 Damages

Fire Turns Olive Into Scene Resembling War   See more photos B-1   (Register photo)

Skeleton Remains Today

By CLAY MILLER
(Register Staff Writer)

A charred skeleton structure is all that remains this morning of the Olive business district that was all but completely destroyed last night in a fiery inferno causing more than $200,000 in damages.

It was like a miniature scene of a bombed out city in Europe during World War II as the entire roof of the 10,000-square-foot structure was caved in, leaving a jagged edge of bricks rimming the building that was located on the northeast corner of Lincoln and Orange-Olive Rd.

Scattered

Bricks and other portions of the building were scattered over the scene. There was hardly anything left of the Olive Market, drug store and Olive Post Office.

Many Christmas cards and packages will not be delivered this year. They were food for the hungry blaze that showed no mercy in its fiery march through the building. A daring band of people risked their lives last night as they carried a valuable gun collection from the drug store minutes before the structure went up in flames.

Market Owner

It was a sad day for Ted Hillers, owner of the market. He and his wife stood in silence in front of the ruins of the store. "Nothing is left. . nothing," Ted said as he bit his upper lip and his wife cleared away tears from her eyes. "You know," he continued, "I made the last payment on the market Saturday . . it was now ours."

"Those were the hardest years of our lives," said Mrs. Hillers, "working from 7:30 in the morning to 9 o'clock at night. Never a chance to let up. . the pressure was always on."

"I don't have the slightest idea how the fire started last night. We had our Christmas party at the fire hall and I carried over the tree, walking right down behind the store at 7:30 and didn't notice anything out of order. Later we came home and then someone told us that smoke was coming out of the back of the store.

"Insurance. . that won't do us any good. It only covers about two-thirds the value of the store, I just don't know what we are

(Turn to Page A2, Column 6)

More About

Fire

(Continued from page A1)

going to do. . no, I don't know what we are going to do."

Firemen Safe

Two firemen were resting safely this morning after being treated for minor injuries after a brick wall collapsed on them. Ray Glassner and Bob Workman will return for special X-rays this morning. Twisted steel helmets were a grim reminder to the two of the episode last night nearly taking their lives.

As the blaze spread through the building, firemen rushed to the west side of the drug store in an attempt to break through a door. Nearly a dozen men crowded around the door as axes were slashed into the wood.

There was a sharp crack and everyone ran for their lives as a portion of the brick wall came crashing down. Men were hit by the falling bricks and concrete as they raced for the other side of the street. Six firemen were treated for injuries.

The building, which housed the three business, was built in Olive in 1920 by Alex Fletcher, N. P. Edwards and Lou Bertz. The farming community was one of the first in Orange County and was established before the turn of the century.

Presently Lee McClland, Mrs. Wade Flippen, Roy Edwards and Maybelle Hammel own a portion of the building.

High Pitch

Terror hit a high pitch midst the roaring flames Sunday night as the heat from the flames began to set off ammuniction in the drug store. The crowd scattered, but the firemen held their ground, having no other choice but to fight the flames.

Hundreds of spectators jammed the scene, with Orange police having a difficult time handling the crowd and directing traffic. Finally Orange County Sheriff's Dept. was called on for assistnce.

Members of the Orange Fire Dept., Olive Volunteer Fire Dept., and California Division of Forestry rushed to the scene as the flames lit up northern Orange County skies.

Firemen are still trying to determine the cause of the blaze that started shortly before 9 p.m. in the rear portion of the market. Firemen first on the scene climbed to the roofs of homes adjoining the building and poured water down on the flames.

The fire ate its way from the back of the store in a northerly direction, then swept through the front of the market into the post office and the drug store.

Lee Custer McClelland died May 4th, 1976.

Obituary – Lee Custer McClelland

"McCLELLAND, LEE CUSTER, 78, of Anaheim, passed away, May 4, 1976. Survived by wife, Lovenia McClelland, one son, Brian McClelland, Anaheim. Family wishes memorials directed to Orange County Heart Association. Graveside services Friday 2 p.m., Anaheim Cemetery."

Lovenia McClelland died January 13th, 1979.

Obituary – Lovenia O. McClelland

"McCLELLAND, Lovenia O., 70, a native of South Dakota but a resident of Anaheim since 1915, passed away at a local hospital January 13, 1979. She is survived by her son, Brian M. McClelland of Anaheim. Graveside services will be held at the Anaheim Cemetery, Tuesday, January 15, 1979, at 10:00 a.m. Donations in her name may be made to the Orange County Heart Association, P. O. Box 1704, Santa Ana, Ca. 92702. Hilgenfeld Mortuary. Anaheim Bulletin, January 15, 1979."

FIFTH GENERATION

Brian Mansell McClelland – Fifth Generation

Brian Mansell McClelland, only child of Lee Custer McClelland and Lovenia O'Toole, was born on October 3rd, 1939. His middle name, "Mansell," is his mother's maiden name.

Esther Minnie McClelland – Fourth Generation

Esther Minnie McClelland, fifth child of Elmer Edward McClelland and Mary Settlemyer, was born on November 17th, 1899 in La Crosse, Wisconsin. She married Ralph Shirey. They had one child, Maxine, who was born on July 26th, 1922. Ralph Shirey died in 1961.

1930 CENSUS, YAKIMA COUNTY, WASHINGTON
ESTHER MINNIE McCLELLAND SHIREY, RALPH SHIREY,
& MAXINE SHIREY

Esther McClelland Shirey married Carl William Howell July 26th, 1960 in Los Angeles County, California. Ruth McClelland was the witness for this marriage.

ESTHER M. SHIREY & CARL WILLIAM HOWELL
MARRIAGE CERTIFICATE – JULY 26, 1960

ESTHER MCCLELLAND SHIREY HOWELL
TEACHING IN WALNUT CREEK, CALIFORNIA

Esther died November 24, 1987 in Martinez, Contra Costa, California.

Obituary – Esther Howell

"Esther Howell, 87, died Wednesday at Kaiser Hospital in Concord.

A retired school teacher, Howell taught clay arts in the Alameda Unified School District for 28 years. A native of Wisconsin, she lived in Walnut Creek for the past 30 years.

She belonged to the Clay Arts Guild of Walnut Creek and her work will be on display at the Walnut Creek Civic Arts Center from Thursday through Sunday.

She is survived by her daughter, Maxine Bacon of Clintondale, New York.

There will be no services. The family suggests donations to the Civic Arts Ceramic Program in Walnut Creek."

FIFTH GENERATION

Maxine Shirey – Fifth Generation

Maxine Lee Shirey, only child of Ralph Shirey and Esther Minnie McClelland, was born on July 26th, 1922 in Lincoln, Nebraska.

LEFT TO RIGHT: RUTH MCCLELLAND, ESTHER MCCLELLAND SHIREY, LEE MCCLELLAND, MAXINE LEE SHIREY, PAUL MCCLELLAND, HARRIET MCCLELLAND REBER, RUTH MCCLELLAND, DR. ELMER MCCLELLAND CIRCA 1925

Maxine was a remarkable person, though she did not think so. She had a BA from UCLA and teaching credentials for grammar school, though she never taught. Instead, she fell in love with dance, studying with Lester Horton in Los Angeles before joining a touring company of *The Waltz King*. That trajectory eventually brought her to New York, where she continued to study and got a job in the Broadway production of *One Touch of Venus* starring Mary Martin in 1943. She traveled to Europe in 1945 as a civilian actress technician with the USO in a group that included Paddy Chayefsky and Howard Keel. They performed in Germany, among other places, winding up in London where she married (briefly) a composer named Edward Underwood. When she returned to New York in 1949, she studied with and soon joined the Charles Weidman Company, the resident dance company at New York's City Opera.

She also met Paul Bacon, whom she married in Tijuana, Mexico on July 5th, 1951. Paul Bacon was born on December 25th, 1923 in Ossining, New York. He attended various public schools on the eastern seaboard—New York, New Jersey, Maryland, and Connecticut—graduating from Arts High School, Newark, New Jersey, in June of 1940. He worked for a while after Pearl Harbor and then went into the Marine Corps in April 1943, serving in the South Pacific and North China. He was honorably discharged in April of 1946.

The couple had one child, Preston, an adopted son born July 16, 1957.

Maxine stopped dancing in the early 1950s to try a number of jobs and various volunteer work. She got a degree in Special Education at SUNY New Paltz when she was fifty-one years old. She later became Board Chairman of the Ulster Ballet Company, before being disabled by Alzheimer's disease. She died in Palenville, New York on August 5th, 2003.

Paul became an apprentice in a New York graphic design studio and later went on his own. He is a specialist in book jackets, record album covers, and posters. He ran a studio until 2002. Paul is a life-long jazz fan, musician, and writer. He is still performing as a musician and singer.

PAUL AND MAXINE BACON
1995

SIXTH GENERATION

Preston Bacon – Sixth Generation

Preston Bacon, adopted son of Paul Bacon and Maxine Shirey, was born on July 16th,

1957. He is dyslexic, though his family did not find out until he had had a rough time in school. He is a designer/draftsman for Central Hudson Power Company, part of the huge grid that runs from Canada to the south.

He married Carol Harcher on May 31st, 1986 in New Paltz, New York, where they still live.

CAROL AND RYAN BACON

Their sons are Ryan, born March 2, 1988, and Matthew, born April 5, 1991. Preston is a demon outdoorsman (skiing, biking, surfing), a car nut, and a fine mechanic and fixer of almost anything; the boys share some of the same traits. Carol runs a childcare center in New Paltz.

LEFT TO RIGHT: RYAN, PRESTON, PAUL AND MATTHEW BACON
2004

Elmer Edward Ellsworth McClelland – Fourth Generation

Elmer Edward Ellsworth McClelland, sixth child of Elmer Edward McClelland and Mary

Settlemyer, was born on August 18th, 1902 in La Crosse, Wisconsin.

Elmer studied medicine at Creighton University of Medicine and did his internship at Buffalo General Hospital in Buffalo, New York.

He married Ruth Laverne Tuttle on October 4th, 1924 in Council Bluffs, Iowa. Ruth was born on March 6th, 1905 in Omaha, Nebraska.

Elmer began his medical practice in the very small village of Elgin, Nebraska during the mid 1920s.

ELMER E. McCLELLAND AND RUTH TUTTLE
MARRIAGE CERTIFICATE
OCTOBER 4, 1924

ELMER AND RUTH McCLELLAND, 1925

RUTH TUTTLE McCLELLAND, 1925

Elmer practiced medicine during the Great Depression. Money was scarce, but the family survived on a meager cash flow supplemented by bartered farm produce. During these years,

---

Alliance, Nebraska
November 10th, 1927

Dr. E. E. McClelland, Jr.
Elgin, Nebraska

Dear Sonnie,

Your cheering letter received and we are pleased with the progress you seem to be making in every way. About the pooch you will find that you have to go after him and his tape about the same as you would a human give him a good physic then take food from him for twenty four hours then give your anthelmentic and in about twelve hours another physic of castor oil and you will gather in the varmin "haid" and all, Tanret's Pell etierine is considered one of the best proprietaries on the market it costs better than two dollars per bottle, Aspidium Male Fern is fairly good but uncertain in its action as regards the removal of the "haid" and unless that portion is gotten rid of it is only a little time until the subject is troubled as much as ever. A dog will according to weight take three to five times the amount of a human of most any medicine and get by with it that is to say if a dog weighed about the same as a human adult he would take the greater dose as above suggested.

Very glad indeed that you enjoyed the roasts and pickles. I love those pickles but they do not set very good with me and so a little taste is all for me.

Surely glad that your knee case is coming on you will have an opportunity to charge in that case if everything goes along well and the outcome is satisfactory.

The fracture report is also very pleasing to us as we are so anxious that everything shall work out for you to your best desires.

Think you are doing fine in prescription writing you plan to have them go wherever they want to is my plan, and the only fair one but our views are not shared by the "docs" here. Noticed Slagle's steps leading up to his office printed in big bold letter Holstens for this and that the three steps up the storm like door have each something that may be purchased at Holstens probably the entire stairway up to the main landing is laden with printed signs extolling the great Holsten store. Haven't much use for Slagle he thinks he is a high brow. I haven't been in his joint since coming to Alliance and should our lot be cast here for years to come he will not have me for a caller. Ma thinks the "Sloogle" outfit are a wonderful bunch of humanity but not so your pop.

Ma thinks we haven't told you about our new floor case $92.00 bucks laid down it is some case believe me and sets our room off nicely on one side eight feet long. We needed it so badly it really helps trade. It is golden oak finish and beautiful we have it well laden with a nice toilet collection. Two hundred would not tempt me to take it out unless selling the whole outfit. We are not carrying a dollar of insurance, am a sport, if it burns up let her go we have had it quite a while and can't sell it; it might burn up some day, I have paid insurance all my life and am tired of it as it is $33.60 gets away from me every month for life insurance quite a bunch of coin but I am old and cannot afford to drop it now as long as I am able to raise the coin each month but with the drug stock it is different let her burn who cares.

Maybe we can get another little bunch of ducks to you before the season closes would like to send with part of the plumage but will have to interview the law before attempting it. Ma is picking feathers to make our Harriet a pair of pillows.

Don't worry about your bills and debts let the other fellow walk the "flure" as the Irish man says. It doesn't do any good to worry and if creditors know you are making effort to be square with them, usually they do not bother much you cannot go out and hold up some one to get money, but after you have it earned it will come in when you are not looking or expecting perhaps, and you can settle as fast it lasts. It has always been a difficult matter for me to carry around money that was owed to someone and I think it will be the same with you.

Love and kisses,

Papa E.E. McClelland

LETTER FROM E. E. McCLELLAND TO HIS SON DR. ELMER McCLELLAND
NOVEMBER 10, 1927

Elmer was affectionately known as "Doctor Mac." It was also during his years in Elgin that Elmer developed an interest in flying and acquired part ownership in a two-seat Piper-Cub. He logged sufficient hours to earn a private license. He was also a member of the Elgin School Board.

Tired of hard times, Elmer left his practice in Elgin, moved, and set up a new practice in Bellaire, Ohio. The family spent a year in Ohio.

Elmer and Ruth Laverne Tuttle McClelland had three children: Lee Custer,

ELMER McCLELLAND'S OFFICE, ELGIN, NEBRASKA - CIRCA 1930

born July 9, 1929 in Omaha, Nebraska; William Dennis, born December 13, 1932; and Paul Joseph, born March 8, 1941 in Elgin, Nebraska.

When Pearl Harbor took the nation into World War II, Elmer joined the Army Air Force and became one of the oldest flight surgeons on record. He was commissioned a Captain and sent overseas to England and Germany after his promotion to Major. He served with distinction and was promoted to Lt. Colonel before his retirement from the service. During his service, he continued to fly and logged enough hours in larger aircraft to later qualify for a commercial pilot's license.

ELMER McCLELLAND WITH AMBULANCE, 1943

ELMER McCLELLAND, 1943

The Depression and the war took its toll on the family. Ruth and Elmer divorced. Ruth had custody of the three sons.

Ruth and the boys lived in Shadyside, Nebraska between August 1941 and August 1942, then in Omaha for a year. Ruth's older sister Goldie Moore was in Omaha at the time, but moved to Portland shortly after Ruth and the boys arrived. Ruth followed the Moores to Portland as soon as the school year closed, in June of 1943. Two of Ruth's older brothers, Richard and Minor Tuttle, lived in Camas, Washington, a short drive from Portland. The Tuttles had been in that area since the late nineteenth century. Ruth's great-grandfather Archibald Tuttle is buried at Fisher's Landing, a short distance from Camas.

As it was wartime, the shipyards of Portland attracted vast numbers of workers, and housing was at a premium. The family moved into a one-room apartment, later finding more adequate housing through Goldie.

Ruth Laverne Tuttle died November 19th, 1977 in Portland, Oregon.

FIFTH GENERATION

Lee Custer McClelland, William Dennis McClelland,
Paul Joseph McClelland

Lee Custer McClelland – Fifth Generation

Lee Custer McClelland, first child of Elmer Edward Ellsworth McClelland and Ruth Laverne Tuttle, was born on July 9th, 1929 in Omaha, Nebraska.

Lee's education began in a small school in Elgin, Nebraska where his father was a member of the school board. He later attended a much larger school in Shadyside, Ohio. Lee did well in mechanical and architectural drafting in high school and spent a great deal of time on the stage crew and with the school's service club. He did not see the need for spending significant hours in some other areas of studies. In college, he learned to hit the books, and exchanged his Architecture major for a major in Sociology. He spent two years at a state extension center, which later became Portland State University, and graduated from the University of Oregon with a Bachelor of Science in Liberal Arts with a major in Sociology and a minor in Psychology.

Lee married Carolyn Fay Reif on June 20th, 1964 in St. Michael's Church, Portland, Oregon. Carolyn Fay was born on October 29th, 1936 in Albany, Oregon, the second daughter of Goldie Ray and Frank Joseph Reif. Her pioneer ancestors, the William Gulliford family, settled in the Oregon Territory in 1852. Some time before 1893, her maternal grandparents Harker and Ray came to Linn County, Oregon. The Reif family homesteaded in Oregon from 1911 until 1942, leaving the Prineville (Central Oregon) area in 1942 for the Willamette Valley. Carolyn's family spent three years on the Oregon coast before settling in Eugene, Oregon. She graduated from a liberal arts school for girls near Portland, then Marylhurst College. Her Bachelor of Arts degree and Sociology major led to the field of social work. She spent four-and-a-half years as a caseworker with the Public Welfare Division.

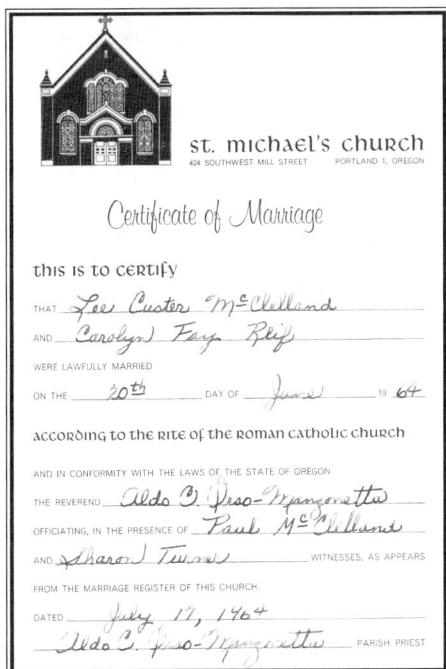

LEE CUSTER MCCLELLAND AND
CAROLYN FAY REIF,
MARRIAGE CERTIFICATE – JUNE 20, 1964

LEFT TO RIGHT: GOLDIE REIF, FRANK REIF, CAROLYN REIF, LEE MCCLELLAND, RUTH MCCLELLAND
WEDDING – JUNE 20, 1964

The couple have two children: Michael Lee, born June 10, 1965, and Joseph Edward, born November 3, 1966.

Lee spent several years at Goodwill Industries while searching for a career, a goal eventually attained when he was hired by the state's welfare agency. Lee spent seven-and-a-half years as a field caseworker in the Portland and Bend areas. He was promoted to casework supervisor and, subsequently, to a number of management positions in the agency's central office at the state capitol in Salem. He spent sixteen years as the agency's chief hearing officer and received recognition awards from two governors and a state court of appeals judge. He took early retirement after thirty years with the state.

Since retirement, Lee and Carolyn have been active in charitable activities, the Boy Scouts, and their parish church.

MICHAEL, LEE AND JOSEPH MCCLELLAND
CIRCA 1967

LEE, MICHAEL, RUTH AND JOSEPH MCCLELLAND
1974

SIXTH GENERATION

Michael Lee McClelland, Joseph Edward McClelland

Michael Lee McClelland – Sixth Generation

Michael Lee McClelland, first child of Lee Custer McClelland and Carolyn Fay Reif, was born on June 10th, 1965 in Salem, Oregon. He was named after his dad and the church, St. Michael's, where Lee and Carolyn were married.

Michael attended primary, middle, and high school in Salem. He was active in the church youth group and Boy Scouts. Michael has since established his own business in the computer field. He builds computers and provides a wide range of supportive help for computer users. As he built his business, he worked in electronics for several big box stores where his major objective was selling and activating wireless phones.

MICHAEL MCCLELLAND - 1971

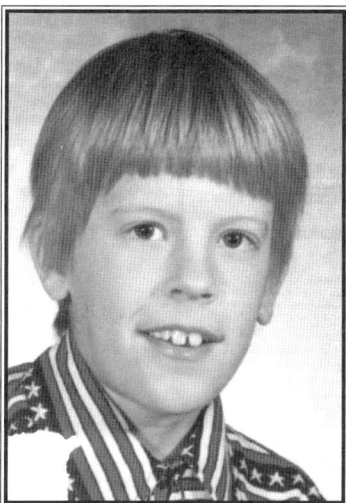

MICHAEL MCCLELLAND

MICHAEL MCCLELLAND
HIGH SCHOOL GRADUATION

Michael married Georgette Yvonne Lusey on January 9th, 1993 in Springfield, Lane County, Oregon. Georgette was born on May 6th, 1969 in Neptune City, Monmouth, New Jersey.

MICHAEL LEE MCCLELLAND AND GEORGETTE YVONNE LUSEY
WEDDING DAY – JANUARY 9, 1993
LEFT TO RIGHT: LEE & CAROLYN MCCLELLAND,
GEORGETTE & MICHAEL MCCLELLAND, AND JOSEPH EDWARD MCCLELLAND

They have four children: Adam Christopher, born November 14, 1994; Gabrielle Anne, born April 17, 1998; Caitlin Ruth, born March 28, 2000; and Emily Renee, born May 5, 2002. The children have done exceptionally well in school, at least in part because of Michael and Georgette's support at home; both parents have also consistently volunteered at the children's grade school. Michael and Adam have been active in the Boy Scout movement, and the entire family is very involved in their church.

FRONT ROW, LEFT TO RIGHT: EMILY RENEE, CAITLIN RUTH, GABRIELLE ANNE, ADAM CHRISTOPHER; BACK ROW: GEORGETTE AND MICHAEL McCLELLAND

SEVENTH GENERATION

Adam Christopher McClelland, Gabrielle Anne McClelland, Caitlin Ruth McClelland, Emily Renee McClelland

Adam Christopher McClelland – Seventh Generation

Adam Christopher McClelland, first child of Michael Lee McClelland and Georgette Yvonne Lusey, was born on November 14th, 1994 in Oregon City, Oregon.

ADAM CHRISTOPHER MCCLELLAND
1995

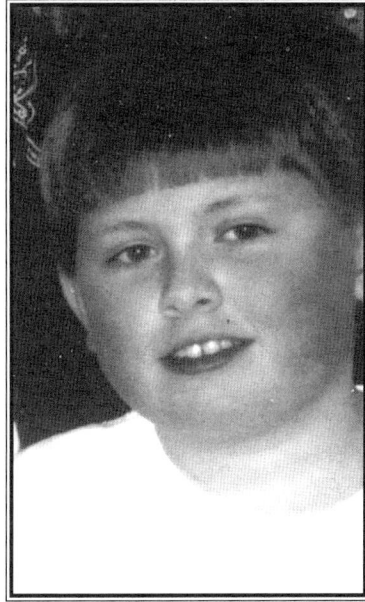

ADAM CHRISTOPHER MCCLELLAND

Gabrielle Anne McClelland – Seventh Generation

Gabrielle Anne McClelland, second child of Michael Lee McClelland and Georgette Yvonne Lusey, was born on April 17th, 1998 in Milwaukie, Oregon.

GABRIELLE ANNE MCCLELLAND

Caitlin Ruth McClelland – Seventh Generation

Caitlin Ruth McClelland, third child of Michael Lee McClelland and Georgette Yvonne Lusey, was born on March 28th, 2000.

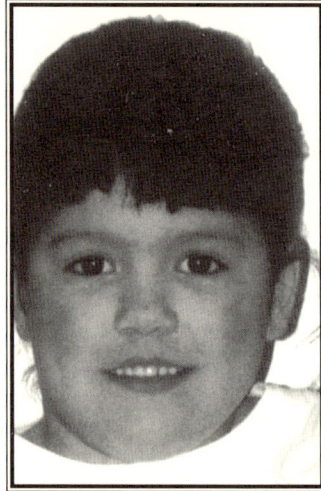

CAITLIN RUTH McCLELLAND

Emily Renee McClelland – Seventh Generation

Emily Renee McClelland, fourth child of Michael Lee McClelland and Georgette Yvonne Lusey, was born on May 5th, 2002 in Salem, Oregon.

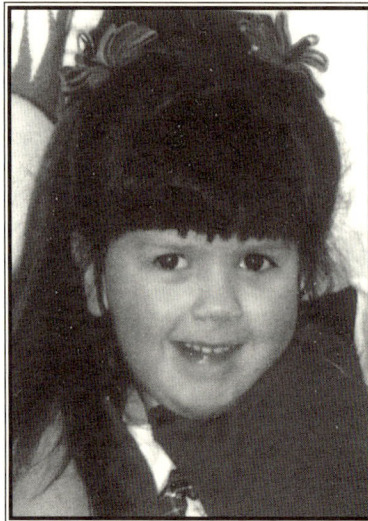

EMILY RENEE McCLELLAND

Joseph Edward McClelland – Sixth Generation

Joseph Edward McClelland, second child of Lee Custer McClelland and Carolyn Fay Reif, was born on November 3rd, 1966 in Salem, Oregon. He was named after his granddad and St. Joseph Church, where the family attended.

Joseph attended primary, middle and high school in Salem. He was active in Boy Scouts and took a real liking to backpacking, camping, and mountaineering. He was an honor student at Portland State University and has plans for further education.

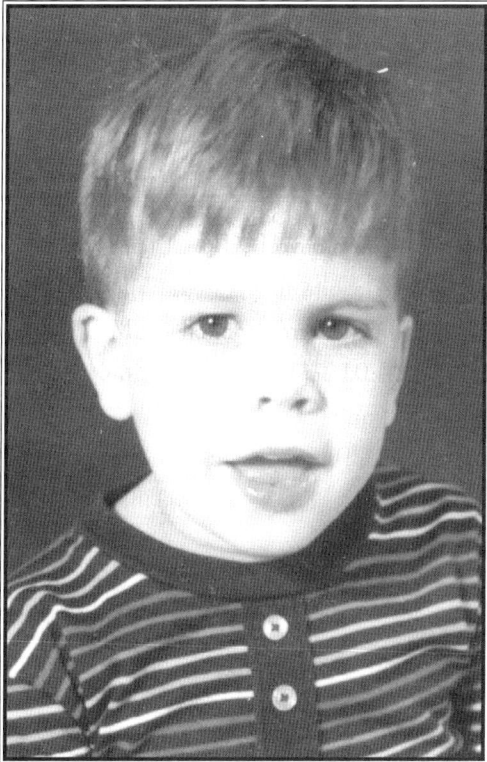

JOSEPH EDWARD MCCLELLAND
KINDERGARTEN, 1971

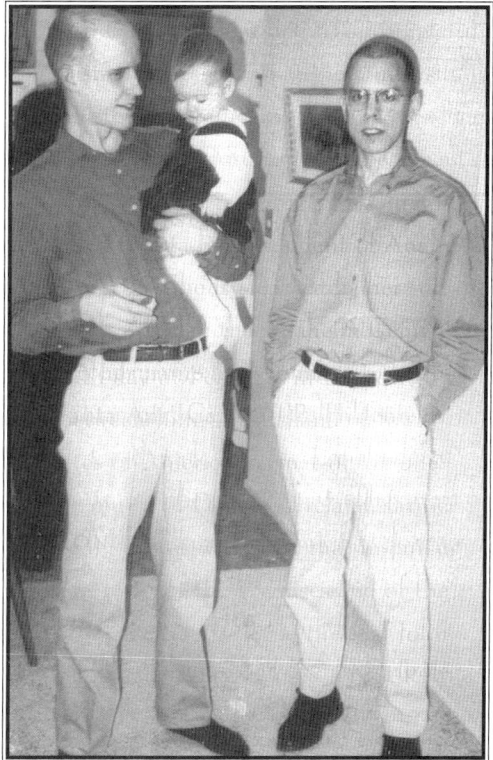

LEFT TO RIGHT: MICHAEL LEE, GABRIELLE ANNE, AND JOSEPH EDWARD MCCLELLAND JANUARY 1999

Joseph remains single and is employed as a buyer for specialty firms in the Portland metro area. His real love is the outdoors, and he spends many weekends and vacations in the Oregon and Washington Cascade Mountains, where he has climbed the major peaks and investigated most of the back country. When the winter fog and rain set in, he occupies a great deal of his spare time reading.

William Dennis McClelland – Fifth Generation

William Dennis McClelland, second child of Elmer Edward Ellsworth McClelland and Ruth Laverne Tuttle, was born on December 13th, 1932 in Elgin, Nebraska. Elgin is still a small town that serves the surrounding farm community, with a population of 900 or so that has not changed a great deal since Elmer McClelland practiced medicine there.

William began school in Elgin and continued in Shadyside, Ohio and Omaha, Nebraska. He completed his grade- and high-school education in Portland, Oregon, where he was a straight "A" student and exceptional in mathematics. He was awarded a scholar-ship to prestigious Reed College in Portland. The Korean War put an end to his educational plans, and he became a member of the Air Force Reserve.

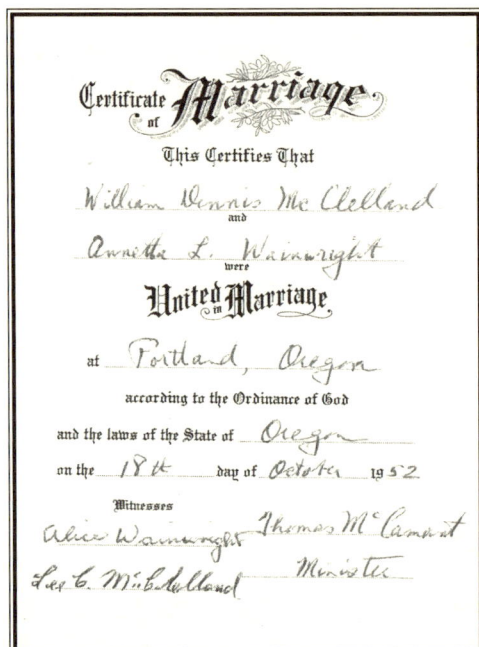

WILLIAM DENNIS McCLELLAND
& ANNETTA L. WAINWRIGHT
MARRIAGE CERTIFICATE – OCTOBER 18, 1952

He married Anne Wainwright on October 18th, 1952 in Portland, Oregon. Anne was born on May 19th, 1933.

WEDDING DAY – OCTOBER 18, 1952
LEFT TO RIGHT: RUTH STRAIN WAINWRIGHT
(ANNE'S MOTHER), ANNE WAINWRIGHT
McCLELLAND , WILLIAM (MAC) McCLELLAND,
AND RUTH TUTTLE McCLELLAND (MAC'S MOTHER)

They have four children: Patricia Ann, born August 3, 1953; Janette Marie, born November 1, 1955; Mary Jordana, born August 6, 1961; and Mark Dennis, born December 22, 1963.

William, known as "Mac," entered the work force as an employee in a street sweeper repair firm. As that job promised little in the way of future development, Mac soon found employment with International Business Machines time division, which was eventually sold to the Simplex Division. After several years working with school clocks and bells, Mac decided that steam fitting was his calling. His major concern in that arena

WILLIAM (MAC) AND ANNE WAINWRIGHT MCCLELLAND 1980s

was large heating and cooling systems in buildings such as hospitals. He developed an area-wide reputation for being able to solve problems that stumped the best. Mac retired from Carrier Corporation as a member of the Steamfitter's Union on December 31st, 1993.

He has spent his retirement representing children through CASA (Court Appointed Special Advocates). On May 1st, 2006, he graduated from college with an Associate in Applied Science degree.

Anne has been a homemaker and raised their children. She also babysat and cared for children during the 1960s and 1970s and spent several years in the real estate industry.

WILLIAM DENNIS MCCLELLAND FAMILY THANKSGIVING 1995 FRONT ROW, LEFT TO RIGHT: MEGAN GERTSON (GRANDDAUGHTER), WILLIAM DENNIS (MAC) & ANNE MCCLELLAND, TYREL NEWTON (GRANDSON), CHELSEA GERTSON (GRANDDAUGHTER); BACK ROW, LEFT TO RIGHT: MARK MCCLELLAND (SON), MARY & LINDSAY GERTSON (DAUGHTER AND SON-IN-LAW), DEAN & JANETTE NEWTON (SON-IN-LAW AND DAUGHTER), & PATRICIA ANN (DAUGHTER)

SIXTH GENERATION

Patricia Ann McClelland, Janette Marie McClelland,
Mary Jordana McClelland, Mark Dennis McClelland

Patricia Ann McClelland – Sixth Generation

Patricia Ann McClelland, first child of William Dennis McClelland and Ann Wainwright, was born on August 3rd, 1953.

Patricia graduated from James Madison High School in Portland, Oregon on June 3rd, 1971. She remains single. She worked for a fraternal benefit life insurance company in Portland for twenty-two years. She currently lives in Milwaukie, Oregon and works for the Oregonian Publishing Company in Portland.

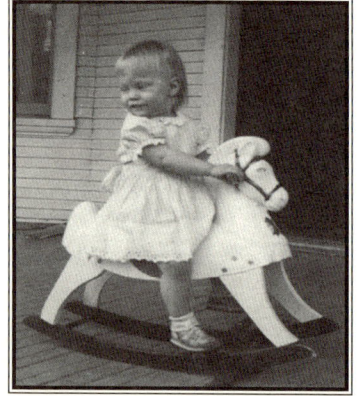

PATRICIA ANN MCCLELLAND, AGE TWO, FRONT PORCH OF HOME ON S.E. STARK ST., 1955

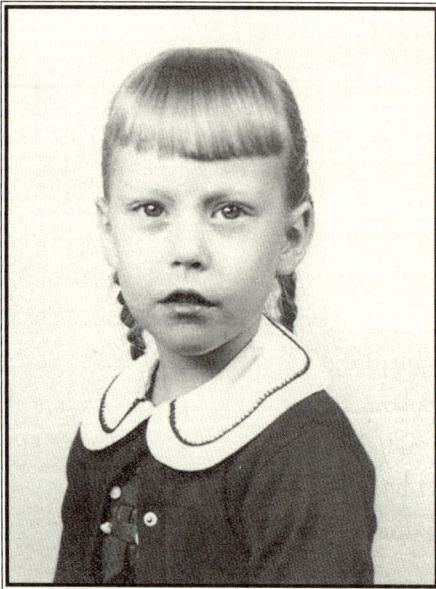

PATRICIA ANN MCCLELLAND, AGE SIX
FIRST GRADE, GLENHAVEN GRADE SCHOOL
PORTLAND, OREGON – 1959

PATRICIA ANN MCCLELLAND
HIGH SCHOOL GRADUATION
1971

Janette Marie McClelland – Sixth Generation

Janette Marie McClelland, second child of William Dennis McClelland and Ann Wainwright, was born on November 1st, 1955.

JANETTE MARIE MCCLELLAND,
JAMES MADISON HIGH SCHOOL
GRADUATION 1973

She married Gregory Dean Newton on August 19th, 1977.

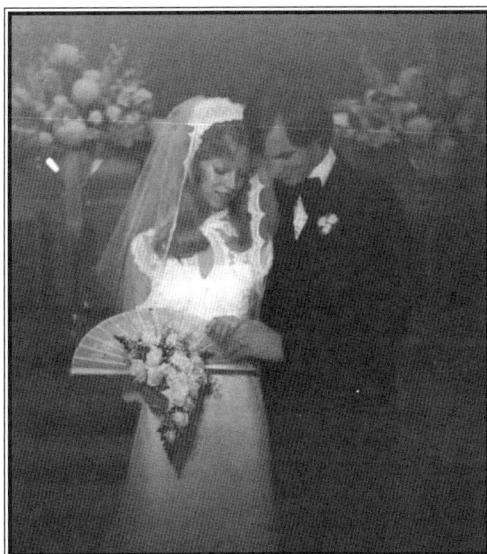

JANETTE MARIE MCCLELLAND
& GREGORY DEAN NEWTON
WEDDING DAY - AUGUST 19, 1977

Mr. and Mrs. William D. McClelland
and
Mr. Glenn A. Newton
request the honour of your presence
at the marriage of their children
Janette Marie
and
Gregory Dean
on Friday, the nineteenth day of August
Nineteen hundred and seventy-seven
at seven-thirty in the evening
Evangelical Congregational Church
Northeast Fifty-fifth and Alberta Street
Portland, Oregon

Reception following

JANETTE MARIE McCLELLAND
AND GREGORY DEAN NEWTON
WEDDING INVITATION
AUGUST 19, 1977

They have one child, Tyrel Dean Newton,
born September 19, 1981.

Janette and her family lived in Gresham,
Oregon until 2000. In 1984, Janette went to
work for Harris Group, an engineering company
in Portland, Oregon. She accepted the position
of Controller in their Seattle office in 1998
and eventually the family moved to Seattle after
Tyrel graduated from high school. Dean works
for King County.

LEFT TO RIGHT: TYREL NEWTON, JANETTE
NEWTON, AND DEAN NEWTON
AT HOME IN GRESHAM, OREGON
1998

SEVENTH GENERATION

Tyrel Dean Newton – Seventh Generation

Tyrel Dean Newton, only child of Dean Newton and Janette Marie McClelland, was born on September 19th, 1981 in Portland, Oregon.

Tyrel grew up in Gresham, Oregon. Once he graduated from high school, he and his parents moved to Seattle, where he enrolled in the University of Washington. He graduated in June of 2004 with a Bachelor's Degree in Electrical Engineering.

Upon graduation, Tyrel started work for Tether's Unlimited, Inc. in Lynnwood, Washington. He and his fianceé Christie Iverson now live in Lynnwood, Washington. Christie was born on January 15th, 1982 in Portland, Oregon. She is pursuing a nursing degree at Everett Community College. They are planning their wedding for August 2007.

TYREL DEAN NEWTON
1984

TYREL DEAN NEWTON
UNIVERSITY OF WASHINGTON
GRADUATION 2004

TYREL DEAN NEWTON AND CHRISTIE IVERSON
ENGAGEMENT, 2005

Mary Jordana McClelland – Sixth Generation

Mary Jordana McClelland, third child of William Dennis McClelland and Ann Wainwright, was born on August 6th, 1961 in Portland, Oregon.

Mary graduated from James Madison High School in Portland, Oregon in June of 1979.

MARY JORDAN McCLELLAND
HIGH SCHOOL GRADUATION
1979

She married Lindsay Alfred Gertson on December 12th, 1987 in Vancouver, Washington. Lindsay Alfred Gertson was born on September 26th, 1962 in Wellington, Colorado.

They have two children: Megan Marie, born January 22, 1983, and Chelsea Lynn, born August 24, 1988.

LINDSAY ALFRED GERTSON AND MARY
JORDANA McCLELLAND
WEDDING DAY – DECEMBER 12, 1987

SEVENTH GENERATION

Megan Marie Gertson, Chelsea Lynn Gertson

Megan Marie Gertson – Seventh Generation

Megan Marie Gertson, first child of Lindsay Alfred Gertson and Mary Jordana McClelland, was born on January 22nd, 1983 in Portland, Oregon.

MEGAN MARIE GERTSON, 1986

MARY & MEGAN GERTSON, 1987

Megan graduated from Skyview High School in Vancouver, Washington in June 2001.

Megan started working part-time for UPS in October of 2001. She also completed a course as a massage therapist and one year of college at Clark Community College. In October 2006 she was promoted to the position of driver at UPS and is now working full-time. Megan currently lives in Vancouver, Washington.

MEGAN MARIE GERTSON
HIGH SCHOOL GRADUATION
2001

Chelsea Lynn Gertson – Seventh Generation

Chelsea Lynn Gertson, second child of Lindsay Alfred Gertson and Mary Jordana McClelland, was born on August 24th, 1988 in Portland, Oregon.

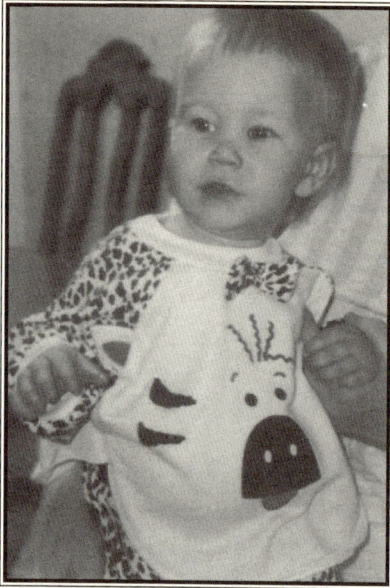

CHELSEA LYNN GERTSON
1ST BIRTHDAY – 1989

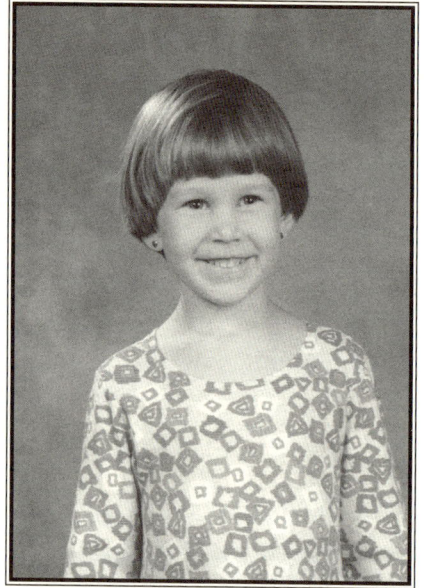

CHELSEA LYNN GERTSON, 1993

CHELSEA LYNN GERTSON
HIGH SCHOOL GRADUATION
2006

Chelsea graduated from Hudson's Bay High School in Vancouver, Washington in June 2006.

Chelsea followed her sister into UPS in September 2006. She is working for UPS part-time and will also be taking advantage of their very generous college tuition program. Chelsea currently lives in Vancouver, Washington.

Mark Dennis McClelland – Sixth Generation

Mark Dennis McClelland, fourth child of William Dennis McClelland and Ann Wainwright, was born on December 22nd, 1963 in Portland, Oregon.

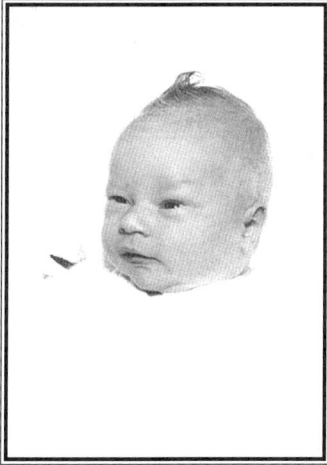

MARK DENNIS MCCLELLAND
AT BIRTH

MARK DENNIS MCCLELLAND, 1965

Mark graduated from James Madison High School in Portland, Oregon in June, 1983.

MARK DENNIS MCCLELLAND, MADISON
HIGH SCHOOL GRADUATION – 1983

MARK DENNIS MCCLELLAND, 1983

After graduation, Mark worked for a number of car/truck dealerships as a parts driver. He completed his apprenticeship program with the Steamfitter's Union in June 2000. He is currently working for AirPride Incorporated and living in Portland, Oregon.

Paul Joseph McClelland – Fifth Generation

Paul Joseph McClelland, third child of Elmer Edward Ellsworth McClelland and Ruth Laverne Tuttle, was born on March 8th, 1941 in Elgin, Nebraska. Paul was an infant when the McClellands moved to Shadyside, Ohio, Omaha, and finally Portland. He has lived in Portland, Oregon since, and attended grade school and technical high school in the Portland school system.

Paul worked as a warehouseman before becoming a marine electrician, and later as a journeyman and foreman as he gained knowledge in his craft. He can spin many a story about his work on large sea-going vessels, as he was often on board when those ships put out to sea for trial runs.

Paul married Francine Jane Schaaf on July 8th, 1961 in Portland, Oregon. Francine was born on December 15th, 1941 in Portland, Oregon. Paul and his wife Francine are a lively couple, almost constantly joking and having fun. This is perhaps why they have come into contact with so many children over the years, particularly as Francine provided daycare. They enjoy travel, movies, and musicals, and seem constantly to be on-the-go.

One of Paul's great loves is his stunning model train, which is set up in the basement of his home.

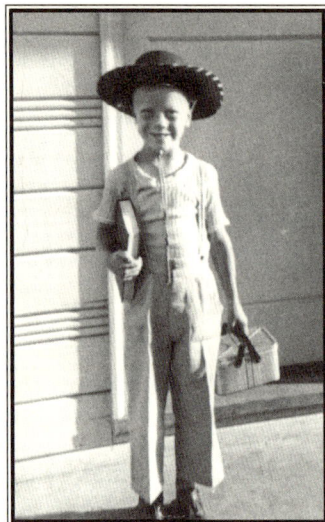

PAUL JOSEPH McCLELLAND
1947

It is truly realistic, down to the smallest detail, with many sidings and switches – a work of art and love.

They have three children: Paul Daniel, born March 9, 1963, Shawn Patrick, born March 17, 1966, and Susan Renee, born June 3, 1967.

PAUL JOSEPH AND FRANCINE SCHAAF McCLELLAND, 1980s

SIXTH GENERATION

Paul Daniel McClelland, Shawn Patrick McClelland,
Susan Renee McClelland

Paul Daniel McClelland – Sixth Generation

Paul Daniel McClelland, first child of Paul Joseph McClelland and Francine Jane Schaaf, was born on March 9th, 1963 in Portland, Oregon.

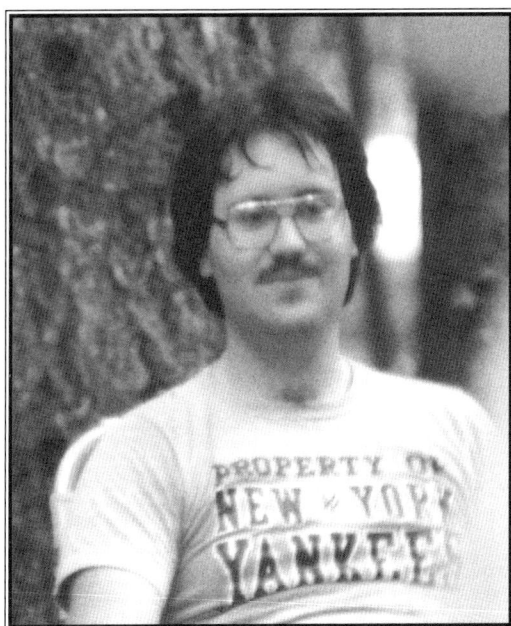

PAUL DANIEL MCCLELLAND

He married Sherry Laverne Akers on October 2nd, 1993 in Hillsboro, Oregon.

Shawn Patrick McClelland – Sixth Generation

Shawn Patrick McClelland, second child of Paul Joseph McClelland and Francine Jane Schaaf, was born on March 17th, 1966.

He married Janette Denise Woods September 24th, 1988 in Troutdale, Oregon.

SHAWN McCLELLAND AND JANETTE DENISE WOODS WEDDING – SEPTEMBER 24, 1988

They have three children: Megan Alysia, born September 11, 1989, Kelsey Ann, born December 5, 1992, and Zackery Ryan, born October 3, 2000.

SEVENTH GENERATION

Megan Alysia McClelland, Kelsey Ann McClelland,
Zackery Ryan McClelland

Megan Alysia McClelland – Seventh Generation

Megan Alysia McClelland, first child of Shawn Patrick McClelland and Janette Denise Woods, was born on September 11th, 1989 in Portland, Oregon.

Megan is a junior in high school.

MEGAN ALYSIA McCLELLAND
MAY 2005

Kelsey Ann McClelland – Seventh Generation

Kelsey Ann McClelland, second child of Shawn Patrick McClelland and Janette Denise Woods, was born on December 5th, 1992 in Portland, Oregon.

Kelsey is in the eighth grade.

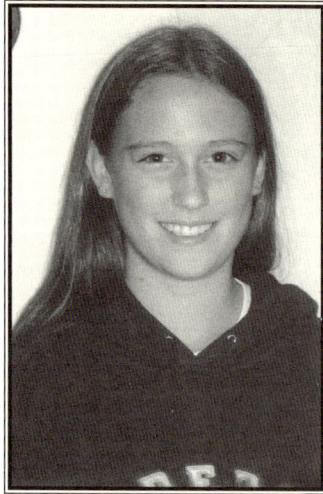

KELSEY ANN McCLELLAND
SEPTEMBER 2006

Zackery Ryan McClelland – Seventh Generation

Zackery Ryan McClelland, third child of Shawn Patrick McClelland and Janette Denise Woods, was born on October 3rd, 2000 in Portland, Oregon.

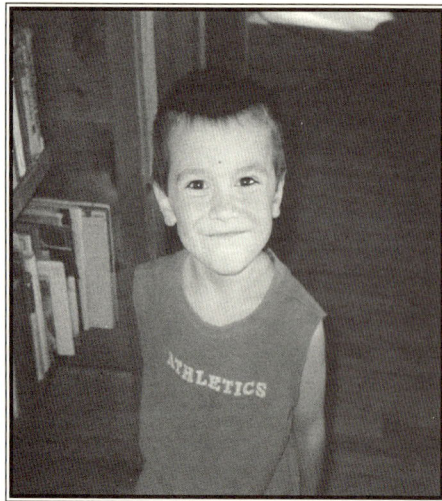

ZACKERY RYAN McCLELLAND, SEPTEMBER 2006

Susan Renee McClelland – Sixth Generation

Susan Renee McClelland, third child of Paul Joseph McClelland and Francine Jane Schaaf, was born on June 3rd, 1967.

She married Charles William Mize on August 24th, 2003 in Troutdale, Oregon.

SUSAN RENEE MCCLELLAND AND
CHARLES WILLIAM MIZE
WEDDING DAY – AUGUST 24TH, 2003

Elmer married Margaret Stella St. Clair (Turner) Hardiman on January 18th, 1947 in East Sussex, England. Margaret Stella was born on November 23rd, 1914 in Bargaed, Wales, United Kingdom.

ELMER EDWARD MCCLELLAND AND STELLA ST. CLAIR (TURNER) HARDIMAN
MARRIAGE CERTIFICATE – JANUARY 18, 1947

PERMANENT STAFF – AAF STATION 342
ENGLAND – JUNE 14, 1944
DR. ELMER MCCLELLAND (7TH FROM LEFT, FRONT ROW)

ELMER AND SHIRLEY MCCLELLAND
PARIS, FRANCE, 1946

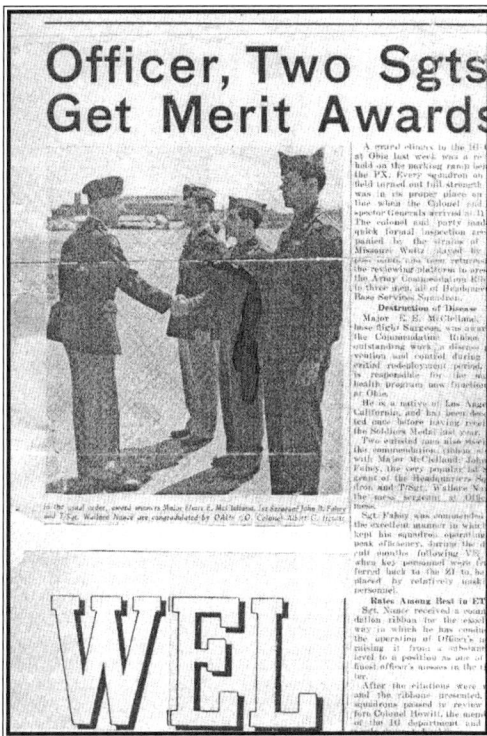

ELMER MCCLELLAND
MERIT AWARD – GERMANY
JULY 6, 1946

Elmer and Shirley had one son, Stephen, born August 3rd, 1945. Following the war, the family took up residence in San Fernando, California, where Elmer was on the staff of the San Fernando Veteran's Hospital. He specialized in pulmonary medicine, later moving into private practice with a specialty in internal medicine.

V.A. HOSPITAL, SAN FERNANDO, CALIFORNIA
DR. ELMER McCLELLAND – FRONT ROW CENTER
1950

Elmer was a director of the Panorama City Chamber of Commerce in 1956 and joined the Panorama Hospital staff in 1960. Elmer and Shirley "Stella" McClelland were very active in the Panorama City Rotary Club.

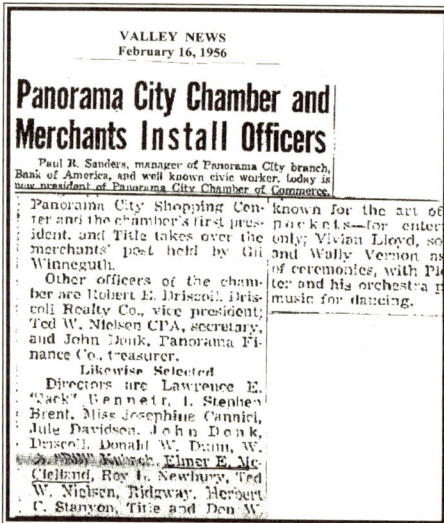

VALLEY NEWS
February 16, 1956

Panorama City Chamber and Merchants Install Officers

Paul R. Sanders, manager of Panorama City branch, Bank of America, and well known civic worker, today is new president of Panorama City Chamber of Commerce.

Panorama City Shopping Center and the chamber's first president, and Title takes over the merchants' post held by Gil Winneguth.

Other officers of the chamber are Robert E. Driscoll, Driscoll Realty Co., vice president; Ted W. Nielsen CPA, secretary, and John Donk, Panorama Finance Co., treasurer.

Likewise Selected

Directors are Lawrence E. "Jack" Bennett, L. Stephen Brent, Miss Josephine Cannici, Jule Davidson, John Donk, Driscoll, Donald W. Dunn, W. [illegible] Kulisch, Elmer E. McClelland, Roy L. Newbury, Ted W. Nielsen, Ridgway, Herbert C. Stanyon, Title and Don W.

known for the art of pockets—for entertainment only; Vivian Lloyd, soloist and Wally Vernon as master of ceremonies, with Pl[illegible] and his orchestra playing music for dancing.

VALLEY NEWS
FEBRUARY 16, 1956

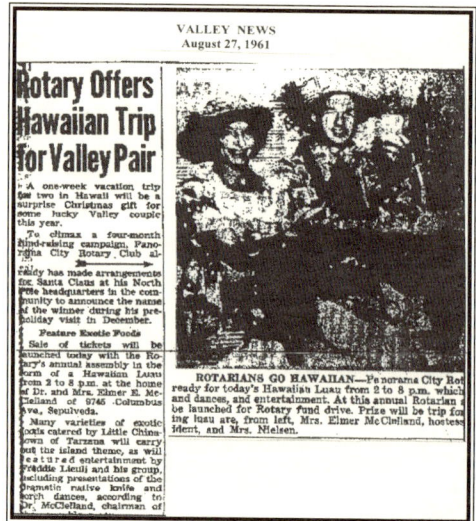

VALLEY NEWS
August 27, 1961

Rotary Offers Hawaiian Trip for Valley Pair

A one-week vacation trip for two in Hawaii will be a surprise Christmas gift for some lucky Valley couple this year.

To climax a four-month fund-raising campaign, Panorama City Rotary Club already has made arrangements for Santa Claus at his North Pole headquarters in the community to announce the name of the winner during his pre-holiday visit in December.

Feature Exotic Foods

Sale of tickets will be launched today with the Rotary's annual assembly in the form of a Hawaiian Luau from 2 to 8 p.m. at the home of Dr. and Mrs. Elmer E. McClelland of 9745 Columbus Ave., Sepulveda.

Many varieties of exotic foods catered by Little Chinatown of Tarzana will carry out the island theme, as will featured entertainment by Freddie Lleuji and his group, including presentations of the dramatic native knife and torch dances, according to Dr. McClelland, chairman of

ROTARIANS GO HAWAIIAN—Panorama City Rotary ready for today's Hawaiian Luau from 2 to 8 p.m. which and dances, and entertainment. At this annual Rotarian be launched for Rotary fund drive. Prize will be trip for ing luau are, from left, Mrs. Elmer McClelland, hostess dent, and Mrs. Nielsen.

VALLEY NEWS
SUNDAY, AUGUST 27, 1961

Sons of Elmer Edward McClelland
Left to right: Paul, William, Lee and
Stephen McClelland
Circa 1960s

Elmer Edward Ellsworth
McClelland, 1961

Elmer, Shirley and Stephen McClelland
Circa 1962 – 1963

A tragic accident took Elmer's life—drowning in his pool September 29th, 1963 in Van Nuys, California.

Friday, October 4, 1963—Van Nuys (Calif.)

Throng Attends Last Rites for 'Doctor Mac' McClelland

More than 150 Rotarians, friends and relatives attended the funeral services at Praiswater Funeral Home, Van Nuys, for Dr. Elmer E. McClelland, prominent Valley

DR. E. E. McCLELLAND
Mourned by Community

phyiscian and Rotarian who passed away suddenly in a swimming pool accident on Sunday, Sept. 29.

"Doctor Mac," as he was affectionately known, was a charter member of the Panorama City Rotary Club and maintained perfect attendance for more than 10 years.

He was born Aug. 3, 1902, in La Crosse, Wis., received his degree from the University of Nebraska Medical School in 1926, and practiced in Bellaire, Ohio, until he entered the service in 1942.

Won Soldier's Medal

McClelland held a commercial pilot's license and while in Ohio became known as the "Flying Doctor." He well remembered many an Ohio farmer signaling for assistance with a bedsheet.

The doctor served in the Eighth Air Force from 1942 to 1947 as a flight surgeon and saw action in England, Germany and France. In 1944 he received the Soldier's Medal for heroism in remaining with the pilot of a crashed, burning aircraft until he could be rescued.

He came to California in 1947 and served as chief of vocational rehabilitation and education on the staff of the San Fernando Veterans Administration Hospital until he established his private practice as an internist in Panorama City in 1950.

Served Community

Dr. McClelland was a staff member of the Valley Presbyterian, Pacoima Lutheran, Van Nuys Maternity, and Sherwood Hospitals and was an FAA medical examiner.

He was active in community affairs and served as director of the Panorama City Chamber of Commerce in 1955.

Dr. McClelland resided at 9745 Columbus Ave., Sepulveda, and is survived by his wife Shirley and son Stephen 18.

OBITUARY – DR. ELMER E.
"MAC" McCLELLAND

Shirley Stella McClelland moved to Laguna Beach, California following Elmer's death and purchased the beach-front apartment property where she currently resides.

FIFTH GENERATION

Stephen Edward McClelland – Fifth Generation

Stephen Edward McClelland, only child of Elmer Edward Ellsworth and Margaret Shirley Turner, was born on August 3rd, 1945 in Cambridge, England.

He married Patricia Jacqueline Short on May 22nd, 1971 in Arundel, West Sussex, England. Patricia was born on February 19th, 1947 in London, England. She lived in the London area up until 1970, excepting the four years she spent in Toronto, Canada.

Stephen met Patricia Jacqueline Short in July 1964 when he and his mother came to England to visit family and friends after the death of his father in 1963. Shirley and Stephen were staying with very good friends in Enfield, Middlesex, a northern suburb of London, who just happened to very good friends and next-door neighbors to Patricia's family. Stephen returned to USC at the end of the summer, and the following summer saw Patricia spending six weeks in California with Shirley and Stephen, initially in the San Fernando Valley, and then in Laguna Beach when Shirley decided to relocate. Stephen and Patricia stayed in touch over the next few years, including Stephen's time in the U.S. Navy (June 1966 to August 1969) when he served in Vietnam on the aircraft carrier Ticonderoga. Patricia returned to Laguna Beach in May 1970 to help Shirley with her apartments during the hectic summer months. By then, Stephen had started back to Saddleback Junior College in Mission Viejo for his AA degree. Patricia returned to England in February 1971 in order to help arrange their wedding, which took place at her parents' local 16th century church, St. Margaret's, in Angmering, Sussex, England. Stephen and Patricia were married May 22nd, 1971, in St. Margaret's Church, Angmering, Sussex, England.

STEPHEN MCCLELLAND
AND PATRICIA SHORT
WEDDING DAY – MAY 22, 1971

Stephen and Patricia returned to California in August 1971 and moved to Riverside in order for Stephen to complete his BA in Psychology at the University of California. They moved to Seattle in August 1973 when Stephen accepted a scholarship at the University of Washington to pursue his PhD in Developmental Psychology. Patricia worked at the University hospital, setting up a Patient Relations Department. They thoroughly enjoyed their twelve years in Seattle, especially the births of their two children: Damien Karl, born February 10, 1979, and Caitlin Jane, born July 31, 1982.

After receiving his doctoral degree, Stephen worked with the severely retarded population at Rainier School in Buckley, Washington, transferring to Fairview Developmental Center in Costa Mesa, California in 1985, where he has continued to work with the severely retarded. He was also an Associate Professor in the Psychology Department at Saddleback College from 1985 – 2000, the first student to return as a professor.

STEPHEN, DAMIEN, CAITLIN AND
PATRICIA MCCLELLAND

Stephen died June 9th, 2006 in a tragic accident hiking in the desert near his home.

SIXTH GENERATION

Damien Karl McClelland, Caitlin Jane McClelland

Damien Karl McClelland – Sixth Generation

Damien Karl McClelland, first child of Stephen McClelland and Patricia Short, was born on February 10th, 1979 in Seattle, Washington.

CAITLIN, STEPHEN, DAMIEN, AND PATRICIA MCCLELLAND
DAMIEN'S COLLEGE GRADUATION—UCLA IRVINE

STELLA AND DAMIEN MCCLELLAND
IN THE GARDEN, 2003

Damien graduated from Fountain Valley High School. He attended the University of California - Irvine and got his BA in Criminology. He is presently employed with Kaiser Permanente.

Caitlin Jane McClelland – Sixth Generation

Caitlin Jane McClelland, second child of Stephen McClelland and Patricia Short, was born on July 31st, 1982 in Seattle, Washington.

Caitlin graduated from Fountain Valley High School. She attended California State University—Long Beach and graduated with a BA in Child Development. She is presently employed as a preschool teacher.

CAITLIN AND DAMIEN MCCLELLAND

DAMIEN, STELLA AND CAITLIN MCCLELLAND
SOUTHERN CALIFORNIA
2004

SHIRLEY "STELLA" MCCLELLAND
90TH BIRTHDAY
2004

Harriet Rose McClelland – Fourth Generation

Harriet Rose McClelland, seventh child of Elmer Edward McClelland and Mary Settlemyer, was born on July 10th, 1904 in Des Moines, Iowa. Harriet married George Reber, born August 19, 1902. They had three children: Barbara Ruth, born November 18, 1929, George William, born March 15, 1932, and Suzanne Lee, born July 26, 1939.

HARRIET & GEORGE REBER
EASTER – EARLY 1920s

FRONT ROW, LEFT TO RIGHT:
UNKNOWN, BARBARA, GEORGE JR.,
HARRIET REBER;
STANDING: GEORGE REBER

1930 CENSUS, BLOOMINGTON, SAN BERNARDINO COUNTY, CA.
GEORGE & HARRIET REBER AND FAMILY

George Reber died March 5th, 1967 in Orange County, California.
Harriet died December 28th, 1991 in Ventura County, California.

FIFTH GENERATION

*Barbara Ruth Reber, George William Reber, Jr.,
Suzanne Lee Reber*

Barbara Ruth Reber – Fifth Generation

Barbara Ruth Reber, first child of George William Reber and Harriet Rose McClelland, was born on November 18th, 1929 in San Bernardino County, California.

George William Reber, Jr. – Fifth Generation

George William Reber, Jr., second child of George William Reber and Harriet Rose McClelland, was born on March 15th, 1932, in Los Angeles County, California. He married Norma Spicer on November 5th, 1958 in Los Angeles County, California. Norma was born on October 1st, 1937. They have three children: George M., born June 7, 1959, Daryl N., born September 20, 1961, and Marla L., born April 15, 1967.

SIXTH GENERATION

*George M. Reber, Daryl N. Reber,
Marla L. Reber*

George M. Reber – Sixth Generation

George M. Reber, first child of George William Reber, Jr. and Norma Spicer, was born on June 7th, 1959 in Los Angeles County, California. He married Eva, born September 1st, 1961.

Daryl N. Reber – Sixth Generation

Daryl N. Reber, second child of George William Reber, Jr. and Norma Spicer, was born on September 20th, 1961 in Los Angeles County, California. He married Irene.

Marla L. Reber – Sixth Generation

Marla L. Reber, third child of George William Reber, Jr. and Norma Spicer, was born on April 15th, 1967 in Los Angeles County, California.

Suzanne Lee Reber – Fifth Generation

Suzanne Lee Reber, third child of George William Reber and Harriet Rose McClelland, was born on July 26th, 1939 in Wheeling, West Virginia.

Suzanne married Edgar Foster on January 14th, 1961 in First Presbyterian Church, Hollywood, California.

Suzanne later married Charles Chuck Brasher on November 28th, 1963, Lake County Courthouse, South Lake Tahoe, California. Chuck was born on November 15th, 1938 in Los Angeles, California.

SUZANNE LEE REBER AND CHUCK BRASHER, WEDDING DAY – NOVEMBER 28, 1963

Chuck and Suzanne started their married life in the San Fernando Valley, California. They lived in an apartment that Chuck and his brother Jim and dad had built. Chuck is a general building contractor.

They have one daughter, Eileen Brasher, born October 24, 1970 in Northridge, Los Angeles, California. They lived in Northridge, California for a time before moving to Grass Valley in 1977.

During their early married years, they often went big-game hunting. Chuck shot a grizzly bear and Suzanne a black bear, among others, in Canada. They no longer hunt and now prefer to only shoot pictures.

They are also major collectors. In 1968, Chuck started collecting toy trains and has a wonderful collection in the attic of his home. Chuck and Suzanne have made friends all over the world in train clubs and go to York, Pennsylvania in the spring and fall, where 10,000 – 15,000 collectors gather at the fairgrounds.

Besides toy trains, the couple also collects old Halloween items, Santas, and baskets dating back to the 1750s – 1800s, as well as furniture and other items.

Suzanne started back to college at the age of 42, taking all of the basic classes and receiving her LVN (Licensed Vocational Nurse) degree in June 1989. In June 1999, she graduated from Sierra College's Registered Nurse's program. She is still working at the local hospital, in the Transitional Care Unit.

Suzanne and Chuck love traveling in the U.S. Ten years ago, they started giving one another surprise

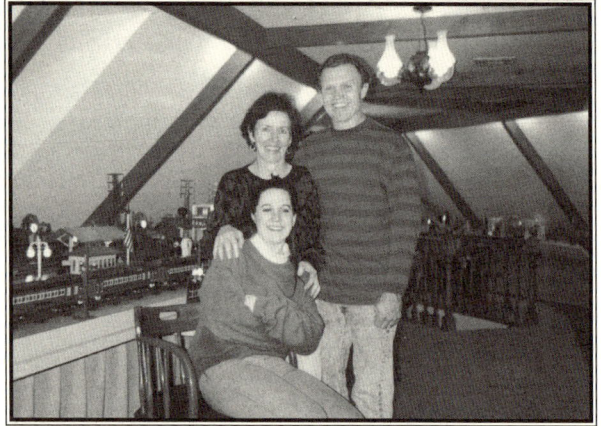

EILEEN, SUZANNE & CHUCK BRASHER IN THE "TRAIN ROOM" IN THEIR ATTIC, JANUARY 1991

SUZANNE BRASHER RN GRADUATION JAN. 1999, WITH GRANDCHILDREN LETICIA AND ROMARIO BAUCUM

SUZANNE AND CHUCK BRASHER TRAIN CONVENTION – PITTSBURGH 2004

trips on their anniversary. They have been to the northern and southern rims of the Grand Canyon; Boston; Williamsburg, Virginia; Wheeling, West Virginia; and the Ohio River via the Delta Queen, to name a few. On each anniversary, depending on whose turn it is to plan the trip, one must announce to the other one when to be ready to go. It is an exciting way to travel.

SIXTH GENERATION

Eileen Marie Brasher – Sixth Generation

Eileen Marie Brasher, only child of Charles Chuck Brasher and Eileen Brasher, was born on October 24th, 1970 in Northridge, Los Angeles, California.

Eileen spent one year as a foreign exchange student and then majored in Oriental Language at U.C. Berkeley. She enjoyed traveling with her parents in Japan and being an interpreter.

She married Richard Allen Baucum on August 3rd, 2001 in Reno, Nevada. They reside in Grass Valley, California. They have four children: Leticia Mireya, born May 29, 1992, Romario Charles, born September 15, 1994, Ximena, born April 21, 2002, and Elizabeth, born August 4, 2004.

RICHARD, ROMARIO AND EILEEN BAUCUM
WEDDING RECEPTION
AUGUST 3, 2001

SEVENTH GENERATION

Leticia Mireya Baucum, Romario Charles Baucum,
Ximena Baucum, and Elizabeth Baucum

Leticia Mireya Baucum – Seventh Generation

Leticia Mireya Baucum, first child of Richard Allen Baucum and Eileen Marie Brasher, was born on May 29th, 1992 in Berkeley, California.

LETICIA BAUCUM
AGE 13

Romario Charles Baucum – Seventh Generation

Romario Charles Baucum, second child of Richard Allen Baucum and Eileen Marie Brasher, was born on September 15th, 1994 in Berkeley, California.

ROMARIO BAUCUM
AGE 11

Ximena Baucum – Seventh Generation

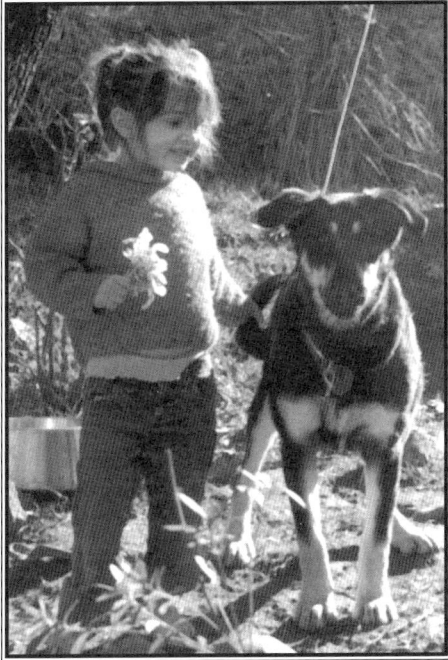

Ximena Baucum, third child of Richard Allen Baucum and Eileen Marie Brasher, was born on April 21st, 2002 in Auburn, California.

XIMENA BAUCUM
AGE 3

Elizabeth Baucum – Seventh Generation

Elizabeth Baucum, fourth child of Richard Allen Baucum and Eileen Marie Brasher, was born on August 4th, 2004 in Auburn, California.

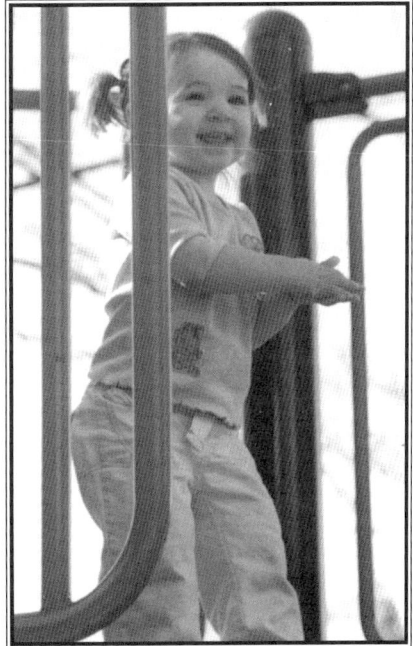

ELIZABETH BAUCUM
AGE 18 MONTHS

Matilda McClelland – Third Generation

Matilda McClelland, second child of John McClelland and Elizabeth McCauley, was born in July 1863 in Pennsylvania. She married Levi W. Hastings on April 23rd, 1884 in Polk County, Iowa. By 1910, Levi and Matilda had moved to South Dakota, where they homesteaded some land. After the death of Levi, Matilda lived with her sister Minnie in Kewanee, Illinois.

```
                        MARRIAGES..POLK COUNTY, IOWA        PAGE      33
                                    BOOK 2
         COPIED BY PIONEER SONS AND DAUGHTERS, P O BOX 2103, DES MOINES, IOWA 50310

   BIDE                      AGE GROOM                        AGE DATE       PAGE

   C CAUGHEY ROSA             20  FROACH WM                    20  08 31 82    61
   C CAULLEY E A - BOYD       63  KELLOGG F S                  73  06 27 83   121
   C CAVLEY JENNIE            24  WEATHERWAX SIDNEY            25  02 06 82   272
   C CLAIN IDA H              24  WARD POWELL                  33  02 22 82   273
   C CLAY SARAH               20  DAVIS JAMES W                20  02 14 83    43
   C CLELLAND MARIA           21  WOOD BENJ                    32  07 14 81   271
   C CLELLAND MATILDA E       21  HASTINGS L W                 32  04 23 84    93
   C CLURE ELLA M             20  HAWKINS JAMES N              45  11 26 84    95
   C CONNAUGHEY CLARISSA      19  SHIFFER CHARLES N            27  02 23 81   215
```

MARRIAGE RECORD OF MATILDA MCCLELLAND AND LEVI HASTINGS

IOWA CENSUS 1900; SHOWS MATILDA
AND LEVI HASTINGS

LEFT TO RIGHT: MATILDA HASTINGS,
MARGARET FULLER TURNER, MINNIE MAY
MCCLELLAND, AND HARRIET TURNER
CIRCA 1934

Susan McClelland – Third Generation

Susan McClelland, third child of John McClelland and Elizabeth McCauley, was born on November 26th, 1865, in Iowa. Susan married Sandy Kane on July 5th, 1886 in Polk County, Iowa.

```
           MARRIAGES..POLK COUNTY, IOWA      PAGE      31
                        BOOK 3
   COPIED BY PIONEER SONS AND DAUGHTERS, P O BOX 2103, DES MOINES, IOWA 50310


   BRIDE                  GROOM                   DATE        PAGE

   MC CAULEY ANNA         GRITTSHALL GEO WM       02 02 86     91
   MC CAULEY MARY         MC KINLEY WILLIAM       -- -- 85    165
   MC CLAIN DAISY         CHIETHAM ELMER          09 22 87     50
   MC CLELLAND EMMA       TOWNSEND W S            07 04 88    268
   MC CLELLAND LAURA      BENNETTE LYCURGUS M     08 06 86     26
   MC CLELLAND LONA L     SHOCKLEY WM P           06 01 86    245
   MC CLELLAND SARAH M    MILLER MAURICE A        03 01 86    168
   MC CLELLAND SUSAN M    KANE SANDY M            07 05 86    145
   MC CLLELLAND ANNETTE   WATTS ROBT M            01 04 86    288
   MC COLLUM HANNAH M     HALL JASON              09 15 86    106
   MC CONKEY ANNA M       THRASH G D              02 09 85    264
```

POLK COUNTY, IOWA
MARRIAGE REGISTRATION – JULY 5, 1886; SUSAN M. MCCLELLAND AND SANDY KANE

They moved to Deadwood, South Dakota, where they lived with John McClelland.

1900 CENSUS - DEADWOOD, SOUTH DAKOTA
SUSAN AND MICHAEL SANDY KANE AND FAMILY
SHOWN LIVING WITH JOHN MCCLELLAND

Susan was a school teacher. She and Sandy moved to Seattle, where Sandy worked for the University of Oregon. Susan died August 17th, 1944 in Tacoma, Washington.

Harriet Hattie McClelland – Third Generation

HARRIET MCCLELLAND AND ERNEST REYNOLDS
MARRIAGE CERTIFICATE - MARCH 31, 1909

Harriet (Hattie) McClelland, fourth child of John McClelland and Elizabeth McCauley, was born on November 26th, 1868, in Iowa. In 1899 she was living in Deadwood, South Dakota. Harriet married Ernest Reynolds on March 31st, 1909 in Seattle, Washington. Mr. S.M. Kane, Harriet's brother-in-law and Susan's husband, and Mrs. L.W. Hastings, Harriet's sister Matilda, were witnesses at the ceremony.

Ernest was born circa 1878, in England. Harriet was a school teacher and a member of Amaranth. She was living in Tacoma, Washington.

1930 CENSUS, KING COUNTY, WASHINGTON
HARRIET MCCLELLAND REYNOLDS & ERNEST REYNOLDS

Harriet died April 29th, 1942.

Obituary – Harriet E. Reynolds

"Mrs. Ernest (Harriet E.) Reynolds, Rt. 2, Bothell, died Wednesday. Besides her husband, she leaves sisters, Mrs. Susan M. Kane of Tacoma and Mrs. Minnie M. Turner and Mrs. Matilda E. Hastings of Illinois. She was a member of Amaranth. Funeral services at 11 a.m. Saturday at the Bothell parlors."

Minnie May McClelland – Third Generation

Minnie May McClelland, fifth child of John McClelland and Elizabeth McCauley, was born on May 4th, 1872 in Polk County, Iowa.

MARRIAGE RECORD, MINNIE M. MCCLELLAND AND WM. TURNER
JUNE 15, 1892

MINNIE MAY MCCLELLAND AND WILLIAM TURNER
WEDDING ANNOUNCEMENT

Minnie May McClelland married William Turner on June 15th, 1892 in Polk County, Iowa. William Turner was born on March 8th, 1859 in Edinburgh, Scotland.

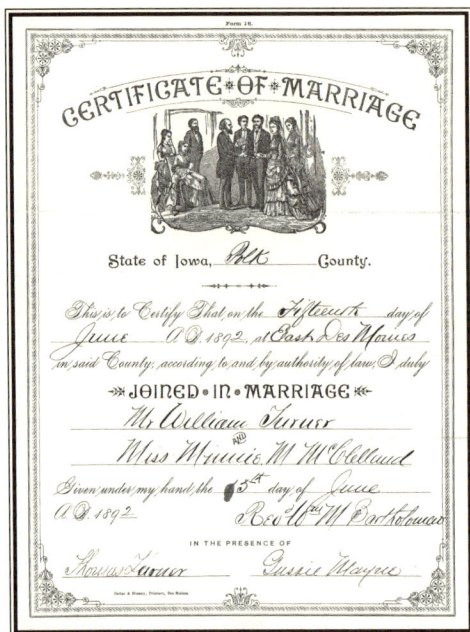

MINNIE MAY McCLELLAND AND WILLIAM TURNER
MARRIAGE CERTIFICATE – JUNE 15, 1892

HOME OF WILLIAM TURNER AND
MINNIE MAY McCLELLAND TURNER
WETHERSFIELD, ILLINOIS

LEFT TO RIGHT: HARRIET, MINNIE MAY
& ROBERT TURNER
CIRCA 1903

HARRIET & ROBERT TURNER
CIRCA 1900

Minnie graduated from East Des Moines High School in 1889. On September 1st, 1890, she was awarded a Second Class Teacher's Certificate authorizing her to teach in Polk County, Iowa.

They had three children: Harriet, born in April 1893, Robert, born August 3, 1895, and William, born January 10, 1911.

William died October 29th, 1927 in Kewanee, Henry, Illinois.

Minnie May died October 15th, 1947 in Kewanee, Henry, Illinois.

1900 CENSUS, KEWANEE, ILLINOIS
LINE 8: SHOWS MINNIE MCCLELLAND AND WILLIAM TURNER

Obituary – Minnie May Turner

"Mrs. Minnie M. Turner. Funeral services for Mrs. Minnie May Turner, 75, 226 W. College Street, will be held at 2:30 p.m. Friday, in chapel of Smith Funeral Home. Dr. Lloyd M. Thompson, pastor of First Methodist Church, will be in charge and burial will be in Pleasant View cemetery.

Friends and family may call at the funeral home Thursday night.

Mrs. Turner died in Kewanee Public hospital this morning. She had been in ill health for some time and was a patient in the hospital for a week.

Minnie May McClelland was born May 4, 1872, in Polk County, Iowa, daughter of John and Elizabeth McClelland. She married William Turner on June 15, 1892, in Des Moines and Kewanee had been her home for 54 years.

She was a member of First Methodist Church, Fortnightly Club, Women's Club, and Rebekah Lodge.

Surviving are a daughter, Miss. Harriet Turner, Baltimore, Maryland, two sons, Robert Turner of Kewanee, and William Turner of Crete, Illinois, also a granddaughter, Nancy Turner of Crete, and a sister, Mrs. Matilda Hastings, living in Kewanee.

Her husband, two sisters, and two brothers preceded her in death."

Obituary – William Turner

"The funeral of William Turner was held from the family home, 226 West College Street, at 2 o'clock Monday afternoon. The Rev. Mr. D. J. Geach, assisted by the Rev. Mr. S.R. Chubb, officiated at the home and at the grave in South Pleasant View Cemetery.

At the home Mrs. William Arnold and Mrs. John Burgland sang "My Ain Countree" and "Some Day the Silver Cord Will Break." Bearers were: Emil Wirth, James Tucker, J. L. P. Wells, Thomas McGrath, William Heideman and E. W. Beckman.

Members of the I. O. O. F. formed an honorary escort while members of the moulders' union and employees of the foundry at the Kewanee Boiler Company, attended the services in a body.

Those from out of the city who attended the funeral were: Robert Turner of Granger, Iowa, Thomas Turner of Ottumwa and F. I. Wells, Mrs. and Mrs. M. J. Dustin and Mrs. E.C. Hunt of Moline.

Mr. Turner was born in Dumbarton, Scotland, March 8, 1859, and came to this country at an early age. He had been a resident of Kewanee since 1891. For many years he had been a foreman at the Haxtun Steam Heather Company, now the Walworth Company, and at the time of his death was superintendent of the foundry at the Kewanee Boiler Company.

He was a member of the moulders' union, Kewanee Lodge, No. 128, I. O. O. F., and of the Kewanee Rebekah Lodge, No. 512.

Surviving, besides the widow, are two sons, Robert M. and William Turner; one daughter, Miss Harriet Turner of Des Moines, Iowa; three brothers, Robert Turner of Granger, Thomas Turner of Ottumwa, and James Turner, and one sister, Mrs. Alfred Gaskell of Los Angeles."

FOURTH GENERATION

Harriet Pauline Turner, Robert M. Turner, William Wallace Turner

Harriet Pauline Turner – Fourth Generation

Harriet Pauline Turner, first child of Minnie May McClelland and William Turner, was born in April 1893, in Illinois.

Harriet graduated from Kewanee High School in 1911. She was Salutatorian of her class and editor of the annual Kewanite in her senior year.

While in the Library School at Western Reserve University, Harriet formed life-long friendships. Her spirit of fun that bubbled forth unexpectedly to relieve the tedium of a difficult assignment was noted in "Kitty Log," the Annual of The Library School:

> She's not Serious Enough that's the Trouble
> And her Chuckle is just sure to Bubble
> When the Rest of the Class Has Reached such a Pass
> That from Work, they are all Seeing Double.

HARRIET PAULINE TURNER
CIRCA 1920

HARRIET & MARGARET TURNER
CIRCA 1920

PHOTO ABOARD THE SS RYNDHAM, APRIL 1953
HARRIET TURNER SAILING TO SCANDANAVIA WITH A GROUP.
HARRIET IS SECOND FROM LEFT IN THE BACK ROW.

Harriet was a favorite of the many friends with whom she corresponded throughout her life. She endeared herself to all with her warmth, charming sense of humor, love of life, and generous attitude toward all.

Upon congratulating Harriet for 25 years of service at the Enoch Pratt Library, Amy Winslow, Director, wrote:

"Let me say that you have helped us maintain good, old-fashioned standards of service, have kept us from too many new-fangled notions and, let us hope, becoming entirely too foolish for sensible librarians to be. Better than that, you have added to the joy of life. What would we do without your spice, your wit, and your astringent, gad-fly common sense!"

One of Harriet's many interests was crafts, which took her on several vacations to the Penland School of Handicrafts in North Carolina. In her self-effacing style, she describes an experience with enamel on copper: "I enameled on copper first getting rid of all frustrations by beating the stuff into a mold. The enameling is not hard, but I lack the artistic sense which would make happy combinations of color and design."

Harriet died on December 10th, 1964.

Obituary – Harriet Turner

"Miss Harriet Turner, a former resident of Kewanee, died on Thursday afternoon in Baltimore, Md., where she had made her home for the past 35 years. Miss Turner recently spent the Thanksgiving holidays in Kewanee visiting relatives and friends.

The daughter of William and Minnie McClelland Turner, she was born in Kewanee in 1893. She attended Kewanee schools, graduating from high school with the Class of 1911. She was a graduate of the University of Wisconsin and Western Reserve Library School.

Miss Turner's library career began in Vevay, Ind., and she continued as librarian in the Kewanee Public Library from 1920 to 1927 and the Des Moines Public Library until she became Director of the Sociology Department of the Enoch Pratt Free Memorial Library in Baltimore. She was a member of the American Library Assn.

Miss Turner was interested in the study of languages, making several trips to Europe to study at the University of Heidelberg during the period prior to World War II. She retired recently from active duty.

Surviving are two brothers, Robert M. of 111 W. Oak Street, Kewanee, and William of Newark, Del.

Funeral services will be held this morning at the SS Phillip and James Church in Baltimore.

Interment will be in Pleasant View Cemetery in Kewanee on Tuesday at 10 a.m., with graveside rites to be conducted by the Rev. John F. Crowley.

All friends may call at the Creamer Funeral Home here on Monday from 7 until 9 p.m."

Robert M. Turner – Fourth Generation

Robert M. Turner, second child of Minnie May McClelland and William Turner, was born on August 3rd, 1895, in Illinois.

ROBERT TURNER
CIRCA 1920

Robert married Margaret Fuller in Kewanee on June 27th, 1934. Matilda Hastings, Robert's aunt, and Minnie M. Turner, his mother, were witnesses to the marriage.

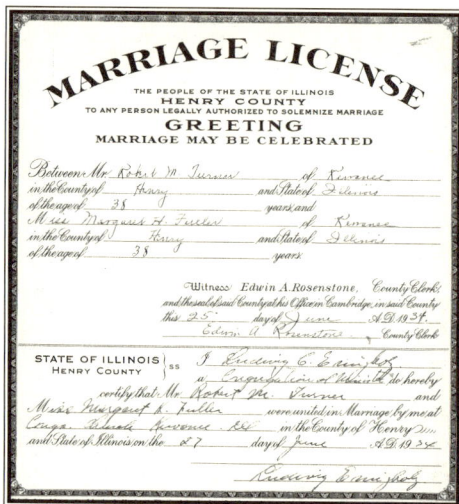

ROBERT M. TURNER AND MARGARET H. FULLER
MARRIAGE CERTIFICATE – JUNE 27TH, 1934

144

Robert Turner & Margaret Fuller
Wedding Day – June 27, 1934

Left to right: Mrs. Edward Quirk, Robert Turner,
Margaret Turner, and Harriet Turner
Thanksgiving 1964

Robert & Margaret Fuller Turner Home
Kewanee, Illinois

Margaret died June 16th, 1973.

Robert died May 31, 1976, in Kewanee, Henry, Illinois.

Obituary – Robert M. Turner

"Robert M. Turner, 80, retired Kewanee Boiler Co. employee living at 515 E. Prospect St., died at 2:55 p.m. Monday, May 31, 1976, in Kewanee Public Hospital.

Services will be at 3 p.m. Thursday, June 3, in the Creamer Funeral Home, with the Rev. Charles Wildman of the First Congregational Church officiating.

Interment will be in the Pleasant View Cemetery, with the Kewanee Veterans Council conducting military rites.

Friends may call 7 to 9 Wednesday, June 2, at the Creamer Funeral Home.

Memorials may be directed to the First Congregational Church.

Turner was born in Kewanee August 3, 1895, the son of William and Minnie McClelland Turner. He graduated from Kewanee High School in the Class of 1913. Before entering military service he was employed by National Tube and also in Detroit, Mich., and Ottumwa, Iowa.

He served in the Army's ordinance department in World War I.

Surviving are a brother, William W. of Newark, Del., and a niece, Mrs. Alonzo (Nancy) Foster of Rochester, N.Y.

He was preceded in death in addition to his parents and wife, by a sister.

Turner had been a member of the old Kewanee Club. Kewanee Elks Lodge 724, Kewanee Knights Templar, Midland Country Club, been a member of the City Board of Review and had served as secretary of Henry County Zoning, Board of Appeals.

He was currently a member of Kewanee Post 31, American Legion, and of the American Society of Mechanical Engineers.

Turner had been employed by Kewanee Boiler Co., retiring in 1961, as head of the engineering department after 42 years of employment."

R. M. Turner Retiring After 44 Years at Boiler

Robert M. Turner, head of the Engineering department, is retiring April 1 after 44 years of service with the Kewanee Boiler plant of the American Standard Industrial Division.

Turner started his engineering career as a draftsman progressing to manager of the Engineering department. He was prepared to retire in 1960 but was asked by the company to stay on for another year, which he agreed to do.

Turner played an important part in the history and progress of Kewanee Boiler Co. and was responsible for many developments in the Boiler industry, a plant official observed in announcing Turner's retirement. He served as a member of the ASME Boiler Code committee for many years.

Turner and his wife, Margaret, intend to travel and "thoroughly enjoy their leisure time."

R. M. TURNER

THE STAR COURIER, MARCH 23, 1966
ROBERT M. TURNER RETIRES

William Wallace Turner – Fourth Generation

William Wallace Turner, third child of Minnie May McClelland and William Turner, was born January 10th, 1911, in Kewanee, Illinois.

WILLIAM WALLACE TURNER
ONE YEAR OLD – 1911

WILLIAM WALLACE TURNER
GRADUATION – UNIVERSITY
OF ILLINOIS, CHAMPAIGN, ILLINOIS, 1932

William graduated from Kewanee High School, where he played football, and in 1932 earned a Bachelor of Science degree in Chemical Engineering at the University of Illinois. There he was a member of A.I.C.E. and the Cavalry Officer's Club, and Captain of the University Brigade.

William married Leona Cook Schweer on June 7th, 1942 in Harvey, Illinois.

LEFT TO RIGHT: ROBERT TURNER, MATILDA HASTINGS, MARGARET TURNER, LEONA COOK (BEFORE MARRIAGE), AND MINNIE MAY TURNER CIRCA 1940

Leona Cook was born on June 27th, 1907 in St. Louis, Missouri, the second of three children. She later moved to Crete, Illinois with her mother Agnes and two brothers, Joseph and Leo. Leona married Otto Schweer on December 12th, 1927 in Crete, Illinois. They had one daughter, Carol, born April 18, 1930. Otto died in the early 1930s.

Soon after their marriage, William, Leona, and Carol moved to Athens, Ohio, where William worked at an ordinance plant in nearby Pt. Pleasant, West Virginia. It was in Athens that Nancy Claire was born March 11, 1944.

William joined Stauffer Chemical Company in 1946 and remained with the company until his retirement in 1976. His work as plants manager was to take

LEONA COOK SCHWEER AND WILLIAM TURNER
WEDDING DAY – JUNE 7, 1942

the family back to the Chicago suburbs, then on to Roanoke and Front Royal, Virginia, and finally to Newark, Delaware in 1960. After retiring, William did consulting work. An assignment in Columbia, South America was a highlight for him, as it gave him an opportunity to explore the country and experience the culture through fellow workers with whom he became friendly.

William and Leona took active roles as Lutheran church members in Roanoke and Front Royal—Leona taught Sunday School and Bible School, and William sang in the choir. William was interested in classical music and opera, and enjoyed collecting stamps as a hobby.

Through the years, the family maintained close ties with the Chicago relatives and made frequent trips back and forth between Virginia and Delaware. Tragedy struck in 1970 when Carol died suddenly of a brain tumor. She left behind her husband of 21 years, William Anderson, and a son, Mark, sixteen years old.

William Turner, Former Kewanee Resident, Weds

The marriage of Leona Dorothy Schweer, daughter of Mrs. Agnes Sovar of Crete, Illinois, and William W. Turner, son of Mrs. William Turner of Kewanee, took place at Harvey, Illinois, Saturday, June 6, at 4 o'clock. The ceremony was performed by Rev. R. T. Gaffert at the Lutheran parsonage.

Attendants were Miss Frances Sovar, sister of the bride and William Stenning of Crete.

The bride wore a navy blue ensemble with white hat and matching accessories and a corsage of white orchids.

Following the ceremony a wedding supper was served at the Shoreland hotel in Chicago. Those present from Kewanee were Mrs. William Turner and Mr. and Mrs. Robert Turner.

The bride is a graduate of Hyde Park high school, Chicago, and has taken special nurses' training.

The bridegroom attended Wethersfield high school, and was graduated from the University of Illinois with the degree of Chemical Engineer. He is a member of Alpha Chi Sigma fraternity. He has been engaged in supervisory work for the General Chemical Company of New York at their Chicago plant and at present is taking special training at the Kankakee Ordnance plant in preparation for similar work at Point Pleasant, West Virginia, where Mr. and Mrs. Turner will reside after Aug. 1.

STAR COURIER
KEWANEE, ILLINOIS – 1942
LEONA DOROTHY SCHWEER &
WILLIAM WALLACE TURNER
WEDDING ANNOUNCEMENT

William and Leona moved back to the Homewood, Illinois in 1983, when William began experiencing the first stages of Alzheimer's disease. When Leona was unable to care for him at home, William entered a nursing home in 1988.

Leona died from the complications of a massive stroke on January 19th, 1989. William died January 14th, 1995.

LEONA & WILLIAM TURNER
25TH WEDDING ANNIVERSARY

FIFTH GENERATION

Nancy Claire Turner – Fifth Generation

Nancy Claire Turner, daughter of William Wallace Turner and Leona Cook Schweer, was born on March 11th, 1944 in Athens, Ohio.

LEFT TO RIGHT: MINNIE MCCLELLAND TURNER,
NANCY TURNER AND MATILDA HASTINGS
CIRCA 1946

NANCY AND CAROL TURNER
CIRCA 1948

William's work as a chemical engineer took the family, including Nancy's half-sister, Carol, from Ohio to Illinois and Indiana, then on to Delaware, where Nancy completed her high school education in 1962.

Nancy studied for two years at Randolph-
Macon Women's College and earned a Bachelor of
Arts degree from the University of Delaware. While
at the University, Nancy met Alonzo (Lon) Foster.

They married in August of 1967.

Soon after the marriage, Lon joined the
Army and was stationed in Berlin, where the
couple spent a year, Lon completing his military
service and Nancy exploring Berlin and observing
German culture. Leave time gave them an opportunity to travel to Paris and Italy, and cruise the
Rhine River from Rotterdam to Basil.

After Lon was discharged from the Army,
he and Nancy returned to Delaware, moving
to Rochester, NY in 1972, where Lon received

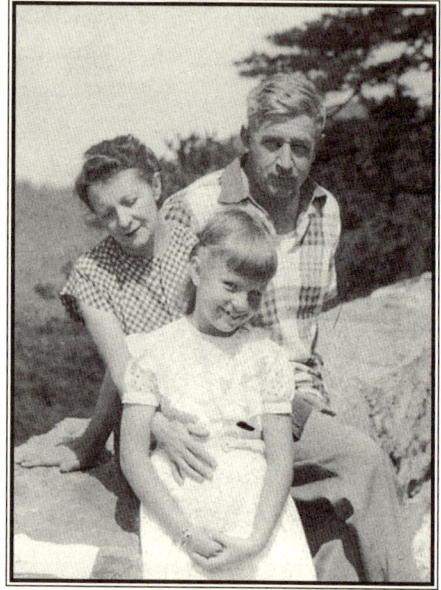

LEONA, WILLIAM AND NANCY
TURNER VACATIONING IN
VIRGINIA, CIRCA 1950s

NANCY TURNER & LON FOSTER
ENGAGEMENT PHOTO – 1966

LON FOSTER AND NANCY TURNER
WEDDING DAY – AUGUST 1967

an MFA from Rochester Institute of Technology. They divorced in 1977. Lon settled in Atlanta, Georgia. He remarried and has three sons.

Nancy remained in Rochester and built a career in residential real estate. She balances the challenges of the business with the opportunity to work with a rich cross-section of people as they move in and out of the Rochester area.

Pursuing art, theater, dance, music and film fills much of Nancy's spare time. She volunteers at the Memorial Art Gallery of the University of Rochester and the George Eastman House, where she has served on the boards of their fundraising organizations.

Nancy seems to have inherited her Aunt Harriet's love of travel. Favorite past destinations range from Paris to Nantucket, New York City to the Caribbean. Her wish-list for the future includes an African safari, the Italian Lake District, the Greek islands and more.

LEFT TO RIGHT: NANCY FOSTER, AUNT FRANCES KEEN, LYNN LOWERY, COUSIN, CELEBRATING AUNT AND UNCLE'S 50TH WEDDING ANNIVERSARY IN MARIN, CALIFORNIA

Samuel Francis McClelland – Third Generation

Samuel Francis (Frank) McClelland, sixth child of John McClelland and Elizabeth McCauley, was born June 7th, 1876 in Polk County, Iowa.

At the time of his mother's death—October 7th, 1899—Frank was living in Victor, California. According to his World War I draft registration, he resided in Washington.

CHAPTER III
William McClelland

William McClelland, third child of Thomas McClelland and Susan Henning, was born on July 20th, 1839, as shown in the Baptism Record of 1st Newry Presbyterian Church, and baptized ten days later.

BAPTISMAL BOOK 1ST NEWRY
PRESBYTERIAN CHURCH

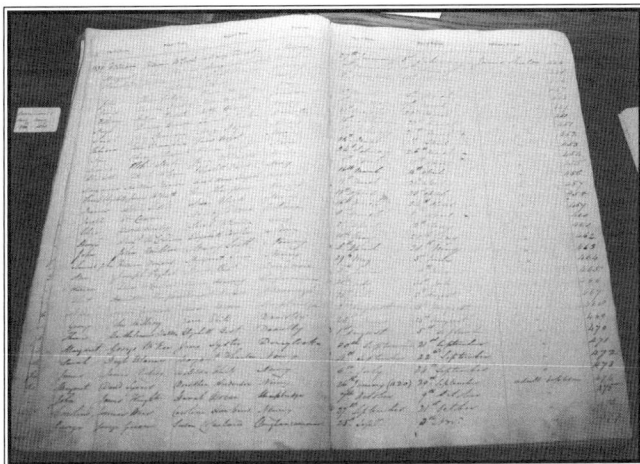

BAPTISMAL BOOK SHOWING THE ENTRY FOR WILLIAM
MCCLELLAND (12TH ENTRY FROM BOTTOM OF PAGE)

The Baptism Book in 1st Newry Presbyterian Church contains the dates of birth and baptisms of all of Thomas McClelland and Susan Henning's children. This register, which dates from the 1820s, is still in use to this day.

Following the death of his mother in October 1864, and his father less than two years later in June 1866, William was left to manage the family farm at Cloughenramer at the age of 27, as well as take responsibility for his surviving siblings.

William McClelland married Sarah Donnelly on February 28th, 1877 at Rostrevor, Kilbroney, County Down, Ireland. Sarah was born in 1845.

WILLIAM McCLELLAND AND SARAH DONNELLY
MARRIAGE CERTIFICATE – FEBRUARY 28, 1877

They had four children: Lucy, born August 1, 1879, Mary Minnie, born June 12, 1881, Sarah Maud, born August 29, 1883, and William, born September 7, 1885.

Memorial No. 46- 224 shows William McClelland purchasing 6 acres, 2 rods and 10 perches from Mercy Glenny on November 12th, 1886.

Memorial No. 46 – 224
November 12, 1886

"Memorial No. 46 – 224

A Memorial of an Indenture made the ninth day of November one thousand eight hundred and eighty six between the Reverend Robert Edmund Glenny of Clonallon Glebe in the County of Down Clerk in Holy Orders thereinafter called the Vendor of the First Part Robert Glenny of Newry in the County of Down Merchant of the second part William McClelland of Cloughenramer in the County of Down farmer thereinafter called Purchaser of the third part and the Irish Land Commission thereinafter called the Commission of the fourth part. Whereby after reciting as therein it was witnessed that in consideration of the sum of one hundred pounds paid by the Commission to the Vendor the receipt thereof the Vendor did thereby acknowledge the Vendor as Beneficial Owner did thereby grant the said Robert Glenny did thereby confirm to the Purchaser that part of the lands of Cloughenramer in the occupation of the Purchaser situate in the Lordship or Barony of Newry and County of Down containing six acres two rods and ten perches statute measure or thereabouts to hold to the Purchaser in Fee simple and said Indenture also witnessed that in pursuance of the agreement therein mentioned and in consideration of the premises the Purchaser covenanted with the Commission to pay to the Commission upon the first day of November one thousand eight hundred and eighty seven interest at the rate of three and one eighth per cent on the said sum of one hundred pounds from the date of said advance up to the first day of May instant also to pay an annuity of four pounds for forty nine years from the first day of May one thousand eight hundred and eighty seven by equal half yearly payments on every first day of May and first day of November in each year without any deductions the first payment of said annuity to be made on the first day of November one thousand eight hundred and eighty seven and thereby charged the said holding with the said interest and annuity. And said Indenture also witnessed that for the same consideration the purchaser as Beneficial owner conveyed to the Commission conveyed to the Commission the said Holding To Hold unto the Commission in fee simple subject to the proviso for redemption therein mentioned which Indenture and also this memorial as to the execution thereof respectively by the said Robert Edmund Glenny, Robert Glenny and William McClelland respectively are witnessed by James Searight Atkinson Solicitor and Jesse Holmes Law Clerk both of Newry County of Down."

Sarah Donnelly McClelland died September 22nd, 1885 in Newry, County Down, Ireland.

Obituary – Sarah Donnelly McClelland

"Deaths, McClelland – On the 22nd of September, Sarah, the beloved wife of Wm. McClelland, Cloughenramer. The remains will be removed for interment in St. Patrick's burial ground, this day (Thursday) at 11 o'clock."

William McClelland died March 20th, 1909 in Newry, County Down, Ireland.

Obituary – William McClelland

"We regret to chronicle the demise of Mr. William McClelland, who passed away at his late residence, Rock View, Cloughenramer, Newry, on Saturday last. The interment took place on Monday in St. Patrick's Churchyard, Newry. The large and representative cortege which followed his remains testified in a striking manner to the worthiness of the deceased gentleman, and to the estimation in which he was deservedly held by a wide circle of neighbors and friends. Although it was known that Mr. McClelland was in delicate health for some time, his death, notwithstanding, came as a painfully sudden surprise, and while Dr. Crossle, the family physician, was unremitting in his attendance upon his patient, the end came to the poignant grief of his bereaved children, his grief-stricken relatives, and his numerous sorrowing friends. Mr. McClelland was one of the largest and most respected farmers in the neighborhood of Newry. He, with his late wife, carried out dairying and butter making very successfully, and the butter from this dairy gained many awards at the principal Irish agricultural shows. Our late friend's life may be regarded as a book in which was written in its every chapter all the characteristics of a genial nature and a noble mind. In his home life he by precept was a loving and indulgent husband and father; to his relations he was an affectionate kingsman; and outside the closer charmed circle of his family and relations those who knew him intimately were encouraged and favoured who could claim him as a friend. His friendship was not of the intangible or evanescent kind, for the late Mr. McClelland was a straightforward and loyal friend. In his home life he be precept led his family along the paths of industry, integrity, and truth; and in his business connections with his neighbors he took for his guiding principles the Sermon on the Mount. Surely such a life and such a character as was lived and possessed by our late friend has left a fragrant memory behind that will never be dissipated by the winds of time. Nor will the impress of his manly and ennobling example and life-work ever be effaced from the remembrance of those he daily came into contact with, no matter what be the changes or vicissitudes that may occur in the days to be. We leave this humble wreath upon his freshly-made grave to keep company with the spring flowers that now star around his tomb, in full assurance of that resurrection morn, that the blooms of each recurring spring tide will always typify till that last trumpet will sound and the dead in Christ will arise."

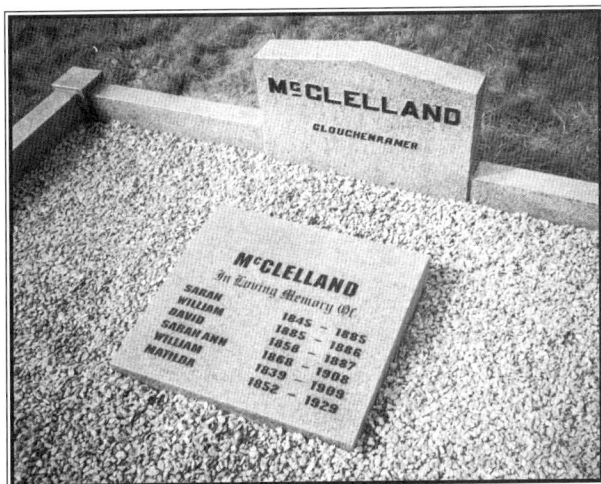

McClelland Grave
St. Patrick's Church
Summer 1996

Church Records of McClelland Name
Left to right: Norman McClelland,
Rev. T. H. Dunwoody & David Irwin
Summer 1996

MCCLELLAND HOMESTEAD
LEFT TO RIGHT: BARBARA MCCLELLAND, MAUD HAWTHORN VALLANCE
& NORMAN MCCLELLAND
SUMMER 1996

THIRD GENERATION

Lucy McClelland, Mary Minnie McClelland,
Sarah Maud McClelland, William McClelland

Lucy McClelland – Third Generation

Lucy McClelland, first child of William McClelland and Sarah Donnelly, was born on August 1st, 1879 at Rockfield House, Cloughenramer, County Down, Ireland. She attended Rockvale School.

LUCY MCCLELLAND
ABOUT 20 YEARS OLD

ROBERT & LUCY HAWTHORNE
ABOUT 1920

Lucy was fairly short, small, and plump. She had dark hair. She was very close to her sister Maud.

Lucy married Robert Hawthorn on November 15th, 1905 in Newry Presbyterian Church, County Down, Ireland. Robert, the first child of William Hawthorn and Anna Watson Hawthorn, was born on March 22nd, 1876 in Newtonhamilton, County Armagh, Ireland. He attended schools there. He was about 5' 9" tall, with brown hair, blue eyes, and a happy disposition. He owned a motorbike and lived in Dennistown, Lanark, Scotland. His brother Albert introduced him to Lucy McClelland. While the Hawthorns had no children, Robert was very fond of his brother Albert's family.

LUCY McCLELLAND AND ROBERT HAWTHORN
MARRIAGE CERTIFICATE – NOVEMBER 15, 1905

In 1895 the family moved to Glasgow. Robert got a job with the transport service as a tram driver.

Lucy died June 27th, 1923, and Robert's spirit died with her. He lost all interest in living and died on September 22nd, 1928.

Mary Minnie McClelland – Third Generation

Mary Minnie McClelland, second child of William McClelland and Sarah Donnelly, was born on June 12th, 1881 in County Down, Ireland.

She grew up on the family farm and attended Newry Female D. Model School. Minnie left school August 3rd, 1897 and was appointed Pupil Teacher at Kingsmills School. She attended the Presbyterian Teachers Training College at Marlborough Street, Dublin.

TEACHER'S TRAINING COLLEGE – CIRCA 1900 MARLBOROUGH STREET, DUBLIN BACK ROW EXTREME LEFT: MINNIE McCLELLAND WITH FELLOW STUDENTS

On January 1st, 1902 Minnie took up a post at Ballykeel National School. She found digs in the townland of Barnmeen, approximately two miles from the school.

THE HOUSE AT BARNMEEN, UNCHANGED SINCE THE DAYS
MINNIE MCCLELLAND LODGED THERE

BALLYKEEL WEST PRIMARY SCHOOL CIRCA 1970, WHEN THE
SCHOOL WAS NO LONGER IN USE. IT IS NOW DEMOLISHED.

It was not long before the young teacher came to the attention of a local man by the name of Sam Wright. Twelve years his junior, Minnie soon found that she had much in common with this progressive farmer. When Sam's home, Finnard Cottage, began to be transformed into a fine two-story house with a roof of Bangor Blue slates, it was evident that the couple had plans for the future.

Sam and Mary Minnie McClelland were married on August 29th, 1906 at Sandy's Street Presbyterian Church, a happy union destined to last for 50 years. Witnesses to the ceremony were R. Sloan and M. Copeland.

ROBERT SAMUEL WRIGHT & MINNIE McCLELLAND
MARRIAGE CERTIFICATE – AUGUST 29, 1906

Given the demanding nature of the job and no doubt influenced by the fact that she was carrying her third child, Minnie decided to retire from teaching in September 1910. The esteem in which she was held is evidenced by the presentation of a gold watch made to mark the occasion.

Robert Samuel Wright (known as "Uncle Sam" to Sara Winifred McClelland and all of the children of James Parker and Margaret Jane "Jenny" Wright), fourth child of Robert Wright and Eliza Sloan, was born on April 27th, 1869 at Finnard, County Down, Ireland. He grew up on the family farm and was educated first at Shinn National School, then Ballykeel National School. Both were less than a mile from the family farm, with tuition fees of three shillings per term.

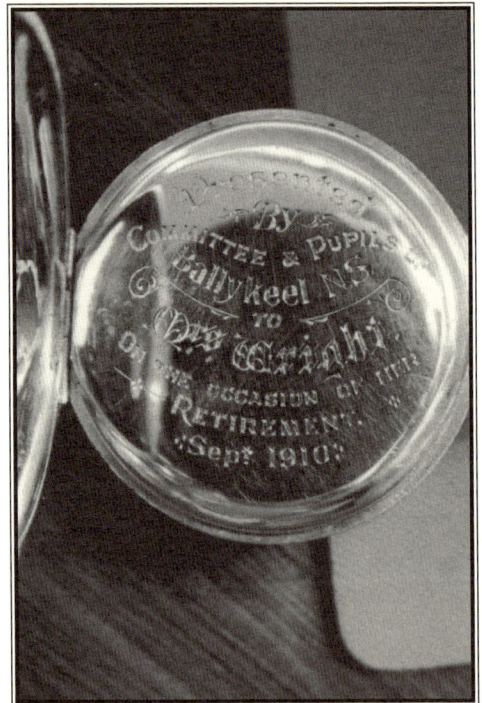

THE INSCRIPTION READS: PRESENTED BY COMMITTEE AND PUPILS OF BALLYKEEL NATIONAL SCHOOL TO MRS. WRIGHT ON THE OCCASION OF HER RETIREMENT. SEPT. 1910

Sam's siblings Sarah, Joseph, and Elizabeth were born in 1871, 1874, and 1877, respectively, while the family unit at Finnard looked set for the future. In 1878, however, when Sam was nine years old, his father, a young man of 45, died suddenly. His mother, not yet forty, was left with seven children ranging in age from a few months to fourteen years. The loss of the main breadwinner must have been a devastating blow to the family, particularly as it coincided with a general economic downturn in farming. The family undoubtedly faced difficult times, not least because land in Ireland at that time was not "freehold," and over £14 of rent had to be found twice yearly.

After his father's death, young Sam was transferred to Ballykeel National School while his older brother Willie John remained at Shinn, where a school report had suggested that his gifts might be best cultivated in the more academic environment. The ground, even at this early stage, was being prepared for Sam to become the farmer, successor to his father.

In 1888, Sam was one of the youngest ever members of Ryan's Presbyterian Church to be elected to the congregational committee, a testament to his reliance on his Christian faith during the difficult years following his father's death.

His young shoulders seemed to have been primed for burdens, and another came on the last day of December 1891 with the death of his mother at 52. His eldest sister Jane had married James Parker in 1889, and Willie John emigrated to the United States in the year of his mother's death; so, on New Year's Day, 1892, Sam effectively found himself head of the family. He was 22 years old.

There were further burdens for Sam to carry before the "tide" of misfortune eventually began to turn. In 1898, his brother Joe emigrated to the U.S.A. and never returned to Ireland. Less than a year later, his sister Annie was to die under tragic circumstances. Further hardship followed in 1901, when news reached Finnard of Willie John's drowning in San Francisco.

A national event changed Sam's life. Land ownership had long been a highly political issue in Ireland. The government of the day sought to solve the conflict with the passing of the Irish Land Act in 1903, whereby larges estates were broken up and the tenants enabled to purchase their land by means of a long-term loan. So for the first time, Sam had the hope that he would soon own the land he and his family had worked for generations. These hopes were realized in 1907, and marked a major turning point in the life not only of Sam, but also of thousands of his fellow Irish farmers.

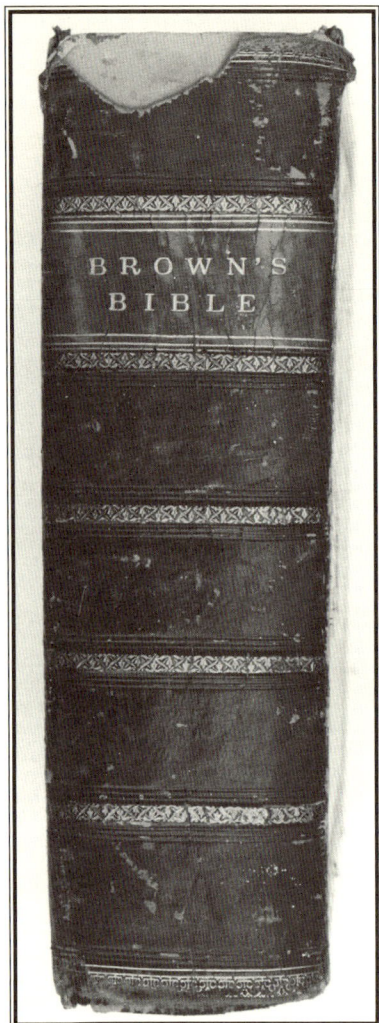

THE SPINE OF BROWN'S BIBLE

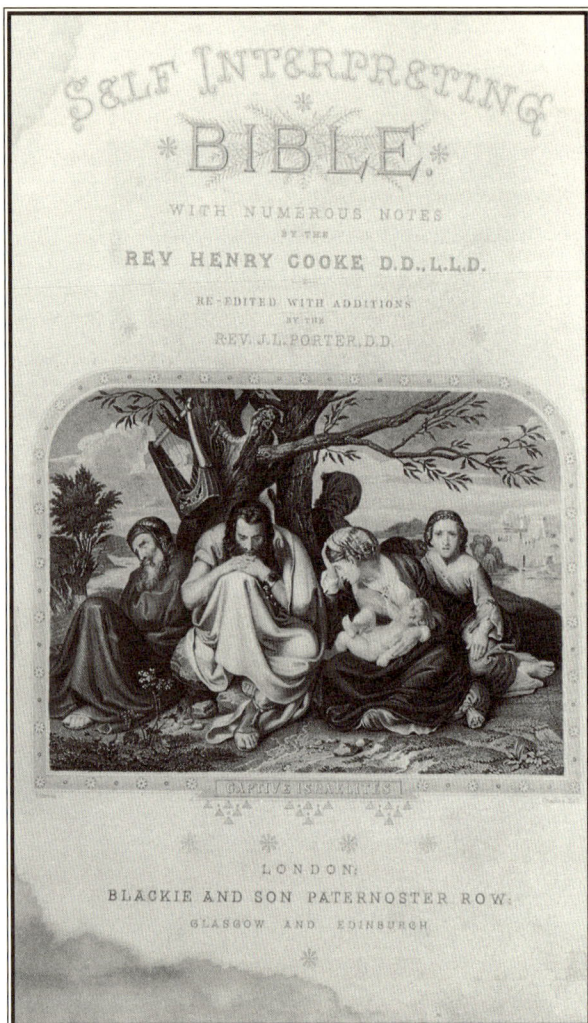

A COPY OF THE TITLE PAGE OF BROWN'S SELF-INTERPRETING BIBLE. THE REST OF THE INSCRIPTION READS, "WITH NUMEROUS NOTES BY THE REV. HENRY COOK, D.D., L.L.D., RE-EDITED WITH ADDITIONS BY THE REV. J.L. PORTER, D.D., LONDON, BLACKIE AND SON PATERNOSTER ROW, GLASGOW AND EDINBURGH."

A "self-interpreting" Bible would have been highly characteristic of 19th-century Presbyterians. The centrality of the "word of God" and the independence to interpret it for one's self would be and still are tenets of Presbyterianism.

The Rev. Henry Cook is regarded as the great architect of modern Irish Presbyterianism and led a crusade for evangelism and orthodoxy in the church during the 19th century. It was not an accident that this particular Bible was on the shelves of Robert Wright and his son, Sam.

DETAILS AS FOUND IN BROWN'S BIBLE, ROBERT
SAMUEL WRIGHT MARRIED MARY MINNIE
MCCLELLAND IN SANDY'S STREET PRESBYTERIAN
CHURCH ON AUGUST 29, 1906

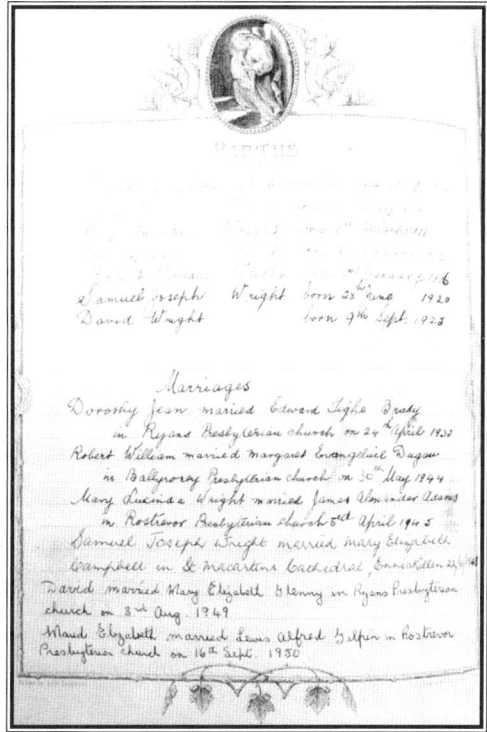

DETAILS AS FOUND IN BROWN'S BIBLE

Birth and marriage details are recorded in the Wright Family Bible as follows: Births: Maud Elizabeth Wright, born 16th June, 1907; Sarah Roberta Wright, born 23rd May, 1909; Mary Lucinda Wright, born 3rd March, 1911; Dorothy Jean Wright, born 23rd November, 1912; Robert William Wright, born 3rd January, 1916; Samuel Joseph Wright, born 28th June, 1920; David Wright, born 9th September, 1925. Marriages: Dorothy Jean Wright married Edward Tighe Brady in Ryans Presbyterian Church on 24th April 1935; Robert William Wright married Evangeline Margaret Dugan in Ballyroney Presbyterian Church on 30th May, 1944; Mary Lucinda Wright married James Alexander Adams in Rostrevor Presbyterian Church on 3rd April, 1945; Samuel Joseph Wright married Mary Elizabeth Campbell in St. Macartan's Cathedral, Enniskillen, 22nd June, 1948; David Wright married Mary Elizabeth Glenny in Ryans Presbyterian Church on 3rd August, 1949; Maud Elizabeth Wright married Lewis Alfred Gilpin in Rostrevor Presbyterian Church on 16th September, 1950.

In the 1911 Census of Ireland, Sam Wright, age 42, Minnie Wright, age 29, Maude Elizabeth, age three, Sarah Roberta, age one, and Mary Lucinda, age one month, are shown living at Finnard.

CENSUS OF IRELAND, 1911

Throughout his life, Sam was an active supporter of the Irish Evangelization Society. In 1893, Ryans Presbyterian Church had called a new minister who laid great emphasis on the "Protestant aspect of our Church's message." Sam was firmly on the evangelical wing of the Church, and differences arose with the minister in 1899 when Sam granted the Faith Mission the use of one of his fields for a tent crusade. Sam left Ryans and joined Third Rathfriland Presbyterian Church, where his work and witness was quickly recognized and where he was subsequently elected to the eldership.

A new minister was appointed to Ryans in 1915 with whom Sam had no doctrinal differences. With a young family situated less than a mile from his former church, it made sense to return, which he did in 1922. He was immediately co-opted onto the Session, and in 1925 he was appointed Congregational Secretary, a post he was to hold for the rest of his life.

ROBERT SAMUEL WRIGHT & MARY MINNIE McCLELLAND WRIGHT

THE WRIGHT FAMILY IN THEIR YARD AT FINNARD, PROBABLY AROUND 1918. LEFT TO RIGHT:
BERTHA, MINNIE (MOTHER) WITH ROBERT, DOROTHY, MAUD, SAM (FATHER) & MOLLY

The photo at Finnard, Wright Home place.

MAUDE HAWTHORNE & MINNIE McCLELLAND, FINNARD, WRIGHT HOME PLACE, 1923-1924

Given his early experience, it is little wonder that Sam successfully negotiated his farm through the economically difficult 1930s. The forties saw the remainder of his family launched on life's path and his eldest son in a position to succeed him.

THE WRIGHT FAMILY, 1930, BACK ROW, LEFT TO RIGHT: BERTHA, MOLLY, ROBERT, MAUD & DOROTHY; FRONT ROW: MINNIE, DAVID, SAMUEL & SAM

A lifetime of hard work had taken its toll, and Sam was increasingly experiencing discomfort from a troublesome knee joint. In 1950, he and Minnie retired to 73 Newry Street, Rathfriland. The couple celebrated their 50th wedding anniversary in the summer of 1956, and on September 25th, while in his 87th year, Sam passed away.

The extended Wright family, circa October 1956, Left to right, Back Row: Alfie Gilpin, David Wright, Samuel Wright, Robert Wright, Jim Adams & Edward Brady; Middle row: Maud Gilpin, Elsie Wright, Molly Wright, Eva Wright, Molly Adams & Dorothy Brady; Seated: Bertha Wright, Minnie Wright & Elizabeth Wright

The Garden Picnic at Finnard, 1932, Left to right, Back row: Dorothy Wright, Maud Wright, Dora Hawthorn, Willie Hawthorn, Bob Irwin & Sam Wright; Middle Row: Sam Wright, Molly Wright, Maud Hawthorn, Eileen Irwin, & Bobby Wright; Seated: Margaret "Maggie" Irwin (Audrey on her knee), Mary "Minnie" Wright, David Wright, Tom Irwin, Myrtle Irwin & the Wright Collie dog, "Sport"

THE GARDEN PICNIC AT FINNARD, 1932, LEFT TO RIGHT, BACK ROW: BOBBY WRIGHT, WILLIE HAWTHORN, BOB IRWIN, SAM WRIGHT; MIDDLE ROW: MAUDE HAWTHORN, MAUD WRIGHT, MOLLY WRIGHT, DORA HAWTHORN, EILEEN IRWIN, TOM IRWIN WITH MYRTLE IN FRONT; SEATED: MARGARET "MAGGIE" IRWIN, MARY "MINNIE" WRIGHT; FRONT: DAVID WRIGHT, AUDREY IRWIN, DOROTHY WRIGHT, & SAM WRIGHT

Following Sam's death, Minnie moved to Newry and lived with her daughter, Bertha. It was during a short visit to her eldest daughter, Maud, that Minnie was taken ill and died on March 31st, 1960 while in her 87th year.

Sam and Minnie were tremendously solid and dependable people, and the community in which they lived held them in great respect. It is still widely held that the funeral of Sam Wright in 1956 was one of the largest gatherings of people ever assembled at Ryans Church.

Minnie in her own right was a gifted and intelligent woman, but in keeping with her time, she chose to subsume her individual gifts with those of her husband, in order to create something even better. The prism through which they both viewed life was that of believing Christians, and as the vicissitudes of life came along they were accepted and interpreted through their living faith.

FINNARD, HOME OF SAM & MINNIE MCCLELLAND

Sam Wright is regarded by many of the nephews and nieces who knew him as a patriarchal figure, one who set a direction for the family in the 20th century. This was in keeping with the values adopted by our ancestors, and those which he and Minnie had tested throughout their lives and believed were sufficient to sustain and guide our lives into the future.

Robert Samuel Wright and Mary Minnie McClelland are buried at Ryans Presbyterian Graveyard, Finnard, County Down, Northern Ireland.

FOURTH GENERATION

Maud Elizabeth Wright, Sarah Roberta Wright, Mary Lucinda "Molly" Wright, Dorothy Jean Wright, Robert William Wright, Samuel Joseph Wright, David Wright

ROBERT SAMUEL & MARY "MINNIE" WRIGHT WITH THEIR FIRST CHILD, MAUD, 1908

Maud Elizabeth Wright – Fourth Generation

Maud Elizabeth Wright, first child of Sam Wright and Mary Minnie McClelland, was born on June 16th, 1907 at the farm at Finnard, Donaghmore, County Down, Ireland. She attended the local Ballykeel West Primary School, where she was remembered as a bright pupil with a particular aptitude for music.

The photograph to the left by H. Allison & Company, taken in 1908, shows Maud as a very young child with her father, Robert Samuel Wright, and her mother, Mary "Minnie" McClelland Wright.

Maud's three sisters, Bertha, Molly, and Dorothy, were born before Robert, the first boy, who arrived in 1916. Sam and David followed. By 1925 there were seven children living on a labor-intensive farm. Upon leaving school, Maud found that she had more than full-time employment in the home helping her mother, and, when time permitted, in the fields helping her father.

She was a committed Christian from an early age and won the prestigious Newry Presbytery Sabbath School Union Gold medal in 1922 and 1923. This was a notable achievement, carried on in the face of stiff competition and won by way of written examination. It is, therefore, of little surprise that she was much sought after, and proved to be a willing worker in the local Ryans Presbyterian Church.

Maud was a founding member of the Girls Auxiliary and was active in the Christian Endeavour. She also taught in the Sunday School, and for a number of years acted as church organist.

On September 16th, 1950, she married Lewis Alfred Gilpin, a farmer from "The Clare" Waringston, County Down, in Rostrevor Presbyterian Church. Alfie, as he was known to one and all, was a hugely gregarious man. Nephews and nieces who went to "The Clare" to stay love to tell stories of the midnight feasts, water fights, and games of every hue initiated and actively engaged in by Alfie.

MAUD ELIZABETH WRIGHT AND LEWIS ALFRED GILPIN
MARRIAGE CERTIFICATE – SEPTEMBER 16, 1950

On January 12, 1980, Maud Elizabeth Gilpin died at home in Lenaderg, Banbridge, County Down, Northern Ireland.

"ALFIE" & MAUD GILPIN AT "THE CLARE"

On September 5, 1989, Lewis Alfred Gilpin died in Lenaderg, Banbridge, County Down, Northern Ireland. Both Maud and Alfie are buried in the Gilpin family plot at St. Mathias Parish Church, Knocknamuckly, Portadown, Northern Ireland.

"THE CLARE" HOME OF MAUD & "ALFIE" GILPIN,
A PLACE OF HAPPY MEMORIES FOR MANY OF THE NEPHEWS AND NIECES

Sarah Roberta Wright – Fourth Generation

Sarah Roberta Wright, known as Bertha by all, second child of Sam and Minnie Wright, was born on May 23rd, 1909 at Finnard, Donaghmore, County Down, Ireland. She attended the local Ballykeel West Primary School for a short time before continuing her education at the Model School in Newry, where many years later she was destined to become Vice Principal.

Bertha was an able child and, no doubt influenced by her mother, a former teacher, also decided on that profession. To gain admission to teacher training college in those days, one had to become a monitor at a school from age 15 to 18 before taking the "King's Scholarship." This general examination lasted 3 days, and in addition to the usual academic disciplines included tests on singing, needlework, and free-hand drawing.

MINISTRY OF EDUCATION FOR NORTHERN IRELAND.

KING'S SCHOLARSHIP EXAMINATION, 1928.

Name of Candidate *Sarah R. Wright* Examination Number 923

Address *Finnard, Ardaragh*
Newry.

NUMBER OF MARKS ASSIGNED IN :—

	Reading	Penmanship	Spelling and Punctuation	Grammar	Composition	English Literature	Geography	Arithmetic and Mensuration	Algebra	Geometry and Trigonometry	Drawing	Theory of Music	Singing	Needlework	Botany, Physics, Chemistry or Domestic Economy	Irish	French	German	Latin	History	Mark for Practice of Teaching
																		OPTIONAL			
Maximum Marks	100	40	40	70	150	100	100	200	100	100	100	50	50	100	100	100	100	100	100	100	150
Marks Obtained	80	27	38	44	70	66	69	129	40	34	66	34	35	77	51c	—	—	—	—	55	125

Result of Examination *First Division*

" F " denotes failure.

" A " signifies advanced course in Languages.
" E " „ elementary „ „

Ministry of Education,
Parliament Buildings,
Belfast.

Entd.
Chkd.

Note :—Qualifications for untrained women assistants and junior assistant mistresses are set forth overleaf.

KING'S SCHOLARSHIP EXAMINATION – 1928

Perhaps it was a spark from this latter activity that led in later life to an interest in art. One of her landscapes is still in the family today.

Bertha gained admittance to Stranmillis Teachers Training College in Belfast in 1928. The new complex was still under construction and her first-year lectures were held in the nearby Queen's University.

The photo shows Sarah Roberta Wright, known as Auntie "B"

SARAH ROBERTA WRIGHT, AUNTIE "B"

Graduating in 1930, Bertha taught for a short time at Mullavilly, Co. Armagh before accepting an offer in 1931 from the Model School in Newry, where she was to teach for the next 33 years. A successful and conscientious teacher, she was noted for her patience and perseverance.

A woman of wide interests, she was actively involved in many charities, particularly Dr. Barnardo's and the Spastic Society. She had a great interest in travel and before and after the Second World War visited many places in the U.K. and Europe. The highlight was a holiday to Switzerland in the 1950s.

A devoted Christian, Bertha was a lifelong member of Ryans Presbyterian Church. She took an active part in many organizations, including Sunday School teaching, singing in the choir, and for a time serving as organist.

3 Windsor Bungalows, Newry, The home of Bertha Wright and her mother, Minnie Wright, from 1957 to her death in 1960

Bertha, in keeping with many generations of the Wright family, had a great interest in creative writing and English literature. Following her death, her sisters collated and published a booklet of favorite quotations and some of her original poetry entitled "Bertha's Poems."

FAIRIES IN MY ROOM

Fairies came into my room today,
Clad in dresses of gold and green;
Frilled and flounced in a beautiful way,
Fairies came into my room today.

I know you would call them daffodils,
With stems of green and heads of gold,
Call them daffodils if you will,
To me they are certainly fairies still.

"We've come to bring you joy," they said
"To cheer you up in your weary bed,
To tell you that winter has gone away
Spring is here, summer is in on the way.

"For long we lay in dark earthly beds,
Soil and withered leaves covered our heads,
We thought we surely were there to stay
But even the dark hours pass away.

"With patience we struggled to the light,
It wasn't easy, we had to fight,
You must be brave if you want to win,
The sunshine's there if you'll let it in.

"Out of the dark earth has brightness come,
After a dark cloud we see the sun.
Joy will come after trial and pain,
Hold up your head and be brave again.

"We are happy in making you glad,
Smile and you won't feel half so bad;
Forget yourself for a little while,
Think of others and raise a smile.

"Indulgence in self-pity makes you feel worse,
Think less of yourself and more of your nurse.
Think of the steps she has walked for you,
Do you deserve such love so true?"

I'm glad they came to my room today,
daffodil fairies dressed so gay.
If you want to be happy your whole life through,
You must scatter sunshine as you go.

A poem by Bertha Wright written in 1943
while she was confined to bed by illness

At the comparatively young age of 55, Sarah was diagnosed with bowel cancer, and following a short illness died in Newry General Hospital on Saturday October 3rd, 1964.

SARAH ROBERTA WRIGHT–RYANS PRESBYTERIAN GRAVEYARD

Mary Lucinda "Mollie" Wright – Fourth Generation

Mary Lucinda "Mollie" Wright, third child of Robert Samuel and Mary "Minnie" Wright, was born on March 3rd, 1911 at Finnard, Newry, County Down, Ireland.

She trained as a teacher at Stranmillis College, Belfast, and came to work in Lisnacreeve Primary School about two miles outside Fintona in County Tyrone. There she met the local veterinary surgeon James Alexander Adams, who qualified from the Royal (Dick) School of Veterinary Studies, University of Edinburgh in December of 1938.

They were married in Rostrevor Presbyterian Church, County Down, Northern Ireland on April 3, 1945. They established a home at 46 Campsie Road, Omagh, where Jim worked from a surgery at the back of their house. It was busy day and night.

JAMES ADAMS AND "MOLLIE" WRIGHT, WEDDING DAY,
APRIL 3, 1945, ROSTREVOR, COUNTY DOWN

MARRIAGE CERTIFICATE OF JAMES ALEXANDER ADAMS & MARY LUCINDA WRIGHT, APRIL 3, 1945

LEFT TO RIGHT: MAURICE, JOHN & DAVID ADAMS

WILLIAM BRIAN ADAMS

They had four sons: David Alexander, born January 20, 1946, Samuel John, born November 24, 1947, Maurice James, born May 19, 1949, and William Brian, born April 23, 1952.

Mollie and Jim were actively involved in the local Presbyterian church organizations. Jim was Clerk of Session and Mollie held the office of secretary of the PWA (Presbyterian Women's Association) for 32 years.

Jim died suddenly on February 28th, 1975. He had no previous history of heart trouble but suffered a fatal heart attack. Mollie was the last surviving member of the Wright family of her generation at the time of her death on December 9, 2000 in Omagh, County Tyrone. Mollie's life was perhaps best summarized by her minister at her funeral service when he said:

"Worship for her was never a merely passive activity; she was prepared to work at it, and she understood that the more she brought to it, the more she would receive from it. Her husband Jim and she had a wonderful partnership – in the home, in his work, in the Church. His had been a relentless courtship and having secured her for himself, his was a valued prize, and theirs a mutuality of respect, devotion and happiness. His comparatively early death left her sore and sad. She was sorry, but never could it be said that she was sorry for herself. For this was a woman of strength and courage, and it was at this very point in her life, at a time of such personal loss and upheaval, that she threw herself wholeheartedly into the establishment of a branch of the Samaritans in this town, something, which many would find remarkable, and most perhaps impossible. For her it was neither of these things; she found help for herself in helping others, and those who knew her as she was, found her reaction quite typical.

MARY LUCINDA (WRIGHT) ADAMS 1911-2000

She played her part also in the Veterinary Wives Association, the Women's Institute, the Red Cross, and particularly as a part of the team which staffed the Hospital Trolley Shop, and the local Animal Welfare Group, in which, like a great many others, she trembled under the authority of the late Miss MacQuillian, and with great good humor, produced scones for a coffee morning upon demand. The life of Mollie Adams was rooted in faith. Nurtured in the Presbyterianism, to which she gave her lifelong allegiance, first, in the congregation of Ryans, near Newry, she knew with the psalmist the delight of the temple of the Lord. But with Him, she also knew the dry valley of hard experience; it was her capacity to make of it a place of springs and as a result to grow stronger as she journeyed nearer and nearer to Zion. The spirit of God was indeed hers – not timid, but filled with power and love. She was one who held firmly to the truths she was taught, and who remained in the faith and love which are ours in union with Christ Jesus. Hers was a life in which was seen the loveliness and the effectiveness of the Christianity which gave it purpose, and which would claim us all. An ambassador for Christ indeed, we give thanks for every remembrance of her, and for the sincerity of faith that was in her. We know that our friend and His now share His peace and joy."

Mollie is buried in the Adams family plot in Dublin Road Cemetery, Omagh, County Tyrone, Northern Ireland.

Fifth Generation

David Alexander Adams, Samuel John Adams, Maurice James Adams, William Brian Adams

David Alexander Adams – Fifth Generation

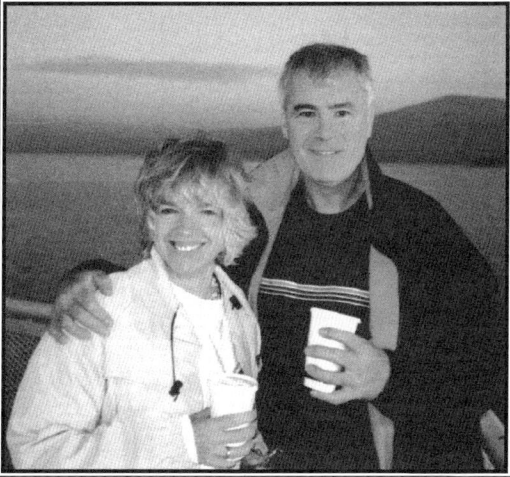

SADIE & DAVID ADAMS,
ON HOLIDAY IN VANCOUVER

David Alexander Adams, first child of James Adams and "Mollie" Wright, was born on January 20th, 1946 in Londonderry Hospital, Northern Ireland.

In March 1968 he married Sarah White, whose family farmed at Thornhill, just outside Omagh, having moved from Cootehill, County Cavan. They emigrated in 1968 to live in Hamilton, Ontario, Canada, and now live in Whitby, Ontario. They have three children, Catherine, Michael, and Joanne.

Sixth Generation

*Jennifer Catherine Adams, Michael James Adams,
Joanne Elizabeth Adams*

Jennifer Catherine Adams – Sixth Generation

Jennifer Catherine Adams, first child of David Adams and Sarah White, was born on September 18th, 1968 in Lagan Valley Hospital, Lisburn, County Down, Northern Ireland. Catherine works as a media projects manager in Whistler Tourism.

Catherine married Edward Francis Haboly on August 14th, 2004 in Whistler, B.C., Canada. Edward is senior engineer in Vancouver. The couple live with their daughter Alison in the city.

LEFT TO RIGHT: PETER WHITESIDE, EDWARD HABOLY, CATHERINE ADAMS, AND JOANNE ADAMS, WEDDING DAY – AUGUST 14TH, 2004

SEVENTH GENERATION

Alison Mae Haboly – Seventh Generation

Alison Mae Haboly, first child of Francis Haboly and Catherine Adams, was born on August 18th, 2005 in Lion's Gate Hospital, North Vancouver, Canada.

ALISON WITH HER MOTHER ON THE OCCASION OF HER 1ST BIRTHDAY

THE HABOLY FAMILY
LEFT TO RIGHT: EDWARD,
CATHERINE, AND ALISON

Michael James Adams – Sixth Generation

Michael James Adams, second child of David Adams and Sarah White, was born on December 26th, 1975 in Hamilton, Ontario, Canada. Michael graduated from the University of Waterloo and now works as a technical writer in Toronto, Canada.

Michael married Casey Matthews in Toronto Botanical Gardens on Friday August 11th, 2006. The couple plan to set up home in Toronto, Canada.

MICHAEL AND CASEY ADAMS

Joanne Elizabeth Adams – Sixth Generation

Joanne Elizabeth Adams, third child of David and Sarah White Adams, was born on March 14th, 1978, in Hamilton, Ontario, Canada. Joanne graduated from Guelph University in 2001 in Honors English. She is now working at the Wheat Marketing Board.

CATHERINE, MICHAEL & JOANNE ADAMS

Samuel John Adams – Fifth Generation

Samuel John Adams, second child of James and "Mollie" Wright Adams, was born on November 24th, 1947 in Omagh, County Tyrone, Northern Ireland.

John followed in his father's footsteps to become a veterinarian, qualifying from Trinity College Dublin in 1971. After several years gaining experience in other practices in Northern Ireland, he returned to work with his dad in the family practice. After his father's death in 1975, he worked the practice single-handedly for some months, eventually finding a partner, then assistants as the practice expanded. In 1986, he joined the Department of Agriculture, which allowed for regular hours and more time with the family at night and on weekends.

John married Kathleen Law on December 29, 1975. Kate grew up on a farm at Grange near Ahoghill in County Antrim, and went to school at Cambridge House in Ballymena, County Antrim, going on to qualify in medicine from Queen's University, Belfast in 1968. Kate specialized in ear, nose, and throat surgery, and came to work in Tyrone County Hospital, Omagh in 1974, where she met John early in 1975.

They live at Ballinamullan, just outside Omagh, about a mile from the family home. They have two children: James Alexander, born November 13, 1978, and Judith Anne, born June 28, 1980.

JOHN ADAMS & KATHLEEN LAW ADAMS, TRINITY COLLEGE, JOHN'S 30TH REUNION

JAMES, JOHN, KATE & JUDITH, WITH GEORGE & BEN ADAMS, CIRCA 1995

JAMES ALEXANDER ADAMS & JUDITH ANNE ADAMS

SIXTH GENERATION

James Alexander Adams, Judith Anne Adams

JAMES GOES FLYING, 2001

James Alexander Adams – Sixth Generation

James Alexander Adams, first child of Samuel John Adams and Kathleen Law, was born on November 13th, 1978 in Omagh, County Tyrone.

James has achieved his ambition of becoming a pilot. Because of the inclement weather in Ireland, he went to Canada to train and now holds both a private and commercial pilot's license.

JUDITH ADAMS GRADUATION, 2002

Judith Anne Adams – Sixth Generation

Judith Anne Adams, second child of Samuel John Adams and Kathleen Law, was born on June 28th, 1980 in Omagh, County Tyrone.

Judith graduated from Edinburgh University with an Honors MA in French and Philosophy. She is now in the shocking situation of having to find a way of earning a living!

Maurice James Adams – Fifth Generation

Maurice James Adams, third child of James Adams and "Mollie" Wright, was born on May 19th, 1949 in Omagh, County Tyrone.

Maurice graduated from Trinity College Dublin with a degree in Philosophy and Psychology. He traveled extensively in India and America before finally settling in Florida with his partner, Imani. He works as a masseur.

MAURICE JAMES ADAMS

IMANI, PARTNER

William Brian Adams – Fifth Generation

William Brian Adams, fourth child of James Adams and "Mollie" Wright, was born on April 23rd, 1952 in Omagh, County Tyrone.

Brian stayed in Omagh and runs a painting and decorating business locally. He keeps in touch with other members of the family more regularly than most. He is interested in computer photography and has reproduced many old family photographs, enhancing them superbly.

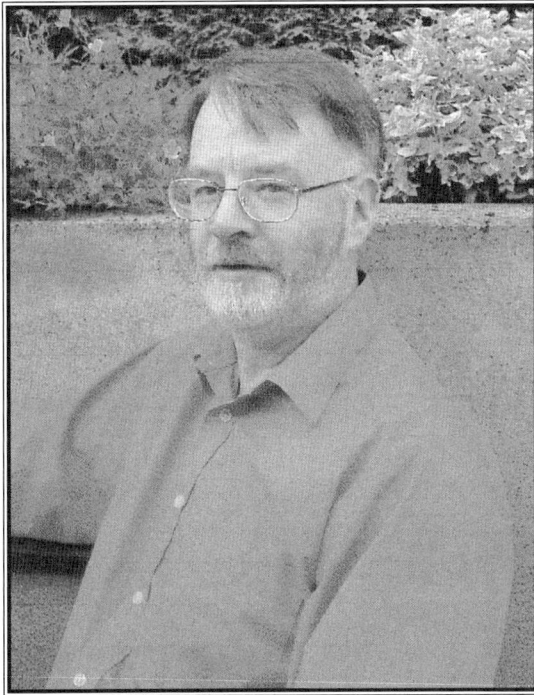

WILLIAM BRIAN ADAMS

Dorothy Jean Wright – Fourth Generation

Dorothy Jean Wright, the fourth child of Samuel and Minnie Wright, was born on November 24th, 1912 at Finnard, Donaghmore, County Down, Ireland. She grew up on her parents' farm with her three older sisters and three younger brothers in a home where family ties and Christian influences were strong. She attended the local primary school at Ballykeel and the nearby Ryans Presbyterian Church and Sunday School. In the evenings and on weekends, she helped with work in the house and on the farm. She particularly enjoyed feeding young calves and other livestock, especially the horses, around the farmyard. A highlight of summer months was an occasional trip over the hills to the fair at Warrenpoint.

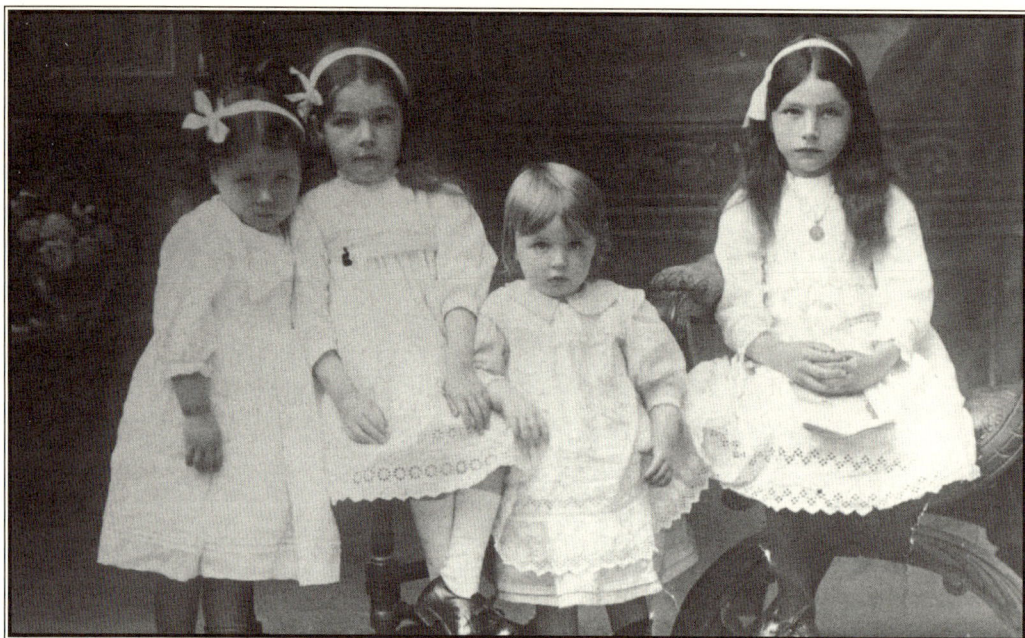

THE WRIGHT SISTERS, CIRCA 1914, LEFT TO RIGHT: MOLLIE, BERTHA, DOROTHY & MAUDE

DOROTHY JEAN WRIGHT
DRIVING LICENSE PHOTO, CIRCA 1935

During her teenage years, Dorothy became seriously ill with what was diagnosed as pleurisy. For many months she was confined to bed at home, and while she eventually made a good recovery, the illness certainly curtailed her life choices in terms of further education, travel, and other social activities. Although essentially quiet and retiring by nature, Dorothy was a very warm-hearted, genuine and sincere person who was universally well liked. Throughout her lifetime and wherever she went, she had the ability to make lasting friendships. Dorothy was five feet six inches tall, of medium build, with brown hair and blue eyes.

In 1933, the future course of her life was set when she met a dashing young colonialist who had returned to his Irish roots from South Africa to live on a nearby farm at Finnard. Edward Tighe Brady was born in 1911 and brought up in South Africa, where his father Thomas, a civil engineering graduate of Queen's College Belfast, was employed on pioneering railroad construction.

Six feet tall and athletic, Edward excelled at most sports, particularly soccer, cricket, and boxing. He enjoyed travel, having accompanied his parents on a couple of long sea trips to Ireland in his childhood. By the time he left Africa, he had traveled extensively throughout much of the territory now controlled by both the Republic of South Africa and Zimbabwe. However, tired of the colonial lifestyle, he came to Ireland seeking a more settled environment in which to pursue his ambitions as a writer. Over a period of two years, Dorothy and Edward got to know each other well and fell in love. They were married in Ryans Presbyterian Church on April 24th, 1935. A reception for family and friends was held at her parents' home at Finnard.

EDWARD TIGHE BRADY AND DOROTHY JEAN WRIGHT, MARRIAGE CERTIFICATE

DOROTHY WRIGHT & EDWARD T. BRADY, WEDDING DAY, APRIL 24, 1935
LEFT TO RIGHT, BACK ROW: JOHN COTNEY & EDWARD T. BRADY
LEFT TO RIGHT, FRONT ROW: BERTHA WRIGHT, DOROTHY WRIGHT, AUDREY IRWIN & NORA MERCER

Edward bought land at Ardaragh and built "Ardeevin," which became the Brady family home. There, Dorothy raised her family of five: Alan, Kenneth, Rosemary, Barbara, and Denis. It was a happy family home and Dorothy was a devoted mother who used all of her energies to give her children the best possible start in life, often at considerable personal sacrifice. With the onset of World War II, times were often hard, and as Edwards's attempts at authorship proved unrewarding, he returned to journalism, the profession in which he had been employed in South Africa. He founded a newspaper and printing business in Rathfriland. This would have been a bold entrepreneurial step in any circumstance, but in the heart of rural Ulster in the later 1930s, it was regarded by some at the time as an extremely risky venture. However, the Outlook Press proved a great success over the years. Now under new management, it continues to provide a weekly news service for that part of County Down, Northern Ireland.

The Brady Family – circa 1964
Left to right, back row: Denis, Kenneth & Alan
Left to right, front row: Rosemary, Edward, Dorothy & Barbara

Dorothy and Edward lived most of their married lives at Ardaragh and contributed much to the local community and to the Church at Ryans, where Dorothy was a member of the Women's Missionary Association, and Edward was an elected Elder and Church Secretary. In later life, they relocated to the County Down seaside village of Dundrum. There they enjoyed a few happy years in retirement together and found time to travel abroad to visit friends and relatives in South Africa and New Zealand. In time, however, declining health overtook them both and Dorothy died on April 8th, 1979. Edward succeeded her for a further seven years, but then passed away suddenly on January 17, 1986. Dorothy and Edward are buried in the Brady family plot in Ryans Presbyterian Church graveyard, County Down.

FIFTH GENERATION

Alan Robert Tighe Brady, Kenneth Edward Brady, Rosemary Muriel Brady, Samuel Denis Brady, Barbara Jean Brady

Alan Robert Tighe Brady – Fifth Generation

Alan Robert Tighe Brady, first child of Dorothy Jean Wright and Edward Tighe Brady, was born on July 19th, 1936 at the family home "Ardeevin" in the townland of Ardaragh, rural County Down, Northern Ireland. Alan is the eldest of five children. He has spent most of his adult life in New Zealand, where, after a career in print, radio, and television journalism, he settled near Queenstown in Central Otago and became a pioneer and one of the leading figures in the winegrowing industry.

Early life in a secure and loving family environment molded values which remained an important influence throughout his life and travels. War came only as close as distant flashes at night from German bombing raids on Belfast, and military exercises by U.S. and British troops in the fields and roads around home. In retrospect, life was austere but never seemed so at the time. Much time was spent on his grandparents Sam and Minnie Wright's farm less than a mile away at Finnard, where he learned something of the rhythm of the seasons and the miracle of nature from his uncles, Bob and David. These were influences which much later were to prove valuable when he planted grapevines in far-off New Zealand.

Alan went to primary school at Ballykeel and Rathfriland before moving on to Newry Grammar School. He was good at English but never a diligent scholar. Sports were important and he was school captain at hockey and cricket. He played hockey for Ulster and Irish schools and later for Ulster at senior men's level. He continued his hockey career with some distinction in New Zealand, representing his province Otago for four years in the 1960s.

With printing ink "in his blood" and an enthusiasm for writing, Alan never looked beyond journalism as a career. He began as a cadet on the *Armagh Guardian* in 1955, and after a two-year apprenticeship joined the family printing and newspaper business, *The Rathfriland Outlook*. But having grown up listening to his South-African born and raised father's stories of travel and adventure, he inevitably had to explore the world for himself.

With a job arranged in advance, he sailed for New Zealand in 1959 at the age of 23. He worked for a while with the *Manawatu Evening Standard* before heading to the South Island and a position on the *Otago Daily Times* in Dunedin. There he met his first wife, fellow journalist Denise Jeavons. They married February 24th, 1962 in St. Paul's Cathedral, Dunedin, New Zealand, and returned to Ireland to visit family the same year. Alan worked as a senior reporter on the *Belfast Telegraph* and Denise obtained a job as a continuity announcer with Ulster Television. They lived in Belfast for two years before sailing "home" to New Zealand in 1964.

Alan and Denise have two children born in Queen Mary Hospital, Dunedin, New Zealand: Susan Jane, born February 2, 1966, and Jennifer Lynn, born December 1, 1967. Alan's marriage to Denise ended in 1971.

In 1973, he married Denise Tocker, and four years later they abandoned city careers to live on 16 acres in the spectacular mountains of inland Otago. Their daughter Tara Dorothy was born January 4, 1978.

Alan worked as a freelance journalist and Denise began psychology practice. They were among the first to plant vines in Central Otago in 1981, and those pioneering efforts led to the development of New Zealand's fastest-growing wine region. They separated in 1987.

Alan went on to found Gibbston Valley Wines, Ltd, and later the Mount Edward Winery, both of which have become important New Zealand brands. He is manager, winemaker, and marketing manager of Mount Edward, and is involved as a consultant to several other companies. He was made a member of the New Zealand Order of Merit in the Queen's Birthday Honours list in 1966 for services to the wine industry.

His three daughters, two granddaughters, and church and community work are important elements in a busy lifestyle. He is an ordained elder and parish councilor at the Wakatipu Presbyterian Parish in Queenstown, and serves on the committees of a number of community groups. Recreation revolves around skiing, gardening, and occasional golfing.

ALAN BRADY WITH HIS THREE DAUGHTERS LEFT TO RIGHT: SUSAN, TARA & JENNY BRADY

SIXTH GENERATION

Susan Jane Brady, Jennifer Lynn Brady, Tara Dorothy Brady

Susan Jane Brady – Sixth Generation

Susan Jane Brady, first child of Alan Brady and Denise Jeavons, was born on February 2nd, 1966 in Queen Mary Hospital, Dunedin, New Zealand. Susan is an actress working on film, television, and stage in New Zealand.

Jennifer Lynn Brady – Sixth Generation

Jennifer Lynn Brady, second child of Alan Brady and Denise Jeavons, was born on December 1st, 1967 in Queen Mary Hospital, Dunedin, New Zealand. She attended Otago University, where she obtained the degree of Bachelor of Commerce, majoring in Economics.

She married Brian David Watson on April 8th, 1993 in Arrowtown, New Zealand. Brian, a native of Tauranga, New Zealand, was born on March 1st, 1967. Brian is also a graduate of Otago University, having completed the same degree course as his wife. He also has a degree in Physical Education, and since leaving Otago University has been involved in the pharmaceutical industry.

Jenny's career to date has been rich and varied and included advertising, personnel consulting, floristry, personal training, and, lately, motherhood. She and Brian have two daughters, Sophie and Emma. They now live in Sydney, Australia.

SEVENTH GENERATION

Sophie Alexandra Watson, Emma Victoria Watson

Sophie Alexandra Watson – Seventh Generation

Sophie Alexandra Watson, first child born of Jennifer Lynn Brady and Brian David Watson, was born on August 26th, 1995 in Auckland, New Zealand.

Emma Victoria Watson – Seventh Generation

Emma Victoria Watson, second child born of Jennifer Lynn Brady and Brian David Watson, was born on May 21st, 1997 in Auckland, New Zealand.

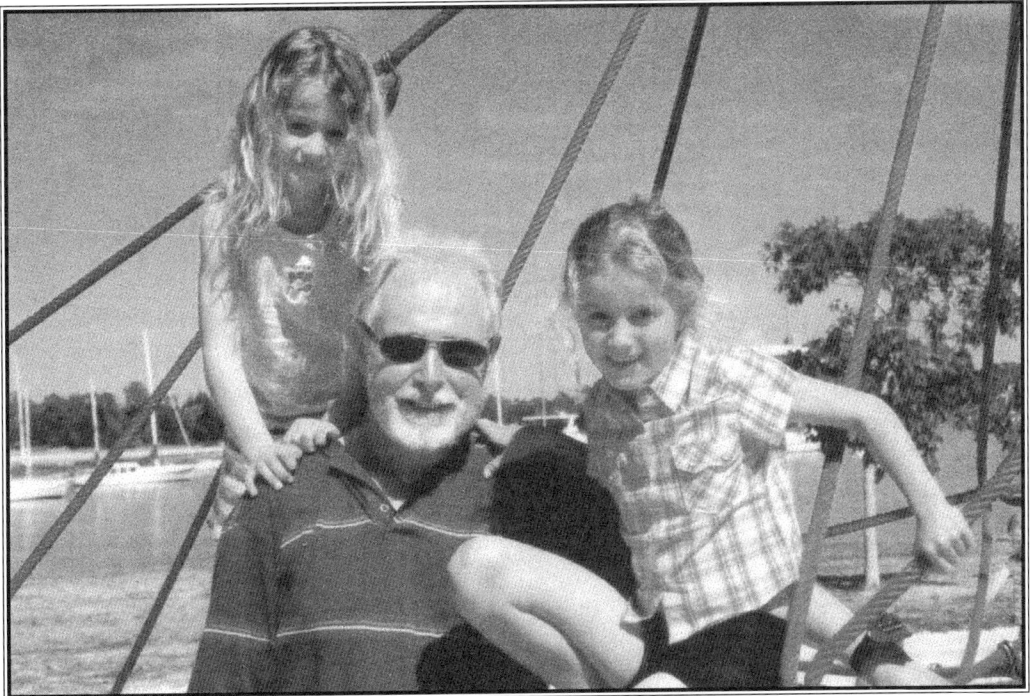

ALAN BRADY WITH HIS GRANDDAUGHTERS SOPHIE & EMMA WATSON, SYDNEY, AUSTRALIA 2002

Tara Dorothy Brady – Sixth Generation

Tara Dorothy Brady, first child of Alan Brady and Denise Tocker, was born on January 4th, 1978 in Queen Mary Hospital, Dunedin, New Zealand. She lives and works in Queenstown and is an outdoor and adventure-sports enthusiast.

Kenneth Edward Brady – Fifth Generation

Kenneth Edward Brady, second son of Edward Brady and Dorothy Wright, was born on July 25th, 1939 in Adrianne Nursing Home, Newry, County Down, Northern Ireland.

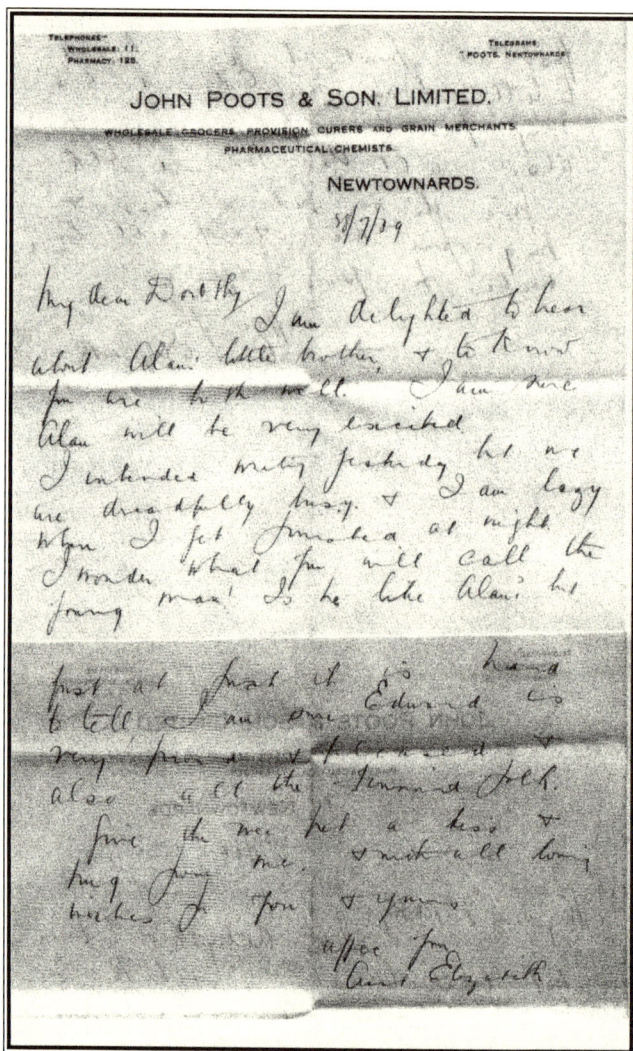

LETTER FROM GREAT-AUNT ELIZABETH "CISSIE" WRIGHT TO DOROTHY BRADY CONGRATULATING HER ON THE BIRTH OF HER SECOND SON, KENNETH, JULY 25, 1939

His childhood years were spent happily in the pleasant rural setting of Ardaragh, remote from World War II influences and sublimely ignorant of the historic times through which the world was passing. His schooling, like so many of his forbearers, began locally at Ballykeel Primary, to which he made the round trip of three miles on foot each day. Later he traveled by bus to Rathfriland where he attended Iveagh Primary School. His secondary education was obtained at Newry Grammar School,

ALAN BRADY & KENNETH BRADY, CIRCA 1940

where he made many life-long friendships. During his time there he took part in several school drama productions, and was heavily involved in sports, becoming captain of the 1st IX hockey team in his final year.

Kenneth and his older brother Alan were the first, and for some years only, grandchildren of Sam and Minnie Wright, whose home at Finnard was within easy walking distance of Ardaragh. Consequently, Kenneth benefited enormously during his formative years from the positive influences of grandparents and numerous aunts and uncles. Many happy and productive hours were spent on the Wright farm helping with crops and livestock, and learning to drive tractors. Attendance at Ryans Presbyterian Church and Sunday school every Sunday was a significant feature of his upbringing and helped to lay early foundations for a lifetime commitment to the Christian faith.

From 1958 to 1963, Kenneth attended Queen's University Belfast, where he obtained a Bachelors Degree in Agriculture and a post-graduate diploma in education. Employment with the Government Department of Agriculture followed, beginning with a post as farm advisor in County Down. Thereafter, Kenneth progressed through various positions in education, forestry, and policy administration to a seat on the management board.

Kenneth is over six feet tall, of slim build, with fair hair and blue eyes. In his final year at school, he fell in love with one of the senior girls, Anne Elizabeth Ferguson from Bessbrook, County Armagh. Thus began a long courtship, which continued through his university years and led to their marriage on March 24th, 1964 at the Friends Meeting House in Bessbrook.

ANNE FERGUSON & KENNETH BRADY, WEDDING DAY, MARCH 24, 1964

Anne is five feet six inches tall, of medium build, with brown hair and blue-green eyes. On leaving school, she first took up a career in banking for two years before returning to college to study for a qualification in child care. Thereafter, and until the arrival of her first child, Anne was employed at the Jordanstown School for Blind and Deaf Children in County Antrim.

Kenneth and Anne have three children: Joanne, born in 1966, Phillip, born in 1967, and Alison, born in 1975. The family lived for 22 years at Stormont, Belfast, convenient to their church and schools and Kenneth's place of employment. Now in retirement, Kenneth and Anne live at Dundonald, County Down, where they are closely involved with the local Presbyterian Church—Kenneth is an elected Elder, Missionary Convener, and choir member, while Anne is the Leader of the Ladies' Fellowship. Their other interests center on family, grandchildren, golf, and caravanning.

KENNETH BRADY WITH JOHN DUNLOP & RICHARD DUNLOP, SUMMER HOLIDAYS, 1958

SIXTH GENERATION

Joanne Linda Brady, Phillip Kenneth Brady, Alison Grace Brady

Joanne Linda Brady – Sixth Generation

Joanne Linda Brady, the eldest child of Kenneth Brady and Anne Ferguson, was born on August 16th, 1966 in Belfast, County Antrim. She spent the first few years of her life at Carryduff, County Down, Northern Ireland, before the family moved to Stormont, Belfast. She attended Dundonald Primary, Sullivan Upper Schools, and then Queen's University Belfast, where she enrolled for a four-year degree course in Psychology. Following graduation in 1989, she moved to the south of England to seek employment and settled in Reading, Berkshire. There she met her partner Anton Rowe, with whom she has been living happily for many years. Anton comes from Derby, England and is a graduate of Warrick University. He trained as an accountant and is currently the European financial controller with Johnson Diversey.

After working for several years in both private industry and the public sector, Joanne decided to go into business on her own and established a very successful consultancy practice in organizational development. Working from her present home in Fleet, Hampshire, she regularly commutes to locations throughout the UK.

LEFT TO RIGHT: ANTON ROWE, JOANNE & KENNETH BRADY, JULY 1999

Joanne is five feet six inches tall, with brown hair and green eyes. She enjoys socializing, reading, cycling, hill walking, and gardening, and is currently developing a talent for various DIY skills. She is an enthusiastic traveler, and together with Anton has traveled extensively in Europe and made several trips to North and South America and Africa.

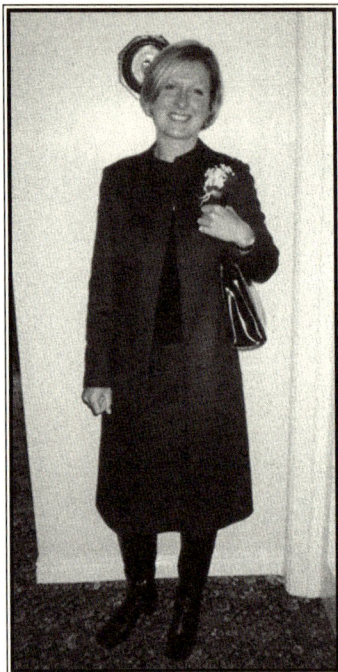

JOANNE BRADY, DECEMBER 2000

Phillip Kenneth Brady – Sixth Generation

Phillip Kenneth Brady, the second child of Kenneth Brady and Anne Ferguson, was born on November 13th, 1967 in Belfast, County Antrim, Northern Ireland. He lived with his parents and two sisters at Stormont, Belfast and attended primary school at Dundonald and Sullivan Upper School at Holywood, County Down, Northern Ireland. Later, he enrolled at the Jordanstown campus of the University of Ulster to study Electronics and Communication Engineering.

On graduating, Phillip commenced employment in Sales and Marketing with F. G. Wilson Engineering, now a subsidiary of Caterpillar, Inc. Working from Larne, County Antrim, he is currently employed in the electric power division of Caterpillar as Product Definition Manager. In connection with his work, he lived for two years in the USA and has traveled to many parts of Europe, the Middle- and Far-East, Pakistan, the Philippines, and North and South America.

Phillip is six feet one inch, of medium build, with fair hair and blue eyes. His interests

include socializing with a large circle of friends, gardening, home improvement projects, power kiting, and cars.

On June 30, 1995, Phillip married Gillian Turner, a medical graduate of Queen's University, Belfast, at Helens Bay Presbyterian Church, County Down.

PHILLIP KENNETH BRADY & DR. GILLIAN TURNER, WEDDING DAY, JUNE 30, 1995

Gillian is currently employed at the Musgrave Park and City Hospitals in Belfast as consultant in anesthetics. They have two children: Anna Jane, born July 5, 1997 in Belfast and Thomas Phillip, born December 2, 1999 in Belfast. The family currently lives in Cairnburn, Belfast.

SEVENTH GENERATION

Anna Jane Brady, Thomas Phillip Brady

Anna Jane Brady – Seventh Generation

Anna Jane Brady, known as Anna, the first child of Phillip Brady and Gillian Turner, was born on July 5th, 1997 in Belfast, County Antrim, Northern Ireland.

Thomas Phillip Brady – Seventh Generation

Thomas Phillip Brady, the second child of Phillip Brady and Gillian Turner, was born on December 2nd, 1999 in Belfast, County Antrim, Northern Ireland.

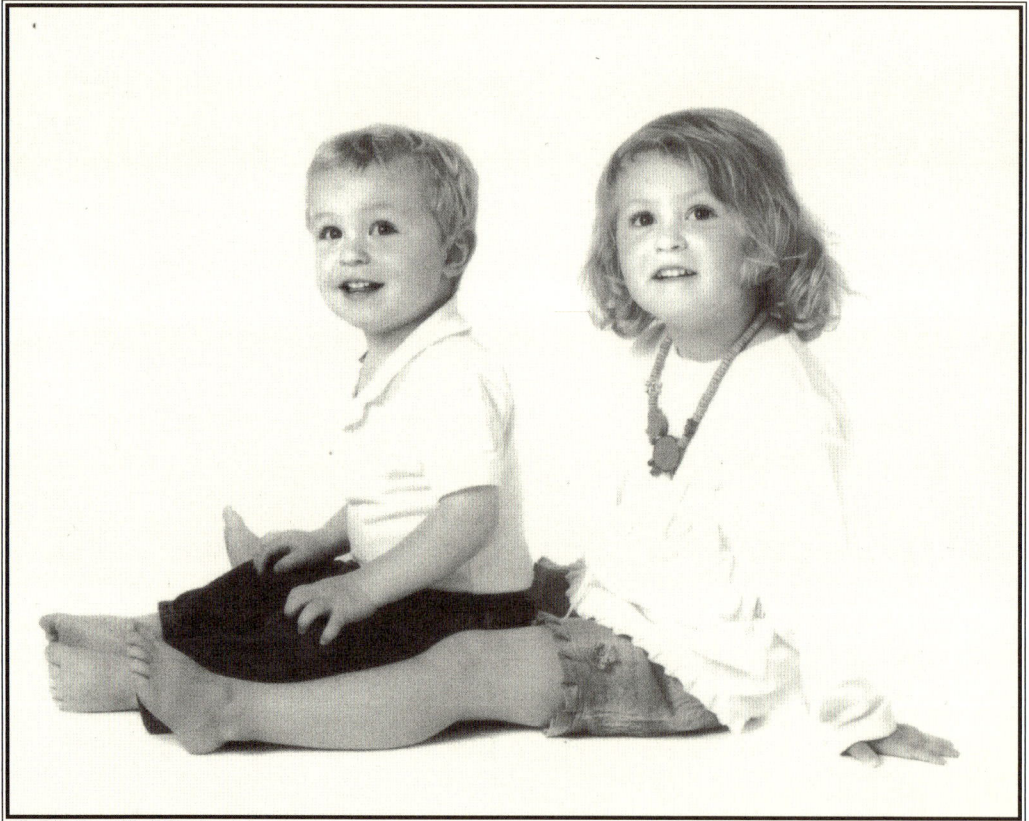

TOM & ANNA BRADY, JULY 2000

Alison Grace Brady – Sixth Generation

Alison Grace Brady, the third child of Kenneth Brady and Anne Ferguson, was born on November 22nd, 1975 in County Antrim, Northern Ireland. She lived with the family at Stormont, Belfast and attended Dundonald Primary and Strathearn Schools. Alison was a regular attendee at Dundonald Presbyterian Church and actively involved in several of its organizations. After completing her schooling, she attended Queen's University Belfast, graduating with a BSc in 1997, and an MPhil in 1999.

KENNETH, ALISON & ANNE BRADY, GRADUATION, DECEMBER 1999

Following completion of a postgraduate diploma in accounting in 2000 at the University of Ulster, Alison trained as a chartered accountant with KPMG and now works as a value-for-money consultant in the health sector in Northern Ireland.

During her time at Queen's, Alison met Stephen Webb, a medical student who was to become her husband. Stephen, now a qualified doctor, is currently working for a year as an anaesthetist at the Papworth Hospital in Cambridge. The couple have two children: Holly Rebekah, born April 25th, 2005, and Max Daniel, born October 2nd, 2006. Alison and Stephen were married at Dundonald Presbyterian Church on December 11, 2000.

STEPHEN WEBB & ALISON GRACE BRADY, WEDDING DAY
DECEMBER 11, 2000

They currently live at Cregagh, Belfast and attend Windsor Baptist church.

Alison is five feet seven inches tall, of slim build, with fair hair and green eyes. She enjoys traveling and during student vacations got involved in charity work, which opened opportunities to spend time in the Republic of Ireland, Scotland, and as far afield as Africa and India. She has also holidayed extensively in Europe, and has toured both the North and South Islands of New Zealand with Stephen. She enjoys sports, marathon running, rowing, cooking for friends, and interior decorating.

SEVENTH GENERATION

Holly Rebekah Webb, Max Daniel Webb

Holly Rebekah Webb – Seventh Generation
Holly Rebekah Webb, first child of Stephen Webb and Alison Brady, was born on April 25th, 2005 in Belfast, Northern Ireland.

Max Daniel Webb – Seventh Generation
Max Daniel Webb, second child of Stephen Webb and Alison Brady, was born on October 2nd, 2006 in Addenbrooks General Hospital, Cambridge, England.

HOLLY WITH HER MUM AND DAD
MAY 2005

LEFT TO RIGHT: STEPHEN, BABY MAX, HOLLY, AND ALISON

Rosemary Muriel Brady – Fifth Generation

Rosemary Muriel Brady, the third child of Edward and Dorothy Brady, was born on May 15th, 1944 in a Belfast Nursing Home. Rosemary enjoyed a wonderful and very happy childhood growing up at "Ardeevin," Ardaragh. She attended Ryans Presbyterian Church and Sunday School and was involved in various church activities, including singing in the choir. Rosemary went to Newry Model School at age five, traveling the seven miles each day by bus, a journey which took about thirty minutes in those days. She qualified to attend Newry Grammar School at age eleven, and though not a great scholar enjoyed all of the sporting activities and represented the school on all of the girls' hockey teams. Rosemary was a house captain in her last year and left school after completing her Senior Certificate at age seventeen.

Alan, Rosemary's eldest brother, who immigrated to New Zealand, planned to get married in 1962, and the family decided that Rosemary should represent them at the wedding. So, in October 1961, Rosemary sailed for New Zealand and the trip of a lifetime. In February 1962 at Dunedin, South Island, she was a bridesmaid at Alan's wedding. She stayed in New Zealand for the remainder of that year, and on return to Northern Ireland spent a year at a college of further education in Belfast.

Thereafter, she went to work in Dublin, where she met her future husband Michael Wilson, a medical student at Trinity College. They married in the summer of 1966 in Rostrevor Presbyterian Church, County Down, while Michael was still a medical student, and had two of their children—Stephen Edward and Jonathan Michael—before Michael qualified as a doctor. Paul Singleton was born in Newry and Peter James McMahon in Craigavon Hospital after the family moved to Lurgan, County Armagh.

Rosemary is five feet five inches tall, with strawberry blond hair and blue eyes. She is blessed with a very happy marriage and she and Michael share many interests, including golf, travel, and entertaining friends. She leads a busy, active life and is a Justice of the Peace and a Lay Magistrate. She is also a member of several charity committees. She and Michael are both active members of Armagh Road Presbyterian Church. While their children were young, the family spent many holidays in Europe, mainly France. They also visited Disney World and Disneyland. Golf is another consuming interest, and Rosemary plays off a handicap of fourteen. On family holidays to California, essential luggage includes several sets of golf clubs!

Rosemary loves cats and dogs and has taken in quite a few strays over the years. At the moment Lynx and Tiger "rule the roost" in the Wilson home. Rosemary has seven grandchildren, with one or more due to be born quite soon. Unfortunately, they all live in England, so she does not get to see them as often as she would wish.

Rosemary and Michael live in Portadown, County Armagh. Michael is a general medical practitioner in nearby Lurgan.

MICHAEL & ROSEMARY (BRADY) WILSON
CIRCA 1971

THE WILSON FAMILY. LEFT TO RIGHT: DR. MICHAEL WILSON, PAUL, STEPHEN, PETER & JONATHAN; FRONT: ROSEMARY BRADY WILSON, 2000

SIXTH GENERATION

Stephen Edward Wilson, Jonathan Michael Wilson, Paul Singleton Wilson, Peter James McMahon Wilson

Stephen Edward Wilson – Sixth Generation

Stephen Edward Wilson, first child of Rosemary and Michael Wilson, was born on March 27th, 1967 in Daisy Hill Hospital, Newry, County Down, Northern Ireland. Stephen was six weeks premature and quite a difficult baby for the first few months. He soon became a lovable, mischievous little boy with red hair and hazel eyes. From an early age, Stephen loved to be the clown and was always in trouble of some sort, but never the serious kind!

Stephen attended Bocombra Primary School and the Royal School Armagh. He also went to Armagh Road Presbyterian Church and Sunday School in Portadown.

Stephen did not work particularly hard at school but enjoyed his school days and loved sporting activities. He excelled at rugby, a sport he still plays, and gained his colours blazer in his final year. After leaving school, Stephen attended Wye College, London University, where he received a degree in Horticulture. He then returned to Northern Ireland and completed a post-graduate qualification in Communication Studies at Loughry College, Queen's University, Belfast. Thereafter, Stephen moved to Kent, England and commenced work with a firm of fruit importers. He still works for this firm and is now in a managerial position which involves extensive travel.

Stephen is almost six feet tall, with curly red hair and a strong physique. On July 22nd, 1995, Stephen and Jo Fenton were married in St. Alban's Church, Frant, East Sussex, England. Jo was Stephen's sweetheart, whom he met at Wye College.

Stephen is a great father and loves being with his three beautiful children: Rory, born August 4, 1996, Angus, born June 5, 1998, and, the apple of his eye, Annabel Emily Rose, born April 16, 2001. All were born in Kent, England.

STEPHEN & JO WILSON, CHRISTENING SERVICE OF BABY RORY, 1996

ROSEMARY BRADY WITH GRANDCHILDREN ELLIE, RORY & ANGUS, 2002

ANNABEL, RORY & ANGUS WILSON, SUMMER, 2002

Seventh Generation

Rory Edward McMahon Wilson, Angus Robert Ramsey Wilson, Annabel Emily Rose Wilson

Rory Edward McMahon Wilson – Seventh Generation

Rory Edward McMahon Wilson, the first child of Stephen Wilson & Jo Fenton, was born on August 4th, 1996 in Kent, England.

Angus Robert Ramsey Wilson – Seventh Generation

Angus Robert Ramsey Wilson, the second child of Stephen Wilson & Jo Fenton, was born on June 5th, 1998 in Kent, England.

Annabel Emily Rose Wilson – Seventh Generation

Annabel Emily Rose Wilson, the third child of Stephen Wilson & Jo Fenton, was born on April 16th, 2001 in Kent, England.

Jonathan Michael Wilson – Sixth Generation

Jonathan Michael Wilson, second child of Rosemary Brady and Michael Wilson, was born on March 26th, 1968 in St. John of God's Nursing Home, Newry, County Down, Northern Ireland. Jonathan was a big, pleasant child, with a questioning side from an early age. Clever and bright at school, he excelled at most things when he wanted to, but had the attitude that there was more to life than being a swot! He attended the Royal School Armagh, where he was involved in all aspects of school life, enjoying sports and achieving his colours blazer for rugby. During his school years, Jonathan went with his family to Armagh Road Presbyterian Church and Sunday School.

Jonathan didn't quite know what course to pursue after completing his schooling but finally went to Aston University, Birmingham, where he took a degree in Human Psychology. The day after his graduation, he left with a rucksack on his back and traveled around Europe, ending up in Barcelona, Spain, where he remained and still lives today. He now teaches English at a university there.

Jonathan is five feet ten inches tall, strongly built, with blond hair and hazel eyes. He has an engaging personality and makes friends wherever he goes. He loves cooking, entertaining and traveling, and generally enjoys life to the fullest. Jonathan and his partner Cristina Delgado Puig continue to live in Barcelona. The couple recently welcomed their first child Carla Tighe Wilson, born February 25, 2005. While attending the family reunion in

2004, Jonathan noticed that the name Tighe kept appearing on his maternal grandfather's side of the family. He made a decision that day to give the name to the first child he and Cristina had.

CRISTINA AND BABY CARLA WILSON

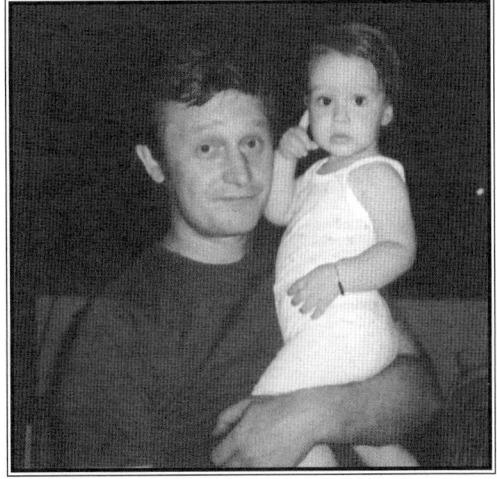

JONATHAN AND CARLA WILSON

SEVENTH GENERATION

Carla Tighe Wilson – Seventh Generation

Carla Tighe Wilson, first child of Jonathan Michael Wilson and Cristina Delgado Puig, was born on February 25th, 2005 in Barcelona, Spain.

Jonathan Wilson, Annabel's Christening, 2001

Paul Singleton Wilson – Sixth Generation

Paul Singleton Wilson, third child of Rosemary Brady and Michael Wilson, was born on August 29th, 1970 at St. John of God's Nursing Home in Newry, County Down, Northern Ireland. He was a beautiful baby with dark hair and big brown eyes. Paul always had a most endearing personality, right from boyhood. As the third child, he was frequently bossed about by his big brothers but always managed to hold his own.

Paul attended Portadown Preparatory School and Royal School Armagh, where sports often took precedence over school work. He played rugby and was a nippy scrum-half, but his real love was golf, which he played with his Mum and Dad. Paul represented both his school and Portadown Golf Club in juvenile golf competitions. He still plays off a handicap of seven.

After completing his exams at school, Paul enrolled at Stratclyde University in Glasgow, where he received a degree in Biochemistry and Immunology. He then went on a year-long trip to New Zealand and Australia, visiting his Uncle Alan's vineyard and working there for some time before moving on to Australia. When he returned home, he went back to Glasgow to study for a Masters Degree in Forensic Science.

After graduation, Paul went to work in California for the District Attorney's office in Bakersfield. He stayed there for three years and enjoyed the life, though he found the climate too hot for his liking. While living in California, Jill Brown, his girlfriend from Portadown, joined him, and they were married in Carmel on September 28th, 1999. They have an American daughter named Rebecca, born July 10, 2000 in Bakersfield, California. Paul now works for a forensic consultancy firm in Durham in the north of England.

Paul is settled in his new life in England and he and Jill have bought a house there. Their second child Joshua Paul Wilson was born January 25, 2003. Paul and Jill are active members of their local church.

JILL & PAUL WILSON

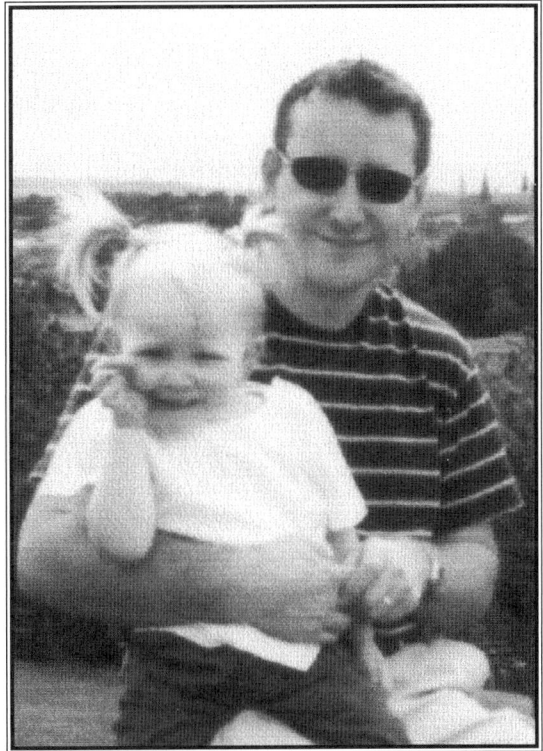

PAUL WILSON & DAUGHTER, REBECCA, 2002

SEVENTH GENERATION

Rebecca Jennifer Wilson, Joshua Paul Wilson

Rebecca Jennifer Wilson – Seventh Generation

Rebecca Jennifer Wilson, the first child of Paul Wilson and Jill Brown, was born on July 10th, 2000 in Bakersfield, California.

Joshua Paul Wilson – Seventh Generation

Joshua Paul Wilson, the second child of Paul Wilson and Jill Brown, was born on January 25th, 2003 in Durham, England.

JOSHUA AND REBECCA WILSON

Peter James McMahon Wilson – Sixth Generation

Peter James McMahon Wilson, fourth child of Rosemary Brady and Michael Wilson, was born on February 21st, 1974 in Portadown, County Armagh, Northern Ireland. At over nine pounds birth weight, Peter was the biggest Wilson baby. He was a very good baby and a helpful child as he grew up. As the youngest in the family, his brothers used to tease him and call him "Joseph," asking when he was getting his coat of many colors!

Peter attended Portadown Preparatory School and was good at maths but experienced some difficulty with reading. It took some time to discover that he suffered from dyslexia, a condition which at that time was little recognized in Northern Ireland. He really struggled at school with some subjects but with the help of a good teacher in a small class he learned to read. Peter joined his brothers at the Royal School Armagh and excelled at sports, particu-

PETER & JOANNE WILSON & ELLIE ROSE, WEDDING DAY, OCTOBER 21, 2000

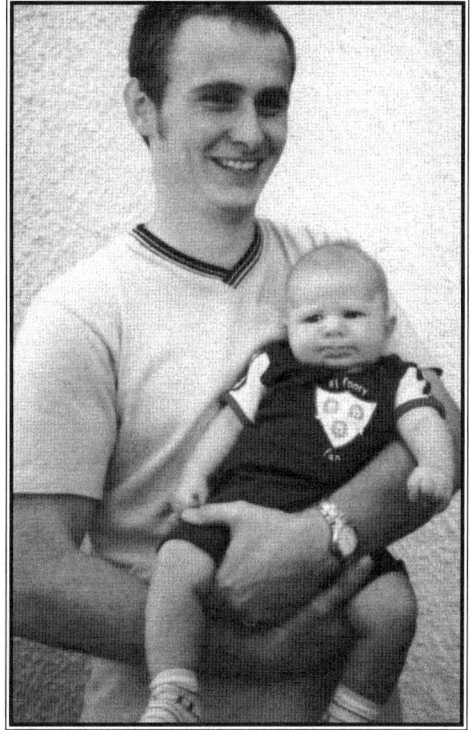

PETER WILSON & BABY ISAAC, 2002

larly rugby and golf. He gained his colors blazer in rugby and golf and is still a keen golfer with a handicap of seven. Peter was also juvenile captain of Portadown Golf Club and represented his club for four years as a juvenile. He was also the only Wilson to become a prefect at the Royal School.

After leaving school, Peter went to John Moore University in Liverpool to study Biomedical Sciences. After graduating he moved to the School of Medicine at Liverpool University to study for his PhD, which he completed in September 2002. Peter is five feet eleven inches tall, of slim build, with dark blond hair, brown eyes, and a rather absentminded professorial attitude—clever but sometimes a man of few words.

Peter met Joanne Prior, his wife-to-be, in his first year at University and fell in love. They have a wonderful daughter named Ellie Rose, born June 14, 1997. She is brown-eyed, dark-haired and just full of sparkle, the first girl in the Wilson clan. Peter and Joanne married in Liverpool on October 21, 2000 and are happily settled there with Ellie Rose and Isaac Michael, born June 20th, 2002.

SEVENTH GENERATION

Ellie Rose Wilson, Isaac Michael Wilson

Ellie Rose Wilson – Seventh Generation

Ellie Rose Wilson, the first child of Peter Wilson and Joanne Prior, was born on June 14th, 1997 in Liverpool, England.

Isaac Michael Wilson – Seventh Generation

Isaac Michael Wilson, the second child of Peter Wilson and Joanne Prior, was born on June 20th, 2002 in Liverpool, England.

Samuel Denis Brady – Fifth Generation

Samuel Denis Brady, the fifth child of Dorothy and Edward Brady, was born on April 1st, 1949 in Banbridge, County Down, Northern Ireland. Like his brothers and sisters, Denis was raised at the family home "Ardeevin" in the townland of Ardaragh, County Down, Northern Ireland.

Denis began his early education at the local Ballykeel Primary School, and then, like some of his cousins, switched to the Model School at Newry, a decision no doubt influenced by the presence of his Aunt Bertha, who taught there.

Denis later attended the Newry Grammar School and Rathfriland High School before completing his education at Renshaws Tutorial College in Belfast. There he learned some of the skills which were to equip him for entry into the family newspaper business in 1966. With his keen interest in sports, he quickly developed the sports pages of the *Outlook*, acting as both reporter and photographer.

Denis married Ruth Meeke July 17th, 1971. Their first child, Richard William Tighe, was born December 13, 1974, Kathryn Clare on April 30, 1976. Denis and Ruth divorced in 1980.

It became apparent early in his career that photography was Denis's chief interest, and in 1972 he opened a photographic studio in Rathfriland, followed three years later by one in Kilkeel, both trading as Outlook Photographic Studios. When the Outlook Press was sold in 1978, Denis moved his photographic business to Kildare Street in Newry. Over the years his ability in the wider photographic world has been recognized by Associateships of The British Institute of Professional Photographers and The Royal Photographic Society of Great Britain. Denis is also a past president of The Professional Photographers Association of Northern Ireland.

On December 31st, 1983 Denis married Norma Butler in Rostrevor Presbyterian Church, County Down. Norma, a native of Clonmel, County Tipperary, was a nursing sister in St. Vincent's Hospital, Dublin. They set up home in the seaside town of Warrenpoint, County Down, their sea-fronting home enjoying spectacular views across Carlingford Lough. Their daughter Olga Denise was born November 30, 1984, followed by a son, Andrew David, born July 7, 1987. Norma now works as a nurse in the local health center in Warrenpoint.

In the late 80s, Denis leased out his photographic business in Newry and opened an art gallery and picture framing business in his hometown of Warrenpoint. In 1992, Denis qualified as an independent financial advisor. Since closing the art gallery in 1993, Denis has continued to manage his photographic business from The Mews Gallery, which is attached to the family home.

His financial business is operated from premises in the County Down town of Banbridge.

Denis, a keen soccer and rugby player in his younger days, retains an interest in many sports, which he enjoys these days from the comfort of his armchair.

An Elder and former Sunday School Superintendent, Denis and Norma are active in the local Warrenpoint Presbyterian Church.

THE BRADY FAMILY. LEFT TO RIGHT: NORMA, KATHRYN, RICHARD, DENIS, OLGA, AND ANDREW BRADY, WARRENPOINT, COUNTY DOWN, JANUARY 2002

DENIS & NORMA BRADY, 2002

SIXTH GENERATION

Richard William Tighe Brady, Kathryn Clare Brady

Richard William Tighe Brady – Sixth Generation

Richard William Tighe Brady, the first child of Denis Brady and Ruth Meeke, was born on December 13th, 1974 in Newry, County Down, Northern Ireland. He is a graduate of the University of Bournemouth with a degree in Financial Management.

Kathryn Clare Brady – Sixth Generation

Kathryn Clare Brady, the second child of Denis Brady and Ruth Meeke, was born on April 30th, 1976 in Newry, County Down, Northern Ireland. She now owns and rents a number of domestic properties in Glasgow, Scotland.

*   *   *

Denis's second marriage to Norma Butler resulted in two children, Olga Denise Brady and Andrew David Brady.

SIXTH GENERATION

Olga Denise Brady, Andrew David Brady

Olga Denise Brady – Sixth Generation

Olga Denise Brady, the first child of Denis Brady and Norma Butler, was born on November 30th, 1984 in Warrenpoint, County Down, Northern Ireland. Olga was educated at Kilbroney Integrated Primary School, Rostrevor, before moving to Shimna College, Newcastle.

Andrew David Brady – Sixth Generation

Andrew David Brady, the second child of Denis Brady and Norma Butler, was born on July 7th, 1987 in Warrenpoint, County Down, Northern Ireland.

Barbara Jean Brady – Fifth Generation

Barbara Jean Brady, the fourth child of Edward Brady and Dorothy Wright, was born on March 20th, 1952 at Banbridge Hospital, County Down, Northern Ireland. Barbara enjoyed a very happy childhood at Ardaragh. She attended Ballykeel Primary School for several years before moving to Newry Model School (where Bertha Wright, her Auntie B., was Vice-principal) to finish her primary education.

Barbara enjoyed the company of her Wright cousins, Eleanor and Uel, who lived just down the road. The summer months provided many opportunities for exploring and getting up to harmless mischief on the farm at Finnard. During her childhood years, Barbara sometimes stayed with her other Wright cousins in Armagh City, and she and Eleanor Wright also occasionally stayed with their Auntie Maud Gilpin at the Clare, Waringstown.

In addition to attending Sunday School and church at Ryans, Barbara was an enthusiastic member of the Youth Club during her teenage years and sang in the choir. After her time at the Model School, Barbara continued her education at Newry Grammar School before entering the Royal Victoria Hospital in Belfast as a student nurse. In 1971, she accompanied her parents on a round-the-world cruise, stopping in New Zealand for four months to visit her eldest brother, Alan. On her return to Ireland, Barbara took up a position at Craigavon Area Hospital.

On September 21st, 1974, Barbara married William John Alexander (Lex) Girvan at Ryans Presbyterian Church. Barbara and Lex had two daughters: Cara Louise, born August 19, 1979 at the Royal Maternity Hospital, Belfast, and Clare Alexandra, born March 13, 1981, also at Royal Maternity Hospital in Belfast. The family lived at Moneyreagh outside Belfast until Barbara and Lex separated in 1986, divorcing in 1989. In 1987, Barbara and the girls traveled to New Zealand to visit Alan and stayed for one year in the Queenstown region of Central Otago. They loved their time there and particularly enjoyed the outdoor life, the climate, and the spectacular scenery. They made many new friends and found it very difficult leaving it all behind to return home in 1988.

Back in Ireland, Barbara and her girls settled in Portadown, County Armagh, and Barbara took up a position as classroom assistant in a local primary school. On July 6th, 1994, Barbara married James Clifford Edgar at Armagh Road Presbyterian Church, Portadown. Clifford, a sales manager with a fertilizer company, had three children from his previous marriage: Lynsey, Suzanne, and Craig. The family bought a new home in Portadown and all lived there until 2001. Barbara and Clifford have recently completed the construction of a new home in the country and now live between Gilford and Waringstown. Barbara is five feet six inches tall, of slim build, with fair hair and blue eyes.

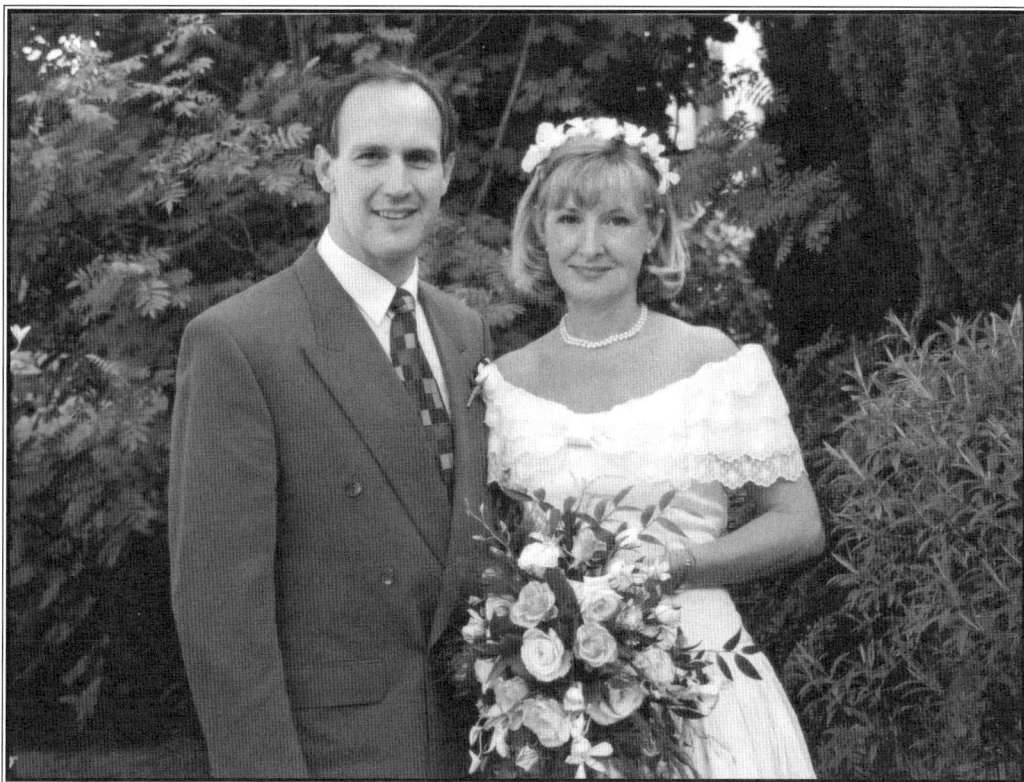

JAMES CLIFFORD EDGAR & BARBARA JEAN BRADY, WEDDING DAY, JULY 6, 1994

SIXTH GENERATION

Cara Louise Girvan, Clare Alexandra Girvan

Cara Louise Girvan – Sixth Generation

Cara Louise Girvan, first child of Barbara Jean Brady and William John Alexander Girvan, was born on August 19th, 1979 at the Royal Maternity Hospital in Belfast, County Antrim, Northern Ireland.

Cara is five feet six inches tall, of slim build, with blue eyes and dark brown hair. She grew up at Moneyreagh outside Belfast and attended Moneyreagh Primary School, Carryduff Presbyterian Church and Sunday School, and Girls Brigade until the age of eight. Between 1987 and 1988, Cara lived in New Zealand, where she attended Arrowtown Primary School. She loved the outdoor life "down under" and during her time there learned to ski.

On return to Ireland, she lived at Portadown, County Armagh, where she attended Bocombra Primary School, Killycomaine Junior High School, and Portadown College. Cara worked hard at school and always attained good marks. She was also a sports enthusiast and excelled especially at cross-country running and hockey, winning many prizes over the years.

On leaving school, Cara attended Queen's University Belfast and graduated in 2001 with a Bachelor of Law degree. In 2001, she successfully completed a course on management, and also attended Sandhurst Royal Military Academy, passing successfully as an officer in the Territorial Army.

CARA LOUISE GIRVAN

At the time of publication, Cara is traveling extensively in Europe and hopes to pursue a career in management when she returns home.

Clare Alexandra Girvan – Sixth Generation

Clare Alexandra Girvan, second child of Barbara Jean Brady and William John Alexander Girvan, was born on March 13th, 1981 at the Royal Maternity Hospital, Belfast, County Antrim, Northern Ireland.

Clare lived with her parents and sister Cara at Moneyreagh outside Belfast until the age of six. While there, she attended Moneyreagh Primary School and Carryduff Presbyterian Church and Sunday School.

In 1987, Clare traveled with her mother and sister to New Zealand, where she lived for a year in the Queenstown area of Central Otago. She was involved in all the fun events run by the community and very much enjoyed Kiwi rural life. While in New Zealand, she attended the local primary school at Arrowtown.

CLARE ALEXANDRA GIRVAN, GRADUATION, JULY 2002

Clare is five feet eight inches tall, of medium build, with blond hair and blue eyes. She attended Hope University in Liverpool and graduated in July 2002 with a joint Sports and Business degree. At the time of publication, she is taking a post-graduate teacher training course at Hope University, with a view to future employment as a PE teacher.

Robert William Wright – Fourth Generation

Robert William Wright, the fifth child and first son of Sam Wright and Minnie McClelland, known to many as Bobby, was born on January 3rd, 1916 in Finnard, County Down, Ireland. Farming in those days was labor-intensive, and the arrival of a first son to help and hopefully inherit would have been greeted with quiet satisfaction, as well as the usual thanksgiving by his parents. His brothers Sam and David soon followed, and the seven children grew up as a strong family unit imbued with Christian values.

He attended the local Ballykeel West Primary School, where he was a good pupil, no doubt aided in his studies by his mother, a former principal teacher at the same school. But farming was his destiny, and he embraced it for the rest of his life with relish and no regrets.

He took an interest in all aspects of the farming industry from an early age and was an active member of the Ulster Farmers Union all his life, serving for a time as Chairman of the South West Down Group. But it was the practical side of farming he loved and through which he proved himself both innovative and progressive. In 1952, he was one of the first farmers in the area to feed silage to cows. In the mid 1960s, he began the system of paddock grazing the dairy herd. For these efforts he was recognized with a farm visit from the then-Stormont Minister of Agriculture, Major James Chichester-Clark.

On May 30th, 1944, he married Evangeline Margaret Dugan in Ballyroney Presbyterian Church, and the couple set up home close to the farm. Eva Dugan was born on May 21st, 1918.

ROBERT WRIGHT AND EVANGELINE MARGARET DUGAN,
WEDDING DAY – MAY 30, 1944

ROBERT WILLIAM WRIGHT AND EVANGELINE MARGARET DUGAN, MARRIAGE CERTIFICATE

Wedding Bells

WRIGHT — DUGAN

A wedding of exceptional local interest was solemnized in Ballyroney Presbyterian Church, on Tuesday, May 30th, when Miss Evangeline Margaret Dugan, 'Whitegates,' Rathfriland, was joined in wedlock to Mr Robert William Wright, of Finnard, Ardarragh, Newry. The bride, who is a leading member in Rathfriland and Ballyroney young people's circles, is the youngest daughter of Mr and Mrs John Dugan, 'Whitegates,' Rathfriland. The bridegroom is the eldest son of Mr and Mrs R. S. Wright, Finnard, and is Secretary of the newly-formed Ardarragh branch of the Ulster Farmer's Union, as well as a popular member of Rathfriland Young Farmers' Club.

CHARMING BRIDE

A large crowd attended the ceremony, which was conducted by Rev. D. McCay Little, M.A., Minister of Ballyroney. The bride, who was given away by her brother, Mr. Robert J. Dugan, was charmingly gowned in a turquoise blue frock with accessories to tone, and carried a bouquet of pale pink carnations. She was attended by one bridesmaid, her cousin, Miss Margaret Magowan Belfast, who wore a dusky pink frock with accessories to tone. Her bouquet consisted of cream carnations.

Mr Samuel Wright, brother of the groom, efficiently performed the duties of groomsman. Miss Gwendoline Groves presided at the organ.

After the ceremony, on coming out of church, the bride was presented with a silver horse shoe by little Miss Dorothy Guest, of Belfast.

A reception was held at the home of the bride's parents, where also numerous handsome wedding presents were on view.

The happy couple later left on their honeymoon, which was spent in the South of Ireland. The bride's travelling ensemble consisted of cherry suit, with black accessories.

RATHFRILAND
'OUTLOOK' NEWSPAPER
JUNE 10. 1944

ROBERT WRIGHT & EVANGELINE MARGARET DUGAN, WEDDING ANNOUNCEMENT – MAY 30, 1944 RATHFRILAND, OUTLOOK NEWSPAPER

Their three children—Iain, Eleanor, and Uel—were born in August 1945, January 1949, and July 1952 respectively. Following the retirement of his father to Rathfriland in 1950, the family moved into the home farm house. Just as his father before him had carried out extensive renovations to the family home in the opening years of the 20th century, so too did Bobby and Eva in the early 1950s.

THE WRIGHTS OF FINNARD, BACK ROW, LEFT TO RIGHT: KAREN LAVERTY, JIMMY LAVERTY, ELEANOR WRIGHT LAVERTY, UEL WRIGHT, JUNE GROVES WRIGHT, IN HER ARMS SARAH WRIGHT; FRONT ROW, LEFT TO RIGHT: EMMA LAVERTY, ROBERT WRIGHT, LOUISE LAVERTY, IAIN WRIGHT, ON HIS KNEE NICOLA WRIGHT, SHIRLEY HILL WRIGHT, ON HER KNEE SUZANNE WRIGHT, JOANNE WRIGHT & EVA DUGAN WRIGHT

Brought up in Ryans Presbyterian Church, Bobby devoted much of his leisure time to the work and witness of the congregation throughout his life. He was elected onto the Congregational Committee in 1948, and ordained as an elder in 1956. He served as Sunday School Superintendent from 1970 to 1990, and was a life-long member of the choir and a founding member of Finnard Faith Mission Prayer Union.

THE FAMILY OF ROBERT & EVA WRIGHT
LEFT TO RIGHT, SITTING: IAIN, EVA, UEL & ELEANOR,
STANDING: ROBERT WRIGHT

Robert took particular interest in the Child Evangelism Fellowship movement and was instrumental in launching the Holiday Bible Club held annually in Ryans Church Hall. He took an active interest both locally and worldwide in Christian missionary work, and supported many charities.

After 43 years of marriage and following surgery for a routine gall bladder operation, Eva died on November 16th, 1987 at the age of 69. This was a devastating blow and completely unexpected. Bobby bore the loss with Christian fortitude, continuing to live alone in the retirement bungalow he and Eva had built in 1973.

Shortly after celebrating his 80th birthday, Bobby was diagnosed with cancer that had already spread to his liver. He died peacefully surrounded by his family in Newry Hospice on July 15th, 1996.

Bobby and Eva are buried in the Wright family plot in Ryans Presbyterian Church graveyard, County Down.

THE THREE WRIGHT BROTHERS
LEFT TO RIGHT: DAVID, ROBERT & SAM

FIFTH GENERATION

John Robert (Iain) Wright, Eleanor Elizabeth Wright, Samuel David (Uel) Wright

John Robert (Iain) Wright – Fifth Generation

When Robert and Eva Wright decided to give their first child the name John Robert Wright (everyday name Iain, which is Scottish for John), they were consciously or subconsciously keeping alive a link to Scotland stretching back over 200 years. Born on August 27, 1945, Iain became the sixth generation of the Wright family to have been born in the ancient townland of Finnard.

He attended Shinn and Ballykeel Primary School before being granted the dubious distinction of completing his primary school education under the watchful eye of his Aunt Bertha, who at that time was teaching at the Model School in Newry. Having completed his secondary education at Newry Technical School, Iain joined his father and a long line of antecedents who had farmed the fertile land of Finnard.

From a mixed base, the farm gradually gravitated towards specialization in dairying, and while Iain was kept busy by day, he also took a lively interest in events in the wider agricultural community in the evening. He was a member of the Rathfriland Young Farms Club and took part in several of their amateur dramatic productions.

Iain married Pamela M. KcKee in Clonduff Presbyterian Church, County Down on July 31st, 1971. The couple had no children and the marriage was dissolved in 1977.

Iain has always maintained a great interest in sports, particularly motor sport. He was actively involved in car rallying and took part in many local and provincial events. The high point came in the mid seventies when he was a class winner in the Northern Ireland Texaco Rally. After hanging up his driving gloves, Iain continued to play an active role in the administration of the sport.

He also played rugby for Banbridge, and, despite the time commitment demanded by farming, managed a credible 16 handicap at golf.

Iain married Shirley Hill on September 27th, 1980 in Redrock Presbyterian Church, Markethill, County Armagh.

Shirley, a native of County Monaghan, had moved with her family to Northern Ireland in the 1950s. Shirley was the owner of a ladies' shop in her adopted hometown of Markethill, County Armagh when it fell victim to the Troubles, destroyed by a terrorist bomb.

Shirley is five feet three inches tall, with blond hair and hazel-green eyes. She is currently working as a care assistant with the local Health Trust in Newry.

Their first child, Nicola, was born August 9, 1982 on the farm at Finnard.

Suzanne, their second child, was also born at Finnard, April 5, 1985.

In 2000, after 36 years of farming and at a time when the industry was beginning to go into economic decline, Iain decided to retire from working the land.

Iain Wright & Shirley Hill, Wedding Day, September 27, 1980

In a complete change of direction, Iain purchased a domestic cleaning franchise called "Cleaning Doctor." He is currently building up a client base in the South Down area.

Iain is five feet eleven inches tall, with brown hair and blue eyes. Iain and Shirley are members of Ryans Presbyterian Church, where Iain has been a choir member all his adult life. They both enjoy the countryside, and are keen walkers.

LEFT TO RIGHT: IAIN WRIGHT, SUZANNE WRIGHT, NICOLA WRIGHT & SHIRLEY WRIGHT (NICOLA IS HOLDING A CUP WON FOR SCRIPTURE ANSWERING)

THE WRIGHTS IN SPAIN, 2002, LEFT TO RIGHT: SHIRLEY WRIGHT, IAIN WRIGHT, NICOLA WRIGHT & SUZANNE WRIGHT

SIXTH GENERATION

Nicola Jane Wright, Suzanne Margaret Wright

Nicola Jane Wright – Sixth Generation

Nicola Jane Wright, first child of Iain Wright and Shirley Hill, was born on August 9th, 1982 in Daisy Hill Hospital, Newry, County Down, Northern Ireland. She attended Iveagh Primary School in Rathfriland before completing her secondary education at Banbridge Academy.

Nicola, a bright and able pupil at school, obtained grade "A" in all of her final year examinations at school. She has just completed a 2.1 Honors Degree in History at the University of Durham.

Nicola has inherited the sandy hair so characteristic of the 19th-century Wrights. She is five feet seven inches tall and enjoys reading, swimming, and music.

Suzanne Margaret Wright – Sixth Generation

Suzanne Margaret Wright, second child of Iain Wright and Shirley Hill, was born on April 5th, 1985 at Daisy Hill Hospital, Newry, County Down, Northern Ireland. Suzanne attended Iveagh Primary School in Rathfriland before beginning her secondary education at Newry High School. She is currently an undergraduate student nurse at The Queen's University Belfast.

Suzanne takes a lively interest in local events and is a Sunday school teacher and choir member at Ryans Presbyterian Church.

Her interests include music, walking, swimming, and horses. She is five feet seven inches tall, with brown hair and blue eyes.

Eleanor Elizabeth Wright – Fifth Generation

Eleanor Elizabeth Wright, the second child of Robert and Eva Wright, was born on January 28th, 1949 on the home farm at Finnard, County Down, Northern Ireland.

She attended the local Ballykeel West Primary School and Newry Grammar School. Following a secretarial course at Rathfriland High School, Eleanor joined the law firm of R.A. Mullan and Sons in Newry, County Down.

While working in Newry, Eleanor met a dashing young police constable named James Atchison Laverty. Jimmy, as he is known, was born on November 14th, 1947 and is a native of Ballycastle in Country Antrim.

The couple married on June 3rd, 1972 in Eleanor's home church of Ryans. This small rural Presbyterian church, set among the rolling Drumlins of County Down, has been home church to at least five generations of Wrights.

Following the birth of their first child Karen on June 1, 1973, the family moved to County Antrim, living briefly in Antrim town before moving to the nearby village of Kells, and then finally settling in Ballymena.

Their second daughter Emma was born August 1, 1975, and their third, Louise, August 8, 1981 in Ballymena, County Antrim, Northern Ireland.

JIMMY LAVERTY & ELEANOR WRIGHT, WEDDING DAY, JUNE 3, 1972

THE FAMILY OF ELEANOR WRIGHT & JIMMY LAVERTY
LEFT TO RIGHT: LOUISE LAVERTY, KAREN LAVERTY & EMMA LAVERTY

Jimmy left the Royal Ulster Constabulary in 1977 and began a new career as a landscape gardener. The business he founded has continued to prosper over the years, and he has won awards for artistic merit and standards of maintenance.

Eleanor, apart from a short spell of part-time work, has been a full-time housewife and mother. She and Jimmy are heavily involved in the work and witness of High Kirk Presbyterian Church in Ballymena. In 2000, Eleanor completed a three-year part-time Women's Study Fellowship course at The Belfast Bible College.

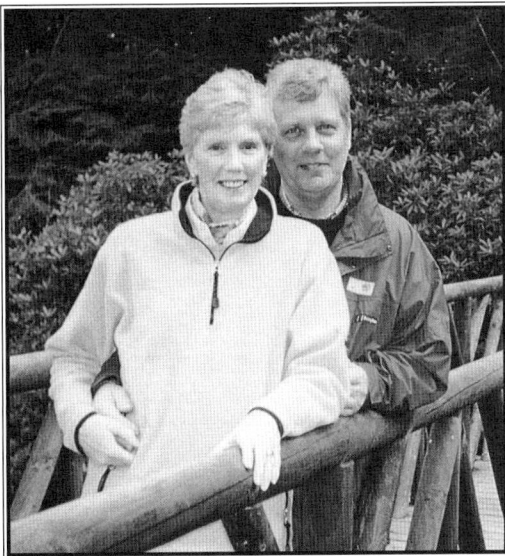

Jimmy has recently given up his landscaping business to go full-time into the work of Christian witness. He and Eleanor are currently studying at the Presbyterian Union Theological College, Belfast and were placed as field workers under the auspices of the Irish Mission towards the end of 2004.

Eleanor is five feet eight inches tall, with brown hair and blue eyes. Her interests include her family, reading, and Church activities.

ELEANOR WRIGHT & HUSBAND JIMMY LAVERTY
TULLYMORE FOREST PARK, APRIL 2000

SIXTH GENERATION

Karen Margaret Jane Laverty, Emma Elizabeth Laverty, Ellen Louise Laverty

Karen Margaret Jane Laverty – Sixth Generation

Karen Margaret Jane Laverty, the first child of Jimmy Laverty and Eleanor Wright, was born on June 1st, 1973 at Rathfriland, County Down, Northern Ireland.

Shortly afterwards, the family moved to Ballymena, County Antrim, where Karen attended Camphill Primary School and then Cambridge House Grammar School for Girls.

She progressed to the University of Ulster at the Belfast Art College campus, where she completed a course in design and communication.

Following graduation, Karen worked for an independent television production company, and then as a trainee with the B.B.C., where she was part of the team that made the critically acclaimed *Eureka Street*, which was shown on network television.

In September 1999, Karen felt a clear call to Christian service and enrolled for a one-year full-time course at The Belfast Bible College. She graduated in June of 2000.

Subsequently, Karen was, for a time, a team leader with the "Exodus Outreach Movement" and visited Peru, Chicago, and central Europe. In 2002, she spent two weeks in Uganda with Evangelical Ministries as part of a work team.

Now living in Ballymena, Karen produces handmade cards with a Christian theme, which she markets as "Karen's Kards." This cottage industry helps fund her outreach work.

Karen is five feet eight inches tall with blond hair and blue eyes. Her interests include music, worship band, traveling, and reading.

Emma Elizabeth Laverty – Sixth Generation

Emma Elizabeth Laverty, the second child of Jimmy Laverty and Eleanor Wright, was born on August 1st, 1975 at Ballymena, County Antrim. Emma attended Camphill Primary School and Cambridge House in her sister Karen's footsteps.

After completing grammar school, Emma took a Higher National Diploma in Leisure Management at Belfast Institute for Higher and Further Education. She then brought this qualification up to full degree level when she attended the University of Luton, graduating in 1997.

Following graduation, Emma worked in the retail sector in both Ballymena and Belfast.

Her life took a dramatic change in direction when she felt called to join the "Teen Challenge U.K." group. This Christian group seeks to work with young people caught up in life-controlling addictions. She was posted to the group's headquarters in Hope House situated outside Swansea, South Wales.

While there, Emma met Simon Evans, a fellow worker who was to become her husband.

Emma Laverty and Simon Evans were married on October 16th, 2002 at High Kirk Presbyterian Church, Ballymena, Country Antrim, Northern Ireland.

Simon and Emma have now moved into their new home at Crosshands a few miles north of Llanelli, South Wales.

Emma is five feet four inches tall, with light brown hair and blue eyes. She retains an interest in sporting activities, is actively involved in church work, and likes reading and music.

SIMON EVANS & EMMA ELIZABETH LAVERTY
WEDDING DAY – OCTOBER 16, 2002

Ellen Louise Laverty – Sixth Generation

Ellen Louise Laverty, third child of Jimmy Laverty and Eleanor Wright, was born on August 8th, 1981 at the Cottage Hospital in Ballymena, County Antrim. Louise attended Carniny Primary School and Cullybackey High School. Her education was interrupted in February 1977 when she developed a form of leukaemia. This was a very difficult time for Louise and her family. With expert medical attention and the prayerful support of family and friends, however, Louise made a full recovery and began to rebuild her life. She became actively involved in the Exodus Outreach Movement and visited Chicago three times to work with homeless and single mothers.

Having completed a two-year course at The Royal School of Dentistry in Belfast, Louise is currently working in a dental practice in Cullybackey, County Antrim.

Louise married Brian William Henry on Monday December 20th, 2004 in High Kirk Presbyterian Church, Ballymena, County Antrim. Brian is an employment support officer for special needs adults.

Their first child, Jonathan William James, was born June 16, 2006 in Antrim General Hospital.

The couple now live in Ahoghill, County Antrim.

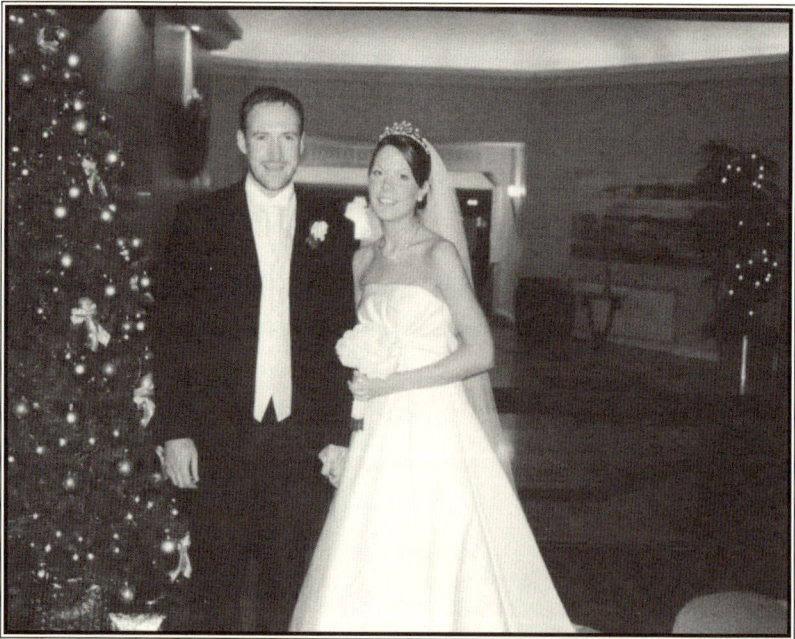

BRIAN WILLIAM HENRY AND ELLEN LOUISE LAVERTY
WEDDING DAY – DECEMBER 20, 2004

SEVENTH GENERATION

Jonathan William James Henry – Seventh Generation

Jonathan William James Henry, first child of Brain William Henry and Louise Laverty, was born on June 16th, 2006 in Antrim General Hospital, County Antrim, Northern Ireland.

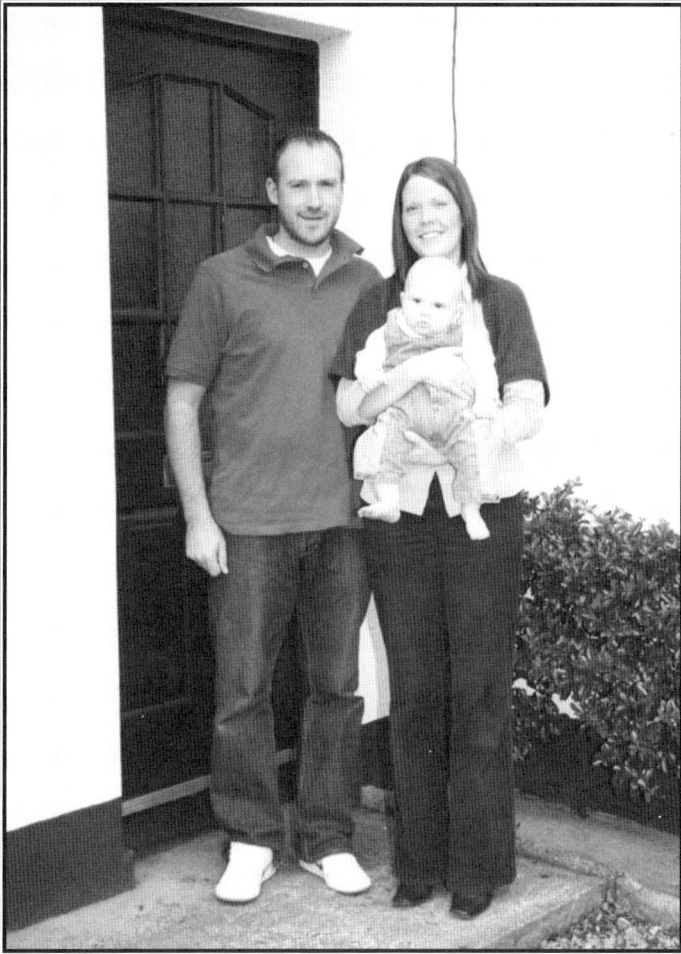

THE HENRY FAMILY
LEFT TO RIGHT: BRIAN, LOUISE, AND BABY JONATHAN AT FINNARD, WHERE BABY JONATHAN IS THE SEVENTH GENERATION CONNECTED WITH THE ANCIENT TOWNLAND

Samuel David "Uel" Wright – Fifth Generation

Samuel David "Uel" Wright, the third child and second son of Robert Wright and Eva Dugan, was born on July 2nd, 1952.

We are indebted to Uel Wright for the following account of his family.

"According to Lizzie Morgan, a 'fields and house' working woman who had a sixty year association with the farm at Finnard, my father threw his cap into the air at the news of my arrival, before going to the agricultural market held on Wednesday of each week in Rathfriland.

"My paternal grandfather was R. S. (Sam) Wright, of whom I have only one memory. During the last few weeks of his life in September 1956, I was taken to see him at his retirement home in Rathfriland. On entering his bedroom, I recall him gesturing at me to go and look in the top drawer of a dressing table, where I found a box of sugar coated jelly sweets. I am glad my only memory of him is such a pleasant one.

"My grandfather had met his future wife, Minnie McClelland, while she was principal of Ballykeel West Primary School, in the opening years of the twentieth century.

"It was to that same single room building where my grandmother had taught, that I began my primary education in 1957. The room, divided by a curtain to produce two teaching areas, was heated by coal fires, and while the days of pupils bringing 'firing' with them to stoke the furnaces were long gone, conditions were primitive, with writing taught by means of wooden pens, steel nibs, and two ink-wells per desk.

"In good weather, I enjoyed the mile long walk from home to school, and while it may be tempting to pander to a rose tinted romantic ideal, and say I went bare footed on good summer days, no such thing happened. My mother, meticulous in the home and in the appearance of her children, ensured that shoes were not only worn, but polished, and on wet or cold mornings my father was called from the farmyard to deliver us to school in the family Vauxhall 2000 car.

"In Irish agricultural circles, primogeniture was, and indeed is, still very much the order of the day, and being the second son on the farm, much speculation surrounded my future career. My Aunt Margaret Dugan (wife of my mother's brother) was a firm advocate of the view that I should become a Presbyterian Minister. To be fair, I think this was her personal opinion, and no pressure to enter the ministry was ever exerted by my parents.

"I was, however, sent to Newry Grammar School and the enjoinder, 'You'll have to make something of yourself', was an implicit reminder that a career on the family farm was not an option.

"My days at Secondary School seemed to pass remarkably quickly and I left with a creditable haul of certificates to study Amenity Horticulture at college. On reflection, this was a decision based more on pragmatism than ambition. My mother had pointed out that environmental type jobs were frequently being advertised in the press.

"After an initial year of study in Northern Ireland, I crossed to England for a further three years study at Askham Bryan College, York.

"Those years in England were to have a major impact on me, and while the qualifications gained quickly secured me employment, I have always held the view that the life experience far outweighed any academic advancement.

"Back on Irish soil and now twenty-two years old, the inevitable question of a wife began to loom large.

"All my adult life I have been involved in fund raising for Third World charities, and it was at one of those events — a twenty-four hour table tennis marathon — that I met my future wife, June Groves.

"June, the daughter of Bertie and Nellie Groves, a farming family of four girls and two boys, lived within five miles of Finnard, and while our parents knew each other, June and I had never met until that charity event in May 1975. We quickly made up for lost time, and were married on February 7, 1976, in Brookvale Presbyterian Church, County Down, Northern Ireland.

SAMUEL DAVID "UEL" WRIGHT & JUNE GROVES
WEDDING DAY, FEBRUARY 7, 1976

"After a brief spell in Banbridge, County Down, I gained promotion and we moved to Portrush on the North Antrim coast where both our children were born, Joanne on March 3, 1980, and Sarah on January 28, 1982.

"In the same year, my job once more necessitated moving, and we were able to design and have built our present home situated in the townland of Finnard, where the Wrights have had a provable presence for 200 years.

"June, having given up her position as a Bank Official when the children were born, returned to banking on a part-time basis in 1986.

"My mother died in November 1987 as a result of complications following a routine gall bladder operation. This was a great blow to the family, not least my father, who continued to live in a retirement bungalow on the family farm until his death in July of 1996.

AN ORIGINAL PAINTING OF FINNARD RING FORT BY MARY CLARK, WHICH HANGS IN THE HOME OF UEL AND JUNE WRIGHT

"My choice of career always dictated that I follow science type subjects though my heart was always with the arts. Aged 39, I decided to indulge my interest and enrolled to study Literature in English at Queen's University in Belfast. After eight years of study two evenings per week, I graduated with a 2.1 Hons Degree in 1998.

Uel Wright & Family, Left to right Seated: Sarah Wright, June Wright & Joanne Wright, Standing: Uel Wright

"Our eldest daughter, Joanne, graduated in 2003 from The University of St. Andrews Scotland, with a Masters Degree in Modern Languages. Our second daughter, Sarah, also graduated in 2003 with First Class Honours from The University of Durham, England. Sarah was also awarded the Gerald Collier Memorial Prize for being the top student in her College of St. Hilde and St. Bede. She is currently teaching in the Preparatory Department of Newcastle-Upon-Tyne Grammar School and shares a flat with her sister who has just completed a teaching qualification at the University of Newcastle-Upon-Tyne.

"I head up the landscaping department of a large public section housing authority, and June continues to work part-time as a bank official."

AUNT MATILDA McCLELLAND "TILLY'S" COTTAGE, FINNARD, JUNE 1999, LEFT TO RIGHT: BARBARA McCLELLAND, MAUD VALLANCE, NORMAN McCLELLAND & UEL WRIGHT

SIXTH GENERATION

Joanne Wright, Sarah Ellen Margaret Wright

Joanne Wright – Sixth Generation

Joanne Wright, first child of Samuel David "Uel" Wright and June Groves, was born on March 3rd, 1980 in Ballymoney, County Antrim, Northern Ireland. Joanne, a 2003 graduate from The University of St. Andrews, Scotland with an M.A. Hons. in Modern Languages, has just completed a post-graduate teaching qualification at The University of Newcastle-Upon-Tyne, England. She took up a post in the St. Venerable Bede Church of England School, Sunderland in September 2004. Joanne has completed her Duke of Edinburgh Gold Award, and was presented with her certificate at Buckingham Palace in July 1999 at a ceremony attended by H.R.H. The Duke of Edinburgh.

Sarah Ellen Margaret Wright – Sixth Generation

Sarah Wright, second child of Samuel David "Uel" Wright and June Groves, was born on January 28th, 1982 in Ballymoney, County Antrim, Northern Ireland. Sarah graduated in 2003 from The University of Durham, England with First Class Honours in Education, and was awarded the Gerard Collier Memorial Prize for being the top student in her College. Sarah has completed her Duke of Edinburgh Gold Award, and was presented with her certificate at a ceremony in Hillsborough Castle, County Down attended by H.R.H. The Duke of Edinburgh in May 2002. Sarah is currently teaching in the preparatory department of Newcastle-Upon-Tyne Grammar School.

Samuel Joseph Wright – Fourth Generation

Samuel Joseph Wright, the sixth child and second son of Robert Samuel Wright and Mary Minnie McClelland of Finnard, Ardaragh, Newry, County Down, was born on June 28th, 1920.

Sam was brought up on the family farm at Finnard with his four sisters and two brothers. Farming in those days was hard work, and with few labor-saving devices every member of the family was allotted tasks around the farm.

Sam attended the local Ballykeel Primary School where his mother had taught until 1910. He was a quick learner with a special aptitude for English and reading. As his elder brother Bob was destined to inherit the family farm, it was decided that Sam should be given a grammar school education. To this end, he was taken from the local primary school at age eight and sent to Newry Model School. This involved leaving home before eight each morning and catching a bus to Newry, followed by a further walk to the school. This daily routine, combined with indifferent health as a child, contributed to Sam missing quite a few days from school, and as such his chance of a grammar school place passed by.

The world of business was seen as a suitable alternative, and in 1936 Sam took up an apprenticeship in the department store Fosters in Newry, where he remained until 1944. Promotion was difficult to achieve at Fosters, and Sam decided to seek new pastures. He applied for a job in Wilson's of Enniskillen and was successful. During his time there he met his future wife Molly Campbell. Molly was a highly intelligent girl, having won one of only four scholarships in all of County Fermanagh for free higher education. However, she passed up the chance of a university education in favour of the Northern Ireland Civil Service. The couple were married in St. Macartan's Cathedral, Enniskillen on June 22nd, 1948.

By this stage, Sam had secured a post in Walker's Department store in Armagh City, which was to be home for the rest of his life. The couple had five children: Helen, born in 1949; Roberta, born in 1951; Clive, born in 1954; Jane, born in 1962; and Emma, born in 1963.

During the period of civil unrest in Northern Ireland known as the Troubles, Walker's shop was destroyed by fire and the owner decided to reduce the size of the new business, offering Sam the soft furnishings part of the business in separate premises. With Molly's help the new venture flourished and is still a principal business in Armagh City today, run by Roberta, her sister Jane, and husband David.

Sadly, Molly did not have long to enjoy the new business—she died at the early age of 57 on June 26th, 1983. Sam's health began to deteriorate from mid-1991 and he died October 26th, 1996 aged 76 years. He and Molly are buried in the Presbyterian Cemetery in Armagh City.

Sam and Molly were members of the Mall Presbyterian Church in Armagh City, where Sam served as Clerk of Session for 18 years. A Christian couple, they leave a legacy for their children of faith in God, hard work, and love for each other.

WEDDING DAY – JUNE 22, 1948, MOLLY CAMPBELL & SAMUEL WRIGHT,
LEFT TO RIGHT: ETHEL MOFFAT, MOLLY CAMPBELL, SAMUEL WRIGHT & DAVID WRIGHT

SAMUEL JOSEPH WRIGHT AND MARY ELIZABETH CAMPBELL, MARRIAGE CERTIFICATE

THE WRIGHTS OF ARMAGH, BACK ROW, LEFT TO RIGHT:
SAMUEL WRIGHT, EMMA WRIGHT, ROBERTA WRIGHT, JANE WRIGHT. FRONT ROW, LEFT TO RIGHT:
MOLLY WRIGHT, HELEN ANNE WRIGHT & CLIVE WRIGHT

FIFTH GENERATION

Helen Anne Wright, Roberta Mary Wright, Clive Samuel Wright, Jane Elizabeth Wright, Emma Margaret Wright

Helen Anne Wright – Fifth Generation

Helen Anne Wright, eldest child of Samuel Joseph Wright and Molly Campbell, was born on March 25th, 1949. Helen was to be the first of five children born into a happy family home.

She was a child with a vivid imagination who loved reading and organizing her siblings and friends into all kinds of make-believe games. She loved to sing and play the piano, and occasionally was called upon to play the organ in church when the organist was absent. She was quite a good sports all-rounder and played hockey and netball for school teams in addition to singing in the choir and acting as a prefect.

She studied French at Queen's University from 1967 to 1972, a four-year honors degree course with an additional year spent as an "assistante" in a French school in the suburbs of Paris. This was an exciting experience and the beginning of a long love affair with Paris, French life, and French culture.

After a year spent teaching French at the secondary school in Armagh, Helen married Gordon McConville, whom she had met through the local youth group at church, and who had just graduated from Cambridge, where he read a degree in modern languages. They were married in the Mall Presbyterian Church on August 8th, 1973 with all three sisters acting as bridesmaids. Gordon was born on April 30th, 1951 in Edinburgh, Scotland. After their marriage Gordon and Helen moved to Edinburgh, where Gordon was to study theology before entering the Presbyterian ministry. Helen found herself unable to teach in Scotland because of the different qualifications, so she supported them both with various jobs until Alistair was born on April 25, 1975. By the time Carys was born on December 10, 1976, the family was back in Ireland, where Gordon was studying for a doctorate in the Old Testament. By then it was clear that his calling was to a teaching ministry, and after the arrival of Andrew on March 14, 1980, he moved the family to Bristol, where he had been appointed lecturer in the Old Testament at Trinity College, an Anglican theological college that trained men and women for ministry both in the Church of England and overseas. There he worked alongside George Carey, who was later to become Archbishop of Canterbury. The family spent nine very happy years there.

Claire was born on January 31, 1983, the same year that Helen's mother died of cancer at the early age of 57.

The family's next move took them to Oxford and another theological seminary, Wycliffe Hall. These were very happy years where the children grew up in the stimulating and cosmopolitan atmosphere of a bustling university city. At school, they were constantly meeting children from different countries and different cultures. Wycliffe Hall had students from all over the world through its doors. It was a very rich experience and a real privilege to be part of a living Christian community. Church life was exciting, too, with a very lively group of 11- to 18-year-olds with which the four young people did everything from drama to music to Bible study and work in the community.

Helen worked for a time on the staff of St. Andrew's Church, her main responsibility the leadership of a large Mums and toddlers group.

These were formative years, and all of their children have since looked for ways of helping those less fortunate than themselves, including gap-year service with Latin Link, a Christian organization working with the Church in various South American countries. They have helped to build churches, orphanages, and teaching centers in Bolivia, Argentina, Peru, Nicaragua and Ecuador.

Their latest move brought them to Cheltenham, the heart of the Cotswolds, where Gordon is now a professor teaching the Old Testament at the University of Gloucestershire, mostly to post-graduate students from all over the world. He is much in demand as a speaker and writer on his specialist subjects of Deuteronomy and Jeremiah, and has recently been to India to give a series of lectures at a seminary in the foothills of the Himalayas. Helen has found a job with a French specialist holiday company, which allows her to renew her love affair with France. All have enjoyed the benefits of frequent holidays in France.

GORDON McCONVILLE & HELEN ANNE WRIGHT
WEDDING DAY – AUGUST 8, 1973

HELEN ANNE & GORDON McCONVILLE WITH GRANDCHILDREN, EWAN, 3 MONTHS &
LOUISA, 4 YEARS, DECEMBER 2002

SIXTH GENERATION

Alistair Gordon McConville, Carys Elizabeth McConville, Andrew Samuel Walter McConville, Claire Alexandra McConville

Alistair Gordon McConville – Sixth Generation

Alistair Gordon McConville, first child of Helen Anne Wright and Gordon McConville, was born on April 25th, 1975 in Edinburgh, Scotland. He graduated from Cambridge in 1997 with a degree in Theology. While at university, he represented his college (Fitzwilliam) in both football and cricket, and has continued to play both games when he has the opportunity. He finally talked his mother into allowing a dog into the family household when they moved to Oxford, and Ben is a much-loved addition.

After graduation, Alistair spent six months working in Paris for a pharmaceutical company so that he could perfect his French and gain business experience in a different country. A year of accountancy followed before he decided to become a teacher. After a year of teaching in London, he married Joanne Griffiths on July 21st, 2001 in St. Phillips Church, Cambridge, England. They have two children: Louisa Kate, born November 25, 1998, and Ewan Patrick, born on September 3, 2002. They returned to Cheltenham for Alistair to take up a post teaching religious studies at Cheltenham Ladies' College, and they live just 15 minute's walk from doting grandparents.

ALISTAIR, LOUISA & JO McCONVILLE, JUNE 2002

SEVENTH GENERATION

Louisa Kate McConville, Ewan Patrick McConville

Louisa Kate McConville – Seventh Generation

Louisa "Lulu" Kate McConville, first child of Alistair McConville and Jo Griffiths, was born on November 25th, 1998 in Cambridge, Cambridgeshire, England.

Ewan Patrick McConville – Seventh Generation

Ewan Patrick McConville, the second child of Alistair McConville and Jo Griffiths, was born on September 3rd, 2002 in Cheltenham, Gloucestershire, England.

Carys Elizabeth McConville – Sixth Generation

Carys Elizabeth McConville, second child of Helen Anne Wright and Gordon McConville, was born on December 10th, 1976 in Newtonards, County Down, Northern Ireland.

Carys has decided on teaching as a career and is just about to start her first teaching job in Nottingham. After leaving the University, she married fellow student Ben Thompson on December 2nd, 2000 in St. Matthews Parish Church, Gloucestershire, England. They have just returned from a year in Portugal, where Ben worked for Mars (Master Foods) outside Lisbon, and Carys taught English. This gave their parents good reason to holiday in Portugal in 2002, although they were glad to have them back in the U.K.

Carys is a keen actress and has spent two summers working with the National Youth Theatre in London. She also took lead roles with the City of Oxford Theatre Guild and has toured with a student production to the Edinburgh Festival. She spent her gap year in Bolivia helping to build dormitories at a school for deaf children, where she learned to "sign," and also took some

BACK, LEFT TO RIGHT: BEN AND CARYS
FRONT: ALICE AND ROSIE

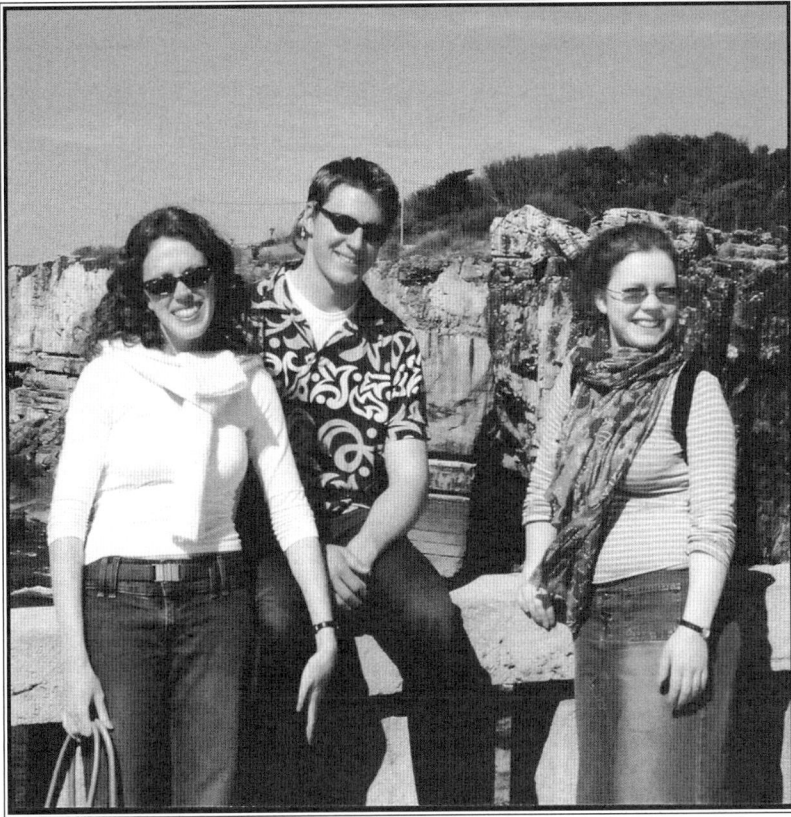

CARYS & BEN THOMPSON & CLAIRE MCCONVILLE, PORTUGAL, FEBRUARY 2002

classes for the younger children at the school, all of which stands her in good stead for her career in the classroom.

Carys and Ben have two daughters: Rosie Grace, born October 13, 2003, and Alice Elizabeth, born November 28, 2005. Both girls were born at Queen's Medical Centre, Nottingham.

SEVENTH GENERATION

Rosie Grace Thompson, Alice Elizabeth Thompson

Rosie Grace Thompson – Seventh Generation

Rosie Grace Thompson, first child of Carys Elizabeth McConville and Ben Thompson, was born on October 13th, 2003 in Nottingham, England.

Alice Elizabeth Thompson – Seventh Generation

Alice Elizabeth Thompson, second child of Carys Elizabeth McConville and Ben Thompson, was born on November 28th, 2005 at the Queen's Medical Center, Nottingham, England.

ROSIE GRACE THOMPSON

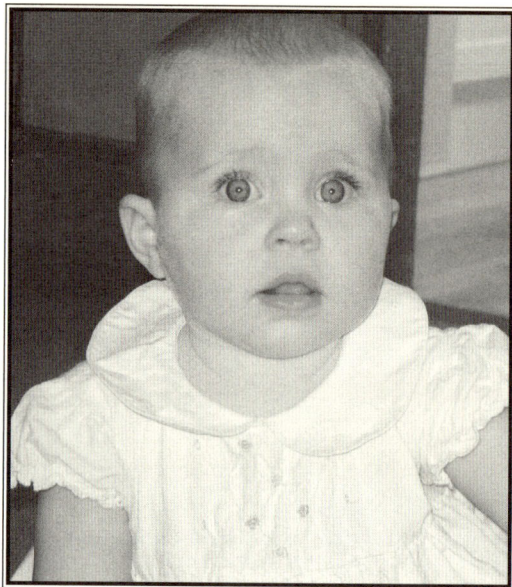

ALICE ELIZABETH THOMPSON

Andrew Samuel Walter McConville – Sixth Generation

Andrew Samuel Walter McConville, third child of Helen Anne Wright and Gordon McConville, was born on March 14th, 1980 in Cambridge, Cambridgeshire, Northern Ireland.

Andrew–Andy to his friends–is a keen sportsman and, along with Alistair, a longtime supporter of The Manchester United football team. He regularly plays football for the church team. Always looking for the next challenge, he has white-water rafted for two weeks in Nepal, hiked the Inca Trail to Machu Piccu in the Andes, and explored ancient cities in the desert in Yemen. He spent his gap year in Peru, where he worked with a team of young people attached to a local mission organization. They helped to build an orphanage in the Andes for children orphaned by the Shining Path guerilla group, and also worked with kids in a shantytown in Lima. Andy pursued theology and religious studies at the University of Gloucestershire, where he was Vice President of the Christian Union.

Andy married Stephanie Ruth Dyke on September 4th, 2004 in Cambray Baptist Church, Cheltenham. Stephanie was born on April 25th, 1981 in Chester, England.

After working for two years with the Cheam Baptist Church, the couple is now back living and working in Cheltenham.

LEFT TO RIGHT: GORDON AND HELEN McCONVILLE, ANDREW SAMUEL WALTER McCONVILLE, STEPHANIE RUTH DYKE, BARBARA AND COLIN DYKE, WEDDING DAY – SEPTEMBER 4TH, 2004

Claire Alexandra McConville – Sixth Generation

Claire Alexandra McConville, fourth child of Helen Anne Wright and Gordon McConville, was born on January 31st, 1983 in Bristol, England.

Claire has just finished her first term at Exeter College, Oxford, where she is studying English. She is very gifted artistically and loves everything to do with the theatre and acting. She has taken leading roles in productions at the Everyman Theatre in Cheltenham. In school productions, she has represented her school in public speaking competitions, and was Head of House in her final year at school. She also loves to read, listen to music (all kinds), and play the piano and violin.

Claire spent four months in Ecuador and Nicaragua working alongside local churches in their outreach to the poor. She took classes in Spanish before going and made great strides in the language while there which enabled her to have very special relationships with the children in the shanty town who came in daily to the feeding centers. She continues to have a real heart for the people she met there and from whom she learned so much about God and His love.

Claire married Nick John Widdows on July 16th, 2005 in St. Michael's Church, Stoke Gifford, Bristol. Nick is training to be an accountant, and Claire is currently pursuing a post-graduate certificate in Education with a view to teaching in the near future. The couple is currently living in Bristol

CLAIRE ALEXANDRA McCONVILLE AND NICK JOHN WIDDOWS
WEDDING DAY – JULY 16, 2005

Roberta Mary Wright – Fifth Generation

Roberta Mary Wright, second child of Samuel Wright and Mary Elizabeth Campbell, was born on May 8th, 1951 at the then family home in Lisnally Gardens, Armagh City, Northern Ireland.

Roberta attended the local Armstrong Primary School and Armagh Girls High School. She progressed to the Belfast College of Business Studies, where she successfully completed a Higher National Diploma.

She began work in the Personnel Department of the Inglis Bakery Group in Belfast, followed by a period of employment in Greater Manchester where she worked as a personnel manager with the firm of Tilly and Henderson.

The family business of Wright's Soft Furnishings, started in 1976 by her father and mother, had by 1980 grown to the extent that her talents could be employed to develop and further expand the business.

Her return coincided with a huge change in the furnishings industry, with the consumer showing an increased interest in designer fabrics and styles. To meet this demand, an extension of the business floor space was required, and in 1994 the premises next door became available, were acquired, and an Interior Design Service launched.

The death of her mother in 1983, and the death of her father just three weeks after the firm celebrated its 20th anniversary, were major blows to Roberta, but the business acumen she had clearly inherited from her parents stood her in good stead. She continues to lead her staff of ten with vigor and foresight.

Further expansion at the turn of the century saw her and a business partner set up a high-quality making-up service. This business currently employs six people in the market town of Tandragee, County Armagh.

Roberta is a member of the Chamber of Commerce in Armagh and Vice President of the City Center Management Committee.

As the only member of her immediate family now residing in Northern Ireland, Roberta continues to live in the family home, a welcoming focal point for gatherings.

ROBERTA MARY WRIGHT, DECEMBER 2002

A lifetime member of The Mall Presbyterian Church, Roberta enjoys traveling and reading. She is five feet five inches tall with brown hair and hazel eyes.

Clive Samuel Wright – Fifth Generation

Clive Samuel Wright, third child of Samuel Wright and Mary Elizabeth Campbell, was born on March 19th, 1954 in Portadown, County Armagh, Northern Ireland.

Clive Samuel Wright and Janet Price Baldwin were married in Trinity Church, Lanark, Scotland on September 4th, 1981.

Janet, born on April 3rd, 1955, the only daughter of Edwin and Marion Baldwin, was transported not only into membership of the Wright clan, but also to a new home in Chester, England, where Clive had a post teaching languages. In 1984, however, the couple returned to Scotland to settle near Stirling. It was there that their children were born. Clive continues to work as a schoolmaster teaching French and German; Janet is a locum pharmacist.

CLIVE WRIGHT & JANET BALDWIN, WEDDING DAY – SEPTEMBER 4, 1981
LEFT TO RIGHT: JANE WRIGHT SEARLE, MOLLY CAMPBELL WRIGHT, CLIVE WRIGHT, JANET BALDWIN
WRIGHT, SAM WRIGHT JR., EMMA WRIGHT MACLEOD

Their eldest, Sheila, remains in a way forever their youngest and one and only little girl, as she died at just two days old. In her footsteps have followed three boys: Michael Edward, and Andrew Donald, born in 1987 and 1988 respectively, and then Philip James, the baby of the family, who arrived in 1996.

Janet's round of pharmaceutical work continues to take her to a wide variety of retail stores, where she has built up a circle of acquaintances both professional and personal. As Philip leaves nursery school, she is beginning to take on work on a more regular basis. When not working, she has links with church groups (the family are members of Chalmers Church in Bridge of Allan) and enjoys reading and some sports.

Clive, in his spare time, enjoys sports, especially golf and tennis. He also has inherited the typical Wright interest in writing. While in no way a professional in the trade, he has had a range of his poetry and short stories published in different periodicals in Britain, as well as at home in Ireland. More recently, he has taken up playwriting, and three of his plays have

LEFT TO RIGHT: MICHAEL WRIGHT, PHILIP WRIGHT &
ANDREW WRIGHT, AUGUST 2001

been performed in local theaters. One of them, *The Long Way Home*, is about an American from Chicago revisiting his roots in Scotland. Rights are available for an American premiere!

The family sends their warmest greetings to all of the wider family and would be delighted to hear from them, whether in Britain, Ireland, or America.

Sixth Generation

Sheila Wright, Michael Edward Wright, Andrew Donald Wright, Philip James Wright

Sheila Wright – Sixth Generation

Sheila Wright, first child of Clive Samuel Wright and Janet Price Baldwin, was born on April 8th, 1985 in Stirling, Scotland, and died on April 10th, 1985.

Michael Edward Wright – Sixth Generation

Michael Edward Wright, second child of Clive Samuel Wright and Janet Price Baldwin, was born on March 24th, 1987 in Stirling, Scotland.

By 1999, both Michael and Andrew had completed their primary education at Beaconhurst School in Bridge of Allan, the school where Clive also teaches. The old man is pleased to report that they didn't give him too much of a hard time there! In 2000, they moved for their secondary education to the nearby Dollar Academy. Little Philip will start at nursery school in Beaconhurst at the same time.

Perhaps energy is the key word for the boys. Never the early-to-bed types (alas!) they fill their free time with sports, rollerblading, and cycling, not to mention TV and Play Station! Both are members of local sports clubs. Michael's main sport is athletics, and he has won medals at Scottish regional level in 100m and 200m. Andrew's first love has always been soccer, and he is showing a lot of promise as he works his way up through the youth teams of the local club, Stirling Albion. Both play rugby and were also in the unusual position in the school team of having Clive as their coach in 1999. They had a good year, with only two defeats and a good number of ties to their names. The family is fortunate, as the cottage where they live is directly opposite a park, big enough for games of all kinds, and also in possession of swings and slides, which suits little Philip down to the ground!

Andrew Donald Wright – Sixth Generation

Andrew Donald Wright, the third child of Clive Samuel Wright and Janet Price Baldwin, was born on October 28th, 1988 in Stirling, Scotland.

Philip James Wright – Sixth Generation

Philip James Wright, fourth child of Clive Samuel Wright and Janet Baldwin, was born on July 2nd, 1996 in Stirling, Scotland.

Jane Elizabeth Wright – Fifth Generation

Jane Elizabeth Wright, fourth child of Samuel Wright and Mary Elizabeth Campbell, was born on April 18th, 1962 in Portadown, County Armagh, Northern Ireland. Her mother said she was her most difficult birth, and Jane believes she has continued with that stubbornness and gritty resistance to change all of her life!

We are indebted to Jane Wright Searle for the following account of her life.

"My childhood was truly very happy. I adored my mother – she had the softest skin and gentlest nature of anyone I have ever known. She encouraged us children to believe we could do anything or go anywhere. She had a love of literature and travel, but mostly it was her love of people that inspired me. She has continued to be my role model throughout life.

"My dad, Sam, was a straightforward farming sort of man. He spoke his mind and in that we were alike! We often clashed but he loved me dearly and I always knew that he wanted the best for my life.

LEFT TO RIGHT: JANE, DAVID, EMILY & LYDIA SEARLE, 1992

LEFT TO RIGHT: JANE, DAVID, LYDIA (AGE 7), & EMILY (AGE 3) SEARLE 1995

"We lived throughout my childhood in Armagh, where my father worked in a large department store, and then in his own soft furnishing business. Armagh is a lovely city – full of history and culture, but it has been badly scarred by the fighting over the past 30 years. Five of the girls in my class at school lost their fathers in the violence. Death and sudden loss were something Armagh people understood well.

"At school I was totally uninspired, although I usually did quite well. I have always loved to write and spent hours putting together comic books with my own stories and interviews. I made up poems and riddles and read them to my younger sister, Emma. My love of writing is something that still continues today.

"I took English, French, and Latin at A level and then followed that with a degree in English and French at the Polytechnic outside Belfast. It was at this point in my studies that my mum, Molly, died of cancer. It really knocked me sideways, but I returned home to Armagh from Belfast and did a one year Personal Assistant's Course at Armagh College of Further Education. I was awarded the top marks for Scotland and Ireland in the London Chamber of Commerce and Industry exams, and went to London for a presentation ceremony.

"In July 1984, I moved to Bristol to take up a secretarial job at the University and to live with my older sister, Helen, and her family. It was whilst I was working in Bristol that I met my husband, David Searle, who was studying for his Doctorate in Engineering. David was born May 1, 1957. We married on December 18, 1985, in Armagh.

"It is perhaps David, more than anyone, who has been responsible for getting me to travel! I am someone who thrives on stability and I have never completely broken my emotional ties with the Ireland I love so much. David was born and raised in Africa and is an adventurous spirit. We are an interesting team.

"Our first daughter, Lydia, was born on March 29, 1988, in Bradford, West Yorkshire, where we were living whilst David continued his studies. In March 1990, when Lydia was two, we moved to Madison, Indiana, USA with David's work for a large American Engine company. After 18 months we were moved again, this time to Charleston, South Carolina, where the warm climate was a welcome change for us British! Our daughter, Emily, was born there on January 30, 1992, and is incredibly proud of her American Passport.

"The girls are my pride and joy! Like all mums I suppose! Lydia is now eleven and is sensitive and gentle natured. She plays the piano and the saxophone. Her teachers say she shows real ability in creative writing. She reads all the time.

"Emily is seven and full of mischief. She plays the piano and goes to gym. She loves animals and wants to be a vet and devote her life to sick dogs. We shall see!

"David and I are both very involved in our church, a smaller inner city Anglican parish. I teach Sunday school, help in a youth group, and am on the leadership team. David is the Treasurer and on the PCC.

"David is a Director in Holset Engineering, which is based in Huddersfield. We live in Shipley, West Yorkshire, in an old four-story Victorian house with lots of creaks and draughts. We have three cats and a hamster who all seem to survive quite nicely amidst the noise.

"My father, Sam, died in October 1996, and he is very much missed by all of us. The children talk fondly of him. He had endless nicknames for them. However, life goes on and I am part of the next generation. As I find out more about those in my family, who have lived in times gone by, I am fascinated by the personalities and the lives they lived. I know that everything I am is through the loving start given to me by my parents. They were good decent, loving people who devoted their lives to their children, and that is the legacy they have left behind. I hope I can do the same."

SIXTH GENERATION

Lydia Catherine Searle, Emily Louise Searle

Lydia Catherine Searle – Sixth Generation

Lydia Catherine Searle, first child of David Earle Searle and Jane Wright, was born on March 29th, 1988 in Bradford, West Yorkshire, England.

Emily Louise Searle – Sixth Generation

Emily Louise Searle, second child of David Earle Searle and Jane Wright, was born on January 30th, 1992 in Charleston, South Carolina.

Emma Margaret Wright – Fifth Generation

Emma Margaret Wright, fifth child of Samuel Wright and Mary Elizabeth Campbell, was born on December 19th, 1963 in Portadown, County Armagh, Northern Ireland. Emma and her sister, Janie, only 20 months older, became the "wee ones"! It was exciting having three older siblings who were off to college when they were still quite young and they always felt spoiled and protected by them. Helen and Roberta used to have Emma and Janie stay in their flats in Belfast. Clive told the most fantastic bedtime stories about Noggin and Nog and scary mythological monsters! Emma and Janie were a double act in many ways and even played piano duets together for assembled family members! Janie was the live-wire and Emma was the quieter one, but they were incredibly close and very loyal to each other. Their parents praised them for being themselves and never compared them to each other, which helped them to be independent whilst remaining best friends. Emma and Janie fought like wild cats at times, with nipping and hair-pulling being the order of the day, but they always made up! Samuel and Molly created a relaxed and happy home filled with love and encouragement. The five children still remain close and continue to love and support each other and their families.

Emma's memories of all those older cousins on her dad's side are vague in some ways, as many were already living away from home by the time she could remember, but Daphne was the nearest in age and everyone enjoyed her visits to the farm. Emma can visualize with pleasure the warmth of those Sunday teatime get-togethers with the aunts and uncles.

Emma kept busy growing up in Armagh with Girls' Brigade, piano, church, and school, where she enjoyed languages and English, and got involved in drama and public speaking. She ended up being Head Girl in her final year, largely because of her diplomatic nature. It was not always easy to act as liason between pupils and teachers, and remain on good terms with both groups! She gained respect for teachers on the whole, and went on to choose teaching as her career.

Emma went to Edinburgh University in 1982 to study French and German and ended up with a degree in French and Spanish. The highlights of her university days were spending a year as a language assistant in Nancy, France and meeting her future husband, John Macleod. John was born on October 24th, 1963. They married August 7th, 1987 in the Mall Presbyterian Church, Armagh City, County Armagh, Northern Ireland. The couple are now divorced. Emma has taught languages in an Edinburgh School for Girls since 1987, but has taken a lot of time off to be with the children over the years. She loves her work and hopes to develop her interest in guidance in the coming years. Meanwhile, Emma does youth and drama work in her church and enjoys doing battle with the garden and never-ending housework.

Emma and John had two children: Rebecca Mary Macleod, born January 12, 1992, and Callum Samuel Macleod, born February 4, 1994. Emma is proud of her children and they are proud to be Scottish, but equally proud of their Northern Irish roots.

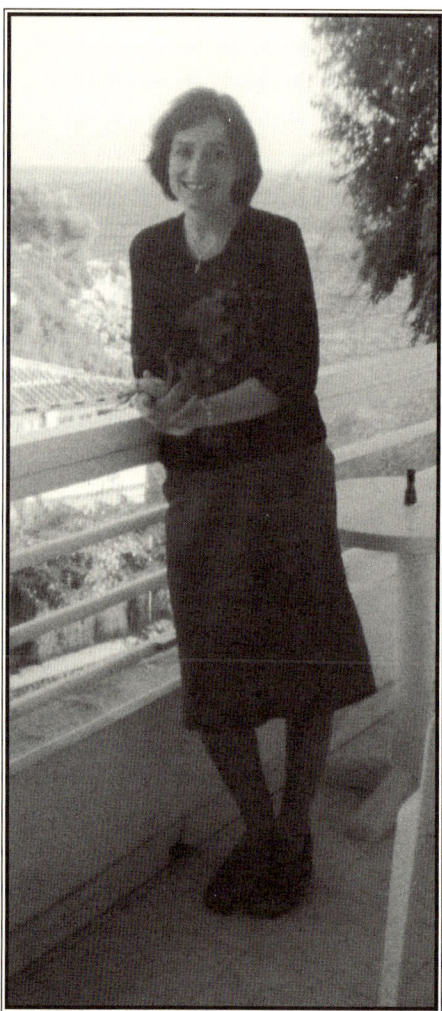

EMMA WRIGHT MACLEOD, OCTOBER 2002

268

SIXTH GENERATION

Rebecca Mary Macleod, Callum Samuel Macleod

Rebecca Mary Macleod – Sixth Generation

Rebecca Mary Macleod, firstborn of John Macleod and Emma Wright, was born on January 12th, 1992 in Edinburgh, Scotland. Rebecca enjoys English in school, plays the flute and hockey, and is very much like her Mum.

Callum Samuel Macleod – Sixth Generation

Callum Samuel Macleod, second child of John Macleod and Emma Wright, was born on February 4th, 1994 in Edinburgh, Scotland. Callum is mad about sports in general, football in particular, and dreams of playing for Scotland (or Ireland if he is not good enough for Scotland)!

REBECCA & CALLUM MACLEOD, DONEGAL, JULY 2002

David Wright – Fourth Generation

David Wright, seventh child of Robert Samuel Wright and Mary "Minnie" McClelland, was born on September 9th, 1925 at Finnard, Donaghmore, County Down, Northern Ireland. As the baby of the family, he was spoiled by his older siblings, who took turns looking after him. He attended Ballykeel West Primary School, a short distance from Finnard. In April 1936, he moved to the Model School in Newry, where his sister Bertha taught, and studied there until July 1938. He was a bright boy, especially good at mental arithmetic. His parents then paid for him to attend Newry Intermediate School, where he had the academic ability to continue his education; however, his love of working on the land was more important, so he left school and achieved his ambition of becoming a farmer.

He is reputed to have met his future wife Mary Elizabeth (Elsie) Glenny when they were in their prams! Certainly they both attended Ryans Church and went to the same school in Newry, often traveling on the bus together. They married on August 3rd, 1949 and set up home in a small holding (formerly the McCracken homestead) just across the fields from Elsie's family farm in Dysart. They started off with a farm, a few cows, some pigs, hens, and sheep, taking more land locally for crops and grazing. They installed a milking machine and gradually built up the dairy herd.

DAVID WRIGHT & MARY ELIZABETH (ELSIE) GLENNY, WEDDING DAY – AUGUST 3, 1949. LEFT TO RIGHT: PAT GLENNY, DAVID WRIGHT, MARY ELIZABETH (ELSIE) GLENNY, FLO GLENNY, SAMUEL CROMIE (BEST MAN)

DAVID WRIGHT AND MARY ELIZABETH GLENNY, MARRIAGE CERTIFICATE – AUGUST 3, 1949

In 1961, after the death of Elsie' father, David and Elsie took over the "Glenny" farm, and with a tremendous amount of hard work built it into a very successful dairy farm. This required an extensive program of building silos, lying-in sheds, and milking parlours, which brought the farm up to a very high standard. However, in 1982, it became impossible to continue with dairy farming because it was so labor-intensive and reliable farm workers were difficult to find. The cows were sold and David fattened beef cattle instead.

The farm at Dysart was only a couple of miles from David's home farm at Finnard where his brother, Bobby, was farming. It was the custom for them to help each other at times of harvesting. When the two "teams" were together, it was always a highly competitive and entertaining time.

David and Elsie were very hard-working and lived their lives quietly with the welfare of their family uppermost in their minds. They were good neighbors, always had time to lend a hand, and were greatly respected by the local community. They both took an active part in the activities of the church at Ryans. David was selected to the Congregational Committee in 1950. Six years later, he was installed as a Ruling Elder and held that office until 1994. He also served as Secretary to the Committee from 1974 to 1985, and held other posts from time to time.

During the Second World War, David and Bobby joined the Home Guard. David was a local councillor on the New No. 1 District Council from 1966 to around 1972. He was also a Governor at Croreagh Primary School, which his daughters attended.

Elsie took an active part in the PWA and was renowned for her work on the cake stall at the Sale of Work each year. She was also a member of the choir for many years. Elsie was always ready to listen when people had problems and give them her advice and help. She later decided to use this valuable experience and undertook training as a member of the Samaritans.

David and Elsie had four daughters: Margaret, Pauline, Brenda and Daphne. It was a very busy and happy home. As their family grew up and left home, David and Elsie started to enjoy some holidays in Europe. They started by going with a local farmer's group and later traveled independently, with Madeira and Portugal as two of the highlights.

Unfortunately, none of the girls was able to take over the farm. They all moved away and married outside the farming community, so in December 1990, the farm at Dysart was sold and David and Elsie retired to Ballygowan. They soon made friends there through the local church, and David joined the bowls club, which he enjoyed immensely. They were now close to their youngest daughter, Daphne, and her young children were able to spend more time with them. However, they still kept in touch with Ryans and their friends and neighbors in Dysart.

LEFT TO RIGHT: DAVID (FATHER), PAULINE, MARGARET, BRENDA, DAPHNE & ELSIE GLENNY WRIGHT (MOTHER)

THE FAMILY HOME OF DAVID & ELSIE WRIGHT, DYSART, COUNTY DOWN

BACK ROW, LEFT TO RIGHT: ADAM SOMAUROO, KAHLIL SOMAUROO, IAN MCCULLA, ROBERT SOMAUROO, MARGARET WRIGHT SOMAUROO, BRENDA WRIGHT MCGARVEY, BILL MCGARVEY, YOUSUF JEETOO, GARY MCGARVEY;
MIDDLE ROW, LEFT TO RIGHT: DAVID WRIGHT, AMY MCCULLA, ELSIE GLENNY WRIGHT;
FRONT ROW, LEFT TO RIGHT: HELEN MCGARVEY, DAPHNE WRIGHT MCCULLA, DAVID MCCULLA, REBECCA JEETOO & PAULINE WRIGHT JEETOO, AUGUST 1994

Their well-deserved retirement was cut short when David died suddenly on April 14th, 1995. Elsie continued to live in Ballygowan supported by her family and friends until she died after a short illness on May 26th, 1996.

BURIAL PLOT OF DAVID & ELSIE WRIGHT, RYANS GRAVEYARD, COUNTY DOWN

FIFTH GENERATION

Margaret Mary Wright, Pauline Elizabeth Wright, Brenda Maud Wright,
Daphne Florence Wright

Margaret Mary Wright – Fifth Generation

Margaret Mary Wright, first child of David and Elsie Glenny Wright, was born on November 21st, 1950 in Dysart, County Down, Northern Ireland. She answers the question, "So how did the Somauroo family happen?"

Margaret went to London in September 1971, having completed a three-year course at the Belfast College of Domestic Science (Garnerville), to continue her studies and qualify as a dietitian. Some friends from Garnerville were working in Epsom, so in January 1972 Margaret came down for the weekend and met Robert (Rahmatool).

Robert was born on January 9th, 1945 in Mauritius and joined their police force when he was 20. All police officers were seconded to the Special Mobile Force (Military Unit) for two years, where they worked with the British Army units (this was before Mauitius became independent). Robert worked as an interpreter and made friends with many of the British soldiers. He wanted an opportunity to travel and decided to come to England. When he arrived in May 1971, he came to stay with friends in Epsom and then applied to train as a nurse – and the rest is "fate."

Margaret Wright and Robert Somauroo were married in Ryans Presbyterian Church, County Down, Northern Ireland on July 5th, 1975.

Margaret then started her new job as senior dietitian at Epsom District Hospital. Robert had qualified and was now a charge nurse at St. Ebba's Hospital in Epsom, which looked after adults with learning disabilities. They bought a house in Epsom and have been there ever since.

RAHMATOOL SOMAUROO & MARGARET WRIGHT, WEDDING DAY – JULY 5, 1975
LEFT TO RIGHT: DAPHNE WRIGHT, RAHMATOOL (ROBERT) SOMAUROO, MARGARET
WRIGHT & RAMAN RAMJAN

Kahlil was born August 28, 1980, followed by Adam, born September 24, 1982. Margaret then gave up her full-time post at Epsom but continued to provide locum cover for the new dietitian until Adam started school in 1987. The children grew up enjoying many visits to the farm at Dysart.

In 1987, Margaret wanted to find a part-time job, but this proved to be impossible as a dietitian on the local level. Instead, she undertook a training course updating office skills first learned at school and found a part-time admin post in another local hospital. At this time, Robert and some colleagues opened a residential home for adults with learning disabilities. Margaret became involved by providing secretarial support, but later took over the invoicing, wages, and basic bookkeeping. She enjoyed this for a few years, but the partnership developed problems and she decided to give this up. The partnership eventually broke up acrimoniously in 1996.

In September 1998, with Kahlil setting off for University and Adam beginning his A-level course, Margaret decided it was time to re-enter the work force. Another crash course in word processing led to a part-time job at a college for training adults with disabilities. This was basically administration work, but also involved meeting and showing new trainees around the college. It was an ideal mix of office work and contact with people.

Robert took early retirement/redundancy in 1997 and is now catching up with all the DIY jobs which have been neglected over the past ten years. He has also had the opportunity to travel more widely. Family holidays have included trips to Ireland, Mauritius, Italy, and Florida. Robert has also traveled to Iran (to visit his sister), Cuba, Beijing, and Finland, with a weekend visit to St. Petersburg. They need more storage space for all of the souvenirs brought back.

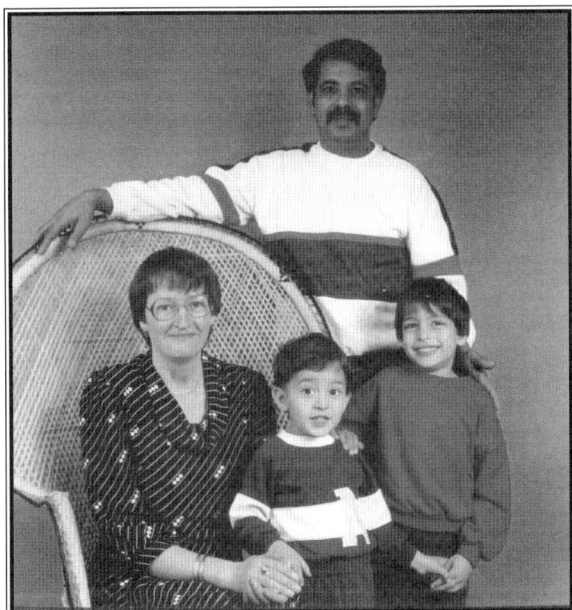

Early Somauroo Family Photo, Circa 1985
Front row Left to right: Margaret, Adam & Kahlil
Somauroo, Back row: Robert Somauro

Somauroo Family Photo, July 2000
Front row: Robert & Margaret Somauroo
Back row: Adam & Kahlil Somauroo

SIXTH GENERATION

Kahlil David Somauroo, Adam Hossen Somauroo

Kahlil David Somauroo – Sixth Generation

Kahlil David Somauroo, first child of Rahmatool Somauroo and Margaret Wright, was born on August 28th, 1980 in Epsom, Surrey, England.

Kahlil has always been ambitious, and from an early age planned to go to Oxford. He is currently studying law at Christchurch and has had a busy but wonderful two years. He probably wishes it could last for more than three years. He is still undecided as to whether he will become a solicitor or pursue a career outside law. Kahlil has been involved in the Scout movement since joining Beavers at age 6. He achieved the Chief Scouts Challenge and Chief Scout Award. He is still a member of the Ventures, and joined them for a second visit to Sweden in 1999. His most interesting trip was a month traveling around Ecuador. His visit to Italy in August 1998 was also a great experience. He plays chess and rugby, and has quite a wide range of interests.

Adam Hossen Somauroo – Sixth Generation

Adam Hossen Somauroo, second child of Rahmatool Somauroo and Margaret Wright, was born on September 24th, 1982 in Epsom, Surrey, England.

Adam has always been an athlete. From an early age, he participated in many sports, most notably football and athletics. This paints a picture of the stereotypical dumb athlete of modern times, but this is not so. In his last year at primary school, his soon-to-be secondary school (Glyn) offered him the chance to join the year above his own. He took this opportunity and has never looked back. From this point, he has gone from strength to strength, taking up the game of basketball. In a few short years he has represented his county in groups above his age bracket. His intellectual development has also continued. He took his GCSEs in 1998 and achieved the third-highest results in his year group of about 200 students. He has undertaken the daunting task of four A levels: Chemistry, Mathematics, English Literature, and Physics. He has chosen to study Physics at university (Nottingham) and will probably base his career on this.

Pauline Elizabeth Wright – Fifth Generation

MOHAMMAD YOUSUF JEETOO & PAULINE ELIZABETH WRIGHT, WEDDING DAY – MAY 9, 1979

Pauline Elizabeth Wright, the second child of David Wright and Elsie Glenny, was born on January 25th, 1954 at the family farm in Dysart, County Down, Northern Ireland.

After completing her secondary education at Newry High School in 1973, Pauline left the farm at Dysart. She attended the Kingston Polytechnic at Kingston upon Thames, where she graduated with a B.A. Hons. Degree in Social Science in 1976.

Pauline met her future husband Mohammad Yousuf Jeetoo in 1974, and they were married in Rostrevor Presbyterian Church, Kilbroney, County Down, Northern Ireland on May 9th, 1979.

Yousuf was born on February 27th, 1952. He studied at The University of Surrey, graduating with a B.Sc. Hons. Degree in Chemistry in 1980.

Pauline worked in the Civil Service from 1977 to 1990, when she left to have her daughter Rebecca Elizabeth, born January 3, 1991. Pauline returned to work in 2002 on a part-time basis as a classroom assistant.

Yousuf has worked in several major pharmaceutical companies as an analytical chemist.

FRONT ROW: PAULINE JEETOO, BACK ROW, LEFT TO RIGHT: REBECCA AND HER FATHER, YOUSUF JEETOO, 2002

SIXTH GENERATION

Rebecca Elizabeth Jeetoo

Rebecca Elizabeth Jeetoo – Sixth Generation

Rebecca Elizabeth Jeetoo, first child of Yousuf Jeetoo and Pauline Wright, was born on January 3rd, 1991 in St. Mary's Hospital, Portsmouth, England.

Rebecca loves music and dance and attends ballet, tap, piano, and flute lessons. She also has a pet rabbit and two guinea pigs.

Brenda Maud Wright – Fifth Generation

Brenda Maud Wright, third child of David Wright and Elsie Glenny, was born on May 18th, 1955 in Newry, County Down, Northern Ireland.

Brenda grew up on a dairy farm, loving every minute of helping with the animals and following her father everywhere he went, with the result that she usually managed to get out of housework. She was very lucky to be the proud owner of a pony, Dinkie, who was the love of her younger days. Life on the farm was made very happy by having such loving parents, and those memories of Dysart will be with her forever.

At the age of 17, she went to work in Gleneyre Portadown Children's Home, as she loved children. After gaining the relevant experience, she went to college in Belfast for a year to train successfully as a residential social worker.

She then took up the third-in-charge post of Knockfergus Children's Home in Carrickfergus, County Antrim, where she enjoyed her work until September 1980. She left to marry William P. McGarvey, whom she had met on holidays in Donegal. And they say holiday romances never last!

The McGarvey story starts with a quiet wedding in Ryans Church on the fourth of October 1980, followed by a honeymoon starting in East Kilbride, Scotland, where a local priest blessed their marriage. Next they headed to the Lake-District, where they had a great time.

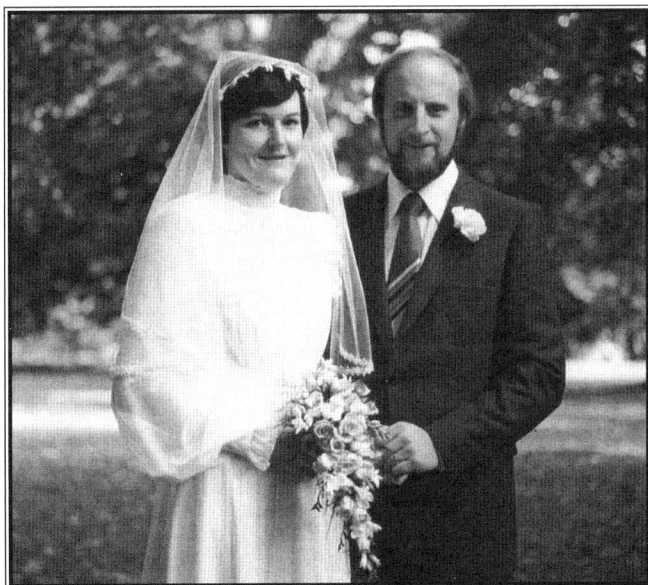

BRENDA WRIGHT & BILL McGARVEY, WEDDING DAY – OCTOBER 4, 1980

LEFT TO RIGHT
BACK ROW: BILL & GARY McGARVEY
FRONT ROW: BRENDA & HELEN McGARVEY

William P. McGarvey was born on August 21st, 1950. He ran his own furniture store in Bunbeg, later moving to Dungloe. He now is in the polyvinyl chloride window and door business.

Brenda and Bill McGarvey have two children. Gary was the first, born October 5, 1981, then Helen Mary, born October 11, 1984.

Bill is a keen fly fisherman and greatly involved with the Rosses Anglers in the area. He helped run the "Junior Fly Fishing World Championships" in 1999, which were held through the Rosses, and a great success. One of his larger achievements in fishing involved winning a seven-foot Sheelin Classic boat by catching a three-pound wild brown trout.

SIXTH GENERATION

Gary McGarvey, Helen Mary McGarvey

Gary McGarvey – Sixth Generation

Gary McGarvey, first child of Bill and Brenda Wright McGarvey, was born on October 5th, 1981 in Letterkenny General Hospital, Letterkenny, County Donegal.

He grew up to become successful at school and developed his love for music, playing the guitar in several local talent competitions with great success. Apart from his music, his other main love and talent is art. He has completed a year's course in art and design in Londonderry, which led him to an HND in Graphic Design in Belfast.

Helen Mary McGarvey – Sixth Generation

Helen Mary McGarvey, second child of Bill McGarvey and Brenda Wright, was born on October 11th, 1984 in Letterkenny General Hospital, Letterkenny, County Donegal.

She is a lively, happy child who made many friends. She loves music and plays the piano accordion in a local marching band. She has always wanted to become a hairdresser and practices on her cousins and friends. She has a part-time job in a hairdressing salon on weekends, which has made her even more determined to train as a hairdresser.

Daphne Florence Wright – Fifth Generation

Daphne Florence Wright, fourth child of David Wright and Elsie Glenny, was born on September 28th, 1959 in Newry, County Down, Northern Ireland.

Daphne left home in September 1977 to commence her general nurse training at Belfast City Hospital. Following her registration as a state registered nurse, she did her Orthopedic Nursing Certificate at Musgrave Park Hospital. On the completion of this course, she remained in Musgrave, staffing on a busy orthopedic ward for three years.

During her nurse training, Daphne met Ian McCulla, born on January 1st, 1960, whom she married April 26th, 1984 in Ryans Presbyterian Church, County Down, Northern Ireland. Later that same year, she undertook her District Nursing Certificate at the University of Ulster, going on to become a District Sister in East Belfast. Daphne held this post until her children, Amy Louise and David, came along June 5, 1987 and February 6, 1989 respectively. Due to family commitments, Daphne gave up her full-time post, but continues to work as a district nurse in East Belfast.

In 1995, Daphne and her husband separated and later divorced. Daphne has just completed a BSc (Hons) Degree in Health Studies at the University of Ulster, which she undertook on a part-time basis.

LEFT TO RIGHT: DAVID McCULLA, DAVID WRIGHT & AMY McCULLA, CIRCA 1994

AMY LOUISE McCULLA, DAPHNE WRIGHT McCULLA & DAVID McCULLA, JULY 2000

Sixth Generation
○─────────○

Amy Louise McCulla, David McCulla

Amy Louise McCulla – Sixth Generation

Amy Louise McCulla, first child of Ian McCulla and Daphne Wright, was born on June 5th, 1987 in the Castlereag District of Belfast, Northern Ireland.

Amy has been involved in various clubs and activities over the years, but at this time the love of her life is her pets. Amy enjoys the family dog and goldfish, has a tortoise, and will soon be getting a hamster to add to her collection. Amy also loves horses and goes riding every Saturday. Amy plays the piano in her spare time and is currently working towards her grade two exams.

David McCulla – Sixth Generation

David McCulla, second child of Ian McCulla and Daphne Wright, was born on February 6th, 1989 in the Castlereag District of Belfast, Northern Ireland.

Apart from enjoying all of the usual sports and activities associated with his age group, David loves taking drum lessons and practicing on his own drum kit. He also took up sailing and water skiing. David enjoys helping his Grandad on his nearby farm on the weekends.

Sarah Maud McClelland – Third Generation

Sarah Maud McClelland, third child of William McClelland and Sarah Donnelly, was born on August 29th, 1883 at Rockfield House, Cloughenramer near Newry, County Down, Ireland. She attended Rockvale School and wanted to be a nurse.

She was fairly tall, with dark brown hair and blue eyes. Quiet and somewhat strict, she liked to read, knit, crochet, and sew. She married Albert Hawthorn on July 2nd, 1906 in Clougenramer, County Down, Ireland.

Albert George Hawthorn, third child of William Hawthorn and Anna Watson Hawthorn, was born on October 11th, 1880 on a horse farm in Newtonhamilton, County Armagh, Ireland. He attended schools there. Albert was six feet tall, very active, with ginger eyebrows and mustache, brown hair, and blue eyes. He was of a happy disposition. His wife referred to him in a letter as "the same jolly boy he always was." His family looked to him as a leader, although he was not the oldest child.

In approximately 1897, after a serious downturn in the business, the William Hawthorn family moved to the East End of Glasgow. Albert left school at an early age and found a job taking care of the horses for the trolley. Albert began as a so-called tracer boy in the Glasgow Transport Department: he would walk to the tram depot at about 5 a.m., prepare his horse (a large Clydesdale), then lead it to one of the hilly sites where he would wait for a horse tram needing assistance to pull up the steep track. He helped his brothers get jobs. Three of them ended up in the transport service. He stayed on with the service and finally became an inspector.

ALBERT HAWTHORN IN MIDDLE GLASGOW
EARLY 1900s

Having settled in Glasgow, Albert still returned to his homeland at every opportunity, usually traveling by bicycle. Albert met Maud when he was on holiday bicycling through Northern Ireland. They married several years later. A frequent visitor to Cloughenramer, Albert also introduced his brother Robert to Maud's family, and he was soon engaged to Lucy. Robert was actually the first to marry, on November 15th, 1905.

ALBERT G. HAWTHORN & SARA MAUD McCLELLAND
MARRIAGE CERTIFICATE – JULY 2, 1906

ALBERT & MAUD HAWTHORN ABOUT 1906

MAUD, WILLIAM ROBERT & ALBERT HAWTHORN,
CIRCA 1910

With Albert established in the Glasgow Transport Department, he and Maud came to live in the Dennistown area, moving later to Shawlands, near his tram depot. The three McClelland sisters were very close to each other, so visits to Ireland were frequent. Maud wrote to her step-brother William and his wife Winnie in a letter dated December 9, 1925: "I had a long holiday in Ireland this summer. I went with Robert on August 1st and stayed nine weeks. Maudie (six at the time) was with me." Later she says, "Maudie has turned out a very clever little scholar. She is a wonderful little reader and counter. Dora is getting on well also, has gone into the Higher Grade. Willie has started his second year at University. Albert is just the same jolly boy he always was—keeps us in lovely potatoes, and vegetables the year round."

Albert and Maud had three children: a son, William Robert, born June 22, 1907, and two daughters—Dora, born June 6, 1913, and Maud, born July 30, 1919.

Albert always said that he and his wife got on well together. Sadly, Maud contracted

HAWTHORN FAMILY – ABOUT 1923-24
LEFT TO RIGHT: MAUDIE, MAUD, WILLIE, ALBERT & DORA

tuberculosis and was ill for a number of years before her death at age 44 on May 14th, 1927, just before they moved to a much larger house in the suburbs. Albert raised the children by himself. The family stayed at Finnard with the Wrights every summer until the start of World War II.

Albert was an enthusiastic gardener and bowler, and organized his days according to his games at Hillpark Club and the various gardening tasks that each season demanded. He had a real green finger and many years of experience, so much of it came naturally to him. During World War II, he worked not one but two fairly large plots of land and was extremely generous with their produce. These allotments were by no means near his home, so he covered many a mile laden with sacks of goodies, much appreciated in war-time by the lucky neighbors.

Albert was a founding member of South Shawland Presbyterian Church. When he retired in 1940, he had progressed to the rank of Inspector, finishing his career in the Underground System. After Dora died on June 4th, 1954, Maud and Robert lived at 59 Merryvale Avenue Giffnock, where Albert died on May 3rd, 1960, aged 79.

Fourth Generation

William Robert Hawthorn, Dora Lucinda Hawthorn,
Maud Elizabeth Hawthorn

William Robert Hawthorn – Fourth Generation

William Robert Hawthorn, first child of Albert George Hawthorn & Sarah Maud McClelland, was born on June 22nd, 1907 in Shawlands, Glasgow, Scotland. He was educated at Shawlands Academy.

William always lived life to the fullest. A keen soccer player, he was also active in the Boys' Brigade (a church-based group organization for Scots boys). Much-needed cash was earned through an early morning newspaper delivery round. In his teens, William took violin tuition to quite an advanced level. That particular artistic interest would persist throughout his life as he played with a number of ensembles, on his own, or with his sister Maud accompanying him on the piano.

William trained for a career in law the hard way, leaving school at fourteen to be apprenticed to Ballantyne, Haddow and McClay. While studying part-time, he was able to bypass the day-school exam system by gaining University Preliminary Passes in enough subjects to earn a place in Glasgow University's Law Department. Since he was apprenticed, he had to attend classes for the old B.L. degree in the mornings and evenings before and after his working day. He succeeded in graduating B.L. in 1927 and joined the Procurators' Fiscal Service as a Deputy P.F. in Glasgow. This Service was responsible for all criminal prosecutions, but, unlike the American district attorney, was administered by the Scottish Office, a government department.

Molly Agnew and William Hawthorn had a true childhood romance, meeting at Finnard while she was still a schoolgirl. Molly, born at Finnard on April 23rd, 1913 was the first of five children born to David Agnew and Sarah Donnelly. Molly and William married by special license granted by the Presbyterian Church at her home, Finnard House, on March 21st, 1936. Molly had just graduated M.A. from The Queen's University of Belfast. William's address at the time of his marriage was 118 Wellmeadow Road, Pollokshaw, Glasgow. The couple began married life in Shawlands, Glasgow. Upon William's promotion to procurator fiscal for Stirlingshire, they moved to the town of Stirling, where they settled permanently and had their two children, Robin and Jane. They regarded their annual sojourn at Killowen Point near Newry, where they could relax and visit their Irish friends, as the highlight of each year.

Molly adopted a practical approach to anything that took her interest, so she became well-known for her charity work and acquired a large circle of friends in Stirling. Her house-keeping was legendary. She also absorbed a great deal about antiques, and became enough of an authority on porcelain to give local lectures.

William had a distinguished career as a P.F., completing 31 years in Stirlingshire before retirement. Thereafter, he did duty as a part-time sheriff (local judge), an appointment of which he was particularly proud. In 1970, William received the Honor of ISO (Imperial Service Order), which was presented by the Queen at Buckingham Palace, London.

A retrial presentation was reported in the *Stirling Observer* on May 3rd, 1972. In it, Sheriff W.C. Henderson detailed Mr. Hawthorn's career, and said he possessed the quality of humanity bred from experience that was so essential in the fulfillment of his duties as procurator fiscal. He also spoke of Mr. Hawthorn's various activities in the town as an elder of St. Columba's Church, a member of the Society of

WILLIAM, ROBIN, JANE & MOLLY HAWTHORN
IN THE GARDEN AT STIRLING

Friends of Stirling Royal Infirmary, and a member of the committee of Whinwell Childrens' Home. Sheriff Principal R. R. Taylor added that William had shown integrity, responsibility, and above all humanity in service, and could be relied upon for his fairness.

Apart from music, William's interest centered round freshwater fishing and antiques. The contents of the Hawthorns' house in Stirling suggest the depth of their knowledge and the value of their taste in antiques. For many years, William also had a season ticket for the local soccer stadium, where he supported Stirling Albion and met up with many of the local characters over whom he had jurisdiction.

William died suddenly on September 6th, 1979 while on holiday at Warwick University, and was cremated five days later. Molly died on March 12th, 2004, after a long illness. Her ashes were scattered in the field to the rear of Ryans Presbyterian Church, the scene of many happy childhood memories where she had first met William, and within view of her beloved birthplace, Finnard House.

FIFTH GENERATION

Robin Hawthorn, Maurine Jane Hawthorn

Robin Hawthorn – Fifth Generation

Robin Hawthorn, first child of William Robert Hawthorn and Molly Agnew, was born on February 12th, 1942.

Robin Hawthorn was educated at Stirling High School and later trained as a laboratory technician, finally settling in the Audio-Visual Department of Stirling University. He has been an enthusiastic pilot of super-light aircraft, and in more recent years became a member of the University Choir. On several occasions at concerts in Dunblane Cathedral, Robin shared the platform with his cousin Pauline Vallance, who was principal flautist in the accompanying Glasgow Chamber Orchestra.

MAUD VALLANCE AND ROBIN HAWTHORN

Maurine Jane Hawthorn – Fifth Generation

Maurine Jane Hawthorn, second child of William Robert Hawthorn and Molly Agnew, was born on February 18th, 1944. She was educated at The Beacon and Stirling High School, eventually graduating M.B.Ch.B. from Glasgow University. For many years she specialized in anaesthetics, but more recently acted as director of a drug rehabilitation unit in a problem area of Glasgow.

Jane married Dr. Jeffrey Louie Jay on July 21st, 1970 in St. Columba's Church, Stirling, Scotland. Anita and Pauline Vallance were bridesmaids, and the reception was held at the Golden Lion Hotel in Stirling, Scotland. Jay is an eye specialist at The Glasgow Gartnavel Infirmary and Sen. Lecturer in the University. Jane and Jay have two children, both born in Glasgow: David Dalyrimple Jay, born December 9, 1975, and Lucy Miranda Jay, born January 3, 1978.

In the 1990s, Jeff was President of the Royal College of Ophthalmologists for the usual three-year stint. He is currently on the General Medical Council. His specialist experience and authority have taken him all over the world in both advisory and executive roles.

Both Jane and Jeff share her parents' enthusiasm for antiques. Also keen on sailing, they spend a great deal of leisure time at their cottage near Inverary, Argyllshire, and have summer anchorage at Crinan on the west coast.

THE JAYS AT AUGHNAGOUL
JEFFREY, JANE, DAVID & LUCY JAY

Sixth Generation

David Dalyrimple Jay, Lucy Miranda Jay

David Dalyrimple Jay – Sixth Generation

David Dalyrimple Jay, first child of Jeffrey Louie Jay and Maurine Jane Hawthorn, was born on December 9th, 1975.

David was educated at Glasgow High School and Winchester. After graduating from Cambridge University, he spent some time in an agency for opera singers in London and trained to teach English as a foreign language. Later, David went to Italy, where he had several positions, including one with the British Council. He is currently teaching English as a foreign language in Cambridge.

Lucy Miranda Jay – Sixth Generation

Lucy Miranda Jay, second child of Jeffrey Louie Jay and Maurine Jane Hawthorn, was born on January 3rd, 1978.

Upon graduating from Cambridge, Lucy trained as a lawyer, a career she is presently pursuing in London.

Dora Lucinda Hawthorn – Fourth Generation

Dora Lucinda Hawthorn, second child of Albert George Hawthorn and Sarah Maud McClelland, was born on June 6th, 1913 in Glasgow, Scotland.

Dora was slightly below average height, with auburn-streaked brown hair which she wore quite close to her head. In the early 1940s, she was an assistant manageress in the restaurant in Copelands', a large Department Store in Glasgow. She then moved to a managerial post at The IONA Community Centre on Clyde Street. By the early 1950s, Dora was managing Works Canteen in a government training center in Hillington Industrial Estate. She was noticeably caring and considerate in her personal relations, always doing things for others. Sadly, when Robert Vallance came on the scene, Dora had lost her two closest friends and her social life was rather restricted. Yet the Hawthorn home was always a pleasure to visit as the conversation was invariably light-hearted and humor always near the surface.

There was considerable stress at all of Dora's work places, a pressure heightened by her own conscientious nature. She was en route to the canteen one morning—June 4th, 1954—when a bus, swerving to avoid a careless young cyclist, mounted the sidewalk and struck her down. Indeed, she should have been on leave the morning of her fatal accident. The circumstances of her death caused deep shock to her small family, already sensitized by the loss of their mother at a very early age.

Maud Elizabeth Hawthorn – Fourth Generation

Maud Elizabeth Hawthorn, third child of Albert George Hawthorn & Sarah Maud McClelland, was born on July 30th, 1919.

DORA LUCINDA HAWTHORN

Following is a memoir written by Maud Elizabeth Hawthorn Vallance:

"If you are a really lucky person—I happen to be one of them—you have certain places where you are simply the person you want to be and happen to be in the place you most desire. My special places have always been where my family and home are and also Ireland in general and Finnard in particular. Each time we went there it was to such a lovely welcome that I'm afraid we dreaded the leaving of it. How my aunt and uncle Wright packed us in as well as their own family of seven, I'll never know but they did it. I remember so well the arrival by pony and trap from Ballyroney Station and the quick run round to see that all the favorite places were still there.

"One year was different. That was when my father's brother, Uncle Bob Hawthorn, took my mother and I packed into the sidecar of his motor bike. The bike wouldn't get started at Ettrick Place where we lived in Glasgow. Soon a crowd gathered and finally they cheered us on our way! The bike was winched aboard the Irish boat in Glasgow and we arrived in some style eventually at Finnard.

"One day of that holiday our cousin, Sam Wright, and I were dispatched to the nearby Heslip's farm to play there all day. When we went back to Finnard there was a new baby. David Wright had been born and became the focus of all my attention to the distress of a rather strict nurse. Never had a child so many people there to worship him. That holiday was memorable in many ways for it was the only time I spent alone with my mother. According to a letter she wrote to Norman's mother in Arizona, she and I stayed for ten weeks.

"When I read that letter not so long ago, (Norman sent me a copy) I realized that I had a very vivid memory of my Uncle Bob trying to catch Norah the pony in the meadow opposite the house. He hid her harness behind him and held out a basin of treats for her, but Norah knew all the answers and she wasn't to be tricked so easily.

"Near the main house a favorite calling in and playing place was Auntie Tilly's house. She was always there for us – and many a penny she gave Sam and I. The day we decided to go up the Cullion Road to buy sweets at a farm there, we became not really lost but we certainly lingered to eat those sweets at the farm fireside, and, of course, we were posted missing and suffered accordingly. That little cottage on the roadside beside a small stream which supplied her cooking, drinking, and washing water, was a great place to visit. However, I have a very real memento of her. When I was about twenty my father told us that when she died we had all been left £10 of Irish Saving Certificates and that they would now be fully matured. I decided to use it for something I would always have and off I went to a little antique shop which I knew in Glasgow and I bought a lovely chest of drawers. It is still there in the bedroom upstairs and is a very real memory maker of a fine old lady.

"There were many events during our time there. Aunt Minnie had picnics in the garden annually and the Irwins from Corgary came to join us. Eileen Irwin and I were always in touch from then on and Bobby also. He and Pearl used to visit us in Uplawmoor and lovely visits they were. Apart from the picnics and the occasional trip to the big stone at Rostrevor, was a yearly visit to the Parkers at Ballykeel. There we were royally entertained and always the space and places to play and things to do. There was never a dull moment. Once I was allowed to go to school for a day with my cousins. I had a wonderful time and was given an abacus to play with. Alas! When I experienced the real school in Glasgow – large classes and not much play – it was a bitter disappointment.

"Sunday evening in the parlor was unforgettable. All work was put aside for a while and we went to the room at the right of the front door. Some sang, some played the piano but the year after I had started piano lessons, I accompanied my brother William on his violin which went everywhere with him. We had been practicing a popular piece at the time (1930s) 'Heyken's Serenade,' and I was so happy to be doing it! We had a good round of applause too. One really memorable time my aunt read to us from Paddy McQuillan. That brought the house down. What I would give for a copy of that book.

"One year when my sister Dora and I were quite young father couldn't get his holiday at the beginning of July when the schools here close, so on his day off he took us to Ardrossan. We crossed to Belfast where Uncle Sam met us. Father then returned to Glasgow straight away and we went by train to Ballyroney, arriving later by trap to Finnard and a big welcome. Later in the month my father and William joined us for probably the last of our family holidays. Willie met and fell in love with Molly Agnew who was in her last year at school and from then on he stayed at the lovely little cottage of Molly's grannie. They called her 'Grannie down the field,' and that was the beginning of another chapter.

"The more one thinks about this the more is remembered. Now I'm amazed that a busy farmer like Uncle Sam took a whole day off to meet Dora and me in Belfast. It's the small events that stand out too like helping Maud (Wright) to carry tea to the men in the hay field. Her homemade scones and the tea in an enamel jug tasted heavenly. Then there was the midday meal round the long table in the kitchen. We were all there us children sitting at the window side on a long stool. Hughie Toal, who worked on the farm, was quietly there and usually there was a collie dog under the table. What a busy room it was – all of us and in front of us a plate of champ (potatoes mashed with butter and milk made by aunt Minnie) and always there the little black stove where all the cooking and baking was done and the reservoir at the side of it to heat the water.

"I wasn't aware at the time of how much I learned. Back in Glasgow I regaled my friends with all the wonderful games and adventures I had known. However, at school whenever I could, my essays were full of Finnard and Ireland. I specially went on about the time I fell into a flax dam and was pulled out smelling – well, smelling the way rotten flax smells. My friends didn't know what flax was and how many fields in Ireland were given over to it. I keep remembering so much now that I've started, but always I return to the great care and kindness we received from such loving relations. Leaving it all behind – all that love and affection left me weeping sadly all the way to the boat. Even my father was much given to nose-blowing as we left everybody there and set off for Ballyroney and the long trip to Glasgow."

Maud was educated at Shawlands School and graduated M.A. from Glasgow University in 1940. During World War II she held two posts teaching Glasgow children who had been evacuated into country areas—one in Pitlochry, Perthshire, the other in Newmilnes, Ayrshire. She then settled in Rockvilla School in a rather poor area of Glasgow.

Maud met her husband Robert through a shared interest in music and performing arts. They were married April 14th, 1949 at South Shawlands Parish Church, Glasgow, Scotland. Robert Climie Vallance was born November 1, 1922 in Clydebank, Glasgow, Scotland, the third child of Alexander Vallance (engineer) and Catherine Climie. His father worked in John Brown's famous ship-building yard. The family moved to Scotstoun, Glasgow in 1929 to be nearer Albion Motors, where Alexander had been transferred. Robert graduated B.Sc. in 1946, beginning a career in science teaching a year later. In 1952, he graduated M. Ed., and moved into the Glasgow Education Department—Psychological Service in 1955. After a short posting in the National Health Service, Robert accepted a consulting position in residential schools with problem children, retiring in 1985. Since his retirement he has had more time for golf, but in recent years began developing his family's history.

MAUD HAWTHORN AND ROBERT VALLANCE
WEDDING DAY – APRIL 14, 1949
FRONT ROW, LEFT TO RIGHT: LYN WILSON, ALEX VALLANCE, MAUD HAWTHORN,
ROBERT VALLANCE, DORA HAWTHORN, FRIEND; MIDDLE ROW, LEFT TO RIGHT:
MOLLY HAWTHORN, KATE VALLANCE, MARY VALLANCE WILSON; BACK ROW,
LEFT TO RIGHT: WILLIAM HAWTHORN, ALEX VALLANCE, ALBERT HAWTHORN

Maud stopped teaching in 1955 when her first child was born. In the early 1970s Maud resumed her teaching career with remedial work in a primary school, retiring in 1986.

Unlike her siblings, Maud physically resembles her father, as she is also of average height with auburn hair. She is passionate about politics, literature, theatre, cinema and music. Like all of her family, she gives much of her time for others. She really does enjoy her friendships and is always pleased when someone drops in at 14 Arthurlie Drive for coffee and a chat.

Maud and Robert have two children: Anita Frances, born March 21, 1955, and Pauline Mary Vallance, born May 16, 1958. Maud and Robert also enjoy many happy and delightful hours chatting and making music with their grandchildren Niamh and Breandan McElhill.

MAUD HAWTHORN VALLANCE &
ROBERT VALLANCE AT THE BIRTH-
PLACE OF PATRICK BRONTE NEAR
RATHFRILAND, COUNTY DOWN IN
JUNE 1999

FIFTH GENERATION

Anita Frances Vallance, Pauline Mary Vallance

Anita Frances Vallance – Fifth Generation

Anita Frances Vallance, first child of Robert Climie Vallance and Maud Elizabeth Hawthorn, was born on March 21st, 1955.

Anita graduated M.A. from Aberdeen University, and after teacher-training in Newcastle settled in London with Gary Gibson, a teacher of science. They have one son, Alexander James, born June 24, 1993.

Until three or four years ago, Gary was a chess enthusiast in a team which reached the national finals. He also played a great deal on the internet and coached his son's soccer team.

LEFT TO RIGHT: GARY, ALEXANDER AND ANITA GIBSON

After several teaching posts in East London, Anita is presently involved in a numeracy project covering eight schools in Hackney.

SIXTH GENERATION

Alexander James Gibson – Sixth Generation

Alexander James Gibson, only child of Gary Gibson and Anita Frances Vallance, was born on June 24th, 1993.

Alexander is now twelve and hoping soon to earn his black belt in karate. He has just completed his first year in high school with good reports.

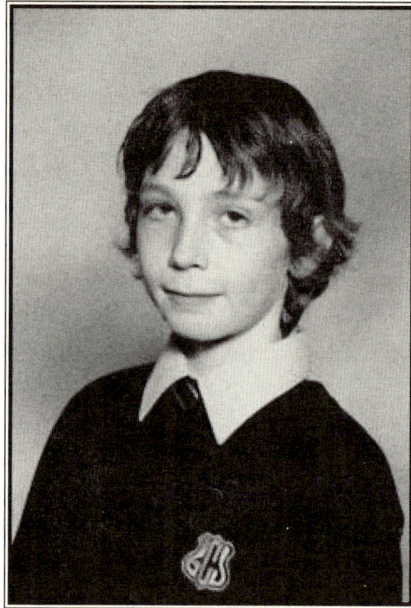

ALEXANDER JAMES GIBSON

Pauline Mary Vallance – Fifth Generation

Pauline Mary Vallance, second child of Robert Climie Vallance and Maud Elizabeth Hawthorn, was born on May 16th, 1958.

Pauline graduated M.A. (Hons) Psychology from Glasgow University. She works in the education system as a health coordinator. While the Youth Centre Manager in Drumchapel, Glasgow West, Pauline met Nick McElhill through their mutual love of music. She and Nick moved to Barrmill, a small village in North Ayrshire, and became the proud parents of twins Breandan and Niamh, born November 25, 1991.

DUNBLANE CATHEDRAL
LEFT TO RIGHT: NIAMH MCELHILL, PAULINE AND MAUD VALLANCE,
ROBIN HAWTHORN AND BREANDAN MCELHILL

SIXTH GENERATION

Breandan Vallance McElhill, Niamh Hawthorn McElhill

Breandan Vallance McElhill – Sixth Generation

Breandan Vallance McElhill, one twin of Nick McElhill and Pauline Mary Vallance, was born on November 25th, 1991.

Breandan is currently very keen on badminton, having already earned a small trophy for excellence at his local club. Since he was quite small, he has been good with construction kits and fixing things. He has just acquired a large remote-controlled bi-plane. Breandan is now settled at high school in Kilbirnie, Ayrshire and particularly involved with playing trumpet and violin in various ensembles.

BREANDAN VALLANCE McELHILL

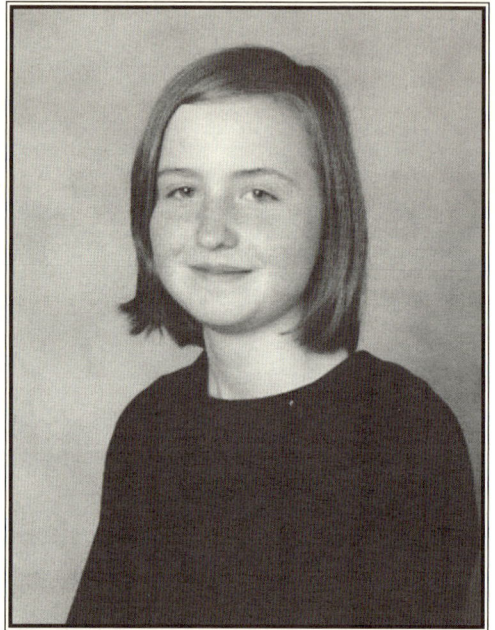

NIAMH HAWTHORN McELHILL

Niamh Hawthorn McElhill – Sixth Generation

Niamh Hawthorn McElhill, one twin of Nick McElhill and Pauline Mary Vallance, was born on November 25th, 1991.

Niamh attends high school in Kilbirnie, Ayrshire, where she also plays trumpet and violin in various ensembles and takes part in the senior choir. Niamh has recently returned from a short tour in Barcelona, Spain with her school music groups, during which she sang and played her trumpet.

William McClelland – Third Generation

William McClelland, fourth child of William McClelland and Sarah Donnelly, was born on September 7th, 1885 in County Down, Ireland. He died December 21st, 1886, at one year of age.

His mother, Sarah Donnelly McClelland, died September 22nd, 1885, after William's birth.

WILLIAM McCLELLAND AND SARAH ANN HENNING
MARRIAGE CERTIFICATE – DECEMBER 12, 1890

William McClelland – Third Generation

William McClelland, third child of Thomas McClelland and Susan Henning, was married a second time, to Sarah Ann Henning, on December 12th, 1890 at Dundalk, Louth, Ireland. Sarah, daughter of Abel Henning and Sarah Ann McKee, was born on August 22nd, 1867 in Tullyvallen, parish of Newton Hamilton, County Armagh, Ireland.

William and Sarah had three children: William Thomas, born October 22, 1891, Margaret McClelland, born June 5, 1894, and David Livingston, born February 11, 1899.

William McClelland & Sarah Henning McClelland Family
Census Of Ireland – 1901

CENSUS SHOWS WILLIAM McCLELLAND, AGE 62, SARAH McCLELLAND, AGE 32,
LUCY McCLELLAND, AGE 21, MARY MINNIE, AGE 19, SARAH MAUD, AGE 17,
WILLIAM THOMAS, AGE 9, MARGARET, AGE 6, AND DAVID LIVINGSTON, AGE 2

Sarah Henning McClelland died August 6th, 1908 at Cloughenramer.
William died March 20th, 1909.

Obituary – William McClelland

"The Late Mr. W. McClelland
Cloughenramer, Newry

We regret to chronicle the demise of Mr. William McClelland, who passed away at his late residence, Rock View, Cloughenramer, Newry, on Saturday last. The interment took place on Monday in St. Patrick's Churchyard, Newry. The large and representative cortege which followed his remains testified in a striking manner to the worthiness of the deceased gentleman, and to the estimation in which he was deservedly held by a wide circle of neighbours and friends. Although it was known that Mr. McClelland was in delicate health for some time, his death, notwithstanding, came as a painfully sudden surprise, and while Dr. Crossle, the family physician, was unremitting in his attendance upon his patient, the end came to the poignant grief of his bereaved children, his grief-stricken relatives, and his numerous sorrowing friends. Mr. McClelland was one of the largest and most respected farmers in the neighborhood of Newry. He, with his late wife, carried out dairying and butter making very successfully, and the butter from this dairy gained many awards at the principal Irish agricultural shows. Our late friend's life may be regarded as a book in which was written in its every chapter all the characteristics of a genial nature and a noble mind. In his home life he was a loving and indulgent husband and father; to his relatives he was an affectionate kinsman; and outside the closer charmed circle of his family and relations those who knew him intimately were encouraged and favoured who could claim him as a friend. His friendship was not of the intangible or evanescent kind, for the late Mr. McClelland was a straightforward and loyal friend. In his home life he by precept led his family along the paths of industry, integrity, and truth: and in his business connections with his neighbours he took for his guiding principles the Sermon on the Mount. Surely such a life and such a character as was lived and possessed by our late friend has left a fragrant memory behind that will never be dissipated by the winds of time. Nor will the impress of his many and ennobling example and life-work ever be effaced from the remembrance of those he daily came into contact with, no matter what be the changes or vissitudes that may occur in the days to be. We leave this humble wreath upon his freshly-made grave to keep company wit the spring flowers that now star around I tomb, in full assurance of that resurrection morn, that the blooms of each recurring springtide will always typify till that last trumpet will sound and the dead in Christ will arise."

FOURTH GENERATION

William Thomas McClelland, Margaret McClelland, David Livingston McClelland

William Thomas McClelland – Fourth Generation

William Thomas McClelland, first child of William McClelland and Sarah Ann Henning, was born on October 22nd, 1891 in Cloughenramer, near Newry, County Down, Ireland. He and Margaret Copeland had one child, Maude, who was born September 16, 1912. Margaret was born on February 17th, 1885.

Copeland Family Census Of Ireland – 1911

CENSUS SHOWS ROBERT, AGE 64, LIZA, AGE 55, SAM, AGE 28, ROBERT JR., AGE 24, MAGGIE, AGE 18, AND WILLIAM JOHN, AGE 13

DONAGHMORE CHURCH OF IRELAND
COPELAND FAMILY'S CHURCH
1977

COPELAND GRAVE
DONAGHMORE CHURCH OF IRELAND
1977

FOURTH GENERATION

Maude McClelland - Fourth Generation

Maude McClelland, only child of William Thomas McClelland and Margaret Copeland, was born on September 16th, 1912 in Newry, County Down, Ireland. She married Samuel Worthington on November 16th, 1938 in Belfast, County Antrim, Northern Ireland. Samuel was born on May 3rd, 1912 in Belfast, County Antrim, Ireland. The couple had two children: Brian, born September 16, 1939, and Patricia, born August 8, 1941.

MAUDE MᴄCLELLAND
18 YEARS OLD – 1930

SAMUEL WORTHINGTON &
MAUDE MᴄCLELLAND – 1938

LEFT TO RIGHT: BRIAN, AGE 2, MAUDE &
PAT, AGE 1 – 1941

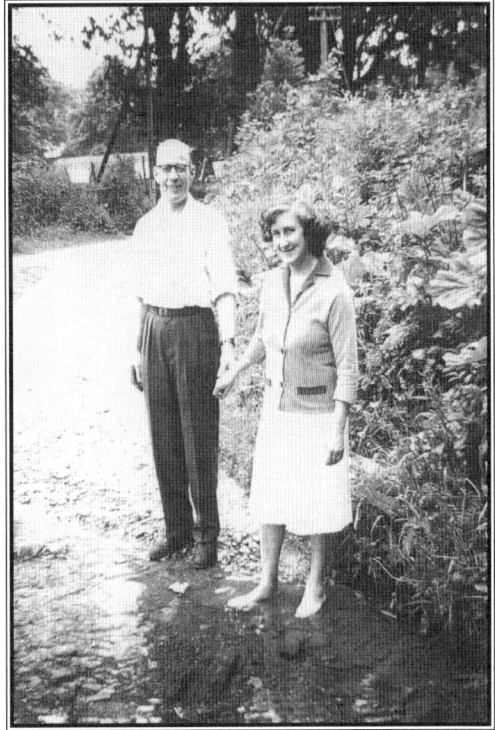

SAM & MAUDE WORTHINGTON
ROSTREVOR, SUMMER 1961

LEFT TO RIGHT: MAISIE HENNING, BARBARA
SIKORA & MAUDE WORTHINGTON – 1977

EILEEN HENNING &
MAUDE WORTHINGTON – 1977

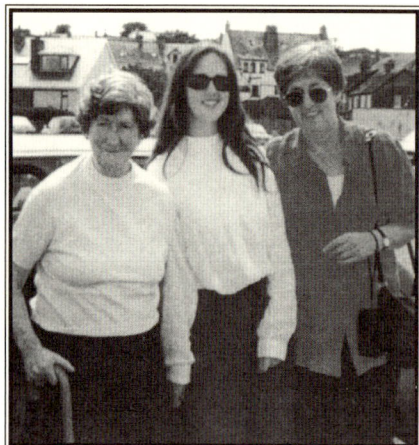

LEFT TO RIGHT: MAUDE WORTHINGTON,
GRACE BROWN & PAT BROWNE – JUNE 1995
GROOMSPORT, NOT FAR FROM BANGOR

WORTHINGTONS/McCLELLANDS
IRELAND – SUMMER 1996

Samuel Worthington died in 1967. Maude died April 6th, 2001.

FIFTH GENERATION

Brian Worthington, Sr., Patricia Worthington

Brian Worthington, Sr. – Fifth Generation

Brian Worthington, Sr., first child of Samuel Worthington and Maude McClelland, was born on September 16th, 1939. Brian married Sarah Elizabeth McKay on September 29th, 1964 in Killaney Parish, Boardmills, County Down, Northern Ireland. Sarah was born on January 27th, 1943.

LEFT TO RIGHT: MAUDE, BRIAN, SARAH &
SAMUEL WORTHINGTON – WEDDING DAY
SEPTEMBER 29,1964

BRIAN WORTHINGTON & SARAH McKAY
WEDDING DAY – SEPTEMBER 29, 1964

Brian and Sarah had three children: Brian Jr., born March 22, 1965, Graeme, born March 25, 1966, and Paul, born January 17, 1970.

WORTHINGTON FAMILY
LEFT TO RIGHT: PAUL, LARA, NICOLA, BRIAN SR., SARAH, RHYS, BRIAN JR., SUSANNE, LOIS, GRAEME AND AUDREY
FEBRUARY 2005

LEFT TO RIGHT: AUDREY, SARAH, LARA, NICOLA, LOIS AND SUSANNE WORTHINGTON
FEBRUARY 2005

LEFT TO RIGHT: PAUL, BRIAN, SR., RHYS, GRAEME, AND BRIAN WORTHINGTON, JR.
FEBRUARY 2005

Sixth Generation

Brian Worthington, Jr., Graeme Worthington, Paul Worthington

Brian Worthington, Jr. – Sixth Generation

Brian Worthington, Jr., first child of Brian Worthington and Sarah Elizabeth McKay, was born on March 22nd, 1965 in Belfast, Northern Ireland. He married Susanne Violet Jordan on June 24th, 1995 in Ballycairn Presbyterian Church, Belfast, Northern Ireland. Susanne was born on February 19th, 1971 in Belfast, Northern Ireland.

STORMONT HOTEL, BELFAST, NORTHERN IRELAND
WEDDING DAY – JUNE 24, 1995
FRONT ROW, LEFT TO RIGHT: MAUDE WORTHINGTON (GRAMMA), BRIAN WORTHINGTON, JR. (GROOM), SUSANNE VIOLET JORDAN (BRIDE), SARAH & BRIAN WORTHINGTON, SR. (PARENTS); BACK ROW, LEFT TO RIGHT: GRAEME WORTHINGTON, UNKNOWN, AND PAUL WORTHINGTON

Brian and Susanne have two children: Lois Susanne, born April 25, 1998, and Rhys Henry, born February 4, 2003.

LEFT TO RIGHT: LOIS, SUSANNE, BRIAN JR., AND RHYS WORTHINGTON
CHRISTMAS 2004

LEFT TO RIGHT: PAUL, SUSANNE, BRIAN, JR.,
GRAEME, AND BRIAN WORTHINGTON, SR.

Seventh Generation

Lois Susanne Worthington, Rhys Henry Worthington

Lois Susanne Worthington – Seventh Generation
Lois Susanne Worthington, first child of Brian Worthington, Jr. and Susanne Violet Jordan, was born on April 25th, 1998 in Belfast, Northern Ireland.

Lois Susanne Worthington with Grandparents, Sarah & Brian Worthington

Rhys Henry Worthington – Seventh Generation
Rhys Henry Worthington, second child of Brian Worthington, Jr. and Susanne Violet Jordan, was born on February 4th, 2003 in Belfast, Northern Ireland.

Left to right: Rhys, Brian, Sr., Lois, Sarah, and Lara Worthington – Christmas 2004

Graeme Worthington – Sixth Generation

Graeme Worthington, second child of Brian Worthington, Sr. and Sarah Elizabeth McKay, was born on March 25th, 1966 in Belfast, Northern Ireland. He married Audrey June Manning on October 4th, 2003 in the Church of Ireland, Belfast, Northern Ireland. Audrey was born on November 20th, 1969 in Bangor, Northern Ireland.

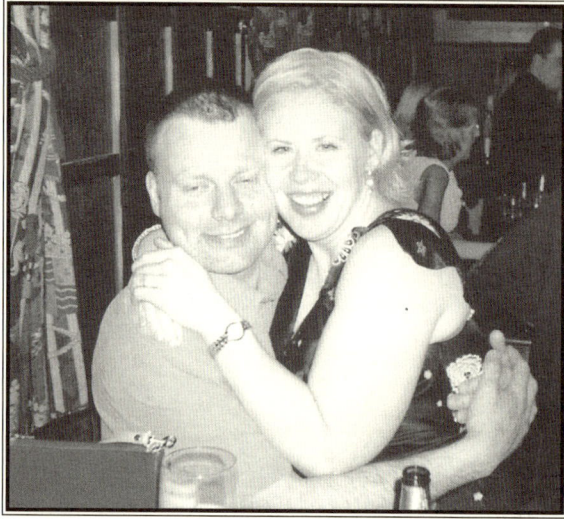

GRAEME WORTHINGTON & AUDREY JUNE MANNING
ENGAGEMENT DAY – 2001
DUBLIN, IRELAND

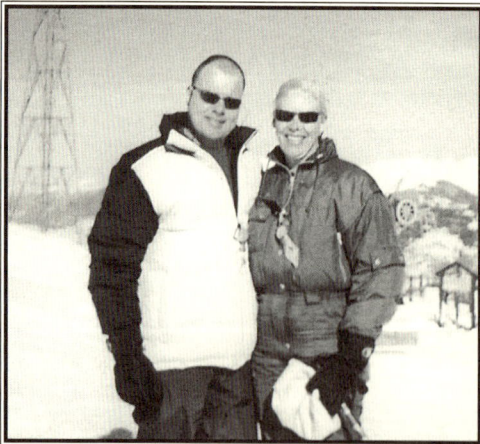

GRAEME & AUDREY WORTHINGTON
FRANCE 2004

AUDREY & GRAEME WORTHINGTON
2005

Graeme and Audrey have one child, Erika Grace, born December 19, 2005.

Erika Grace Worthington – Seventh Generation

Erika Grace Worthington, first child of Graeme Worthington and Audrey Jane Manning, was born on December 19th, 2005 in Belfast, Northern Ireland.

Paul Worthington – Sixth Generation

Paul Worthington, third child of Brian Worthington, Sr. and Sarah Elizabeth McKay, was born on January 17th, 1970 in Belfast, Northern Ireland. He married Nicola Warren on August 18th, 2001 in the Church of Ireland, Belfast, Northern Ireland. Nicola was born on June 11th, 1976 in Belfast, Northern Ireland.

PAUL WORTHINGTON AND NICOLA WARREN
WEDDING DAY – AUGUST 18, 2001

PAUL WORTHINGTON AND NICOLA WARREN
WEDDING DAY – AUGUST 18, 2001

They have one daughter, Lara Rebekah, born June 16, 2004 in Belfast, Northern Ireland.

PAUL, NICOLA, AND
LARA REBEKAH WORTHINGTON
CHRISTENING – OCTOBER 2004

Lara Rebekah Worthington – Seventh Generation

Lara Rebekah Worthington, first child of Paul Worthington and Nicola Warren, was born on June 16th, 2004 in Belfast, Northern Ireland.

LARA REBEKAH & GRANDFATHER, BRIAN WORTHINGTON
FEBRUARY 2005

Patricia Worthington – Fifth Generation

Patricia Worthington, second child of Maude McClelland and Samuel Worthington, was born on August 8th, 1941. Patricia married Roy Browne on April 29th, 1960.

They had five children: Stephen Robert, born August 30, 1961; Kevin Neil, born July 1, 1963; Julia Fiona, born November 25, 1967; David Michael, born February 19, 1969; and Grace Patricia Browne, born November 20, 1978.

PATRICIA BROWNE FAMILY & FRIENDS AT THE
CHRISTENING PARTY FOR CAMERON WORTHINGTON BROWNE
SOMERSET, ENGLAND – APRIL 1995
IN CHAIRS, LEFT TO RIGHT: KEVIN, KATE, & CAMERON BROWNE
BACK ROW, FOURTH FROM LEFT: PATRICIA BROWNE, MOTHER OF KEVIN

SIXTH GENERATION

Stephen Robert Browne, Kevin Neil Browne, Julia Fiona Browne,
David Michael Browne, Grace Patricia Browne

Stephen Robert Browne – Sixth Generation

Stephen Robert Browne, first child of Patricia Worthington and Roy Browne, was born on August 30th, 1961. Robert married June Anne Davis in September 1988.

They have one daughter, Jessica Rose Browne, born in August 2003.

SEVENTH GENERATION

Jessica Rose Browne – Seventh Generation

Jessica Rose Browne, only child of Stephen Robert Browne and June Anne Davis, was born in August of 2003.

Kevin Neil Browne – Sixth Generation

Kevin Neil Browne, second child of Patricia Worthington and Roy Browne, was born on July 1st, 1963. Kevin married Kate Walker Lewis in September 1991.

They have two sons: Cameron Worthington Browne, born December 1994, and Owen Lewis Browne, born May 1997.

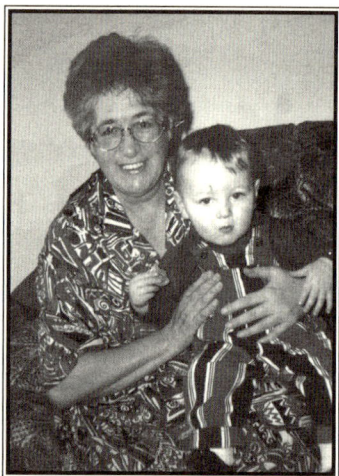

PATRICIA BROWNE AND GRANDSON
CAMERON – MARCH 1996

KEVIN & CAMERON WORTHINGTON BROWNE
1996

SEVENTH GENERATION

Cameron Worthington Browne, Owen Lewis Browne

Cameron Worthington Browne – Seventh Generation

Cameron Worthington Browne, first child of Kevin Neil Browne and Kate Walker Lewis, was born in December of 1994.

Owen Lewis Browne – Seventh Generation

Owen Lewis Browne, second child of Kevin Neil Browne and Kate Walker Lewis, was born in May of 1997.

Julia Fiona Browne – Sixth Generation

Julia Fiona Browne, third child of Patricia Worthington and Roy Browne, was born on November 25th, 1967.

Julia and David have two sons: Ben Harry, born in April 1999, and Sam Alfie, born in July 2000.

SEVENTH GENERATION

Ben Harry Browne, Sam Alfie Browne

Ben Harry Browne – Seventh Generation

Ben Harry Browne, first child of Julia Fiona Browne and David Henry Horne, was born in April of 1999.

Sam Alfie Browne – Seventh Generation

Sam Alfie Browne, second child of Julia Fiona Browne and David Henry Horne, was born in July of 2000.

David Michael Browne – Sixth Generation

David Michael Browne, fourth child of Patricia Worthington and Roy Browne, was born on February 19th, 1969. David married Lucinda Joanne Webb in August 1992.

They have two daughters: Chloe Patricia, born December 1993, and Emily Lucy, born May 1995.

SEVENTH GENERATION

Chloe Patricia Browne, Emily Lucy Browne

Chloe Patricia Browne – Seventh Generation

Chloe Patricia Browne, first child of David Michael Browne and Lucinda Joanne Webb, was born in December of 1993.

Emily Lucy Browne – Seventh Generation

Emily Lucy Browne, second child of David Michael Browne and Lucinda Joanne Webb, was born in May of 1995.

Grace Patricia Browne – Sixth Generation

Grace Patricia Browne, fifth child of Patricia Worthington and Roy Browne, was born on November 20th, 1978.

THIRD GENERATION

William Thomas McClelland, Margaret McClelland, David Livingston McClelland

William Thomas McClelland – Third Generation

William Thomas McClelland, first child of William McClelland and Sarah Ann Henning, was born on October 22nd, 1891 at Cloughenramer near Newry, County Down, Ireland. He lived on a better-than-average farm that had a little bit of everything, including chickens, pigs, cows, sheep, potatoes, oats, and wheat. The family had 18 to 20 cows and supplied milk to the Newry General Hospital.

William received an education equivalent to eighth grade. He was an orphan at age 18 and overnight had responsibility for his younger sister Margaret, 15, and brother David, 11. Two uncles—Abel Henning and Sam Wright—helped William immigrate to Tucson, Arizona in 1912, when Arizona was still a United States territory. A. W. Smith, brother to Joseph Henning's first wife, and his wife Elizabeth "Smithy" befriended young William. They were "family" in Tucson.

William's first job was with Triple C Ranch, near Oracle. In the fall of 1913, he started driving a truck for Henry Peterson, who operated the Holstein Dairy. He worked for Mr. Peterson until 1916, when he returned home. He had previously rented out the farm, which he inherited as the oldest son. This time he sold it, and made some settlement for his sister, and probably his brother as well. Margaret came out to the United States c1912. She went back to Ireland, planning to return, but met, married, and settled down with Thomas Irwin instead.

William served in the army of occupation in Germany for almost a year. It was probably during this period that he took a leave to return to Ireland and renewed acquaintance with Sara Winifred Parker. Sara Winifred accepted a proposal of marriage and left her home in Northern Ireland for America with her brother William Joseph Parker on the *Baltic Liner*.

Sara Winifred Parker was born on August 4th, 1894 at Ballykeel, Drumgath, County Down, Ireland. She lived and grew up on the family farm. Her parents had ambitions for their children. The farm, in keeping with tradition, went to the eldest son, and Winnie was encouraged to become a teacher. She received her training in Dublin and taught school near her home at Ballykeel. Her family attended church in Rathfriland.

Winnie and Bill Parker arrived in New York on the *Baltic* steamship December 19th, 1920 and traveled by train to Tucson, arriving December 26th. Winnie and William Thomas were married the next day, December 27th, 1920.

BALTIC
BUILT BY HARLAN & WOLF, BELFAST, NORTHERN IRELAND, 1904. 23,884 GROSS TONS; 726 (BP) FEET LONG; 75 FEET WIDE. STEAM QUADRUPLE EXPANSION ENGINES, TWIN SCREW. SERVICE SPEED 16 KNOTS. 2,875 PASSENGERS (425 FIRST CLASS, 450 SECOND CLASS, 2,000 THIRD CLASS).BUILT FOR WHITE STAR AND DOMINION LINES, IN 1904. LIVERPOOL-NEW YORK SERVICE. LARGEST SHIP AFLOAT, 1905-05. TROOPSHIP DURING WORLD WAR I. SCRAPPED IN 1933. PHOTO CREDIT – FRANK PICHARDO COLLECTION

WILLIAM T. McCLELLAND & SARA WINIFRED PARKER
MARRIAGE CERTIFICATE – DECEMBER 27, 1920

William J. Parker continued to Sausalito, California, where he lived until 1933.

Sara Winifred Parker was about 5 feet 5 inches tall and of medium build. She had dark brown hair and sparkling brown eyes. She was a kind, gentle person and was always very encouraging. She believed that one could get people to do much more by complimenting and encouraging than by criticizing.

Winnie had a very good mind and was a whiz at figures. She could add a column of figures in the wink of an eye and was always able to do that. She helped with the bookwork in the dairy office as it grew, and was very supportive of W. T. and the dairy, and interested in the Guernsey herd, though she preferred to work in the office. She enjoyed it and she felt that housework and cooking were things that had to be done. She loved to read, and later she learned bridge and loved it. It was a challenge to her. So she could have someone to play with, she taught the whole family.

Sara Winifred was always interested in children's organizations and felt that those programs should be supported. She felt education in a child's early years was very important to his or her total development. She would drill her children in spelling and arithmetic. They were pretty good in those skills because of that.

The Parkers are very easy-going, gentle people. They got along well with others. Willie and Winnie were well matched.

Sara Winifred found quite a contrast in climate when she came to Arizona. She was used to a lot of rain and lovely green countryside. She came to the desert where it was very hot in the summer. Smithy, an old friend, had to tell her that one didn't wear straw hats except in summer. Winnie figured that since the weather was so nice, she should be able to wear a straw hat anytime.

Winnie must have thought she was going to the end of the world when she came to Arizona. She always kept close contact with her family and was a good correspondent. The family was able to go back to Ireland periodically. They went in 1928 and took both Frances and Norman. She went back again in 1937 and took Norman.

Both McClellands went back in 1946. Winnie and Frances went back in 1953, the year of the coronation. The McClellands went back in 1962 when they went to the Isle of Guernsey and bought Daisy Dawn. Winnie and Frances returned again in 1969.

Various members of the Irish family have been to Arizona over the years. There has always been close contact.

The photos below are of A. W. Smith, his wife, Elizabeth "Smithy", and their daughter, Bessie, who married Earl Davis. A. W. Smith was an uncle by marriage to W. T. McClelland. He was the brother of Sarah Ann Smith, the first wife of Joseph Henning.

A.W. SMITH & HIS WIFE, "SMITHY"

"SMITHY" & DAUGHTER, BESSIE

MARRIAGE CERTIFICATE OF E. EARL DAVIS & ELIZABETH L. SMITH DAVIS

In 1919, W. T. bought some land on Ruthrauff Road at the dairy. It was very inexpensive at that time, though the price then probably seemed as high to him as a much higher price might seem now. Over the years he continued to buy land. He accumulated quite a bit of acreage around the dairy, which is located about seven miles outside of town. For a long, long time it was a dirt road. During the rains it would become like corduroy and one just bumped along it.

The McClellands sold the Modern Dairy in 1921 and moved to California where they lived for seven months. They liked California, but they returned because the buyer of the Modern Dairy was not making payments, so they had to take it back. Together they started Shamrock Dairy in November of 1922.

SARA WINIFRED PARKER & W. T. McCLELLAND,
CIRCA 1918-1920

William Thomas McClelland was 5 feet 8 or 9 inches tall, with light brown hair and blue eyes. He was of stocky build. He was a very hard worker and ambitious. He was honest, quite frank, and not too long on patience. He was progressive. If there was new equipment for the plant or new ways of doing things, he was among the first to try it. He was quite innovative through the years at the dairy. He was instrumental in starting the Credit Union, the Welfare Benefit Association and the profit sharing plan. He was usually ahead of the other companies. He didn't believe in credit; you didn't buy something unless you could pay for it.

W. T. was very patriotic and loyal to his newly adopted country. He felt America was good to him and that he should "pay back." He was generous with his gifts – to the church, the medical school and various civic organizations.

W. T. was fond of animals and particularly loved the Guernsey cow, and she did very well for him. He was an early riser. When he woke up, he would go out and admire his cows, talk to them, and pet them. He enjoyed his time with them.

The McClellands built a small adobe house at the dairy in 1921. It had a living room, dining room, kitchen, one bedroom, a bath and a sleeping porch. Later they built two frame houses and an office nearby. In the late thirties, they moved to a nearby house that Mr. Parker bought, and stayed there until after World War II began. In 1942, they moved downtown because of gas rationing.

THE McCLELLAND ADOBE HOME, EARLY 1920s

LEFT TO RIGHT: FRANCES McCLELLAND, FRANCES PARKER, HARRY PARKER, NORMAN McCLELLAND & WINIFRED PARKER McCLELLAND, 1928

LEFT TO RIGHT, BACK ROW: SARA W. McCLELLAND, W. T. McCLELLAND, FRANCES PARKER, BOB WADDELL, OLIVE PARKER; FRONT ROW: NORMAN McCLELLAND, FRANCES WADDELL, KATHLEEN WADDELL & JIM WADDELL, SUMMER OF 1946

W. T. spent a lot of his time at the dairy and with the cows. His social life was more or less tied into them and the dairy . He and Winnie became very close friends with an Irish family named McCandless who owned Rockview Dairy in Downey, California. They were also good friends with Buck and Cossie Roberts, who had started Tucson Bottle Exchange. His other friends were tied to the cow organizations. He was active in the Arizona Guernsey Cattle Club and in the American Guernsey Cattle Club. He became friends with Cliff Knight, who dealt in cattle over in California. He enjoyed any group that was connected with cows. He traveled around the country looking at cows and different herds, attending sales and buying and selling animals. He attended fairs and judgings. There were a number of judging classes at the dairy over the years. He had a close association with the University of Arizona. He knew a number of men in the Agriculture department, mostly the Dairy department and the dairy scientists. He cooperated with university projects over the years. The University in turn has been helpful to Shamrock.

LEFT TO RIGHT: FRANCES PARKER, WINIFRED PARKER MCCLELLAND, W. T. MCCLELLAND, DAISY DAWN, NORMAN MCCLELLAND, FRANCES MCCLELLAND & W. J. PARKER, 1962

MR. W. T. McCLELLAND
1891 - 1968

In Memorium

Last Monday he died, Mr. W. T. McClelland, our beloved Mr. Mac, and a part of Shamrock Dairy died with him.

He was a quiet man, unassuming, yet firm and resolute, a man of dedication.

He was loving and beloved, a good man who kindled a feeling of family among all who worked for him.

When he spoke with that hint of Ireland in his voice he seemed an ordinary man, yet it has been said, "The truly extraordinary man is the truly ordinary man."

He was St. Francis' man, whose pleasure came in caring for the cattle he so prized.

The humility in which he lived his life belied the distinction that was his in the eyes of family, friends, community.

We all felt we knew him and though he walks no longer among us, the memory of his being will live in our hearts in timeless years to come.

April 12, 1968

OBITUARY OF MR. W. T. McCLELLAND

A Tribute
to a
Great Lady
Winifred McClelland
1894-1977

Special Memorial Issue, Shamrock News, December 1977

TRIBUTE TO WINIFRED McCLELLAND,
SPECIAL MEMORIAL ISSUE OF *SHAMROCK NEWS*
DECEMBER 1977

William McClelland

AN EXPRESSION OF APPRECIATION
FOR THE LIFE OF WINIFRED McCLELLAND

Scripture Readings: Psalm 90, Proverbs 31, I Corinthians 13, Romans 8, Psalm 23

We have come to express our appreciation for the life of Winifred McClelland and all that her life and work, her faith and love have meant to us. We have known her as mother and grandmother, as sister and aunt, as one with whom we worked and laughed and lived. And we are grateful to God for all the experiences we have shared with her.

Born in County Down, Ireland, she always cherished her roots and her family there. There was a little bit of Ireland wherever she went. But she came here to fulfill her hopes and dreams. And she rejoiced in all the accomplishments of 57 years in Arizona. Almost 47 of those years were spent sharing and developing a dream with "Mr. Mac". A home and family, a dairy with prize Guernsey cows, American citizenship, the joy of work, people to work with to build a dream to reality, church, friends, community-- all were important.

She was the kind of person who was gentle but hard-working; who liked to praise and support others so they could do their best. She particularly cared for youth in the church; at Boys' Ranch or Girls' Ranch; at the University where a McClelland Scholarship Fund will always be helping someone; in the public schools, where the new Flowing Wells Junior High and adjacent recreation area are on land given by the Mc- Clellands.

And she enjoyed her friends at home, playing bridge; in the American Guernsey Cattle Club; at work; in the church and community.

It was our privilege to meet other members of her family in Northern Ireland last summer. One enjoys just being with them. The part she brought from Ireland and the part she developed here, all went into the life, faith and love of one we have appreciated.

There is a verse from Matthew's Gospel that is particularly appropriate: "Well done, good and faithful servant. You have been faithful even in that which is least; enter into the joy of your Lord."

AN EXPRESSION OF APPRECIATION FOR THE LIFE OF WINIFRED McCLELLAND

331

FIFTH GENERATION

Frances Helen McClelland, Norman Parker McClelland

Frances Helen McClelland – Fifth Generation

Frances Helen McClelland, first child of Sara Winifred Parker and William McClelland, was born on August 4th, 1923 (her mother's birthday) at the Stork's Nest in Tucson, Arizona. She grew up in the country, about seven miles out of town, playing in the fields and trees and riding the cows. The only admonition was, "Don't go near the bull"!

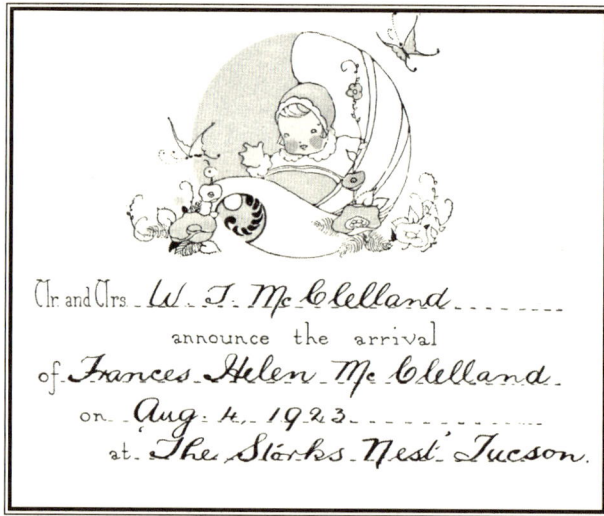

Mr and Mrs *W. J. McClelland*
announce the arrival
of *Frances Helen McClelland*
on *Aug. 4, 1923*
at *The Storks Nest Tucson*.

FRANCES HELEN MCCLELLAND BIRTH ANNOUNCEMENT

At eight years of age, Frances came down with poliomyelitis and spent five years in Los Angeles doing physical therapy and hydrotherapy, and undergoing several surgeries.

At fourteen, she joined her family in Tucson and attended high school at St. Joseph's Academy. She later attended the University of Arizona and majored in Accounting, graduating in 1944.

After working for two years at Trinity Presbyterian Church as the financial secretary, Frances joined Shamrock Dairy and worked around the office on a variety of tasks. Frances eventually became active full-time as Secretary-Treasurer of Shamrock Foods, and a member of the board of directors.

LEFT TO RIGHT: FRANCES HELEN McCLELLAND, JEAN PARKER
SCHUERMAN, ALICE PARKER & KATHLEEN LUTTON 1991

FRANCES HELEN McCLELLAND
SEMI-RETIREMENT PARTY 1991

Frances was 5 feet 3 ½ inches tall, of a stocky build, with light brown hair and blue eyes. As the first child of W. T. and Winifred McClelland, she was encouraged to learn new things and tackle new jobs. She had her mother's mathematical ability, and was known for her quickness with figures.

Frances lived her life to the fullest. Her love for her family and friends was widely felt, and each knew how special (s)he was in her life.

Although life was a challenge to her, Frances never let it get in her way. She traveled around the world with family and friends and continually pushed herself and others in pursuing excellence and appreciating the importance of learning. In quieter moments, she enjoyed reading, working with figures, and playing bridge.

Frances was a warm, caring, intuitive person who felt strongly about helping the less fortunate. She encouraged those around her to value what they had, to live within their means, and to help others. She was a rock that anyone could turn to, with a level head and a calming mien.

Frances was a trustworthy person whose opinions were highly valued, not only by her family, but also by business, academic, and religious communities. She was active in her church, serving as both an Elder and a Trustee, and in the YWCA, where for a number of years she served as Treasurer, and then President. She also served on the University of Arizona's Foundation Board, as well as the board of Amity, Inc.

Frances passed away in her sleep on Wednesday July 6th, 2005 after a brief illness. Her special memorial edition of the *Shamrock News* follows.

In Loving Memory

Frances H. McClelland

August 4, 1923 – July 6, 2005

Special memorial edition of SHAMROCK NEWS

EXCERPTS FROM FRANCES' MEMORIAL SERVICE

"July 4th was a glorious day. I rode down to Tucson with two of my sisters-in-Christ silently wondering what my heavenly Father was going to do. When I walked into the waiting room, I saw family and friends in various stages of grief. I hugged each one and gave a holy kiss to them. My father then gently took my hand, and we went to see our beloved Frances, who now was in intensive care.

My father stayed for a short time and then I was left in the room alone with Frances. I leaned in close to her and asked forgiveness for so many lost years with her and tears began to flow as she gently assured me that she loved me. When Barbara walked in, I felt a stirring in my spirit, and I became very still inside. Barbara asked Frances what her favorite scripture was. She contemplated and finally said:"I don't have one, but I do have one word…LOVE. She went on to say that LOVE solves everything. Another scripture ran through my mind that LOVE never fails. Then Barbara asked Frances what her favorite song was. She had to really sort through many of them but finally said: "Rock of Ages." Barbara began to sing and Frances and I joined in. There was a bit of humor, always a quality of Frances, because all three of us began to hum at the same time because for a moment we all forgot the words. There was such a beautiful smile on Frances's face as she sang. When we stopped singing, I could tell by her expression she was reflecting, which she had been doing for 3 days. Finally, I said to Frances, "You know that we will know each other in heaven," and she said, "I hope so." The Holy Spirit's still small voice let me know that His work was still not completed. Frances went on to say that there was only one thing she was thinking about and that was, "How am I going to get there?" I looked at her and asked if she wanted me to pray with her. I prayed the CROSS where Jesus took upon himself all of our sins that we might be saved and have eternal life. I prayed that Frances would receive Him as her personal Savior and that He would make His home in her heart. In the silence after that, I thought of Zephaniah 3:17 where God says:"The Lord your God is with you, He is mighty to save. He will take great delight in you, He will quiet you with His love, He will rejoice over you with singing." I knew then that Frances was finally home, and there was great rejoicing in heaven. No more adversities to deal with in this world, no more pain, no more sorrow, simply peace. Her joy was finally complete, yet I knew that I would miss her until we were re-united again."
– *Kathe McClelland*

"Frances McClelland – who was she? I'm sure that everyone here today will agree with me that –'Frances McClelland was the First Lady of Shamrock Foods Company.'

During the mid 70's to the mid 80's, Frances and I worked together a lot in our Colorado Division. That's when I started to see and really enjoy her personal side. She was a lot of fun to be with. I soon discovered she had a unique way of getting information from me or anyone else. At times we were not even aware she was doing it.

One of her greatest roles was leading by example. She was a strong willed lady who never gave up. She always saw each task through to completion.

Frances developed relationships with as many of her co-workers as possible. It was important to her to maintain these relationships. She wanted to know and fully understand each course of action the company was undertaking or involved in.

I could go on and on sharing thoughts about this giant of a lady but, I will bring my thoughts to a close. In doing so, let me say this – some might think Frances had a physical obstacle, let me share with you, if she did, I never observed it and I'm sure you didn't observe it either.

Think about her and talk about her often. Let's keep her MEMO-RIES alive within us. We will remember her leadership and overall contributions to the continued success of Shamrock Foods Company. The high standards she established for herself and for Shamrock Foods Company, will always continue with each of us."
– *Charlie Roberts*

"Of the McClellands, she said they were hard working with tremendous capacity for accomplishment, intelligent, determined, and once a course was set, immovable in the pursuit of a goal or objective, and of high integrity.

Of the Parkers, she said, again, they were hard working, but also gentle and fun loving with a great sense of humor, more quiet and reserved, with a passion for education and helping others. My grandmother, Mrs. Mac, was a whiz at figures and Frances certainly had that quality in abundance; but she had all the others as well, any one of which would be a blessing to any of us.

When you work for a family business, particularly one in which family members are very active, or also in leadership positions, I think it's important to know what they stand for, what they are made of. And all those things Frances mentioned, she is and was. And for that, we honor her and will honor her most of all if we continue to live those values she mentioned. We will also miss her – I certainly do – that gentle voice in meetings that reminded us of what we are all about and what is really important.

But there is one value which she missed and again, this is typical of Frances because she wouldn't think of it for herself.

Many, many years ago, a holy man was asked "Who does God bless and smile upon?"

And he replied, "He, or she, who is Humble when endowed with Greatness." For me, that is Frances. She was endowed with greatness as all of her many activities and awards show, yet she preferred a cheery conversation, sprinkled with humor, at the kitchen or bridge table with good friends or family to the garish trappings which so often accompany greatness. It was her humility which I think was and is her greatest gift. I never saw her in anger, or heard her say anything bad about anyone. She was a remarkable and special woman.

And so I think God smiled down on Frances all her life. And now that she is with him, I think he is beaming."
– *Kent McClelland*

Frances Helen McClelland

Our very good friend, sister, cousin and aunt, Frances Helen McClelland, joined with Jesus and her parents on July 6. Her extraordinary life will be remembered for her integrity, humor, generosity and strong will.

Frances was born in Tucson, Arizona on August 4, 1923, and was the first child of W.T. and Winifred McClelland. Her Irish immigrant parents taught her the values of hard work, honesty and Christian ethics that she would embody over her life time.

Frances was stricken with polio in her youth and while the disease left her without the complete use of her legs, she was able to accomplish a full life. She traveled the world, was a western business pioneer, a philanthropist and community leader.

She graduated from St. Joseph's Academy in Tucson in 1940. Upon her graduation from the University of Arizona with an Accounting degree in 1944, she initially worked as Financial Secretary of Trinity Presbyterian Church in Tucson. She was a life long member of Trinity where she also served as Clerk of the Session, President of the Board of Trustees and Treasurer. She also served as Treasurer and Chairman of Finance for Presbytery de Cristo.

In 1946 she joined her parents and brother at Shamrock Dairy where she has been actively involved ever since. This small family owned dairy farm, has grown into Shamrock Foods Company, with farming, dairy and foodservice operations throughout the western United States. Her integrity, honesty, and loving spirit, are continuing values she will leave to her associates at Shamrock. They will remember her leadership as a director and officer of the company for nearly sixty years. Shamrock is recognized by Forbes magazine annually as one of the largest private businesses in the United States.

Frances was also active with the University of Arizona throughout her life. She served on the University of Arizona Foundation Board for a number of years and was recognized in 2003 with an Honorary Doctorate Degree. The business school building at the University of Arizona is named in honor of the McClelland family as recognition of their involvement, and support over several generations. She was honored many different times for her active support and involvement by the University of Arizona.

Her community involvement included long service to the YWCA in Tucson where she served as Treasurer, Finance Chairman and President. She was the recipient of the YWCA 1991 Woman On the Move Award. The YWCA also had presented Frances with a Lifetime Achievement Award.

Frances was also active with the Tucson Library Board, the Amity, Inc. Board and Beta Sigma Phi. Additionally, she has been active in the Arizona Astronomy Board, the University of Arizona Institute for Children, Youth and Family Board, and the Arizona Senior Academy Board.

In addition to her many community and business accomplishments, her strong intellect will be remembered by her many friends and bridge partners. She had a curiosity about the world reflected by her travels and love of reading. Her most recent trip abroad was to visit friends and family in Ireland in the fall of 2004. On that trip she was able to share a genealogy of her family that was co-authored with her brother, Norman.

Frances is survived by her brother, Norman P. McClelland, her niece, Kathe McClelland, nephew, W. Kent McClelland, and cousins, Jeanie Parker Schuerman and James Parker.

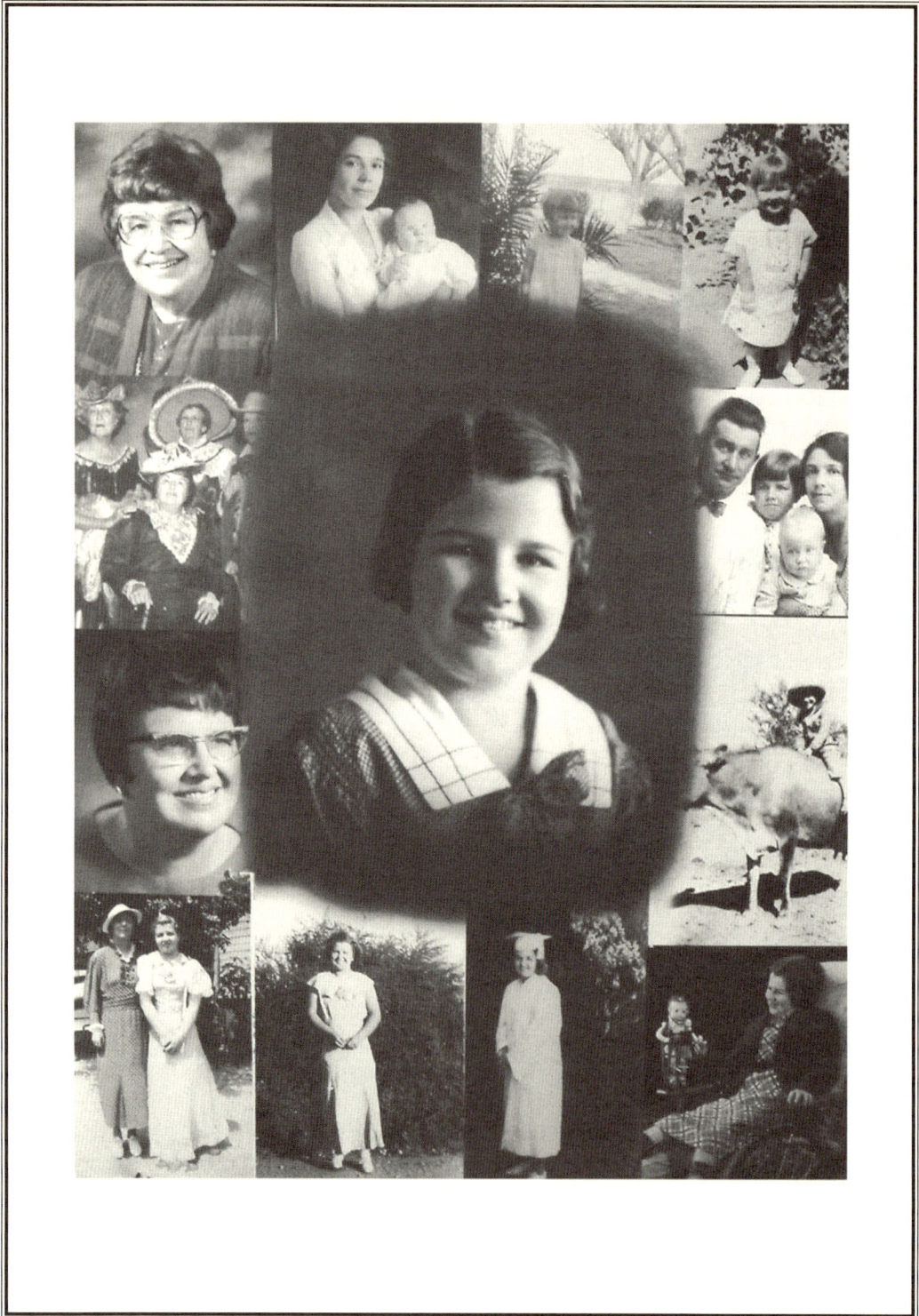

Norman Parker McClelland – Fifth Generation

Norman Parker McClelland, second child of Sara Winifred Parker and William McClelland, was born on June 21st, 1927 at the Stork's Nest in Tucson, Arizona. It was the best life, a childhood on the farm—a playground—and he spent a lot of time by himself growing up.

Norman attended school at Amphitheater Elementary, Junior High, and High School through grade eleven. It was during the Second World War, and due to gas rationing, that the family moved seven miles to downtown Tucson, where he completed his last year at Tucson High School. The family were members of Trinity Presbyterian Church, and membership in various church youth groups helped Norman make the transition from a class of twenty students at Amphitheater to twenty-five hundred at Tucson High.

At age seventeen, Norman volunteered for and joined the United States Air Force. Hostilities were rapidly coming to a close and his service time was spent in Wiesbaden, Germany in the 89th Air Force Station Complement Squadron. Norman was honorably discharged in early 1947. During his service time he spent a week's leave at Ballykeel, Northern Ireland with his Irish relatives and his parents, who took the opportunity to return home for a visit.

The University of Arizona was home for the next few years, and Norman graduated in 1949 with a Bachelor of Science in Business Administration and a minor in Agriculture.

Norman joined the small family business following graduation. With the help of other family members and many Shamrock associates, the business has grown to annual revenues in 2006 of more than 1.5 billion dollars.

Norman continued a tradition of dairy farming, which has grown as a part of Shamrock Farms to a milking operation of 10,000 animals, including registered Guernseys. He served on the Board and as President of the American Guernsey Cattle Club. Over the years, he has been a very active leader in numerous civic, political, and philanthropic organizations.

Norman has always had a very positive, determined outlook on life. He is 6 feet in height, slim of build, with blue eyes. He has inherited the gentle manner of all Parkers.

He has been active in various church organizations, played a leadership role in church development, and served on several occasions as an Elder of the Presbyterian Church.

Norman has received numerous business and civic awards during his career, including the National Conference of Christians and Jews 1988 Human Relations Award, an Honorary Doctor of Laws degree from the University of Arizona in 1991, and a 1997 Ellis Island Medal of Honor. On April 23rd, 1998, he was inducted into the Arizona Business Hall of Fame.

★

NORMAN P. McCLELLAND
Dairy Farmer and Food Distributor
(Born 1927)

Norman McClelland's parents, along with his mother's brother, opened
Shamrock Dairy in Tucson in 1922. Norman was born five years later in
1927 and was raised in the family business along with his sister, Frances.

In 1949, after serving in the military and earning two degrees from the
University of Arizona, Norman joined the family business. He assumed the
post of president in 1954 and became Chairman and CEO in 1992. Under
his guidance, Shamrock Farms evolved from a small dairy farm to a multi-
million dollar food distribution company. In the course of its growth and
expansion, McClelland took three major risks where the success or failure
of the company hinged on the outcome of his actions.

In 1954, McClelland addressed union issues without a strike or confronta-
tion by establishing a credit union and adopting an innovative distributor
system which was framed to protect both the company and the individual
distributors. In 1956, he invested all the revenue Shamrock had generated
since 1922 into building a milk processing plant in Phoenix. McClelland
moved the offices to Phoenix in the face of dire predictions of failure, but
within 15 years Shamrock controlled 40 percent of the Arizona milk market. The third risk involved McClelland's refusal to settle a federal anti-
trust litigation which dragged on from 1972 to the company's total vindi-
cation of the charges in 1984.

In 1966, Shamrock expanded into a full-line food service company. As the
company grew, its personality changed and became more compartmental-
ized. To combat this, McClelland and his son Kent, who became president
in 1992, instituted a system of team management intended to give all
employees a sense of purpose and build stronger client relationships.

McClelland was awarded an honorary Doctor of Laws degree from the
University of Arizona in 1991, and Shamrock was listed among Forbes top
400 private companies in the U.S. in 1993. In 1987, the family donated
$2.5 million toward the construction of McClelland Hall at the University
of Arizona Business College.

BIOGRAPHY OF NORMAN P. McCLELLAND

"If we have been part of the American dream, I believe it has been due in no small measure to having honored my father's wishes: to treat our employees like family and our customers like friends." — Norman P. McClelland

NORMAN P. McCLELLAND

In January 1951, Norman married Barbara Stark of Wynnewood, Pennsylvania. They lived first in Tucson and later in Phoenix, Arizona. Two children were born of this union: Katherine McClelland and Kent McClelland. Norman and Barbara were divorced in May 1990.

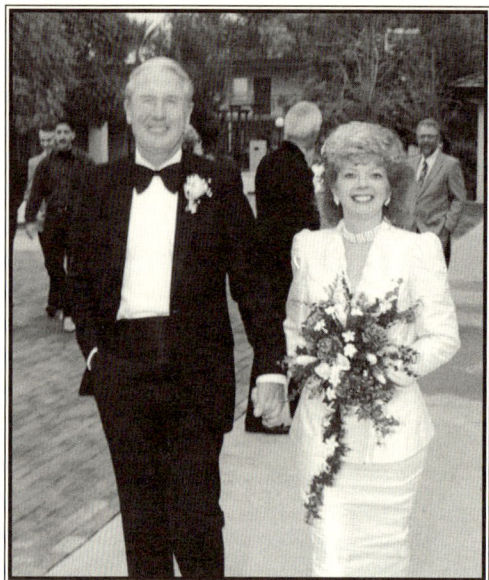

NORMAN McCLELLAND & BARBARA MOUDY
WEDDING DAY, DECEMBER 21, 1991

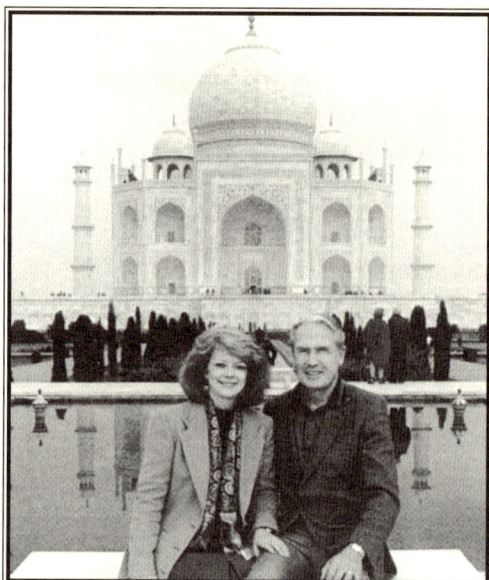

BARBARA & NORMAN McCLELLAND
TAJ MAJAL, 1994

Norman married Barbara Ann Moudy on December 21st, 1991 at Church of the Beatitudes, Phoenix, Arizona.

Barbara was born in Council Bluffs, Iowa and grew up on a farm near Harlan, Iowa. She was the third child in her family and has two brothers and three sisters. Barbara is five feet two inches with red hair and blue eyes. She is friendly, outgoing, and sociable. She particularly enjoys talking to friends and family one-on-one and has a positive, helpful personality. Here are some of her comments about her life:

"My parents gave me the name Barbara Ann Rold. I'm a country girl from a picture-book land of small green farms, blue lakes, and gentle rolling countryside. To even think of my homeland gives me a sense of peace, and also, freedom. It was a vast playground where we could ice skate in the winter and look for tadpoles in the Nishnabotna River in the summer, climb a large evergreen tree, make our favorite mud pies, or just run the green fields. That is, we did when there was no work to be done.

Our life centered around work, family and church. Since our family's Danish roots
had been established in this area for over a hundred years, we knew everyone and had a
marvelous sense of community.

"After graduating from Harlan High School, I attended Patricia Stevens Career
College in Omaha. Immediately afterwards, I married and moved to Kansas City where
I worked at Hallmark Cards, an international family-owned business. The building I
worked in employed 5,000 persons, but we were the family of J. C. Hall and of each
other. Every year, at Christmas, he greeted each of his employees personally in his office.
My last position here was as Senior Secretary to the Senior Vice President of Sales and
Marketing who managed the four U.S. district managers and over 1,000 sales managers.

"Later, after moving to Phoenix, Arizona, I found another family-oriented business
where we were all part of one large family – Shamrock Foods Company. Many of the
employees were from the Midwest and I felt like I had found another home. Their
customs, values, attitudes and behaviors made me feel at home in the vast desert
landscape of the Southwest, which felt so foreign when first moving here.

"My marriage fell apart in 1988 after almost twenty years of struggling to be a
cohesive family. The bright spot and the joy that came from this union was the birth of
Heather Marie Moudy on October 15, 1970, in Kansas City, Missouri.

"Since my marriage to Norman, a fine gentleman who shares my basic belief system
of family and Christianity, I pursued an English major and graduated summa cum laude
in August 1998. I continue to enjoy many great literary works. In recent years I have
taken an interest in exploring the great truths of the Bible, and have met many of God's
people along the way. Their marvelous stories of their walk with God exemplify love,
courage, strength, hope, and a great faith."

A few words from Norman:

"We have met many new Parkers, Wrights, and McClellands in the search for our
roots. We welcome old and new family members and hope you enjoy the information
so many relatives have provided. It has been our pleasure. As a reminder to all who
attended our family reunion in Arizona, 1997, our photo is included.

"Since the family reunion at Lustybeg in Ireland, 2002, we have experienced many
challenges and opportunities for growth within our family and the community. In faith,
we have embraced our Lord, and are confident in His abiding love.

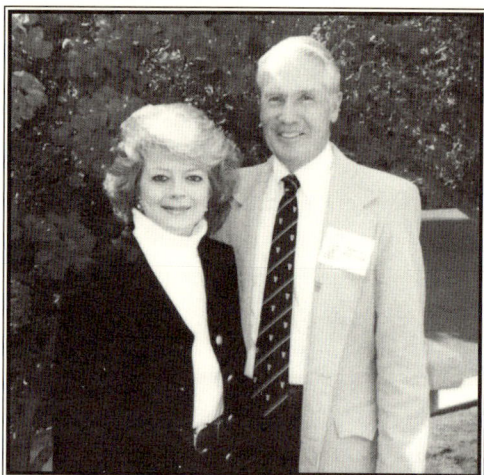

"We are blessed to have all our family living in the same city, and continue to enjoy moments amidst busy schedules. Chandra and Joy have completed their Bachelors degrees at Kenyon College and Northern Arizona University, respectively. Kera is now a freshman at Williams College, and Devon a sophomore at Brophy College Preparatory. Occasionally, we catch up with them.

BARBARA & NORMAN McCLELLAND, FAMILY REUNION, 1997

"Harlan and Jaelyn, Heather's children, continue to delight us at age six with rapid-paced learning, though nothing compares to the love they freely give.

"We're looking forward to the publication of *The McClellands of Cloughenramer* in the spring of 2007, and hope to see many family members and renew strong ties once again in Ireland and America in celebration of this publication. We plan to publish *The Hennings of Ireland* in 2008."

BARBARA & NORMAN McCLELLAND, 2003

McCLELLAND FAMILY 2006
FRONT ROW, LEFT TO RIGHT: CHANDRA, DEVON, BARBARA, KATHE McCLELLAND, JOY ALVAREZ; BACK ROW, LEFT TO RIGHT: KENT, NORMAN, KERA, CELIA McCLELLAND AND JOSHUA ALVAREZ

SIXTH GENERATION

Katherine McClelland, William Kent McClelland

Katherine McClelland – Sixth Generation

Katherine McClelland, the first child of Norman McClelland and Barbara Stark, was born on July 21st, 1952 at Tucson Medical Center in Tucson, Arizona. She was full of vigor and life. Her nickname, Kathe, has been with her for years. Tucson was a wonderful city to raise children in. At the beginning of Kathe's sophomore year in high school, the family moved to Paradise Valley, Arizona. It was a huge change for everybody.

Years went by before she married Elias Baray Alvarez. They had two children: Joshua David, born August 3, 1981 and Joy Rebekah, born January 11, 1984.

The pictures below reflect her faith, her two beautiful children, the beauty of her favorite place to go, the beach, and the one true love of her life, Roxy Anne, born on February 3rd, 2000. She was an angel in disguise and passed away April 15th, 2005.

Jesus came to set the captives free

Joshua & Joy Alvarez, September 1985

The comfort and peace given
by the Holy Spirit

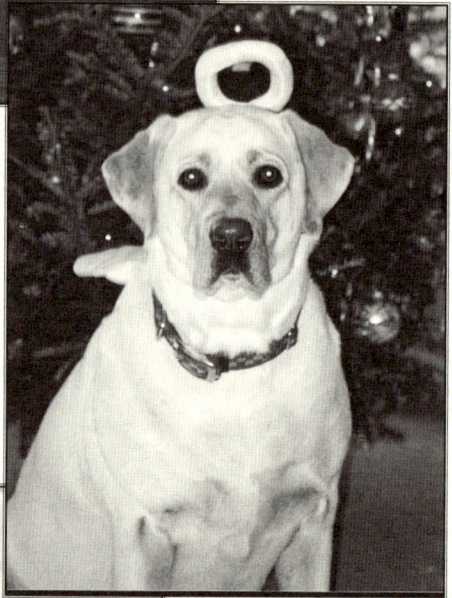

Roxy Anne's angelic
love as she walks on the
streets of gold

Kathe is 5'4" with blond hair and brown eyes. Not all of her years were good, but in 1994, her life truly began. She lived in Solana Beach for three years raising not only her own children but a few others along the way. Her heart has always been for the children and the older ones. In August 1997, she finally made the decision to move to Gilbert, Arizona, and begin her journey with Shamrock Farms.

The children were in high school and, as always, there were about six other kids, both boys and girls, living at the house. It had to be God's gift that saw Kathe through the toughest years, parenting teenagers as a single mother. Every one of the kids that she raised is well and happy.

After Roxy died, she finally surrendered every bit of herself to her Savior and Lord, Jesus Christ. It is through Him that she has been set free from years of bondage. Her shattered heart has been pieced back together with His love.

With the nest never quite empty, she has had more time to devote to the Farms. She has a great love, not only for the Farms, but also for the people who have been there for many years. Her only prayer is that she is a mirror, a reflection of her Heavenly Father. She is also involved with the vineyards in Lodi, California.

She loves being with her kids and her family. They are number one, as far as she is concerned. Her father, Norman McClelland, has made the biggest impact in her life. As she reflects, "When you truly love someone, it takes a tremendous amount of humility and perseverance to really know how they think and feel about life. You find out that they are not always on the same page as you are but that doesn't matter. You have to work through it". They have and she is so very grateful for that.

Norman and Kathe in Carmel, July 1999

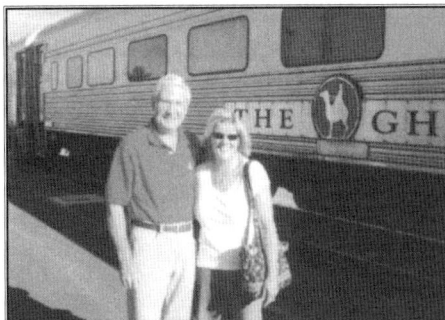

Norman and Kathe in Australia, June 2006

Kathe's mother, Barbara Stark McClelland, is one of the many joys in her life. The most special bond between them is having a personal relationship with Jesus. There is so much to learn about Him, so many discussions are about just that. She is a great grandmother to both of her children and the strays that she has grown to love very much.

She has a heart for education and The Lost Boys of Sudan. Full of energy, she has something going on all the time.

Kathe's aunt, Mary Elizabeth Hall, shares the same bond. She is a great listener and "can lift up your spirit without you even knowing it." She has blessed Kathe throughout the years. After all, she is the one who led Kathe to the Cross where Jesus died for her sins, even though she didn't deserve it.

Kathe and her mom on Thanksgiving Day, 2005

Kathe's mom, her daughter, Joy, and her Aunt Betty, January 2005

SEVENTH GENERATION

Joshua David Alvarez, Joy Rebekah Alvarez

Joshua David Alvarez – Seventh Generation

Kathe on her son Josh:

"Joshua was born two weeks early; however, he did not want to come out. He is my love. Deep inside, Joshua is a very gentle, loving, shy, son. He has always watched over me and his sister. We are a triangle, me, Joshua, and Joy, and there is no one who can break us apart. The three of us have made it together without a husband or father.

"If you want his shyness to disappear, just bring up sports or cars. He knows every person on every team, be it football, basketball, or baseball. He loves the Suns basketball team and goes to as many home games as possible. The challenge before him is to find out what he wants to do with his life. He will find his way. As of late, to my surprise and others, he has become an avid golf player.

"Joshua and Rachel, his girlfriend, have been together for over five years. He met her ten years ago when his sister, Joy, was at a soccer practice. I believe it was love at first sight. It took them some time before they finally got together. They have three dogs, Remy, Cain, and Kaida Lynn, that keep them very busy."

Josh and Rachel at Christmas, December 2005

Joy and Rachel enjoying the ocean, July 2006

Josh and Rachel going to *Phantom of the Opera*, August 2005

The Grande Finale, Joshua's pride and joy

Joy Rebekah Alvarez

Kathe on her daughter Joy:

"Joy was born nine weeks early and weighed three pounds. Contrary to Joshua, she couldn't wait to see the world. What can a mother say about her, except she is the joy of her life. She is the outgoing one, who never lets a new experience pass her by. Joy had watched Joshua play soccer for years, and at the age of ten, she said to me, 'I think I can do this.' She was right. Soccer came so naturally to her, and she advanced to the highest level by the age of fourteen.

"She was an excellent student as well. She had many offers to play soccer for various universities, but she chose Northern Arizona University. In her freshman year, she was a starter at every soccer game, which is very rare indeed. In May of 2002, she was asked to play with her old competitive team, the Sereno Golden Eagles, at regionals held in Oahu. She made the only goal at their last game and walked off the field saying, 'I am done.'

"From that point on she began pursuing a degree in Biology and will graduate December 15, 2006. I am so proud of her. She has been in school for seventeen years, including summer school, so a rest is well deserved."

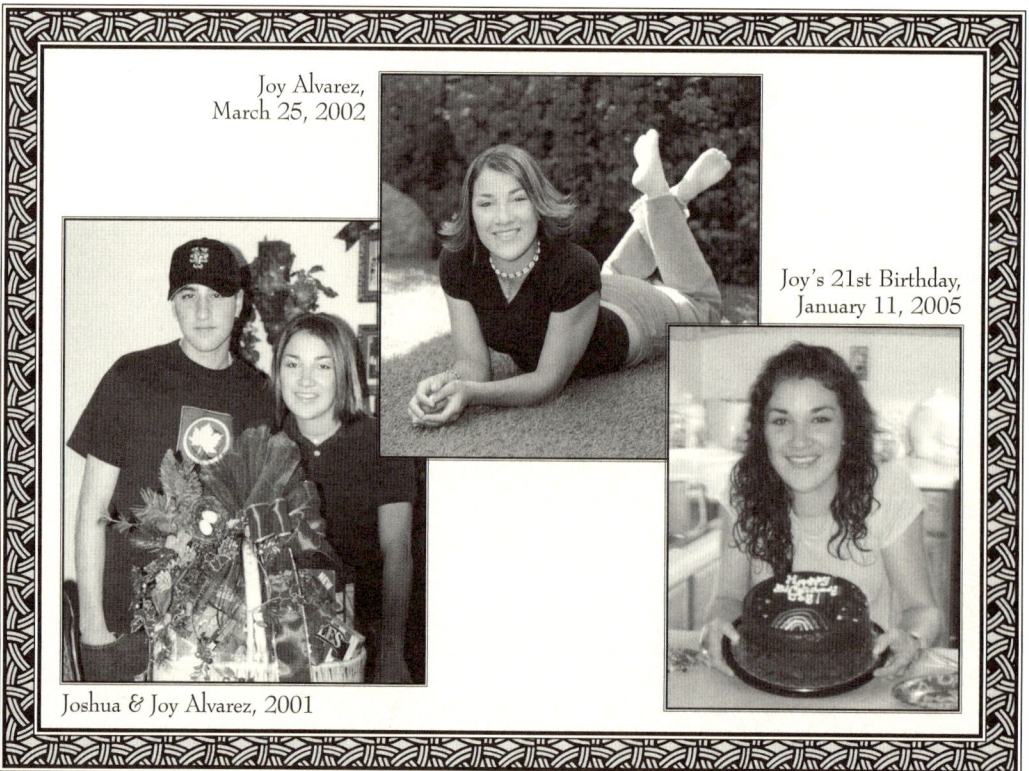

Joy Alvarez,
March 25, 2002

Joy's 21st Birthday,
January 11, 2005

Joshua & Joy Alvarez, 2001

Joy's Best Friend, Ryan Tierney

Joy's 22nd Birthday with Joshua

Joy's 22nd Birthday with Kathe

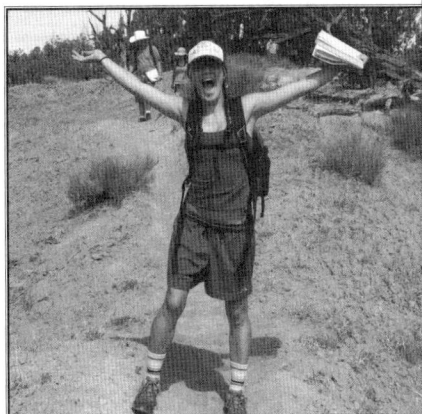

Silly Joy in Utah, Summer School,
Bryce Canyon 2006

Joy & Janna's Friendship

Joy and Janna met their freshman year and neither one of them knew anyone. Joy had moved with her mother and brother from California, and Janna's family had moved from Oregon. They became fast friends and have been for ten years.

A year ago, Janna delivered a beautiful baby girl and named her Olyvia Joy, making Joy her godmother. She has brought more love and joy into her entire family's life. Janna was one of Kathe's kids and will be part of the family forever.

Joy and Janna on New Year's Day, 2006

Joy & her Goddaughter, Olyvia Joy, April 2005

Janna McVicker and Olyvia Joy, November 2006

Nana, aka Kathe, and Olyvia Joy, November 2006

William Kent McClelland – Sixth Generation

William Kent McClelland, the second child of Norman McClelland and Barbara Stark, was born on March 10th, 1954 at Tucson Medical Center, Tucson, Arizona. He attended schools in Tucson and Phoenix, and graduated with a Bachelor of Arts in Physics from Colorado College in 1976. He received a Master of Business Administration from the University of California Los Angeles in 1981.

Kent grew up as part of a family in private business, and worked in various jobs during summer vacations. He spent a brief period as a management trainee with Shamrock before leaving the Company in 1978.

After receiving his Masters degree, Kent spent three years working for the Mercantile Bank of Canada in their Los Angeles real estate lending division. He returned to Shamrock in 1984 and moved to Colorado, where he served in various capacities and finally became President and General Manager of the Colorado Division in 1986. From there he moved to Phoenix as President and Chief Operation Officer of Shamrock Foods Company in 1992.

On December 13th, 1980, Kent married Celia Susan Evans in Denver, Colorado. Celia was born on June 2nd, 1955 in Denver, Colorado to Elsie Little and Charles Evans. Elsie Little grew up in Cedar City, Utah and moved to Denver with Charles in the 1940s. They had five children: Chloe, Bonnie, John, Reed, and Celia. Charles died of cancer at a very young age, and after a time Elsie married Rawlen T. Smith of Denver. Rawlen had a real cowboy-type youth in north central Wyoming, where his family farmed and ranched. He moved to Denver in the 1940s and started a successful manufacturing business in implements for tractors and other farm equipment. Rawlen had two children from a previous marriage, Brent and Michelle.

Celia graduated from the University of Utah in 1977 with a Bachelor of Science in Accounting. She worked for the McGladdrey-Hendrickson accounting firm in Denver, where she received her CPA. In the fall of 1979, she moved to southern California and worked for First Interstate Bancorp in their internal auditing and tax departments while pursuing her Masters in

KENT MCCLELLAND

353

CELIA & KENT MCCLELLAND, 2001

LEFT TO RIGHT: CHANDRA, KENT, DEVON, CELIA, & KERA MCCLELLAND – LAKE LOUISE, ALBERTA, CANADA, JULY, 2003

LEFT TO RIGHT: KENT, CHANDRA, SAM, DEVON, KERA & CELIA MCCLELLAND, NOVEMBER, 2001

Business Taxation, which she received in 1984 from the University of Southern California (USC).

At present, Kent is an active member of All Saints' Episcopal Church, having served as chairman of the school board for All Saints' Episcopal Day School while his children attended. He and Celia were also very active in the Arizona chapter of the Young Presidents Organization, and graduated to the World Presidents Organization in May of 2006. Celia remains involved in the YPO spousal forums, along with other community service groups.

Kent is 5'10" with a muscular build, brown hair, and brown eyes. He plays the piano and enjoys tennis, golf, and reading. He is also an avid mountain climber and has summitted peaks all over the world: Mt. McKinley, Mt. Rainier, and the Grand Teton in North America; Cotopaxi in Ecuador; Ixtachautl, Popocatpetl, and Orizaba in Mexico; as well as Mt Vinson in Antarctica and Mt. Kilimanjaro in Tanzania, Africa. Kent has a strong McClelland personality, touched with the sensibility of his Parker heritage.

Celia is 5'8" with brown hair and blue-green eyes. She is slightly built, with a very gentle manner, a warm, friendly personality, a great sense of humor, and a good-natured way of encouraging those around her. Yet she also has a feisty side, and is very firm in her convictions. Celia enjoys reading, music, visiting family and friends, and rooting for her children in their many endeavors.

Three children were born of this union: Chandra, born May 11, 1984 in Los Angeles, Kera, born April 30, 1988 in Denver, and Devon, born July 13, 1991, in Denver.

MARK & MARION HUME'S HOME
BELFAST, IRELAND – JULY 2005
BACK ROW, LEFT TO RIGHT: KENT McCLELLAND, MARK &
MARION HUME, CHANDRA, DEVON, CELIA & KERA McCLELLAND
FRONT ROW: STEPHEN & JONATHAN HUME

CHANDRA McCLELLAND GRADUATION
KENYON COLLEGE – MAY 2006
BACK ROW, LEFT TO RIGHT: KENT, CHANDRA, NORMAN, CELIA,
DEVON & KERA McCLELLAND; FRONT ROW: LOTTE DUNNELL

SEVENTH GENERATION

Chandra Elise McClelland, Kerani Alysa McClelland, Devon Thomas McClelland

Chandra Elise McClelland – Seventh Generation

Chandra Elise McClelland, firstborn of William Kent McClelland and Celia Susan Evans, was born on May 11th, 1984 in Los Angeles, California.

Chandra graduated summa cum laude with high honors in English from Kenyon College in May 2006, having spent most of her final year researching and writing about musical theatre and literature (which, consequently, meant seeing as many shows as humanly possible). She returned home and is currently spending mornings with three- and four-year-olds as a preschool teaching assistant for Christ Church School. The rest of her time is engaged with riding, writing, learning to cook non-college food, negotiating "real life," and, most importantly, reconnecting with family and friends.

CHANDRA ELISE MCCLELLAND, 2002

Kerani Alysa McClelland – Seventh Generation

Kerani Alysa McClelland, secondborn of William Kent McClelland and Celia Susan Evans, was born on April 30th, 1988 in Denver, Colorado.

Kera graduated from Phoenix Country Day School in June 2006. She was accepted early decision into Williams College in Massachusetts, one of the nation's top liberal arts schools, and is currently diving, socializing, singing with an a cappella group, and studying ridiculously hard. In answer to the inevitable, she plans to pursue the college's pre-med program, balancing a great deal of science with her other core requirements and interests, which include music, history, and possibly yoga, one of the winter-study offerings. Her family misses her a great deal, especially Jack.

KERANI ALYSA McCLELLAND, 2002

Devon Thomas McClelland – Seventh Generation

Devon Thomas McClelland, thirdborn of William Kent McClelland and Celia Susan Evans, was born on July 13th, 1991 in Denver, Colorado.

Devon graduated from All Saints' Episcopal Day School in 2004 and is presently a sophomore at Brophy College Preparatory. Time not spent at school goes straight to the tennis court, as he plays nearly every day of the week and is working on creaming the rest of his family in singles and doubles. Devon recently achieved Eagle Scout status with the completion and review of a service project that involved renovating and planting a community garden. Scouting still has him hiking on the weekends, a pastime he shares with his dad and sisters; all four summitted Mt. Kilimanjaro in the summer of 2006.

DEVON THOMAS MCCLELLAND, 2002

SIXTH GENERATION

Heather Marie Moudy – Sixth Generation

Heather Marie Moudy was born on October 15th, 1970 in Kansas City, Missouri. Heather is energetic and enthusiastic, and loves the world of drama. She has red hair and blue eyes. Heather completed her college education at Arizona State University, with an additional year at the Academy of Dramatic Arts in New York City.

Heather married Nathan Helser on February 14th, 1998. They separated in 2004.

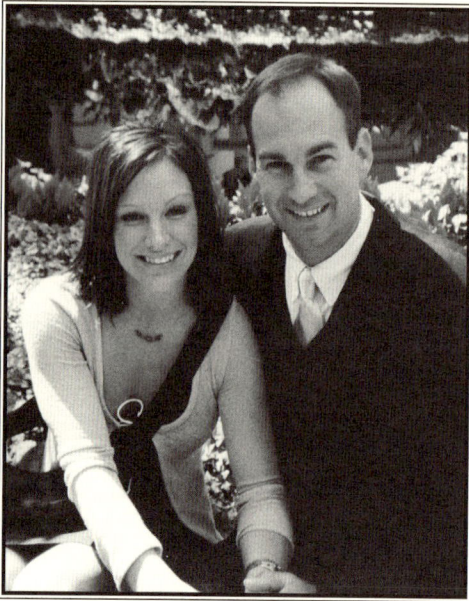

HEATHER & NATE HELSER

There were two children from this union, twins, born September 29, 2000.

Harlan Bleu Helser was born first, followed closely by his sister Jaelyn Navy Helser. The twins are a delight.

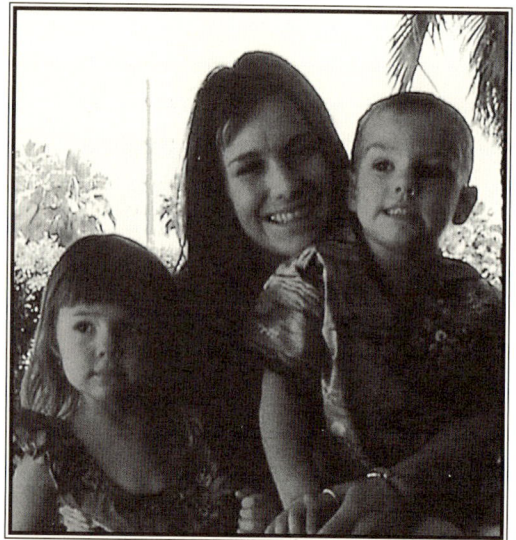

LEFT TO RIGHT: JAELYN NAVY HELSER, HEATHER AND HARLAN BLEU HELSER, 2004

SEVENTH GENERATION

Harlan Bleu Helser, Jaelyn Navy Helser

Harlan Bleu Helser – Seventh Generation

Harlan Bleu Helser, firstborn of twins, was born on September 29th, 2000 to Heather Marie Moudy and Nathan Daniel Helser in Phoenix, Arizona.

HARLAN BLEU HELSER
DRESSED AS A MAN ABOUT TOWN
MAY 2005

Jaelyn Navy Helser – Seventh Generation

Jaelyn Navy Helser, second of twins, was born on September 29th, 2000 to Heather Marie Moudy and Nathan Daniel Helser in Phoenix, Arizona.

JAELYN NAVY HELSER
DRESSED FOR THE BALL
MAY 2005

Margaret McClelland – Third Generation

Margaret McClelland, second child of William McClelland and Sarah Ann Henning, was born on June 5th, 1894 in County Down, Ireland. She married Robert J. Irwin on February 29th, 1916 at Jerrettspass Presbyterian Church. Robert was born on March 1st, 1889.

MARGARET McCLELLAND AND ROBERT J. IRWIN
WEDDING DAY

Margaret was living with her widowed uncle Joseph Henning when she met Robert Irwin, having come to Ireland on a "short" visit from Arizona, where she had accompanied her brother William and planned to return. She never left Ireland again, and was married to Robert from Barkston Lodge, the family homestead of the Henning family.

The Irwins had eight children: Robert William, born May 3, 1918; Eileen May, born November 12, 1919; Emma Margaret, born April 24, 1921; Thomas Alexander, born August 24, 1922; Myrtle Elizabeth, born June 28, 1925; Audrey Jean, born January 19, 1927; David Brown, born November 4, 1931; and Albert Edward, born January 26, 1936.

THE IRWIN HOMESTEAD AT CORGARY

LEFT TO RIGHT: DAVID BROWN IRWIN, ROBERT
JAMES IRWIN, ALBERT EDWARD (BERTIE) IRWIN

FRONT ROW: EMMA, TOM;
BACK ROW: BOB AND EILEEN IRWIN

TOP: MARGARET IRWIN; LEFT TO RIGHT: AUDREY IRWIN,
MYRTLE IRWIN AND BERTIE, AGED 4 MOS., IN MYRTLE'S ARMS

BACK ROW: TOM LOY, ROSE McSHANE, ANNIE McQUAID O'HARE (NEIGHBORS);
FRONT ROW, LEFT TO RIGHT: ROBERT IRWIN, MYRTLE IRWIN, AUDREY IRWIN &
THOMAS IRWIN

The Robert Irwins lived on the family farm. Margaret died on August 19th, 1937, and Robert was left to raise the family with the help of the older children.

Obituary – Margaret Irwin

"IRWIN – 19th August, 1937, at her residence, Corgary, Donaghmore, Margaret, dearly loved wife of Robert Jas. Irwin. Funeral from late residence today (Saturday) at 2:30 P.M., TO First Drumbanagher Presbyterian Churchyard. Deeply regretted by her sorrowing husband and family."

The Irwins were all tall with wavy hair. At 6'2" Robert William was the smallest of the four sons! They were soft-spoken, caring, and gentle people with a strong sense of family duty.

Robert J. Irwin died on September 30th, 1971. He and Margaret are buried in the graveyard at Jerrettspass Presbyterian Church.

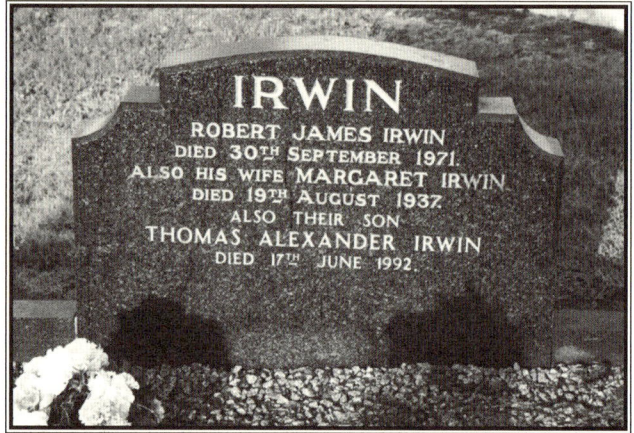

THE GRAVE OF MARGARET AND ROBERT JAMES IRWIN AND THEIR SON TOM ALEXANDER IRWIN

LEFT TO RIGHT: MYRTLE, EILEEN, EMMA AND TOM IRWIN ABOUT 1988

FOURTH GENERATION

Robert William Irwin, Eileen May Irwin, Emma Margaret Irwin,
Thomas Alexander Irwin, Mrytle Elizabeth Irwin, Audrey
Jane Irwin, David Brown Irwin, Albert Edward Irwin

Robert William Irwin – Fourth Generation

Robert William Irwin, first child of Margaret McClelland and Robert J. Irwin, was born on May 3rd, 1918 in Corgary, Donaghmore, County Down, Ireland, and grew up on the family farm. He was educated at The Model School, Newry, and upon leaving school worked on the family farm until 1941, when he joined the Department of Agriculture. He was initially based in County Fermanagh before being transferred to County Antrim in 1943, where he bought his first motor car.

Motor cars needed petrol and servicing, in this case at the local garage and filling station in Ahoghill. That was where Robert met his future wife, the only daughter of the garage owner S. H. Dunlop. He married Pearl Ann Dunlop on July 29th, 1947 at the Presbyterian Church, Ahoghill, County Antrim, Northern Ireland.

ROBERT (BOB) IRWIN AND PEARL DUNLOP IRWIN
WEDDING DAY – JULY 1947

367

Robert and Pearl settled on the edge of the village of Ahoghill, County Antrim. They had five children: Samuel Alexander, born May 22, 1948; Robert James, born July 21, 1949; Agnes Barbara Dunlop, born March 7, 1953; and twin sons, David Wiley and John Dunlop, born May 5, 1957. They were all educated in Ballymena grammar schools.

Robert continued to work for the Ministry of Agriculture based in Ballymena. His work with farm building and drainage schemes took him all over County Antrim, where he became highly respected in the farming community for his fair, helpful, and conscientious approach to his work. Outside of work, he had close links with the local Presbyterian church. He loved his family, home, and garden, and took great time and patience tending to his flowers and vegetables. Robert had a quiet sense of humor and enjoyed hearing and telling anecdotes, particularly of country life.

BOB IRWIN & PEARL DUNLOP IRWIN

Robert died November 9th, 1984, Pearl Ann on November 8th, 1997. They are buried in the graveyard at Brookside Presbyterian Church, Ahoghill, County Antrim.

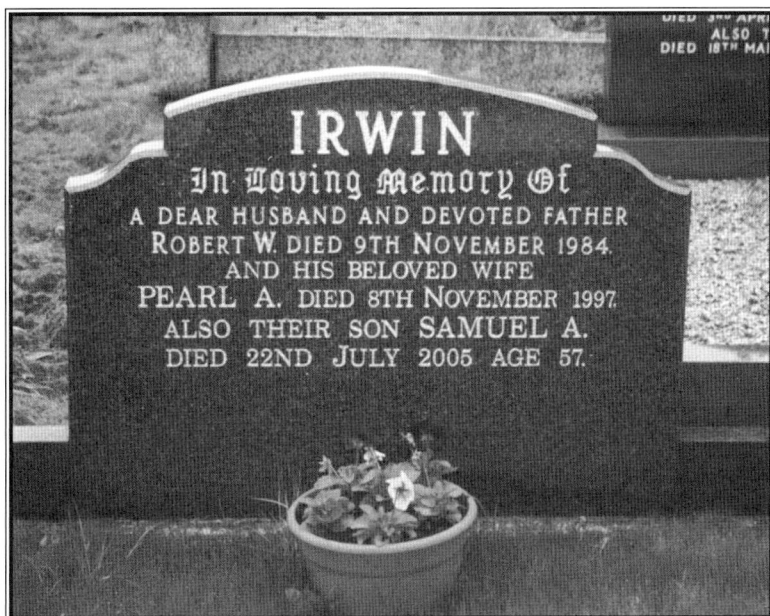

The Irwin Grave in Brookside Presbyterian Church
Ahoghill, County Antrim

Front row, left to right: Victoria Irwin, Pamela (Chapman) Irwin,
Barbara (Brand) Irwin, Pearl (Dunlop) Irwin, Heather Brand (on
Pearl's knee), and Anne (Thompson) Irwin; back row, left to right:
David Irwin, Robert Irwin, Gordon Brand, Robert William Irwin,
Samuel Irwin & John Irwin

FIFTH GENERATION

Samuel Alexander Irwin, Robert James Irwin, Agnes Barbara Dunlop Irwin, David Wiley Irwin, John Dunlop Irwin

Samuel Alexander Irwin – Fifth Generation

Samuel Alexander Irwin, first child of Robert William Irwin and Pearl Ann Dunlop, was born on May 22nd, 1948 in Ballymena, County Antrim, Northern Ireland. Samuel attended Ballybeg Primary School and Fourtowns Primary School, Ahoghill, before going on to Ballymena Academy Grammar School. Samuel graduated from Trinity College, Dublin, and then followed a career in accountancy.

He married Anne Elizabeth Thompson, a school teacher, on August 4th, 1982 in Stormont Presbyterian Church, Belfast. Samuel and Anne have one child, Rachel Ann Elizabeth, born May 1, 1986.

THE WEDDING OF SAMUEL IRWIN AND ANNE THOMPSON
LEFT TO RIGHT: DAVID, JOHN, SAMUEL IRWIN, ANNE THOMPSON IRWIN
PAMELA CHAPMAN IRWIN, ROBERT IRWIN, BARBARA IRWIN BRAND

Samuel passed away on July 22nd, 2005 at the age of 57. He is buried with his parents at Brookside Presbyterian Church, Ahoghill.

Rachel Ann Elizabeth Irwin – Sixth Generation

Rachel Ann Elizabeth Irwin, only child of Samuel Alexander Irwin and Anne Elizabeth Thompson, was born on May 1st, 1986 in the Royal Jubilee Maternity Hospital, Belfast, Northern Ireland.

Rachel went to Hollywood Nursery School and then Cygnet House, the prep school of Glenlola Collegiate School, before progressing to the main campus at Glenlola. Following school, Rachel chose to study English at the University of Liverpool, where she is currently in her final year.

RACHEL WITH HER MUM, ANNE

RACHEL AND HER HORSE "REGGIE"

Rachel has had her own horse since she was twelve. He is called Reggie, though his show name is Cleverly Dun, per his color. Rachel has represented her school and riding club at show-jumping events, and has also competed at the prestigious Balmoral Agricultural Show. Reggie is currently on loan, and next year Rachel intends to take a year to complete her Riding Teacher Qualification. She also intends to travel before attempting a Masters Degree.

Rachel is outgoing and popular with her peers. She loves music and has attended pop festivals in Glastonbury and Reading, and the Oxegen festival at Punchestown Racecourse, South Dublin. She has been to the U.S.A. several times and hopes to work on a museum project in Washington D.C. in the summer of 2007.

Robert James Irwin – Fifth Generation

Robert James Irwin, second child of Pearl Dunlop and Robert W. Irwin, was born on July 21st, 1949 in Ahoghill, County Antrim, Northern Ireland. A beautiful child, Robert had a tumble of fair curls and blue eyes. Robert attended the local primary school in Ahoghill and, later, Ballymena Academy. Formal education held little interest for Robert; his undoubted ability and drive found little stimulation behind a desk, and school reports were of the "could do better" variety.

The world of work found Robert employed with the Northern Ireland Electricity Service as a surveyor. By the late 1960s, the last remote parts of Northern Ireland were connected to the Grid. Robert was part of a team which, for the first time in Britain, used a Wessex RAF helicopter to lift, carry, and plant poles for an overhead cable stretching to the top of Slieve Gallion. Those challenging days in the electricity service were to become rare, leaving Robert unsettled.

On July 5th, 1975 Robert married Pamela Elizabeth Chapman in Portglenone Presbyterian Church, County Antrim. Pamela was the third child and first daughter of Ron and Elizabeth Chapman. Educated at Cambridge House Grammar School in Ballymena, Pamela continued her education at Stranmillis Teacher Training College in Belfast. Pamela freely admits that, at 6'2" and riding a 600 cc Triumph Motorbike, Robert literally swept her off her feet when they first met. After marriage, the couple lived in the nineteenth-century stone cottage in Gracehill that Robert had spent two years restoring. Soon after, Robert decided to be self-employed, and for the next sixteen years spent long hours establishing his own business. "Irwin Metalcraft" culminated in a purpose-built factory at Galgorm on the outskirts of Ballymena, where it still flourishes. After teaching for a few years, Pamela joined Robert in the business and remained there until his death in 1992.

On February 26, 1979, the couple's first child Victoria was born. A son, Russell Robert, followed on October 9, 1980, but passed away in May 1981.

LEFT TO RIGHT: PAMELA CHAPMAN AND VICTORIA IRWIN

Robert had a love affair with motor-bikes from the 1960s onward, but business pressures prevented him from indulging his passion for many years. His last bike, a K100 LT BMW, saw 8,000 miles in the 3 months he owned it, most of them gained on a trip to the Balearic Islands.

ROBERT IRWIN ON ONE OF HIS BELOVED BIKES

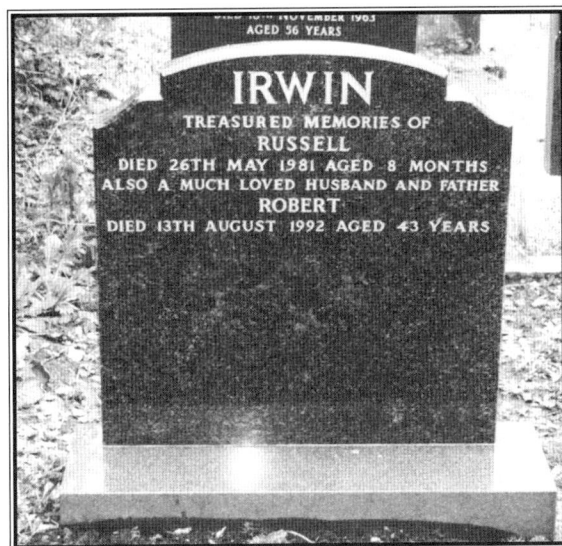

THE FINAL RESTING PLACE FOR ROBERT IRWIN AND HIS INFANT SON RUSSELL IN TOWNHILL CEMETERY, PORTGLENONE, COUNTY ANTRIM

Robert died very suddenly from a heart attack in August of 1992. He was just 43.

He and Russell Robert are buried in the old "Townhill" graveyard on the edge of Portglenone village.

Following Robert's death, Pamela sold the business and Tullygarley House, and she and Victoria moved back to Gracehill, where they restored an early Victorian house in the heart of the village. Pamela took up work part-time, teaching children in a special-needs unit. She also developed an interest in violin and Irish traditional music, and now teaches in a fiddle school of some 85 pupils. Her other interests include piano, gardening, and crafts. She shares her home with Tess, a black-and-white Collie dog.

SIXTH GENERATION

Victoria Elizabeth Ann Irwin, Russell Robert Irwin

Victoria Elizabeth Ann Irwin – Sixth Generation

Victoria Elizabeth Ann Irwin, first child of Robert James Irwin and Pamela Chapman, was born on February 26th, 1979 in Ballymena Cottage Hospital. Her first six months were spent in the Moravian village of Gracehill, two miles from Ballymena, County Antrim before the family moved to Tullygarley House, where they lived until her father's death.

During her early years, Victoria had a great interest in pets, and kept an assortment of dogs, cats, fish, and guinea-pigs, as well as a 12-hand gray pony named Smokie.

Apart from a memorable trip to Phoenix, Tucson, and Sonoma, Victoria's family holidays were mostly spent in Europe, where the seeds of her future career as a linguist were sown. Indeed, a special interest in foreign languages emerged early on, even at the Ballymena Academy grammar school, where she was a good "all-rounder." Victoria followed up that interest at The Queen's University of Belfast, where she studied French and Spanish, and further in Caceves, Spain, where she worked as a language assistant. A year of post-graduate study followed, and she received her Post-Graduate Certificate in Education, which enabled her to make a career as a language teacher. Victoria has been teaching French and Spanish to eleven- through eighteen-year-olds in an integrated school for the past five years.

Victoria is a petite 5'2" with an outgoing, bubbly personality. Her lovely light-brown curly hair comes from the Irwin side, the dark brown eyes from the Chapmans.

VICTORIA IRWIN – 2005

Victoria's interests include travel, both through work and during leisure time; she regularly takes school groups to Paris, Barcelona and Seville. Tennis, cycling and walking with friends keeps her fit, and an ongoing university course in Spanish keeps the accent in good shape.

Victoria has owned her own house for five years and enjoyed turning it into a home.

Russell Robert Irwin – Sixth Generation

Russell Robert Irwin, second child of Robert James Irwin and Pamela Elizabeth Chapman, was born on October 9th, 1980 at the Waveney Hospital, Ballymena. Russell died on May 26th, 1981 at Belfast Hospital for Sick Children. He is buried in the old "Townhill" graveyard on the edge of Portglenone village beside his father, Robert.

Agnes Barbara Dunlop Irwin – Fifth Generation

Agnes Barbara Dunlop Irwin, third child of Robert William Irwin and Pearl Ann Dunlop, was born on March 7th, 1953 in Ballymena, County Antrim, Northern Ireland. She was the only daughter of five children.

Barbara attended the local primary school in the village of Ahoghill and went on to Cambridge House Grammar School in Ballymena. From 1971 – 1974 she attended Stranmillis Teacher Training College in Belfast and received her teaching certificate, with a specialization in the teaching of pre-school and lower primary-school children. During the summer vacation of 1973, Barbara was very fortunate to spend three months in the U.S.A. with Frances McClelland and Bill and Alice Parker from Tucson.

On January 1st, 1975, Barbara married Thomas Gordon Brand. Thomas Gordon Brand was born on June 29th, 1946 in Belfast, Northern Ireland. They both began their married life as teachers. Barbara taught from 1974 -1981 in Northern Ireland primary schools.

BARBARA DUNLOP IRWIN AND THOMAS GORDON BRAND
MARRIAGE CERTIFICATE – JANUARY 1, 1975

Barbara is a friendly, caring, and thoughtful person who is happiest when at home with her family. She is 5'5" with medium-brown hair, green eyes, and sallow skin. Her looks favor the Irwin side of the family, her stature, the Dunlop side.

Gordon is the eldest son of the late Robert and Doreen Brand. He was born in Belfast, Northern Ireland. He is 6'1" with light brown hair and blue eyes. Gordon is a caring and charming person with a strong sense of family duty. An avid sportsman who enjoys playing and refereeing rugby football, he continues to be interested in sport of all kinds. He reads widely and has a particular interest in Anglo – Irish Literature. Gordon has recently retired from teaching and had the satisfaction of seeing a number of years of editorial work come together in the publication of a book about Irish author William Carleton.

The William Carleton Summer School Committee

cordially invites you to the launch of their book

William Carleton
The Authentic Voice

Edited by Gordon Brand, illustrated by Sam Craig

Corick House Hotel

Clogher, County Tyrone, BT 76 0BZ,
Monday, 7th August 2006, at 8.00 p.m.

William Carleton, The Authentic Voice is published by Colin Smythe Ltd. More details at www.colinsmythe.co.uk (Recent Publications) The reverse reproduces three typical illustrations from the book. These drawings depict places that William Carleton would have known.

INVITATION TO THE LAUNCH OF THE NEW BOOK ON THE IRISH WRITER WILLIAM CARLETON, EDITED BY GORDON BRAND

Barbara and Gordon's first daughter, Heather, was born on March 10, 1980 in Magherafelt, County Londonderry, where Gordon and Barbara were teaching at the time.

In 1981, the family went overseas for a teaching spell in Zimbabwe and lived on the campus of Falcon College, Essexvale, where Gordon taught English and History and Barbara became headmistress of the local primary school. They found it a real pleasure to teach in a place where education was so highly valued and children were very eager to learn. During school holidays, the family enjoyed traveling to neighboring countries and fell in love with the African landscape and people.

Alison, Barbara and Gordon's second daughter, was born on September 3, 1983 in Bulawayo, Zimbabwe.

During the summer of 1984, the family returned to Ireland when it was clear that Barbara's father was unwell. Barbara, Heather, and Alison traveled back from Zimbabwe in November to be with her father before he died. When Gordon arrived soon after, he and Barbara settled in County Fermanagh and spent a short spell with the National Trust at Florence Court before both of them returned to teaching.

Barbara joined the staff of Enniskillen Model Primary School in September 1987 as a primary one teacher. She became Head of Early Years in 2000. In her spare time, she enjoys gardening and attending art classes. She has produced many oil paintings of local landscapes and buildings.

BRAND FAMILY
LEFT TO RIGHT: GORDON, ALISON, BARBARA & HEATHER – 1992

SIXTH GENERATION

Heather Sarah Margaret Brand,
Alison Emma Ruth Brand

Heather Sarah Margaret Brand – Sixth Generation

Heather Sarah Margaret Brand, first child of Agnes Barbara Dunlop Irwin and Thomas Gordon Brand, was born on March 10th, 1980 in Londonderry, Northern Ireland.

Heather has great memories of her first four years living in Zimbabwe, Africa, running around in her bare feet in the sunshine.

Heather spent the next part of her life in Enniskillen, Northern Ireland where she attended the Model School Primary and Enniskillen Collegiate Grammar School. Here she enjoyed playing the violin in the Western Schools Orchestra, rowing with the local ladies' team, and singing in the school choir.

Heather attended the University of Dundee, Scotland, graduating in 2002 with L.L.B.[Hons].

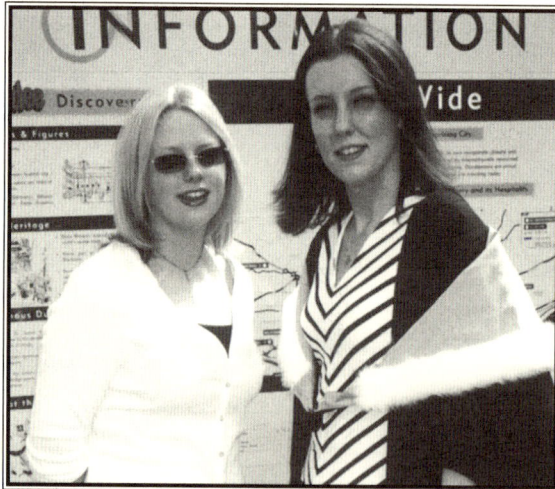

LEFT TO RIGHT: ALISON & HEATHER BRAND
JULY 12, 2002

Heather now works for an insurance company in Cavan, Republic of Ireland as a business analyst. She also enjoys Royal National Lifeboat Institution charity work. She is 5'8"tall with mousy brown hair and green eyes.

Alison Emma Ruth Brand – Sixth Generation

Alison Emma Ruth Brand, second child of Agnes Barbara Dunlop and Thomas Gordon Brand, was born on September 3rd, 1983 in Bulawayo, Zimbabwe.

Alison began her education at the Model Primary School, Enniskillen and Enniskillen Collegiate Grammar. In 2002, Alison attended the University of Wales, Cardiff, where she received a degree in Optometry and Vision Sciences. Her professional training was carried out in her hometown of Enniskillen, where she is now working as an optician.

LEFT TO RIGHT: ALISON, GORDON, BARBARA & HEATHER BRAND
JULY 12, 2002

Alison enjoys many sports, especially hockey, netball, and squash. She is a keen traveler and has visited many countries, including Australia, New Zealand and Thailand. She is 5'6"tall with blond hair and blue eyes.

David Wiley Irwin – Fifth Generation

David Wiley Irwin, fourth child of Robert William Irwin and Pearl Ann Dunlop, was born on May 5th, 1957 in Ballymena, County Antrim, Northern Ireland.

David attended the local primary school in Ahoghill before graduating to Ballymena Academy Grammar School. At school, he always had an inclination towards science and engineering. This trait was likely inherited from his maternal grandfather S.H. Dunlop, who in the early twentieth century was a keen "radio set" builder and amateur photographer. His interest in science and engineering continued into higher education at Queen's University in Belfast where he received a BSc in Electrical and Electronic Engineering in 1980. After a short spell in local industry, David moved across the Irish Sea to Greenock, Scotland, to work in the development of microchips for a multinational corporation based in California (National Semiconductor Corp).

In 1981, David was fortunate to travel to the U.S.A., where he spent time meeting various members of the McClelland and Parker clans. In 1984, he took up jogging rather seriously and completed five full-distance marathons in three years. His first marathon was run in Belfast in 1984. Also competing in that marathon was a youthful U.S.A.-based athlete by the name of Norman McClelland (fourth generation) of Phoenix, Arizona.

After six years in Scotland, David moved south to Lincolnshire in England where he met and married Catherine Lindsay Swinscoe on March 27th, 1989 in West Retford, Nottinghamshire, England.

Catherine, the eldest of two daughters of Peter and Jean Swinscoe, was born in Nottingham, England. On leaving college, Catherine joined the Police Service as a "front desk" civilian. The Police Service was not new to Catherine—she had grown up as a policeman's daughter. Her father Peter "retired" from the Police Force as Detective Chief Inspector, but at the age of 78 still works full-time in a local lawyers office. In the summer of 2000 Catherine, her sister Elizabeth, and her mother Jean were very proud to accompany Peter down to Buckingham Palace to receive the MBE (Member of the Order of the British Empire) award personally from Queen Elizabeth II.

Still in the microchip industry, David moved with Catherine to Bedford (about 50 miles north of London) to work for another U.S.A.-based microchip corporation (Texas Instruments). It was here that their three boys were born: Matthew, born September 21, 1990, and twins Benjamin and Jonathan, born January 14, 1993.

In 1994, David, Catherine, and their three boys were on the move again. The destination this time was Livingston, Scotland, where, regardless of further job-location moves within Scotland, they live today. David has recently taken up a new position in a "home-grown" microchip company (Wolfson Microelectronics) based in Edinburgh, near Livingston. David continues to work in New Product Development, where he specializes in the development of software and electronic hardware used for the production testing of microchips. After a break to bring up the children, Catherine has returned to full-time employment in a local microelectronics company.

DAVID IRWIN FAMILY
LEFT TO RIGHT: MATTHEW, CATHERINE (SWINSCOE),
BEN, DAVID AND JONATHAN – 2006

SIXTH GENERATION

Matthew David Irwin, Benjamin Peter Irwin,
Jonathan Robert Irwin

Matthew David Irwin – Sixth Generation

Matthew David Irwin, first son of David Wiley Irwin and Catherine Swinscoe, was born on September 21st, 1990 in Bedford, England.

Matthew attends school at Stewart's Melville College in Edinburgh. He has completed his standard-grade examinations and is continuing with his higher studies, specializing in science and engineering. He is a keen chess player and enjoys badminton and cycling.

Benjamin Peter Irwin – Sixth Generation

Benjamin Peter Irwin, second son of David Wiley Irwin and Catherine Swinscoe, was born on January 14th, 1993 in Bedford, England.

Benjamin (known as Ben) attends school at Stewart's Melville College in Edinburgh. He is working towards his standard grade examinations. He is a very keen on computing and an avid reader.

Jonathan Robert Irwin – Sixth Generation

Jonathan Robert Irwin, third son of David Wiley Irwin and Catherine Swinscoe, was born on January 14th, 1993 in Bedford, England.

Jonathan attends school at Stewart's Melville College in Edinburgh. He is working towards his standard-grade examinations. He is also a keen badminton player, and has represented the school in rugby. Jonathan enjoys designing and building various wooden contraptions.

John Dunlop Irwin – Fifth Generation

John Dunlop Irwin, fifth child of Robert William Irwin and Pearl Ann Dunlop, was born on May 5th, 1957 in Ahoghill, County Antrim, Northern Ireland.

John is qualified as a chartered structural engineer and principal of the firm of John Irwin Consulting Engineers, which he runs from his home at 4 Killane Road, Ahoghill, County Antrim.

LEFT TO RIGHT: DAVID AND JOHN IRWIN ON THE OCCASION OF DAVID'S WEDDING

Eileen May Irwin – Fourth Generation

Eileen May Irwin, second child of Margaret McClelland and Robert J. Irwin, was born on November 12th, 1919. She married John Cochrane on June 25th, 1947 at Jerrettspass Presbyterian Church, Newry, County Down, Northern Ireland. John was born on November 4th, 1911 in Ballymoney, County Antrim, Ireland.

LEFT TO RIGHT: EMMA IRWIN, BRIDESMAID, JOHN & EILEEN COCHRANE, AND JAMES COCHRANE, BEST MAN, WEDDING DAY – JUNE 25, 1947

EILEEN IRWIN AND HER FATHER TOM IRWIN WEDDING DAY – JUNE 25, 1947

John was a farmer on the Cochrane family farm outside Ballymoney, County Antrim, Eileen a cook in Hopefield Hospital, Portrush.

Eileen and John had four children: Kenneth John, born May 18, 1948; Harold Robert, born April 26, 1951; Hazel Margaretta, born April 26, 1951; and Johanne Elizabeth, born September 14, 1962.

John died February 15th, 1995, Eileen on June 3rd, 2002. They are buried in the Cochrane family grave in Ballymoney Cemetery, County Antrim.

The Cochrane family grave, Ballymoney Cemetery, Country Antrim

Back row, left to right: Eileen (Irwin) Cochrane, Alice (Coleman) Parker; front row, left to right: Frances McClelland, John Cochrane, Frances (Parker) Hume, and John Hume.

Top row, left to right: Jeanie Parker, Heather Killen, Brian Killen, Alice Parker, Kathleen Lutton, Richard Lutton; bottom row, left to right: John Cochrane, Olive Parker, Frances Hume, Amy Moore, Eileen Cochrane & Frances McClelland

Fifth Generation

Kenneth John Cochrane, Harold Robert Cochrane, Hazel Margaretta Cochrane, Johanna Elizabeth Cochrane

Kenneth John Cochrane – Fifth Generation

Kenneth John Cochrane, first child of Eileen May Irwin and John Cochrane, was born on May 18th, 1948 in Ballymoney, County Antrim, Northern Ireland. He married Neisha Merydeth Alford on February 18th, 1977 in Adelaide, Australia. Neisha was born on March 17th, 1951.

They have three children: Renee, born April 5, 1980, Ben, born October 10, 1982, and Matthew, born April 9, 1984.

Neisha and Ken separated in 1997 and divorced in 2000. Neisha is now a dental receptionist and has her own home in Perth, a suburb of Ballajura. Matthew lives with her.

Ken is a professional executive coach and works primarily with corporate clients in mining oil and gas. He lives in the Perth suburb of Padbury with Renee, when she is in Perth.

KEN JOHN COCHRANE & NEISHA MERYDETH ALFORD
WEDDING DAY – FEBRUARY 18, 1977

KENNETH COCHRANE FAMILY
LEFT TO RIGHT: MATTHEW, KEN, BEN, NEISHA & RENEE – 1994

SIXTH GENERATION

Renee Marie Cochrane, Ben Michael Cochrane,
Matthew Cameron Cochrane

Renee Marie Cochrane – Sixth Generation

Renee Marie Cochrane, first child of Kenneth John Cochrane and Neisha Merydeth Alford, was born on April 5th, 1980.

Renee has a gregarious temperament and enjoys organizing events, whether social or work-related. She now works in Dampier in northwest Australia. Renee takes after her mum when it comes to culinary skill, and has worked as a cook on pearling and mining sites. She now works as an assistant camp manager and administrator for a western Australian company that provides catering and accommodation services to construction and mine sites. She works a six-week roster, five weeks in Dampier and a one-week leave, which she spends with her dad in Perth.

DAVID HARTRIDGE & RENEE COCHRANE
AUGUST 2004

She is presently saving money to travel abroad, rather following in her father's footsteps.

Ben Michael Cochrane – Sixth Generation

Ben Michael Cochrane, second child of Kenneth John Cochrane and Neisha Merydeth Alford, was born on October 10th, 1982.

Ben has a gentle and harmonizing temperament and is presently living and working in Darwin in the Northern Territory of Australia. He and his girlfriend (of three years) Belinda Cunningham are working their way around Australia.

Ben, a very competent concrete worker with six years of experience, is learning how to go into business for himself. He loves the outdoors, four-wheel driving, camping, hiking, fishing, and exploring Australia.

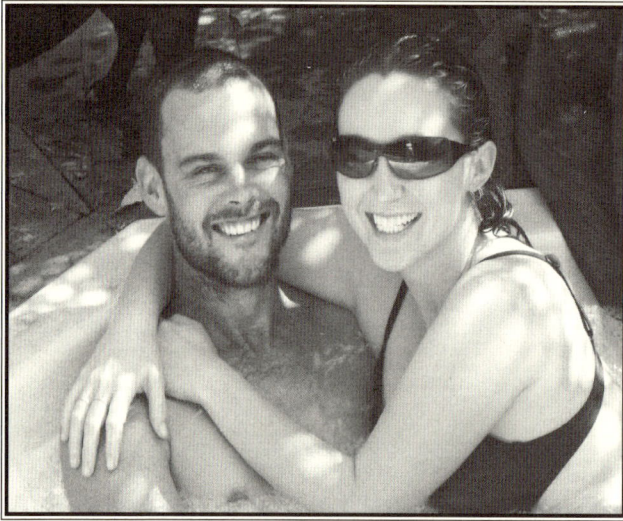

BEN COCHRANE AND BELINDA CUNNINGHAM – SEPTEMBER 2006

Matthew Cameron Cochrane – Sixth Generation

Matthew Cameron Cochrane, third child of Kenneth John Cochrane and Neisha Merydeth Alford, was born on April 9th, 1984.

Matthew has a decidedly extroverted temperament. He completed two years of a carpentry apprenticeship before deciding to study marketing at university level. He supports his studies by working part-time in building. Outside of his studies, Matthew's social life takes priority, followed by a love for the outdoors, camping, fishing, and four-wheel driving.

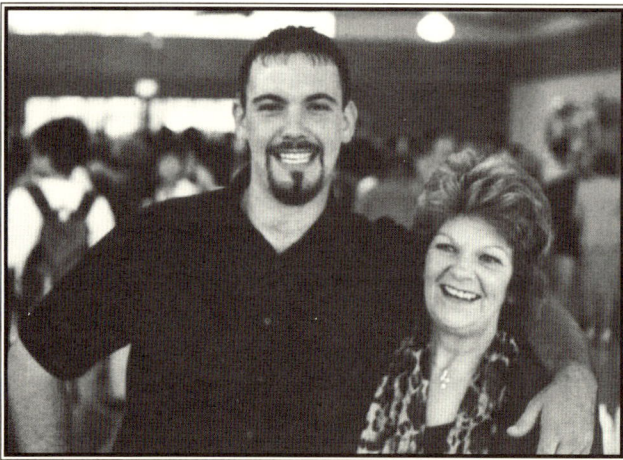

MATTHEW AND HIS MOM, NEISHA COCHRANE

Hazel Margaretta Cochrane – Fifth Generation

Hazel Margaretta Cochrane, second child (and ten minutes older than her twin brother, Harold) of Eileen May Irwin and John Cochrane, was born on April 26th, 1951 in Ballymoney, County Antrim, Northern Ireland. She married John Copeland on August 19th, 1980 in St. James Presbyterian Church. They divorced in 1991.

Hazel graduated as a social worker from Lanchester Polytechnic Coventry in 1973. She received further training and in 1979 became self-employed as a reflexologist and electrologist.

Hazel and John had two children: Johanna Nicola, born August 11, 1981, and Niall Samuel John, born September 27, 1985.

LEFT TO RIGHT: NIALL, JOHANNA, AND HAZEL COPELAND ON THE OCCASION OF JOHANNA'S COMMISSIONING AT THE ROYAL MILITARY ACADEMY SANDHURST – DECEMBER 16, 2005

SIXTH GENERATION

Johanna Nicola Copeland, Niall Samuel John Copeland

Johanna Nicola Copeland – Sixth Generation

Johanna Nicola Copeland, first child of Hazel Margaretta Cochrane and John Copeland, was born on August 11th, 1981.

Having finished secondary education, Johanna went to The University of Leeds to study Environmental Management. During a "year out," Johanna traveled extensively in southeast Asia, China, Mongolia, Australia, and the U.S.A. She then enrolled at The Royal Military Academy, Sandhurst and was commissioned as a Second Lieutenant in the Signals Regiment of the British Army in December 2005. She is currently stationed in York, England.

Niall Samuel John Copeland – Sixth Generation

Niall Samuel John Copeland, second child of Hazel Margaretta Cochrane and John Copeland, was born on September 27th, 1985.

Niall is a third-year student of Electrical Engineering at The University of Bristol, England. He has passed the Admiralty interview board and will take up a place in the Royal Naval College, Dartmouth, England in 2008.

Niall is a keen rugby player and has turned out for both Ballymena and his University team.

Harold Robert Cochrane – Fifth Generation

Harold Robert Cochrane, third child of Eileen May Irwin and John Cochrane, was born on April 26th, 1951. He married Robyn Lees on April 23rd, 1983 in Perth, Australia.

Harold and Robyn have two children: Maya, born December 20, 1976, and Nari, born September 20, 1978.

Harold graduated from Reading University in 1972. He is a soil scientist at Perth University. Robyn is a potter whose work is unique and highly sought after, as evidenced by her presence at many exhibitions.

HAROLD ROBERT COCHRANE AND ROBYN LEES
WEDDING DAY – APRIL 23, 1983

LEFT TO RIGHT: HARRY, JOHANNA COPELAND, MAYA, ROBYN &
NARI – DECEMBER 29, 1996

LEFT TO RIGHT: HARRY COCHRANE, JOHANNA COPELAND, NARI, KEN COCHRANE,
HAZEL COCHRANE, NIALL COPELAND (HAZEL'S SON)

HARRY AND ROBYN'S HOME-IN-THE-MAKING
DENMARK, WESTERN AUSTRALIA

ROBYN COCHRANE AT THE
POTTER'S WHEEL

SIXTH GENERATION

Maya Lees, Nari Lees

Maya Lees – Sixth Generation

Maya Lees, first child of Harold Robert Cochrane and Robyn Lees, was born on December 20th, 1976. Maya obtained her teaching qualification at Perth University and is living in Cairns, Australia at present.

MAYA LEES AND MARLU HARRIS, CAIRNS, AUGUST 2005

MAYA'S 29TH BIRTHDAY
LEFT TO RIGHT: LEIGH HARRIS, NARI LEES, ROBYN LEES, SEN HARRIS,
HAROLD COCHRANE , MARLU HARRIS, MAYA LEES

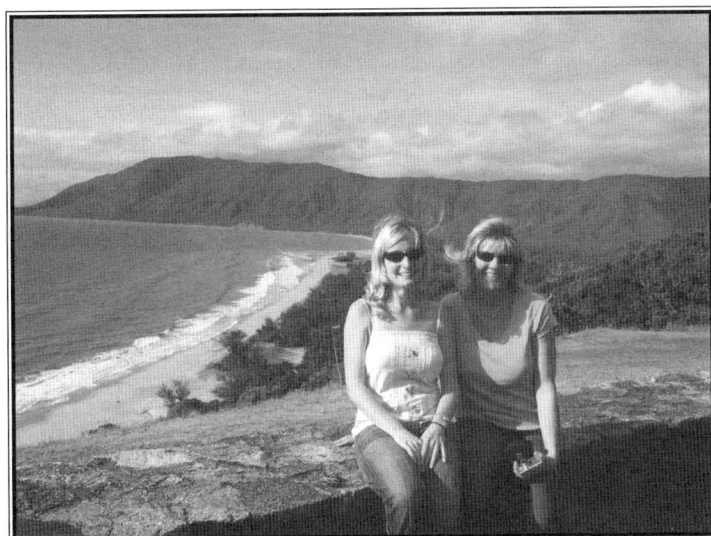

LEFT TO RIGHT: MAYA LEES AND KATHE MCCLELLAND
CAIRNS, AUSTRALIA – JULY 2006

Nari Lees – Sixth Generation

Nari Lees, second child of Harold Robert Cochrane and Robyn Lees, was born on September 20th, 1978. Nari has toured Europe with a ballet company but is undecided as to her career.

Nari and Leigh Harris have two children, Marlu Harris and Sen Harris.

SEVENTH GENERATION

Marlu Harris, Sen Harris

Marlu Harris – Seventh Generation

Marlu Harris, first child of Nari Lees and Leigh Harris, was born on October 22nd, 2001.

Sen Harris – Seventh Generation

Sen Harris, second child of Nari Lees and Leigh Harris, was born on January 17th, 2005.

Johanne Elizabeth Cochrane – Fifth Generation

Johanne Elizabeth Cochrane, fourth child of Eileen May Irwin and John Cochrane, was born on September 14th, 1962 in Ballymoney, County Antrim, Northern Ireland.

Johanne Elizabeth graduated from the University of Dundee, Scotland in 1986. She received a Master's Degree in 2001 and currently works as a medical practitioner in Sydney, Australia, specializing in women's health and addiction medicine.

DR. JOHANNE COCHRANE

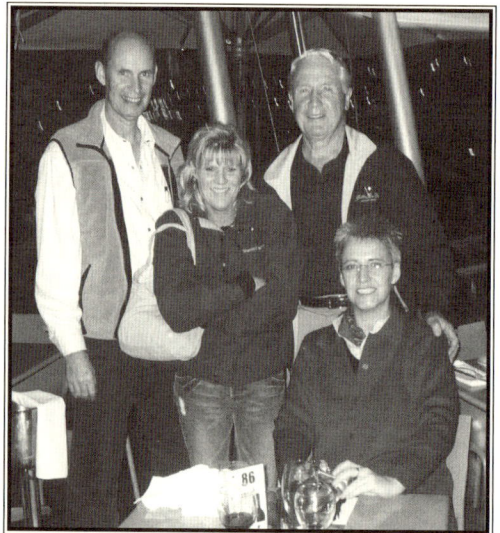

LEFT TO RIGHT: KEN COCHRANE, KATHE McCLELLAND, NORMAN McCLELLAND AND JOHANNE COCHRANE SYDNEY, AUSTRALIA – JULY 2006

Emma Margaret Irwin – Fourth Generation

Emma Margaret Irwin, third child of Margaret McClelland and Robert J. Irwin, was born on April 24th, 1921. She married Henry R. Clarke November 24th, 1948 in Jerrettspass, Newry, County Down, Ireland.

EMMA IRWIN – AGE 12

HENRY CLARKE & EMMA MARGARET IRWIN – WEDDING
DAY, NOVEMBER 24, 1948, LEFT TO RIGHT: HENRY,
EMMA, TOM CLARKE (HENRY'S BROTHER) & MYRTLE

Henry's business included a grocery and general hardware store. He also sold cement, sand, meal, and coal. He was very fond of gardening and woodwork. His parents were farmers.

Henry and Emma had three children: Alan Robert Clarke, born March 27, 1951, Thomas Henry Clarke, born May 14, 1954, and Margaret Isobel Clarke, born August 15, 1955.

EMMA & TOM CLARKE, HER SON – 1996

DAVID IRWIN AND EMMA IRWIN CLARKE – 2006

FIFTH GENERATION

Alan Robert Clarke, Thomas Henry Clarke,
Margaret Isobel Clarke

Alan Robert Clarke – Fifth Generation

Alan Robert Clarke, first child of Emma Margaret Irwin and Henry R. Clarke, was born on March 27th, 1951.

Alan received a B.Sc degree in Physics from The Queen's University of Belfast in 1972. He then moved to Cambridge, England, and still lives there with his partner, Pat.

He is currently a business analyst with a Cambridge software company.

Thomas Henry Clarke – Fifth Generation

Thomas Henry Clarke, second child of Emma Margaret Irwin and Henry R. Clarke, was born on May 14th, 1954. Thomas did not marry.

Tom helped Emma run the family business. He died suddenly on December 21st, 1999 and is buried with his father in the Jerrettspass Presbyterian Church graveyard, County Armagh.

Obituary – Thomas Henry Clarke

"Thomas Henry Clarke died suddenly December 21, 1999, at Daisy Hill Hospital. Very dearly loved son of Emma and the late Henry Reside Clarke, and dear brother of Alan and Margaret. Funeral from his home at 49 Railway Street, Poyntpass tomorrow, Thursday at 2:00 p.m. for service in Poyntpass Presbyterian Church. Internment afterwards in adjoining Churchyard. House private. No cards or letters, please. Family flowers only. Donations in lieu of flowers may be sent, if desired, to William Bell & Company, Funeral Directors, 23 Kenils Street, Bainbridge, BT32 LR for Poyntzpass Presbyterian Church Building Fund and Newry Hospice. Very deeply regretted by his loving mother, brother, sister and the entire family circle."

Margaret Isobel Clarke – Fifth Generation

Margaret Isobel Clarke, third child of Emma Margaret Irwin and Henry R. Clarke, was born on August 15th, 1955. Margaret married Robert (Robin) Owen Convery on November 25th, 1980 in Fourtowns Presbyterian Church, County Down, Northern Ireland. Robin, a member of the famous St. Ledger family on his maternal grandmother's side, was born on October 8th, 1954 in Belfast, Northern Ireland.

MARGARET ISOBEL CLARKE AND ROBERT OWEN CONVERY
MARRIAGE CERTIFICATE – NOVEMBER 25, 1980

Margaret attended Newry Model and High School, progressing to Queen's University in Belfast in 1974 to study Geography. She received her first degree in 1978, and then attended St. Katherine's College in Liverpool from 1978 to 1979, where she obtained her Post-Graduate Certificate in Education. She taught in Markethill High School for 1 ½ years.

Margaret met Robin in her first year at Queen's. They were married 5 ½ years later. Robin was an engineering student who graduated from Queen's in 1977. He went on to complete his MSC and PhD. Having worked for ICL and Lear Fan in Northern Ireland, he and the family moved to Saffron Walden in Essex in 1985. Saffron is an ancient town 15 miles from Cambridge. In the Middle Ages, it was a thriving center for the production of saffron and trading of wool.

Robin worked for STC in Greenwich, London, and then for an American company, SDRC, in Hitchin, Hertfordshire.

Margaret and Robin have four children: David Andrew Convery, born March 9, 1981, Stephen Robert Convery, born July 6, 1984, Kathryn Helen Convery, born January 13, 1990, and Michael Thomas Convery, born July 3, 1992.

EILEEN'S HOME, BALLYMONEY, NORTHERN IRELAND
FRONT ROW: KATHRYN, MARGARET, MICHAEL AND ROBIN CONVERY;
BACK ROW: AUDREY DAVIS AND EILEEN COCHRANE
1994

Robin died suddenly on January 23rd, 1998 near Leicester while away on business. He was just 43 years old. It was a devastating blow for everyone, as the children were just 5, 8, 13, and 16. The Convery's marriage was blissfully happy and the children were devoted to a wonderful, caring father.

HOLIDAY IN IRELAND
FRONT ROW: MICHAEL, KATHRYN, STEPHEN;
BACK ROW: DAVID, MARGARET AND ROBIN
1997

FIFTH GENERATION

David Andrew Convery, Stephen Robert Convery,
Kathryn Helen Convery, Michael Thomas Convery

David Andrew Convery – Fifth Generation

David Andrew Convery, first child of Margaret Isobel Clarke and Robert (Robin) Owen Convery, was born on March 9th, 1981 in Banbridge, County Down, Northern Ireland.

David is 6'2" with blond hair. He graduated from the University of Leeds in 2002 with a degree in Biology. He is currently working at a Border's bookstore in Cambridge, England.

DAVID ANDREW CONVERY

Stephen Robert Convery – Fifth Generation

Stephen Robert Convery, second child of Margaret Isobel Clarke and Robert (Robin) Owen Convery, was born on July 6th, 1984 in Belfast, County Antrim, Northern Ireland.

Stephen is 5'10" with blond hair. He graduated from the University of Nottingham in 2005, where he studied Politics. He is currently working in London as an underwriter.

Kathryn Helen Convery – Fifth Generation

Kathryn Helen Convery, third child of Margaret Isobel Clarke and Robert (Robin) Owen Convery, was born on January 13th, 1990 in Cambridge, England.

Kathryn is 5'10" with blond hair. Like her brothers before her, Kathryn is a pupil at Saffron Walden County High School where she is studying biology, chemistry, mathematics, and history for "A" Level. She also has a keen interest in Japanese animated Manga books and films.

Michael Thomas Convery – Fifth Generation

Michael Thomas Convery, fourth child of Margaret Isobel Clarke and Robert (Robin) Owen Convery, was born on July 3rd, 1992 in Cambridge, England.

Dogged by health problems as a baby—he did not talk until he was three, and could barely communicate in his first school year—Michael now attends mainstream school as an above-average, delightful boy with wonderful qualities.

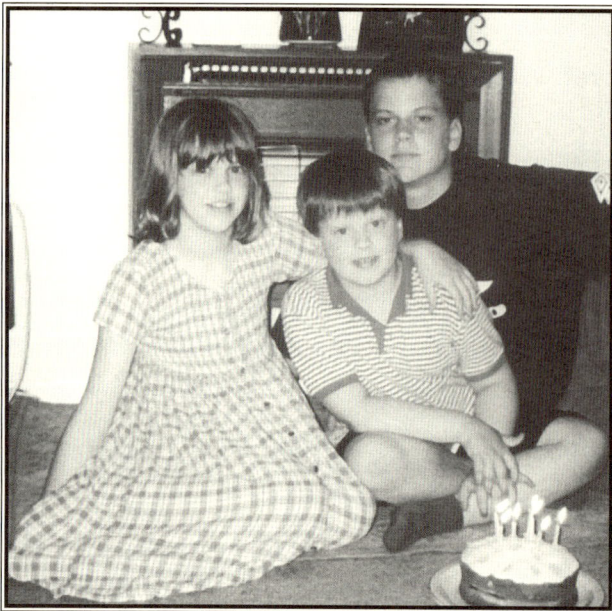

Michael is currently a pupil at Saffron Walden High School and has a keen interest in cooking—he is actually becoming something of a gourmet chef.

KATHRYN, MICHAEL, AND STEPHEN
MICHAEL'S 7TH BIRTHDAY – 1999

Thomas Alexander Irwin – Fourth Generation

Thomas Alexander Irwin, fourth child of Margaret McClelland and Robert J. Irwin, was born on August 24th, 1922 in Corgary, Donaghmore, County Down, Northern Ireland.

Thomas worked for a few years for John Kelly Ltd. coal importers in Warrenpoint, County Down. He returned to the farm in 1941 after his brother Bob joined the Ministry of Agriculture in Northern Ireland.

Tom remained a farmer for the rest of his working life. He married Mary McGrath, a widow, on September 21st, 1966 in St Patrick's Roman Catholic Church, Dundalk, the Republic of Ireland. Mary, born on September 8th, 1924 was previously married to James McGrath. Their son Dermot William McGrath was born December 2, 1949. Dermot is now retired from British Telecom and married to Una, who is also retired, from teaching. The couple have two grown daughters—Sinaid and Orla.

TOM IRWIN

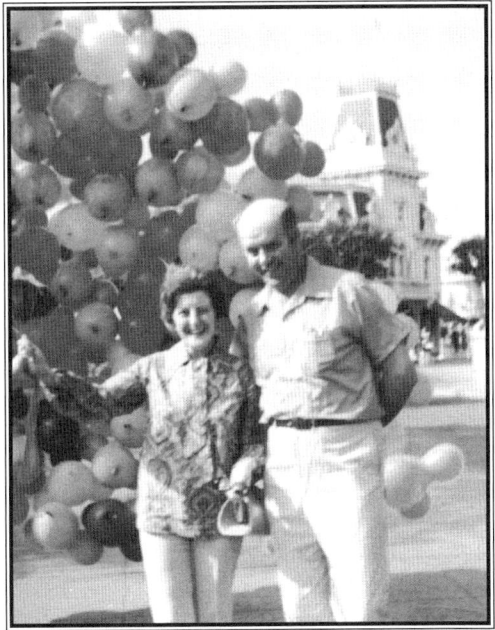

MARY AND TOM IRWIN

403

TOM AND MARY IRWIN – CORGARY, NEWRY

TOM IRWIN WITH DOGS, SHEF AND SHANE

When Tom retired from farming, he moved to Warrenpoint for a time before returning to Cloughenramer, where he lived until his death on June 17th, 1992.

IRWIN BOYS
LEFT TO RIGHT: BERTIE, THOMAS, DAVID & ROBERT IRWIN

LEFT TO RIGHT: FRANCES MCCLELLAND, TOM IRWIN, MARY (MCGRATH) IRWIN

In Loving Memory of

Mary Irwin

who died on 7th July 2006

Aged 81 Years

May She Rest In Peace

+

We cannot bring the old days back,
When we were all together;
The family chain is broken now
But memories last forever.

We Give Our Loved Ones
Back to God

We give our loved ones
back to God.
And just as He first gave
them to us
and did not lose them
in the giving,
so we have not lost them
in returning them to Him...
for life is eternal,
love is immortal,
death is only a horizon...
and a horizon is nothing
but the limit
of our earthly sight.

THE MARY IRWIN MEMORY CARD

Tom is buried in the family plot at Jerrettspass Presbyterian Church, County Armagh with his father and mother. Mary died on July 7th, 2006 and is buried in the Poyntzpass Roman Catholic graveyard.

In Loving Memory Of
JAMES McGRATH
DIED 9TH SEPTEMBER 1956 AGED 35 YEARS
EDWARD McGRATH
DIED 7TH APRIL 1963 AGED 81 YEARS
ANNIE McGRATH
DIED 2ND OCTOBER 1976 AGED 80 YEARS
MARY IRWIN (RELICT OF JAMES McGRATH)
DIED 7TH JULY 2006 AGED 81 YEARS

REST IN PEACE

McGRATH

THE RESTING PLACE
OF MARY IRWIN

Myrtle Elizabeth Irwin – Fourth Generation

Myrtle Elizabeth Irwin, fifth child of Margaret McClelland and Robert J. Irwin, was born on June 28th, 1925 in Corgary, Donaghmore, County Down, Northern Ireland. She married James Harshaw on September 2nd, 1952 in Jerretspass Presbyterian Church, County Armagh.

WEDDING – SEPTEMBER 2, 1952
LEFT TO RIGHT: JAMES HARSHAW, MYRTLE IRWIN, EMMA IRWIN,
HUGH HARSHAW & HUGH HARSHAW'S DAUGHTER, AGE 7

Myrtle and James had four children: Daphne Elizabeth, born February 4, 1954, Mavis Irene, born June 26, 1955, Robert James, born June 21, 1957, and David Thomas, born January 22, 1962.

MYRTLE ELIZABETH IRWIN

MYRTLE & JAMES HARSHAW
CHRISTMAS 1996

HARSHAW FAMILY – 1992
LEFT TO RIGHT: DAPHNE, ROBERT, DAVID,
MAVIS; FRONT ROW: MYRTLE & JAMES

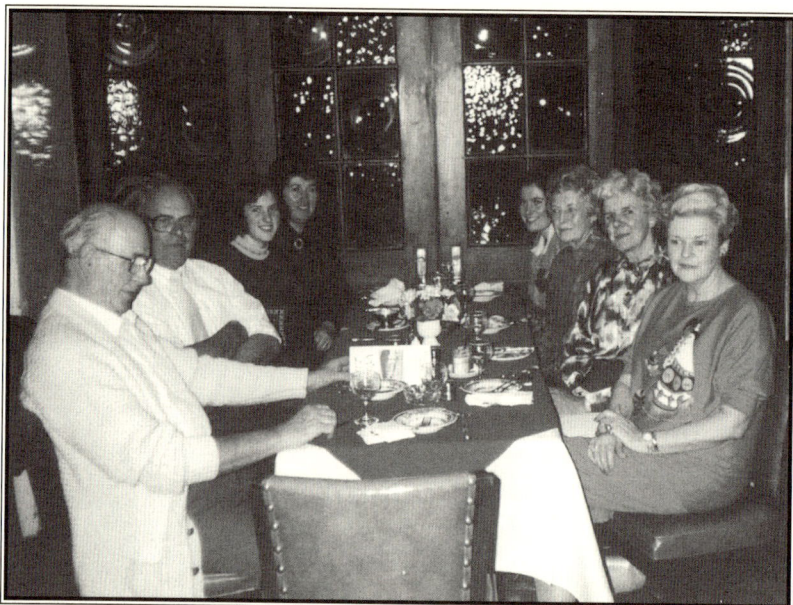

THIS PHOTOGRAPH WAS TAKEN IN THE DOWNSHIRE ARMS HOTEL, BANBRIDGE,
COUNTY DOWN ON THE OCCASION OF AUDREY'S TRIP TO IRELAND, SEPTEMBER 1989
LEFT TO RIGHT: TOM IRWIN, JAMES HARSHAW, ORLA McGRATH, UNA McGRATH,
DERMOT McGRATH, SINAID McGRATH, MARY McGRATH, MYRTLE HARSHAW, AUDREY
DAVIS

LEFT TO RIGHT: JAMES HARSHAW, FRANCES McCLELLAND, NORMAN McCLEL-
LAND, DAVID IRWIN, FLORENCE (McBRIDE) IRWIN, EMMA (IRWIN) CLARKE &
MYRTLE (IRWIN) HARSHAW

THE HARSHAW FAMILY PLOT AT DONAGHMORE PARISH CHURCH, THE FINAL RESTING PLACE OF MYRTLE IRWIN HARSHAW

Myrtle died January 13th, 2006 and is buried in the Harshaw family grave in the Donaghmore Parish Church graveyard, County Down.

FIFTH GENERATION

Daphne Elizabeth Harshaw, Mavis Irene Harshaw, Robert James Harshaw, David Thomas Harshaw

Daphne Elizabeth Harshaw – Fifth Generation

Daphne Elizabeth Harshaw, first child of Myrtle Elizabeth Irwin and James Harshaw, was born on February 4th, 1954 in Bainbridge Maternity Hospital. She married Robert Acheson on April 3rd, 1975.

Daphne attended Donaghmore Primary School from age four to eleven. She then left school and became a sales assistant in a drapery store in Banbridge.

Daphne and Robert have four children: Lynn, born August 15, 1976, Neill, born November 28, 1979, Jill, born October 2, 1982, and Amy, born April 20, 1988.

Daphne is a registered child-minder and works in her own home. The family lives in Gilford, County Down, Northern Ireland.

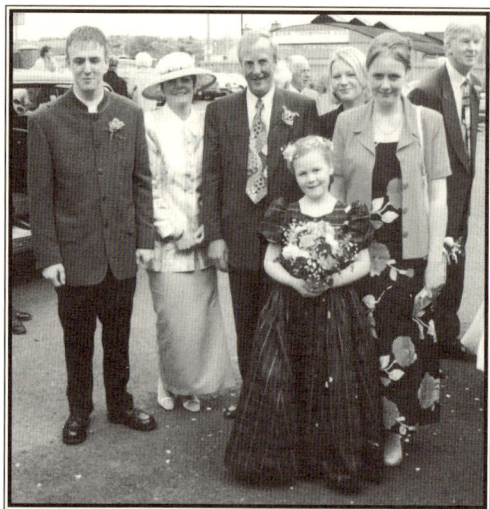

ACHESON FAMILY – MAY 1996
NEILL, DAPHNE, ROBERT, LYNN,
JILL AND AMY (IN FRONT)

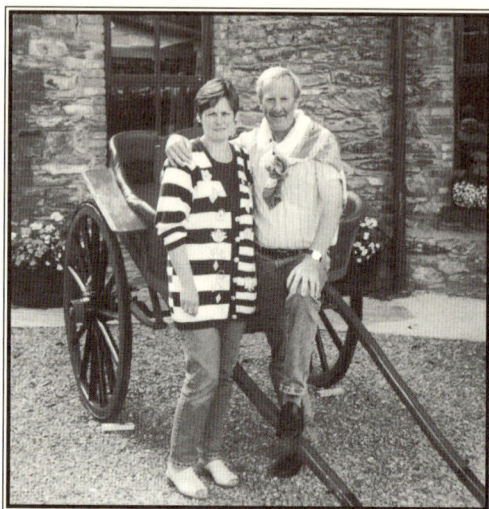

DAPHNE & ROBERT ACHESON
JULY 1996

SIXTH GENERATION

Lynn Elizabeth Acheson, Neill Robert Acheson,
Jill Emma Acheson, Amy Mavis Acheson

Lynn Elizabeth Acheson – Sixth Generation

Lynn Elizabeth Acheson, first child of Daphne Elizabeth Harshaw and Robert Acheson, was born on August 15th, 1976.

Lynn married Marc Montgomery on August 28th, 2002 in All Saints Parish Church, Gilford, County Down. Marc is a civil engineer for Powershield, which operates from Lisburn City. Lynne, a graduate in Food Technology, works for the Portadown food-processing company Moy Park as a product development manager.

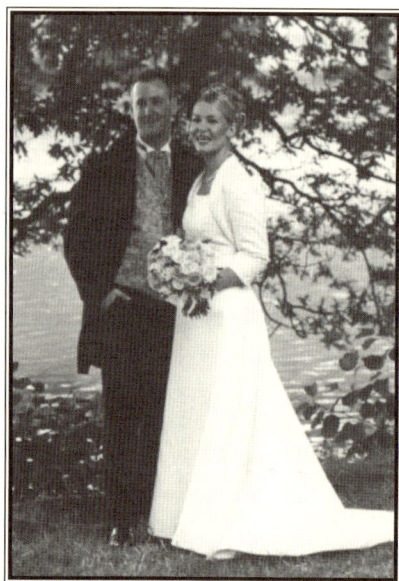

MARC MONTGOMERY AND
LYNN ELIZABETH ACHESON
WEDDING DAY – AUGUST 28TH, 2002

410

Neill Robert Acheson – Sixth Generation

Neill Robert Acheson, second child of Daphne Elizabeth Harshaw and Robert Acheson, was born on November 28th, 1979.

Neill attended Craigavon Primary School and Portadown College, then The Queen's University of Belfast, where he graduated in 2001 with a BSc in Agriculture and Economic Management. He currently works with Farmrite in Portadown and farms part-time. His hobbies include motorbiking, football and reading.

NEILL ACHESON

Jill Emma Acheson – Sixth Generation

Jill Emma Acheson, third child of Daphne Elizabeth Harshaw and Robert Acheson, was born on October 2nd, 1982.

Jill attended Craigavon Primary School and Tandragee Junior High before progressing to Craigavon Senior High School. She graduated from Belfast Institute in November 2003 with a HND in Beauty and related therapies.

Jill currently runs her own business from home on the Loughbrickland Road, Gilford.

Her hobbies include walking, shopping, and playing badminton. She also sings in her church choir and helps with the Crusaders.

JILL ACHESON

Amy Mavis Acheson – Sixth Generation

Amy Mavis Acheson, fourth child of Daphne Elizabeth Harshaw and Robert Acheson, was born on April 20th, 1988.

Amy attended Craigavon Primary School, Tandragee Junior High, and Craigavon Senior High School. She has just completed a two-year course at Armagh Technical College and has been accepted by the Queen's University of Belfast for Nursing. Amy has a bubbly personality and a love for her elders, both of which will undoubtedly make her a very good nurse. She enjoys singing and dancing and works part-time in a supermarket. Like her sister, she sings in the church choir and helps out with the Crusaders.

AMY ACHESON

Mavis Irene Harshaw – Fifth Generation

Mavis Irene Harshaw, second child of Myrtle Elizabeth Irwin and James Harshaw, was born on June 26th, 1955 in Banbridge Maternity Hospital. She married Trevor Turkington on June 17th, 1978.

Mavis attended Donaghmore Primary School and then moved to Windsor Hill Primary School for one year. The next five years were spent at Newry High School, with another two years at Newry Technical School for secretarial courses. She then worked in a group accounts office in Banbridge before studying for and receiving her ALCM (Associated London College of Music). She taught piano for a number of years.

Mavis and Trevor have three children: Gary, born January 28, 1981, Colin Henry, born March 21, 1982, and James Robert, born October 17, 1993. They live in Portadown, Craigavon, County Armagh, Northern Ireland.

TURKINGTON FAMILY
GARY, JAMES, COLIN, TREVOR & MAVIS

SIXTH GENERATION

Gary Trevor Turkington, Colin Henry Turkington,
James Robert Turkington

Gary Trevor Turkington – Sixth Generation

Gary Trevor Turkington, first child of Mavis Irene Harshaw and Trevor Turkington, was born on January 28th, 1981.

A graduate from the New University of Ulster (Jordanstown) in Business Studies, Gary is currently working in the family business as manager in Turkington Precast.

Gary and Natalie Hill plan to marry in March 2007. Natalie is a primary school teacher.

Colin Henry Turkington – Sixth Generation

Colin Henry Turkington, second child of Mavis Irene Harshaw and Trevor Turkington, was born on March 21st, 1982.

Colin is a professional car racing driver, and competes in the British Touring Class Championship. He completed a degree in Business Studies at Sterling University, but his ambition was always to race cars. The 2006 British Touring Car championship has just been completed, with Colin securing third place.

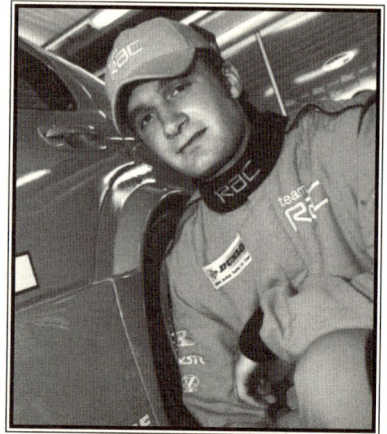

COLIN TURKINGTON

James Robert Turkington – Sixth Generation

James Robert Turkington, third child of Mavis Irene Harshaw and Trevor Turkington, was born on October 17th, 1993.

James is currently a second-year pupil at Clounagh Junior High School in Portadown. He has a great social and sports life centered around the Boys' Brigade, football and swimming. His mum says he also has an encyclopedic knowledge of motorsports—any series, any driver, any year.

Robert James Harshaw – Fifth Generation

Robert James Harshaw, third child of Myrtle Elizabeth Irwin and James Harshaw, was born on June 21st, 1957 in Banbridge Maternity Hospital, County Down. He married Wendy Elizabeth Milne on June 27th, 1981 in St. Columba's Parish Church, Elgin, North Scotland.

Robert attended Donagmore Primary School, Newry Model School, and Newry High School, where he joined the Cadets. He then enlisted in the Royal Air Force on April 24th, 1974. He was a year young, so the first year did not count. He has been in the Forces for 25 years, with many camps in England, Scotland and Wales. He is Sergeant on the Tornadoes, as well as a chief technician. He served in the Gulf for three periods, in addition to the Falkland Islands, Canada, and the United States. He has also been in Germany R.A.F. Bruggen and R.A.F. Loarbruch for three periods. He is now back in the U.K. and stationed in R.A. Rossiemouth.

Robert and Wendy have three children: Mark James, born April 11, 1985, David Michael, born April 24, 1987, and Joanne, born November 12, 1989.

FRONT ROW, LEFT TO RIGHT: JOANNE, WENDY, ROBERT, MARK JAMES; BACK ROW: DAVID MICHAEL – SEPTEMBER 1992

SIXTH GENERATION

Mark James Harshaw, David Michael Harshaw,
Joanne Harshaw

Mark James Harshaw – Sixth Generation

Mark James Harshaw, first child of Robert James Harshaw and Wendy Elizabeth Milne, was born on April 11th, 1985.

After leaving school, Mark had a variety of jobs in the fast-food/entertainment sector. He is currently working for the mobile phone company Phones 4 You as a shop salesman. His main interests away from work are computing and his girlfriend, Jo.

David Michael Harshaw – Sixth Generation

David Michael Harshaw, second child of Robert James Harshaw and Wendy Elizabeth Milne, was born on April 24th, 1987.

David is currently a second-year student at Edinburgh University studying Accountancy and Business Studies. He enjoys university life and keeps fit by playing squash and golf.

Joanne Harshaw – Sixth Generation

Joanne Harshaw, third child of Robert James Harshaw and Wendy Elizabeth Milne, was born on November 12th, 1989.

Joanne is in her final year at Elgin Academy, Scotland, where she is studying science. She has a part-time job in the local McDonalds and lists cooking as one of her hobbies.

David Thomas Harshaw – Fifth Generation

David Thomas Harshaw, fourth child of Myrtle Elizabeth Irwin and James Harshaw, was born on January 22nd, 1962 in Banbridge Hospital, County Down.

David attended St. John's Primary School for one year before transferring to Windsor Hill Primary School in Newry, moving on to Newry High School. He received further education at Banbridge Technical School, where he obtained a City & Guilds certificate. He then worked in a wholesale furniture store, specializing in carpet fitting. He also worked at Allied Maples as a sales consultant for a number of years before the firm closed down. Now he works full-time fitting carpet and other floor coverings, and is a sales representative for Rainbow Domestic Cleaner.

David married Mechelle Boyd at St Mary's by the Sea, Port Douglas, Cairns, Australia on November 8th, 2001. They have three children: Alannah, born August 10, 2002, Bradley, born November 9, 2004, and Alyssa, born October 5, 2006.

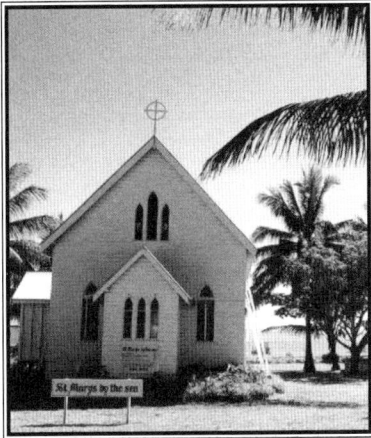

THE NON-DENOMINATIONAL CHURCH OF ST. MARY'S BY THE SEA, PORT DOUGLAS, CAIRNS, AUSTRALIA

LEFT TO RIGHT: MECHELLE WITH ALYSSA, ALANNAH, DAVID WITH BRADLEY

SIXTH GENERATION

Alannah Sarah Elizabeth Harshaw, Bradley David Leonard Harshaw, Alyssa Mechelle Audrey Harshaw

Alannah Sarah Elizabeth Harshaw – Sixth Generation

Alannah Sarah Elizabeth Harshaw, first child of David Thomas Harshaw and Mechelle Boyd, was born on August 10th, 2002.

Bradley David Leonard Harshaw – Sixth Generation

Bradley David Leonard Harshaw, second child of David Thomas Harshaw and Mechelle Boyd, was born on November 9th, 2004.

Alyssa Mechelle Audrey Harshaw – Sixth Generation

Alyssa Mechelle Audrey Harshaw, third child of David Thomas Harshaw and Mechelle Boyd, was born on October 5th, 2006.

Audrey Jean Irwin – Fourth Generation

Audrey Jean Irwin, sixth child of Margaret McClelland and Robert J. Irwin, was born on January 19th, 1927 in Corgary, Donaghmore, County Down, Northern Ireland.

Audrey attended Beech Hill, Rockvale School, and Newry Municipal High School. She trained at McMullans, Castle Arcade in Belfast as a beautician and worked in Brighton and Nottingham, England until moving to California in 1955. At Hughes Market, Audrey trained as a grocery clerk and continued in this occupation for twenty years. It was there that she met Bill Hughes in 1964. She married William P. Hughes in 1964 in Los Angeles, California. They divorced in 1979.

Audrey has lived in Tucson, Arizona since 1980, when she resumed work as a beautician and nail technician. Audrey retired in 1994.

DOROTHY WRIGHT AND EDWARD T. BRADY – WEDDING DAY, APRIL 24, 1935
BACK ROW, LEFT TO RIGHT: JOHN COTNEY AND EDWARD T. BRADY; FRONT ROW, LEFT TO RIGHT: BERTHA WRIGHT, DOROTHY WRIGHT, AUDREY JEAN IRWIN AND NORA MERCER

AUDREY IRWIN
16–18 YEARS OLD

AUDREY IRWIN

David Brown Irwin – Fourth Generation

David Brown Irwin, seventh child of Margaret McClelland and Robert J. Irwin, was born on November 4th, 1931 in Corgary, Donaghmore, County Down, Northern Ireland. He married Florence McBride on April 4th, 1955 in Sandy's St. Presbyterian Church, Newry, County Down, Northern Ireland. Florence was born in Newry, County Down, Northern Ireland.

DAVID BROWN IRWIN

DAVID & FLORENCE "FLORRIE" MCBRIDE
WEDDING DAY – APRIL 4, 1955

WEDDING DAY – APRIL 4, 1955
ANNE JACKSON, DAVID IRWIN, FLORENCE "FLORRIE" McBRIDE,
AND GEORGE JACKSON

David and Florrie had two children: Hilary Florence, born April 16, 1956 and David Bryan, born June 21, 1961.

FRONT ROW, LEFT TO RIGHT: MADELEINE, COLIN, FLORRIE & DAVID
BRYAN IRWIN; BACK ROW, LEFT TO RIGHT: DAVID BROWN IRWIN &
SARAH IRWIN – NOVEMBER 1966

Back row: David Irwin & David Bryan Irwin;
front row: Hillary Irwin Lockington & Florrie Irwin

Florence "Florrie" Irwin passed away Sunday October 6th, 2002 and is buried in the Presbyterian Cemetery on Armagh Road, Newry City.

The resting place of Florence Irwin in the Presbyterian Cemetery, Armagh Road, Newry City

FIFTH GENERATION

Hilary Florence Irwin, David Bryan Irwin

Hilary Florence Irwin – Fifth Generation

Hilary Florence Irwin, first child of David Brown Irwin and Florence "Florrie" McBride, was born on April 16th, 1956 in Daisy Hill Hospital, Newry. Hilary attended Jerrettspass and Newry Model Primary Schools before completing her secondary education at Newry High School. She began work at R.W. Toase and Co. Ltd in Merchant's Quay, Newry.

Hilary married Neil Lockington on September 11th, 1975. The couple, now separated, have three boys: Andrew, born May 8, 1978, David, born September 17, 1980, and Alan, born March 25, 1984. Hilary now lives in Ardnamara, Blackrock County, Dublin where she runs a child-minding service.

BACK ROW: NEIL (DAD), ANDREW, 17, DAVID, 15;
FRONT ROW: ALLAN, 13, HILARY (MUM)

SIXTH GENERATION

Andrew Neil Lockington, David Irwin Lockington,
Alan Bryan Lockington

Andrew Neil Lockington – Sixth Generation

Andrew Neil Lockington, first child of Hilary Florence Irwin and Neil Lockington, was born on May 8th, 1978.

Andrew attended Dundalk Presbyterian School and Dundalk Grammar School. A sports enthusiast, Andrew went to an outdoor activity centre in Galway and spent an enjoyable working holiday in Australia. After a spell in the sports complex of the Fairway Hotel, Dundalk, Andrew is now working in Kinsale, County Cork.

David Irwin Lockington – Sixth Generation

David Irwin Lockington, second child of Hilary Florence Irwin and Neil Lockington, was born on September 17th, 1980.

David is currently working as a bar manager in Blackrock County, Dublin.

Alan Bryan Lockington – Sixth Generation

Alan Bryan Lockington, third child of Hilary Florence Irwin and Neil Lockington, was born on March 25th, 1984.

In his youth, Alan was a keen cyclist and accomplished pianist. He is currently working as a service manager for BMW cars in Belfast.

David Bryan Irwin – Fifth Generation

David Bryan Irwin, second child of David Brown Irwin and Florence "Florrie" McBride, was born on June 21st, 1961 in Newry General Hospital. He married Madeleine Murdock on July 5th, 1986 in Donaghmore Presbyterian Church, County Down, Northern Ireland.

LEFT TO RIGHT: FLORENCE IRWIN, DAVID BRYAN IRWIN,
MADELEINE MURDOCK & DAVID IRWIN
WEDDING DAY – JULY 5, 1986

Bryan spent seven years at Newry Model School before moving on to Newry High School. Afterwards, he took a job as storeman with a local firm from 9:00 a.m. to 1:00 p.m., and an evening job (2:00 p.m. to 10:00 p.m.) in a store beside his home. He saved all of his own money, bought a car at seventeen, and went to car rallies with his many friends. He eventually changed jobs for a firm in Bainbridge, where he remained for about three years. Following this, he worked for a precast concrete company in Portadown, County Armagh for twelve years. He then worked for a construction firm in Magherafelt, County Tyrone and currently works for an engineering firm in Tandragee, County Armagh.

COLIN, MADELEINE, SARAH, & BRYAN IRWIN – NOVEMBER 1996

Bryan and Madeleine live in Portadown, County Armagh. They have two children: Sarah, born May 15, 1987, and Colin, born April 10, 1991.

Madeleine worked for Timber Merchants in Newry, County Down for four years. She is currently a P.A. with a computer software development company in Tandragee, County Armagh.

POYNTZPASS RAILWAY CABIN, LAST ONE IN NORTHERN IRELAND. PHOTO TAKEN BY BRYAN IRWIN ON SATURDAY NOVEMBER 2, 1996

Sixth Generation

Sarah Madeleine Irwin, Colin David Irwin

Sarah Madeleine Irwin – Sixth Generation

Sarah Madeleine Irwin, first child of David Bryan Irwin and Madeleine Murdock, was born on May 15th, 1987 in Craigavon Area Hospital.

Sarah attended Seagoe Primary School and Killicomaine Junior High School in Portadown. She completed her secondary education at The Upper Bann Institute and is now working in Craigavon Area Hospital.

Colin David Irwin – Sixth Generation

Colin David Irwin, second child of David Bryan Irwin and Madeleine Murdock, was born on April 10th, 1991 in Craigavon Area Hospital.

Colin went to Seagoe Primary School and Killicomaine Junior High and is currently a pupil at Portadown College. A keen golfer, Colin is a member of Knocknamuckley Boy's Brigade, through which he is taking part in the Duke of Edinburgh Award Scheme.

Albert Edward Irwin – Fourth Generation

Albert Edward Irwin, eighth child of Margaret McClelland and Robert J. Irwin, was born on January 26th, 1936 in Corgary, Donaghmore, County Down, Northern Ireland. He married Margaret Singleton on June 12th, 1962 in County Armagh, Northern Ireland. Margaret was born in Loughgilly, County Armagh.

Albert "Bertie" was reared on the farm at Corgary. He attended Rockvale Primary School and Newry Model School before starting work in Martin Nesbitt & Irwin, a grocery firm, then Ulster Farmers Bacon Co. Ltd. until he contracted diabetes and had to finish work. Margaret worked with Bertie in the same firm. Both are now retired and live on Latt Road on the outskirts of Newry City.

ALBERT EDWARD IRWIN & MARGARET SINGLETON, WEDDING DAY – JUNE 12, 1962

MARGARET & BERTIE IRWIN – 1986

David Livingston McClelland – Third Generation

David Livingston McClelland, third child of William McClelland and Sarah Ann Henning, was born on February 11th, 1899 in Cloughanramer, County Down, Ireland.

David was orphaned at eleven, and lived with his older brother William and sister Margaret on the family farm at Cloughanramer.

His guardian Abel Henning, an uncle, watched over the young family from a neighboring farm. But David had a mind of his own, as reflected by the ditty he would sing to his uncle from a tree in the family orchard:

> There was a man from Barkston Lodge
> He tried on me to work a dodge,
> So I went up a chestnut tree
> And there he couldn't follow me.
>
> To the old bog shed I will not go
> There's nothing there I need to know.
> So I'll stay here the rest of the day
> Until that man will go away.

DAVID LIVINGSTON MCCLELLAND

David was later sent to live with an older half-sister, Maud, and her husband Albert Hawthorn in Glasgow, Scotland.

David joined the United States Army September 22nd, 1917 and was honorably discharged with the rank of Corporal on June 3rd, 1919.

David was employed by the United States Air Force as a civilian worker for more than 34 years. On November 17th, 1961, Rear Admiral Frank O'Beirne recognized his service with a letter of appreciation:

The New Chieftain – *November 17, 1961*
Albuquerque, New Mexico

LEFT TO RIGHT: REAR ADMIRAL FRANK O'BEIRNE PRESENTING A LETTER OF APPRECIATION TO DAVID L. MCCLELLAND

"**Veteran Worker Cited:** David L. McClelland, civilian employed at Sandia Base for six years, receives a letter of appreciation from Rear Adm. Frank O'Beirne, USN, Commander, Field Command, Armed Forces Special Weapons Project, as he prepares to retire after more than 34 years in Civil Service. Born in Newry, County Down, Ireland, 58 years ago, McClelland attended school there and in Glasgow, Scotland, before coming to the U.S. in 1916. He joined Civil Service in 1922 and worked in California, Hawaiian Islands, and Ohio before coming to Albuquerque. He and his wife live at 1304 Tijeras NW."

David married Myrtle Wilhelmina Haller on January 3rd, 1921 in San Diego, California.

DAVID LIVINGSTON McCLELLAND AND MYRTLE WILHELMINA HALLER MARRIAGE CERTIFICATE

Myrtle Wilhelmina Haller was born on April 29th, 1899 in Midlothian, Texas to Leona Belle Maddox Haller and Frederick Haller. There were three other children: Archibald Orben Haller, Mary Haller, and Elva Haller.

Myrtle's father was a section foreman, and Myrtle grew up in a small railroad town along the Southern Pacific Railroad. As she was the eldest, her siblings called her "Sis." Myrtle was brought up by her mother to be a lady, and she truly always was. She learned to play the piano and was taught embroidery and hat making. Her English was flawless. She was an excellent seamstress and an exceptional cook. She spoke Spanish. She was a pretty woman, 5' 6" tall, slender, with brown hair and eyes. She never left the house unless she was looking her best.

Myrtle became a secretary and worked for President Von Kleinschmidt at the University of Arizona. When her family moved to San Diego c. 1919, she remained in Tucson, where she rented a room from Mrs. Lyle on Alameda Street. She met David there, as he was living with the Smith family just across the road.

As a young couple, David and Billie (as he called her) loved to dance. He was very outgoing, she more reticent. She never had a close friend, although she had many friends of long standing. As years went by, Myrtle became more reserved, and coping with social activities became a real strain for her. She seemed frail but had a quietly strong will—enough to suffer depression and hide it.

Billie and David enjoyed playing bridge and Scrabble. Word games and anything educational, such as travel, were indulged in when possible. Billie's life after her stroke at thirty-two changed her life. She was secluded because David, trying to keep himself occupied and use his boundless energies, bought a small old farm and began to remodel it. It became a lovely place after many years of work, but Billie never drove a car and so remained distant. The house was torn up with all of the remodeling, so entertaining was not possible. Her two daughters were in high school, and their social life suffered as well. All during this time, Billie was struggling to regain her mobility in living conditions which were very difficult. Depression must have been a greater problem for her then, though people doubtless never knew what a struggle she made to recover. Part of the difficulty, of course, was that there was no therapy, and she certainly could have used it. She created her own therapy instead, a particularly admirable accomplishment for one who was not brought up for such hardships.

David and Billie had two children: Patricia Leah McClelland, born September 27, 1922 in National City, California, and Jacqueline Joan McClelland, born March 26, 1925 in San Diego, California.

PATTY & JACKIE McCLELLAND
HONOLULU, HAWAII – CIRCA 1930s

THE McCLELLAND GIRLS
PATTIE & JACKIE – OHIO

DAVID LIVINGSTON McCLELLAND

MYRTLE (BILLIE) HALLER McCLELLAND

David Livingston McClelland died January 26th, 1967 in Albuquerque, New Mexico. Myrtle (Billie) Wilhelmina Haller McClelland passed away on January 2nd, 1986 in Tucson, Arizona.

FOURTH GENERATION

Patricia Leah McClelland, Jacqueline Joan McClelland

Patricia Leah McClelland – Fourth Generation

Patricia Leah McClelland, firstborn of David Livingston McClelland and Myrtle Wilhelmina Haller, was born on September 27th, 1922 at 1850 East 16th Street, National City, California.

Pat's family moved to Honolulu, Hawaii in 1928. The family later moved to Dayton, Ohio in 1932. Pat graduated from Bath Township High School in 1940 and progressed to Miami Jacobs Secretarial College.

PATRICIA LEAH MCCLELLAND

Pat married Marion J. Caple on November 2nd, 1940 in Erlanger, Kentucky. They had one child, Karen Louise Caple, born December 21, 1943 at Mercy Hospital in San Diego, California. Pat divorced Marion J. Caple in May 1948.

Karen Louis Caple – Fifth Generation

Karen Louise Caple, first child of Patricia Leah McClelland and Marion Joseph Caple, was born on December 21st, 1943 in San Diego, California.

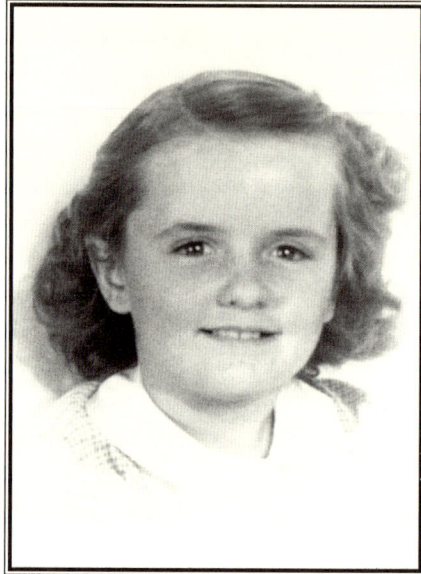

KAREN CAPLE

Patricia married Robert C. Stephens on September 2nd, 1948 in Lordsburg, New Mexico. They have three children: Robert C. Stephens, Jr., born May 20, 1951 in Tucson, Arizona, Ann Elizabeth Stephens, born November 28, 1954 in Tucson, Arizona, and David T. Stephens, born September 4, 1962 in Denver, Colorado. The family moved to southern Peru in 1958, and returned to Tucson September 4th, 1962. They adopted David T. Stephens in 1974. Pat divorced Robert Stephens in 1983.

Pat moved to Lakeside, Arizona where she and her daughter, Ann, had a fabric store. She returned to Tucson in 1986 after five years as a shopkeeper and began teaching needlework in shops at Pima Community College and Green Valley.

Richard & Karen Stephens

Stephens Family
Front row, left to right: Robert, David
Thomas, Patricia; back row, left to right:
Ann Elizabeth & Robert Stephens, Jr.

Four Generations
Front row, left to right: Patricia Stephens, Catalina Stephens,
Ann Willert, Ana Stephens; back row: Alissa and Keeley Willert

Patricia L. Stephens
was born September 27, 1922 in San Diego, CA to the parents of David and Myrtle McClelland. Patricia passed away April 21, 2002 in the loving arms of her family. Patricia was a loved daughter, sister, wife, mother, grandmother, aunt and cousin. Those who were fortunate enough to know her, knew she lived her life with dignity no matter what the obstacles. Patricia's family called her the bravest woman they have ever known. Patricia's strength came from her faith in God, and she was an active member of St. Marks Presbyterian Church. Patricia had many outside activities, which included teaching, volunteering, parenting her children and was always active with her grandchildrens' lives. Patricia is survived by children, Robert C. (Joni) Stephens, Ann (Richard) Willert, and David T. Stephens; grandchildren, Jill D. and Robert C. Pearson, Keeley C., Kent C., Alissa B. Willert, and Catalina Stephens. The celebration of her life will be held at St. Marks Presbyterian Church, 3809 E. 3rd St, SUN, April 28, at 2:00 p.m.

OBITUARY – PATRICIA L. STEPHENS
APRIL 21, 2002

ROBERT & PAT STEPHENS
FAMILY REUNION 1997

Pat was a member of the Order of Eastern Star and St. Mark's Presbyterian Church.

Pat was shy, reserved and beautiful, though she never saw her outward beauty. She conquered every obstacle in life with humility and perseverance. Her life was difficult, and the situations that faced her often very painful. She left a legacy to her children and grandchildren of a life lived with love, faith, service, kindness and generosity.

Pat passed away quietly with her children and grandchildren at her side on April 21st, 2002 in Tucson, Arizona.

FIFTH GENERATION

Robert Coleman Stephens, Jr., Ann Elizabeth Stephens, David Thomas Stephens

Robert Coleman Stephens, Jr. – Fifth Generation

Robert Coleman Stephens, Jr., first child of Patricia Leah McClelland and Robert Coleman Stephens, was born on May 20th, 1951 in Tucson Medical Center, Tucson, Arizona. He married Jeanette LaValle, born in June of 1973. They have two children: Jill Dion Stephens, born May 27, 1977 in Tucson, Arizona, and Robert Coleman Stephens, III, born September 5, 1979 in Tucson, Arizona. Robert divorced Jeanette LaValle.

JILL, JANETTE & ROBERT STEPHENS
DECEMBER 1977

SIXTH GENERATION

Jill Dion Stephens, Robert Coleman Stephens, III

Jill Dion Stephens – Sixth Generation

Jill Dion Stephens, first child of Robert Coleman Stephens, Jr. and Jeanette LaValle, was born on May 27th, 1977 in Tucson, Arizona.

Jill studied at Northern Arizona University and graduated in May of 2004 with a degree in Business.

Jill is lovely, kind, and sensitive and has gracefully overcome every obstacle in her life.

JILL DION STEPHENS

PAT STEPHENS, JILL STEPHENS, AND KEELEY WILLERT
JULY 2000

Robert Coleman Stephens, III – Sixth Generation

Robert Coleman Stephens, III, second child of Robert Coleman Stephens, Jr. and Jeanette LaValle, was born on September 5th, 1979 in Tucson, Arizona.

Robbie studied at the University of Arizona and graduated in 2003. Robbie is intelligent, handsome, kind, and charming.

ROBERT COLEMAN STEPHENS

KENT WILLERT AND ROBBIE STEPHENS JR.

Ann Elizabeth Stephens – Fifth Generation

Ann Elizabeth Stephens, second child of Patricia Leah McClelland and Robert Coleman Stephens, was born on November 28th, 1954 in Tucson, Arizona.

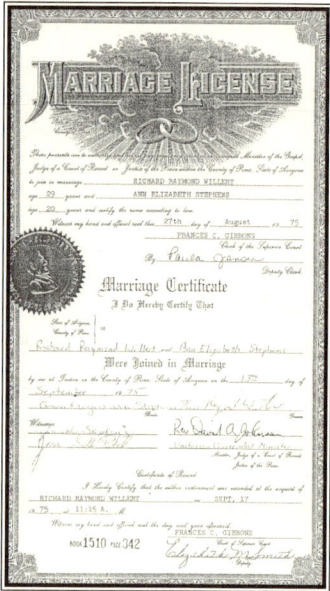

Ann moved with her family to Ilo, Peru at age four for 3 ½ years, returning to Tucson in 1962.

Ann married Richard Raymond Willert on September 13th, 1975 in Tucson, Arizona.

ANN ELIZABETH STEPHENS AND
RICHARD RAYMOND WILLERT
MARRIAGE CERTIFICATE

WILLERT WEDDING DAY
LEFT TO RIGHT: PATRICIA & ROBERT STEPHENS, ANN STEPHENS WILLERT, RICHARD
RAYMOND WILLERT, CECILIA WILLERT AND WILL WILLERT

442

Richard Raymond Willert was born in Little Falls, New York on August 10th, 1946 to Elmer and Cecilia Willert. At age nine, he and his family relocated to Orange County, California. After college and service in the United States Navy, Richard moved to Tucson, Arizona.

FRONT ROW, LEFT TO RIGHT: ANN, ALISSA, & KEELEY; BACK ROW: RICHARD & KENT WILLERT

In 1977, Ann and Richard moved to Pinetop-Lakeside, Arizona for ten years. They have three children: Keeley Crystal Willert, born July 7, 1978 in Tucson, Arizona, Kent Christian Willert, born April 17, 1981 in Show Low, Arizona, and Alissa Beth Willert, born December 1, 1991 in Guatemala City, Guatemala and adopted July 7, 1994 in Tucson, Arizona.

The family returned to Tucson in 1987 to start Desert Hues Painting with Ann's brother, David Stephens. Ann worked as the office manager for eighteen years until they sold the business in May 2005. Richard, Ann, and Alissa relocated to Lake Monticello in Palmyra, Virginia in 2005. Richard has taken up hunting with his son-in-law, Billy.

LEFT TO RIGHT: KENT, ALISSA, ANN, RICHARD & KEELEY FAMILY REUNION – 1997

VILLERFRANCHE, FRANCE – JUNE 29, 2003
LEFT TO RIGHT: KEELEY, ANN, ALISSA, RICHARD & KENT WILLERT

SIXTH GENERATION

Keeley Crystal Willert, Kent Christian Willert, Alissa Beth Willert

Keeley Crystal Willert – Sixth Generation

Keeley Crystal Willert, first child of Ann Elizabeth Stephens and Richard Raymond Willert, was born on July 7th, 1978 in Tucson, Arizona.

Keeley studied at the University of Arizona and Northern Arizona University. She was a flight attendant for Delta Airlines and is currently working in retail management. Keeley is bright, beautiful, kind, and generous, a natural leader.

KEELEY CRYSTAL
WILLERT – 1980

444

RICHARD & KEELEY WILLERT
RICHARD PINNING FLIGHT WINGS AT DELTA GRADUATION
FEBRUARY 28, 2000

Keeley married William Scovel Shear on December 29th, 2003 in Edinburgh, Scotland.

KEELEY & WILLIAM SHEAR
WEDDING DAY – DECEMBER 29, 2003

RICHARD & ALISSA WILLERT, KEELEY & WILLIAM SHEAR, ANN &
KENT WILLERT, WEDDING DAY – DECEMBER 29, 2003

William "Billy" Scovel Shear was born on September 1st, 1975 in Washington, D.C.
to Marta and Richard Shear. Billy graduated from the University of Arizona College of
Medicine in May of 2004.

Keeley and Bill relocated to Charlottesville, Virginia in 2004 for Billy to begin residency
in Internal Medicine at the University of Virginia. Billy recently received a Fellowship in
Gastroenterology Research and Clinical from the University of Virginia, to begin in the year
2007. Billy is a dedicated doctor and an avid hunter and fisherman, and is enjoying rural life
in Virginia. His has an imaginative personality, and his pranks bring comic relief!

Kent Christian Willert – Seventh Generation

Kent Christian Willert, second child of Ann Elizabeth Stephens and Richard Raymond Willert, was born on April 17th, 1981 in Show Low, Arizona.

KENT CHRISTIAN WILLERT – 1986

Kent grew up in the White Mountains and moved with his family to Tucson in 1987. He studied at Pima Community College and Trinity Western University in British Columbia, Canada. Kent worked with his father for many years managing and supervising his business. He is taking a sabbatical from his degree in Fine Arts and putting his experience and talents to work in retail management. Kent is bright, handsome, intuitive, kind, artistic, funny and engaging.

Kent married Emily Ingham on October 10th, 2004.

KENT, ALISSA & RICHARD WILLERT
NIAGARA FALLS – 2000

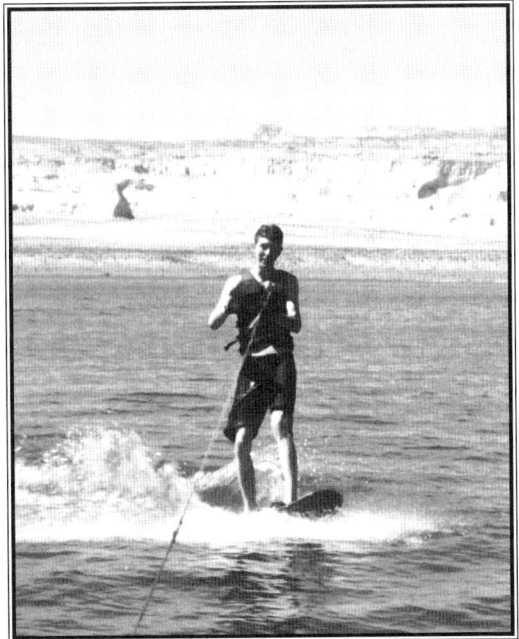

KENT WILLERT – 2000

447

KENT & EMILY WILLERT – WEDDING DAY, OCTOBER 10, 2004
BACK ROW, LEFT TO RIGHT: DAVID STEPHENS, KEELEY SHEAR, WILLIAM SHEAR,
EMILY INGHAM WILLERT, KENT WILLERT, ANN WILLERT, RICHARD WILLERT;
FRONT ROW, LEFT TO RIGHT: ALISSA WILLERT AND CATALINA STEPHENS

Emily Mae Ingham was born in Tucson, Arizona on July 23rd, 1982 to Rex and Wendy
Ingham. Emily is currently working on her Fine Arts and Interior Design degree at the
University of Arizona. Emily is graceful, beautiful, tenderhearted, kind and very artistic.
Emily's mother and Kent's mother went to high school together and were acquaintances—
small world!

Alissa Beth Willert – Sixth Generation

Alissa Beth Willert, third child of Ann Elizabeth Stephens and Richard Raymond Willert, was born on December 1st, 1991 in Guatemala City, Guatemala, and adopted on July 7th, 1994 in Tucson, Arizona. Alissa arrived in Tucson on Christmas Eve, 1993.

ALISSA BETH WILLERT – AGE TWO
DECEMBER 1993

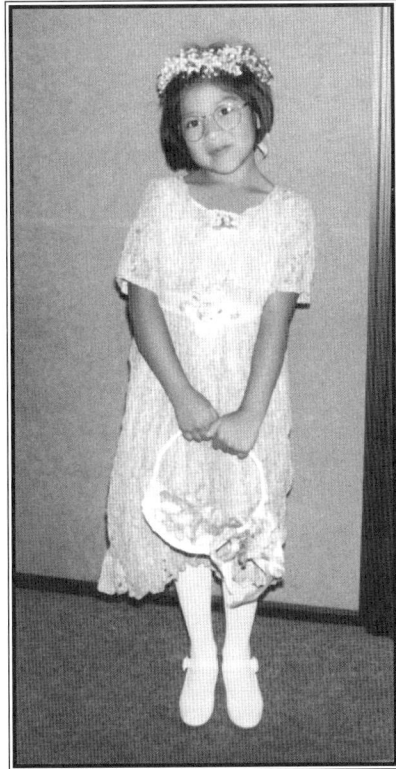

ALISSA BETH WILLERT – 1996

The above (left) photo of Alissa at the age of two was placed on Ann's pillow just before Alissa's twelfth birthday with the following note attached.

"Remember when I was this age? This December 1, 2003, I will be twelve. I thank you for everything you have done in my life you changed it to be better. You have taught me how to be all I can be and never stop trying. Some day I will learn how to drive and live my life, but when I do I will remember everything you have taught me.

I love you with all my heart,

Alissa"

Alissa loves to play soccer. In 2005 she was selected to play on the SOCA U14 Express Travel Team in Virginia. The move to Virginia has helped her to pursue soccer at a much higher level. She traveled and played soccer with her team in Italy the summer of 2006. At fourteen years of age, Alissa is growing up to be a beautiful, kind, graceful, talented and sensitive young woman

David Thomas Lyle Stephens – Fifth Generation

David Thomas Lyle, firstborn of Karen Louise Caple (Stephens) and Harry Thomas Lyle, was born on September 4th, 1962 in Colorado General Hospital, Denver, Colorado.

Patricia L. Stephens and Robert C. Stephens (David's grandmother and step-grandfather) returned to Tucson from Peru on September 4th, 1962, the day David was born. Two years later, David moved to Tucson, Arizona, where he was raised by the Stephens family.

In 1975, Patricia and Robert legally adopted their grandson David (age 13), and he chose to officially change his last name from Lyle to Stephens. While Ann Elizabeth Stephens and Robert C. Stephens, Jr. were naturally his aunt and uncle, David grew up as a little brother to Annabeth and Robbie, with Pat and Bob as his mom and dad.

In Tucson, David attended a Lutheran pre-school, Peter Howell Elementary School, Alice Vail Junior High School, and Rincon High School. Family outings often centered on boating activities, with his dad and brother building and racing boats. As David grew older, he learned the basics of the construction business from his big brother. David credits Robbie for helping him learn how to work until the job got finished. In just three years, at the age of 16, David graduated from Rincon High School.

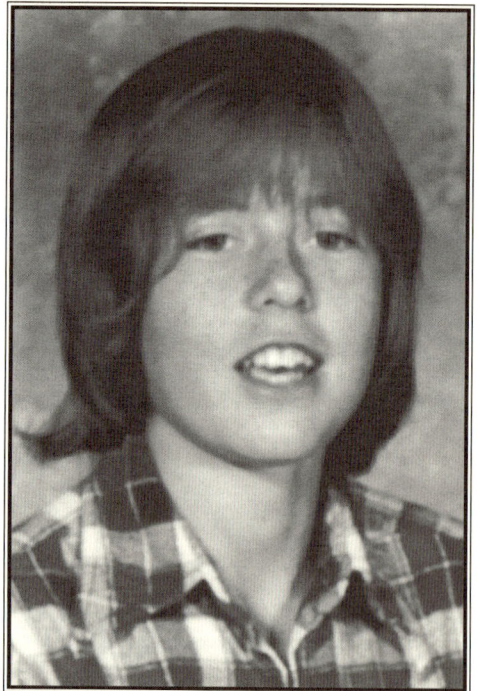
DAVID THOMAS STEPHENS
CIRCA 1974

The next fall, David moved to Flagstaff, Arizona, into Peterson dormitory, and began attending Northern Arizona University. David's girlfriend Ana Morales was already attending N.A.U., and David had family there (Aunt Jackie Priser and her family). David enjoyed welding, photography, and industrial arts classes, as well as lifting weights, studying martial arts, and learning to snow ski at Snowbowl. He ultimately found that marketing and business classes were challenging, and focused his efforts in those areas. David worked his way through college: five years at Schlotzky's sandwich shop and summers at his sister Ann and her husband Richard Willert's painting contracting company in the White Mountains. Only once did he step into a full five-gallon bucket of paint and tip it onto the shag carpet of a country-club home. With the help of school loans, grants, and scholarships, David graduated from NAU in 1984 with a Bachelor's degree in Business Administration.

After college, Richard offered David the opportunity to join him in his painting business. Richard and David formed Desert Hues Painting and moved the company from Lakeside to Tucson. Richard's easy going nature and ability to accomplish almost anything helped them build the company into a thriving business.

In 1988, David began taking real estate classes while Ann and Richard continued to successfully run Desert Hues Painting. David then decided to go back to college, where he attended the University of Arizona's Karl Eller Graduate School of Management.

In 1990, David moved to Congress, Arizona and began working for his cousin Jimmy Parker at the new Parker Dairy. Over the course of two years, Jimmy taught him the 24/7 life of a dairyman—everything from building water systems to buying one-ton bales of alfalfa hay and raising replacement heifers.

In 1992, David and his girlfriend, Ana Morales, moved back to Flagstaff, and he began his career selling real estate. For the past 14 years, David has enjoyed working as a realtor in Flagstaff. He has also worked with partners renovating historic commercial properties in downtown Flagstaff and creating several new residential subdivisions.

David married Ana Luisa Guadalupe Padilla Morales on May 10th, 1997 at the Catholic Newman Center in Flagstaff, Arizona. They divorced in June 1999.

On May 26, 1999, David and Ana were blessed with the birth of their only child, a beautiful daughter they named Catalina Nicole Stephens. Ana chose her name in remembrance of her own grandmother, also named Catalina. She has been nicknamed "Cali."

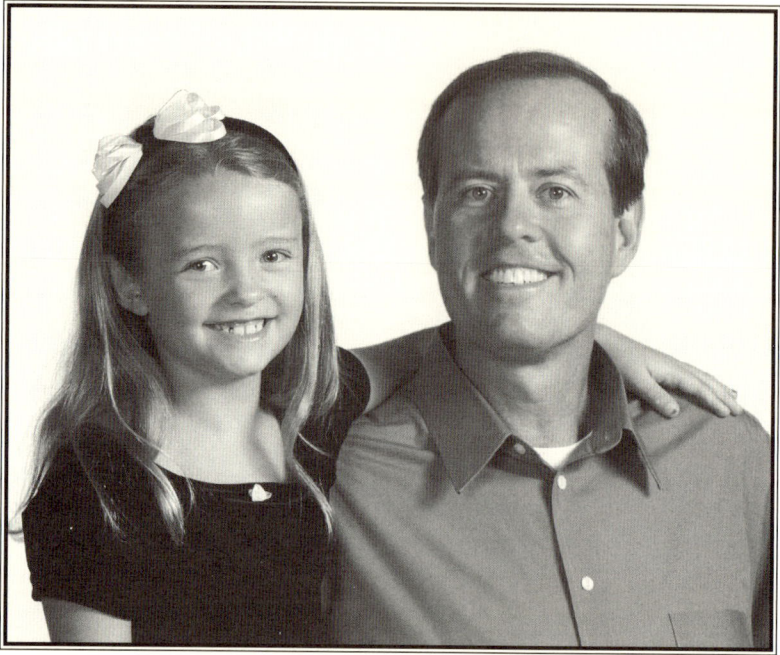

CALI AND DAVID STEPHENS

When he's not selling real estate, David's favorite activities revolve around raising Cali—reading her books, coaching her Micro-Soccer team, ice-skating, and riding bikes at Buffalo Park. An avid water-skier, David enjoys trips to Lake Powell and Flagstaff's Lake Mary when the water's not too cold. David and Cali, now a second-grader at Sechrist Elementary School, enjoy worshipping at Mountain View Christian Church.

SEVENTH GENERATION

Catalina (Cali) Stephens – Seventh Generation

Catalina Nicole Stephens, nicknamed "Cali," firstborn of David Thomas Stephens and Ana Luisa Guadalupe Padilla Morales, was born on May 26th, 1999 at 3:39 a.m. in the Flagstaff Medical Center, Flagstaff, Arizona. She weighed 8 lbs. 6 oz. and was 19 ½ inches long.

Catalina's mother, Ana, was born on December 12th, 1960 in Tucson, Arizona. David and Ana divorced in 1999. Ana works for a plastic surgeon's office as a recovery room nurse and has remarried. Catalina lives with both her mother and her father in Flagstaff, Arizona.

CATALINA NICOLE STEPHENS
CIRCA 2000

CATALINA NICOLE STEPHENS
CIRCA 2004

Catalina attended Peace Lutheran Preschool and now attends Sechrist Elementary School, where she is a second-grade student. At age seven, Catalina's favorite activities include swimming, dancing, playing Micro-Soccer (she's played for five seasons), going to the movies and playing with her Polly Pockets.

She excels in school and has completed two science-fair events: her kindergarten project about melting marshmallows was selected to compete at N.A.U. and won third place in the school district, and her first-grade project about suntan lotions (she experimented with hot dogs in a sun-tanning salon) won second place in the district. Her artwork has been exhibited in the Flagstaff district offices. Catalina has an outgoing personality, a flair for fashion, and a love for animals, especially cats. She attends both Christ's Church of Flagstaff and Mountain View Christian Church.

Jacqueline Joan McClelland – Fourth Generation

Jacqueline Joan McClelland, second child of David L. McClelland and Myrtle Wilhelmina Haller, was born on March 26th, 1925 at Mercy Hospital in San Diego, California. Jackie had scarlet fever as an infant, and the family had to live under quarantine for a number of weeks. As an adult, Jackie was 5' 6 ½" and small-boned. Her hair was brown, her eyes, also brown. She was creative and an above-average student. She skipped 7th grade and graduated in 1942 from Bath Township High School in Fairborn, Ohio. After graduation, she worked for the government during World War II.

JACQUELINE JOAN MCCLELLAND

JOHN BENJAMIN PRISER &
JACQUELINE JOAN MCCLELLAND
WEDDING DAY – MAY 16, 1944

On May 16th, 1944, Jackie married John Benjamin Priser. John was born on August 15th, 1918 in Pueblo, Colorado.

John and Jackie had a home in Vandalia, Ohio where their first child, Michael J. Priser, was born March 18, 1945.

Four children followed: Susan Jean, born July 31, 1946, Jane born September 26, 1952, Patty, and David. The family moved to Tucson, where they spent several years before moving back to Ohio.

1952 found the family in Albuquerque, then White Sands, New Mexico in preparation for a move to Argentina, where John was to work at a satellite tracking station for nine months.

Albuquerque Journal
August 27, 1958

ARGENTINA BOUND: John B. Priser and his family lined up for the camera a few minutes before boarding a plane here for Argentina Tuesday afternoon. There he will work as an observer at one of the Smithsonian Institute's satellite tracking stations. The family includes, left to right, Priser; his wife, Jackie; Mike, 13; Jane, 5; Patty, 3, and Susan, 12. They lived here at 9901 Claremont NE. (Staff photo)

FRONT ROW, LEFT TO RIGHT: JANE, PATTY;
BACK ROW, LEFT TO RIGHT: MIKE, JACQUELINE AND SUSAN PRISER

It was in Argentina that Jackie became fluent in Spanish. John and Jackie's final home was in Flagstaff, where John was an observer at the Naval Observatory.

Jackie served on the Flagstaff school board for five years and was urged to run for office again but refused. She was offered a position with the State Board of Education in Phoenix, but John did not want to move. She went to work for the Northern Arizona Council of Governments when John retired on disability. Her talents were recognized and she was trained to succeed the personnel director. When Coconino County was looking for a personnel director, Jackie did not apply because she did not have the required formal education, but the County Manager sought her out and hired her. She initiated many programs which were of benefit to the approximately 400 county employees. When she became ill with cancer and died on January 18th, 1987, the County held a memorial service for her.

Jacqueline J. Priser, the second woman in history to serve on the Flagstaff School Board, died Jan. 18 at her home. She was 61.

Mrs. Priser, who had been ill for a year, was at the time of death personnel director of Coconino County, a post she had held since June 1984. Prior to that, she had worked almost a decade for the Northern Arizona Council of Governments (NACOG) and had ended her career there as personnel director.

In 1967, Mrs. Priser was elected to a five-year term on the school board. At that time, she was only the second woman to serve on the board. The first was Mary Morton Pollock who served in the 1920s and 1930s.

"Jackie brought county government to a higher plane of decency by her mere presence," County Manager Catherine R. Eden said today. "In many ways, she was the conscience of this county."

"Jackie brought many changes to our personnel system, but she was proudest of starting an employee assistance program which has been widely accepted by our workers.

"It feels today as if there is a huge gap in our organization."

Memorial services will be private.

Mrs. Priser was born March 26, 1925, in San Diego, and grew up and was educated in Ohio. She moved to Arizona first in 1937 and lived for three years in Tucson. She returned in 1960 with her husband, John B. Priser, now a retired astronomer with the U.S. Naval Observatory, and the family settled in Flagstaff.

She was a member of the Flagstaff Symphony Guild and the Art Gallery Association.

In 1967, she was elected to the school board to replace Dr. Doyle Bladon, Sedona, handily defeating a field of six other male candidates to win the seat.

During her board term, she was a member of the Social Health Committee and the advisory committee for selection of school sites. She also served on the joint board-administration professional administration team and was a member of the Arizona School Board-Administrators Joint Study Committee on Professional Guidelines. She also was named to the State Board of Education.

In 1972, she sought re-election to the local board and was defeated.

Survivors are her husband, a Flagstaff resident; two sons, Michael, Maryland; David, Flagstaff; and three daughters, Susan Prins, South Africa; Jane, Flagstaff; and Patty Pasco, Colorado; and a sister, Pat Stevenson, Tucson.

JACQUELINE J. PRISER

COCONINO COUNTY PERSONNEL
DIRECTOR PRISER DIES

THE PRISER FAMILY
JACQUELINE, SUE, JANE,
JACQUELINE PRINS, JOHN
PRISER, PATTY PRISER, AND
DAVID PRISER IN FRONT
FLAGSTAFF, ARIZONA – 1970

John Priser worked as an astronomer at the Flagstaff Station from 1963 to 1975 and was a key figure in the establishment of the 61-inch and its program.

He was fascinated by satellites and "slapped together" a telescope from surplus optics and junk from old automobiles. He built a sidereel drive from clock parts and taught himself to compute satellite orbits with a straight edge and graph paper. He learned photography, built a darkroom in his garage, and obtained some of the first satellite photographs.

The Smithsonian Observatory discovered this humble man and moved him and his family to their satellite tracking station in Argentina. He returned to the U.S. as station chief of the Las Cruces, New Mexico tracking station.

In 1960, John applied for a job at Lowell Observatory and began working as a research assistant, learning photo-electric photometry from Harold Johnson.

John's energy was enormous—he fairly bustled everywhere. He co-authored the test paper of the 61-inch, tested new equipment, set up the photographic program, and produced a definitive set of "pretty pictures," many of which are found in encyclopedias and text books.

In the early days of the station, John taught the family photography, astrometry, drafting, electronics and lunch-time pinochle. He repaired watches, dug cars from the snow, patted people on the back when they excelled and kicked them in the butt when they did not.

When the decision to build the 8-inch transit circle was made, John was named the project manager and acted as observatory liaison with contractors. He was observing variable stars at the time. Nonetheless, he applied his enthusiasm to the 8-inch project, documented the progress, and maintained a discipline and expertise that resulted in one of the most precise instruments owned by the U.S. Navy.

SUE PRINS, JANE PRISER, PATTY PRISER AND JOHN PRISER IN FRONT

John retired in 1975 and worked on contract with IBM writing many of the first programs for the newly developed personal computers . . . all self-taught. In his spare time, John made fine jewelry and painted, painted, painted.

After Jackie's death, John moved to Sedona, Arizona and explored religion and art, and collected an immense entourage of friends. He influenced many people, was generous with his time, had boundless energy, and became a loving "father" to all he came in contact with.

After 78 orbits about the sun, John Benjamin Priser stopped running. He died in his sleep on the 25th of February, 1997. John and Jackie Priser are survived by five children and nine grandchildren.

FIFTH GENERATION

Michael John Priser, Susan Jean Priser, Jane Priser, Patricia Priser, David Priser

Michael John Priser – Fifth Generation

Michael John Priser, first child of Jacqueline Joan McClelland and John Benjamin Priser, was born on March 18th, 1945 in Vandalia, Ohio.

Michael's first memories were of living on a farm on Shaker Road, Dayton, Ohio owned by David (Pop) and Myrtle (Tootsie) McClelland. Mike went to elementary school and had his first job selling "Spud Nuts" until age 12, when John and Jackie Priser moved with the children to Albuquerque, New Mexico. Mike attended Jackson Junior High School and pursued interests in science, astronomy, and mathematics.

In 1959, the Prisers moved to Argentina for a year, and Michael went to elementary school and learned basic Spanish. He has studied and habla Espanol con gusto (speaks Spanish with gusto). In Villa Dolores, Argentina, there was lots of horseback riding and swimming.

Michael and the family moved to Las Cruces, New Mexico, where he attended junior high school and was selected to go to the New Mexico State Science Fair Contest for his homemade spectroscope. He continued learning Spanish.

After the family moved to Flagstaff, Arizona, Michael had a paper route and enjoyed climbing Mt. Elden. He was active in Boy Scouts and received the coveted Eagle award.

From a Flagstaff Newspaper

SCOUT AWARDED — Mike Priser, Explorer Post 31, Federated Church, receives the coveted Eagle award from Scout Executive Robert M. Bishop while Mike's parents, Mr. and Mrs. John B. Priser, 3335 N. Jamison Blvd., watch proudly. Post Advisor is W. H. Troxell, active in Scouting in Flagstaff since 1947.

MIKE PRISER – EAGLE SCOUT AWARD

Mike was an honor student at Flagstaff High School. During the summers, he worked with a survey team and had jobs all over northern Arizona. Michael graduated a year early to study at Northern Arizona University and the University of Arizona, graduating in 1966.

Michael joined the Navy in 1966 and was commissioned as an ensign and trained as a naval aviator during the war in Vietnam. He served one year at Barber's Point in Hawaii.

The G.I. Bill paid for Mike's subsequent schooling at Stetson Law School and the

University of Baltimore. He received his law degree, passed the bar, and started his own law office at Bel Air, Maryland in 1975.

Michael danced contras and reels to old-time country music at Lovely Lane Methodist Church. It was there that he met his bride Nancy Joanne Travers, whom he married on June 15th, 1983 in Baltimore, Maryland.

Nancy Joanne Travers Priser was born on August 21st, 1945 at Women's Hospital in Baltimore, Maryland.

MICHAEL JOHN PRISER

459

Nancy lived with her mother, Irma Rohe, grandma, Edith Laird, and grandfather, Irving Laird. Nancy loved the piano, accordion-playing, dancing, and acting. She attended Eastern High School and graduated in 1963. She then attended college at Toneson University where she graduated in 1967 with a double major in Acting and History. Nancy worked from 1961 until 1966 at Lakin's Jewelry. She was in many productions in college and a member of Alpha Psi Omega, an honor fraternity.

Nancy worked for Liberty Mutual as a claims representative, the Medical Commission on Human Relations, and Maryland CEA as a Union representative, in addition to performing at the Rock Theater of the Peabody Conservatory and the Free Theater of Chicago, which led to her performances at the Institute of Contemporary Arts. Nancy also danced with the Cub Hill Cloggers in the late 1970s to early 1980s and performed up and down the east coast; her dance team was even selected to perform at the White House for President Jimmy Carter.

Nancy worked for the American Friends Service Committee to protest the Vietnam War.

Nancy enjoys playing piano and mandolin and knitting. She now works at Michael's Arts and Crafts as an events coordinator and teaches knitting and crafts for children and adults of all ages. She is also an avid bead collector.

LEFT TO RIGHT: JACQUI PRISER, NANCY JOANNE TRAVERS,
MIKE PRISER AND JOHN PRISER
WEDDING DAY – JUNE 15, 1983

Michael and Nancy have three children: Sean Michael Priser, born July 17, 1986 in Havre de Grace, Maryland, Naomi Alison Priser, born November 22, 1988 in Havre de Grace, Maryland, and Sara Elizabeth Priser, born September 27, 1990 in Baltimore, Maryland.

Sean and Naomi were both adopted when they were only a few days old.

SEAN, NAOMI & SARA PRISER

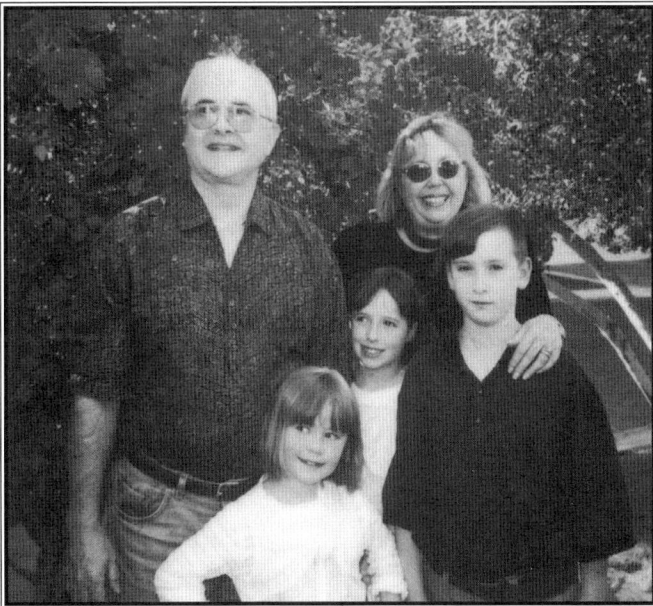

LEFT TO RIGHT: MICHAEL, SARA, NAOMI, NANCY & SEAN PRISER

PRISER FAMILY – 2005
LEFT TO RIGHT: NANCY, SARA, SEAN, NAOMI & MIKE

Michael continues to practice law and loves to cook and barbecue on the deck.

SIXTH GENERATION

Sean Michael Priser, Naomi Alison Priser, Sara Elizabeth Priser

Sean Michael Priser – Sixth Generation

Sean Michael Priser, adopted son of Michael John Priser and Nancy Joanne Travers, was born on July 17th, 1986 in Harford Memorial Hospital, Havre de Grace, Maryland and adopted a day later.

Growing up, Sean loved Christmas lights and car washes. He played baseball, soccer, and basketball.

Sean graduated from C. Milton Wright High School in June of 2004. He enjoys computer games and playing both acoustic and electric guitars. He is very interested in Japanese drift racing and hanging out with his friends.

Naomi Alison Priser – Sixth Generation

Naomi Alison Priser, adopted daughter of Michael John Priser and Nancy Joanne Travers, was born and adopted on November 22nd, 1988 at Harford Memorial Hospital, Havre de Grace, Maryland.

Naomi played t-ball, basketball, karate, and soccer. At twelve, she was determined to learn all of her father Mike's swimming strokes and is an avid swimmer who loves the beach. She is also interested in horror movies, using her computer, and spending time with her friends.

Sara Elizabeth Priser – Sixth Generation

Sara Elizabeth Priser, third child of Michael John Priser and Nancy Joanne Travers, was born on September 27th, 1990 at Franklin in Baltimore, Maryland.

Sara loves art of all kinds and admires the bead work of her Aunt Patty Hoisch. She is a fantastic artist, painter, and photographer. She has a wide circle of friends and loves to listen to all kinds of music.

Susan Jean Priser – Fifth Generation

Susan Jean Priser, second child of Jacqueline Joan McClelland and John Benjamin Priser, was born on July 31st, 1946 in Tucson, Arizona. Susan married Franciscus Xaverius Prins on June 23rd, 1967 in Stellenbosch, Western Province, South Africa. They have three children: Jacqueline Prins, born November 22, 1969 in Cape Town, South Africa, Judith Prins, born July 1, 1971 in Pretoria, South Africa, and Nicola Prins, born October 26, 1973 in Johannesburg, South Africa.

Sue grew up in Arizona, Ohio, and New Mexico, with an additional year in Argentina. She graduated from Flagstaff High School in 1964 and attended Northern Arizona University from 1965 to 1966, changing her major several times. She also spent a semester at the University of Arizona in 1966, where she studied computer science.

Sue met Frans Prins in early September 1966 while she was doing vacation work as a shop assistant at The Wigwam, an Indian art and craft shop in Flagstaff. Frans had just completed a Master's degree at Northwestern University (on a fellowship) and was travelling around the U.S. before heading back to South Africa. In the middle of the desert, his car's engine blew up and his car towed to the nearest town – Flagstaff. While waiting for a new engine, he wandered into The Wigwam and chatted with Sue. He later returned and asked her out to dinner. It took ten days for Frans' car to be repaired, during which time Sue took

Frans home to meet her family and have some of her mom's good cooking. Later that year Frans proposed over the phone, and the following year saw Sue travelling to South Africa to marry Frans.

SUSAN JEAN PRISER AND
FRANCISCUS XAVERIUS PRINS
MARRIAGE CERTIFICATE
JUNE 23, 1967

Franciscus Xaverius is a family name, but most people just call him Frans. Frans was born on August 16th, 1936 in Stellenbosch, South Africa and raised on the wine farm "Prinshof" just outside town. He matriculated at Paul Roos Gymnasium in 1953 and completed a Bsc Eng and Msc Eng from Stellenbosch University in 1958 and 1960 respectively.

After working for the firm Van Niekerk, Kleyn and Edwards for a few years in design, and later as a site engineer in Cape Town and Port Elizabeth, Frans won a fellowship to study at Northwestern University in the U.S.A. He completed his second Master's degree in Transportation Engineering in 1966. Upon his return to South Africa, he again worked for VKE, now as a consulting transportation engineer.

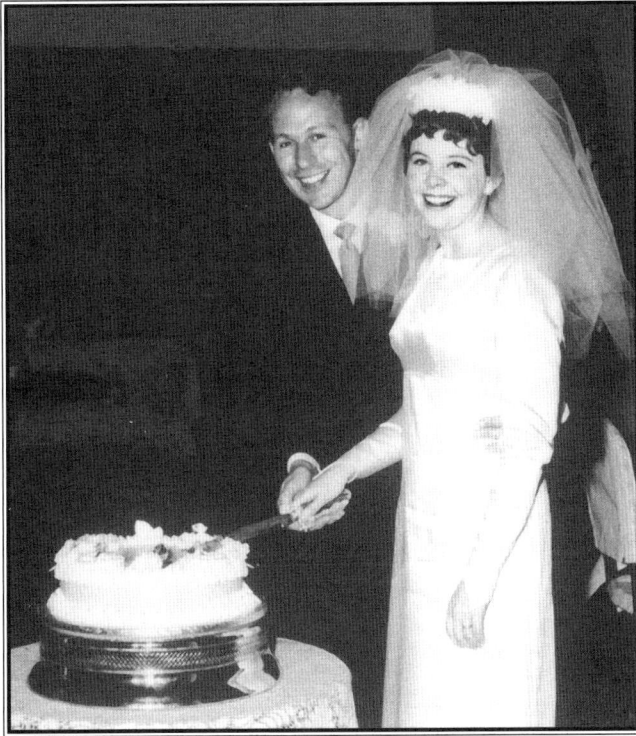

SUSAN AND FRANS PRINS
WEDDING DAY – JUNE 23, 1967

For the two years before Sue and Frans started a family, Sue worked as a computer operator at an engineering firm. When all of the girls were in school, Sue returned to work as a computer programmer for various engineering firms.

In 1970, Frans transferred to VKE'S head office in Pretoria. After two years there, he was approached to start a new engineering firm, founded in 1972. This necessitated a move to Johannesburg, where the family lived for nearly 30 years. Frans was the head of this new firm – Uhlmann, Withaus & Prins (later to be called UWP Consultants) – for 27 years. He retired in 1999.

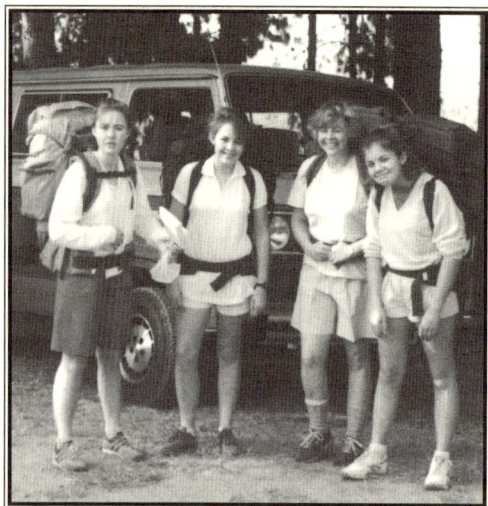

JACQUELINE, JUDY, SUSAN AND NICOLA PRINS
HIKING MAGUBA'S KLOOF, NEAR PILGRIMS' REST,
MPUMALANGA, SOUTH AFRICA

SUE AND FRANS PRINS FLYING MICROLIGHT OVER
VICTORIA FALLS, ZIMBABWE & ZAMBIA – JUNE 1996

FRANS AND SUSAN PRINS – 1998

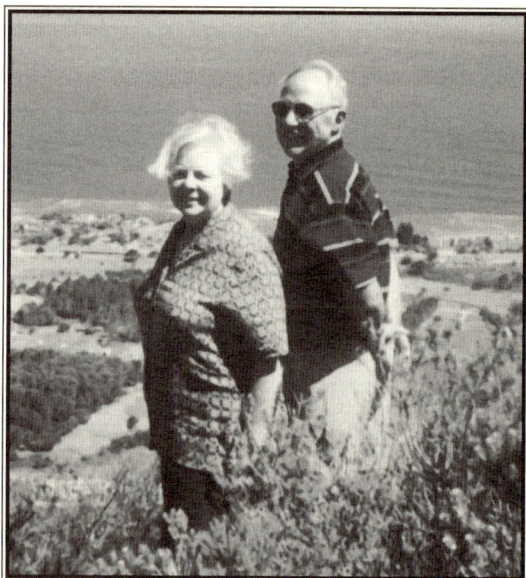

SUE AND FRANS PRINS
HERMANUS, SOUTH AFRICA – JAN. 2001

A year after Frans retired, he and Sue moved to Hermanus, a lovely coastal resort town in the Western Cape, famous for its visiting Southern Right whales and unique Cape Fynbos Floral Kingdom. Frans has had a soft spot for Hermanus from his days as a youngster when the family took an annual fishing vacation after the harvest.

PATTY PRISER, SUE PRINS, JANE PRISER – 1999

Sue continued to program for a few years, then retired to devote more time to her passionate hobby—quilting. Sue now teaches quilting all over South Africa and is a qualified quilt judge. She is also a doting grandmother. When not quilting, Sue enjoys line dancing, reading, painting icons, and hiking.

SUSAN PRINS DOING WHAT SHE LOVES: QUILTING – 1999

Frans likes to garden with indigenous flora, play golf, watch the stock market, and hike. He is a keen camper and a connoisseur of good wine.

Living in a sleepy coastal town has its excitements. At the end of 2001, a raging bush fire came close to the Prins's home. Then, in April 2005, they were inundated by a flood from the mountain behind their home, which caused major damage. Even so, Hermanus remains a wonderful place to live.

Jacqueline Prins – Sixth Generation

Jacqueline "Jacqui" Prins, first child of Susan Jean Priser and Franciscus Xaverius Prins, was born on November 22nd, 1969 in Cape Town, South Africa.

Jacqui married Peter Andrew Conry on August 17th, 1996 in Johannesburg, South Africa. They have two children: Daniel Paul Conry, born May 8, 1997, and Tarryn Conry, born March 3, 2001.

PETER ANDREW CONRY AND JACQUELINE PRINS
WEDDING DAY – AUGUST 17, 1996

Daniel Paul Conry – Seventh Generation

Daniel Paul Conry, first child of Jacqueline Prins and Peter Andrew Conry, was born on May 8th, 1997 in Johannesburg, South Africa.

JACQUI, PETER, DANNY AND TARRYN CONRY
IN TRADITIONAL SAUDI GARMENTS – 2004

Tarryn Conry – Seventh Generation

Tarryn Conry, second child of Jacqueline Prins and Peter Andrew Conry, was born on March 3rd, 2001 in Riyadh, Saudi Arabia.

DANNY AND TARRYN CONRY
MARCH 2005

Judith Prins – Sixth Generation

Judith Prins, second child of Susan Jean Priser and Franciscus Xaverius Prins, was born on July 1st, 1971 in Pretoria, South Africa. She married Bryan McKay on April 22nd, 2001 in Johannesburg, South Africa. They have two children: Megan Adair McKay, born August 21, 2002 in Johannesburg, South Africa, and Amy, born November 2005.

BRYAN McKAY AND JUDY PRINS
WEDDING DAY – APRIL 22, 2001

SEVENTH GENERATION

Megan Adair McKay, Amy McKay

Megan Adair McKay – Seventh Generation

Megan Adair McKay, first child of Judith Prins and Bryan McKay, was born on August 21st, 2002 in Johannesburg, South Africa.

TARRYN CONRY AND MEGAN MCKAY
HIDING IN GRANNY SUE'S PANTRY
MARCH 2005

Amy McKay – Seventh Generation

Amy McKay, second child of Judith Prins and Bryan McKay, was born in November of 2005 in Johannesburg, South Africa.

Nicola Prins – Sixth Generation

Nicola Prins, third child of Susan Jean Priser and Franciscus Xaverius Prins, was born on October 26th, 1973 in Johannesburg, South Africa.

Nicola received a BA in Arts and Honors International Relations from the University of Cape Town. For the past four years, she has been working as an economist in London, presently for the Economist Intelligence Unit.

LEFT TO RIGHT: BRYAN AND JUDY McKAY, SUE PRINS, NICKY PRINS AND MARK KIRKNESS, FRANS PRINS
NICKY AND MARK'S ENGAGEMENT – MARCH 2005

Nicola is engaged to Mark Kirkness, a civil engineer from Pietermaritzburg, South Africa who currently works in property development in London. Nicola is an enthusiastic cook, avid reader, and keen walker. Mark is a keen hockey player and enjoys golf. They both have a passion for traveling.

Jane Priser – Fifth Generation

Jane Priser, third child of Jacqueline Joan McClelland and John Benjamin Priser, was born in 1952 in Dayton, Ohio. Jane married Robert Gonzales and had one son, Adrian Gonzales, born February 13, 1974 in Flagstaff, Arizona.

Jane divorced Robert Gonzales.

JANE AND PATTY PRISER WITH DON ALVINO NEAR BUENOS AIRES, SOUTH AMERICA – 1958

JANE AND PATTY PRISER – 1999

Jane has always shown an extraordinary artistic talent and shares her father's insatiable curiosity about the natural world. Over the years, Jane has used various media in her paintings, drawings, sculpture, and pottery. She studied at the Medocino Art Center for eight years during the 1980s.

Jane currently lives in Fort Bragg, Colorado with Rich Clayton. Jane and Rich enjoy gardening and looking after their pet dogs, cats, and birds. They also have a pottery studio.

JANE PRISER AND RICHARD CLAYTON

Adrian Gonzales – Sixth Generation

Adrian Gonzales, only child of Jane Priser and Robert Gonzales, was born on February 13th, 1974 in Flagstaff, Arizona.

ADRIAN GONZALES AND ARTHUR KEYS

Adrian is an accomplished musician and composer. He currently lives in Fort Bragg, California.

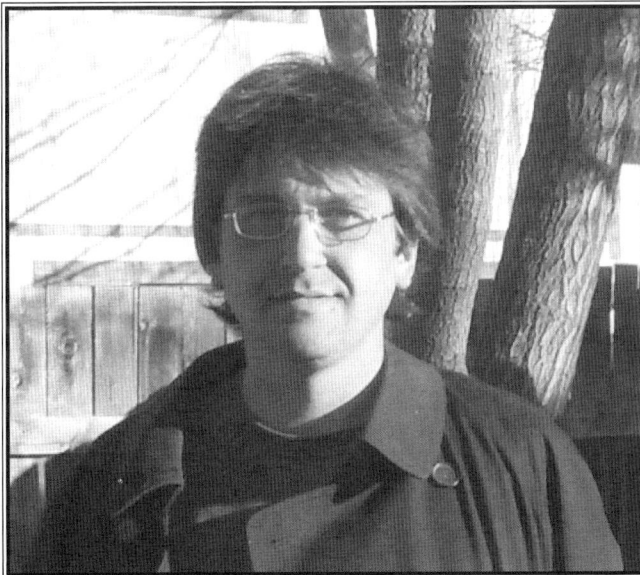

ADRIAN GONZALES

Jane Priser married Charles Keys and had one son, Arthur Keys.

Arthur Keys – Sixth Generation

Arthur Keys, only child of Jane Priser and Charles Keys, was born on December 13th, 1978 in Phoenix, Arizona. Arthur was an intelligence agent in the Air Force. When he left the service, he worked as a systems administrator in Seattle with the computer skills that he had acquired both on his own and in the military.

Arthur married Marisa in 2003. They have two daughters: Rebecca Lynn, born October 20, 2003, and Elizabeth, born July 20, 2005.

Arthur is currently attending the University of Oregon in Corvallis, Oregon.

SEVENTH GENERATION

Rebecca Lynn Keys, Elizabeth Keys

Rebecca Lynn Keys – Seventh Generation

Rebecca Lynn Keys, daughter of Arthur Keys and Marisa, was born on October 20th, 2003.

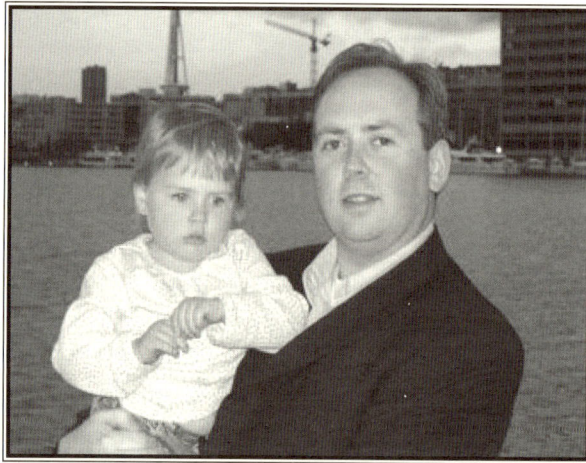

REBECCA LYNN AND ARTHUR KEYS

Elizabeth Keys – Seventh Generation

Elizabeth Keys, daughter of Arthur Keys and Marisa, was born on July 20th, 2005.

Patricia Jo Priser – Fifth Generation

Patricia Jo Priser, fourth child of Jacqueline Joan McClelland and John Benjamin Priser, was born on April 18th, 1955 in Flagstaff, Arizona.

The family moved out West to live in New Mexico. John Priser, Patty's father, took a job tracking satellites in Argentina in about 1958, and they lived there for a year. When they returned to the States in 1959, the family finally settled in Flagstaff.

Patty's first job after graduating from high school was as a lapidarist in Flagstaff. She moved between the Verde Valley, Flagstaff, and Prescott working as a lapidarist and doing other odd jobs.

Patty was married in 1980 and moved to Durango, Colorado, where she found work in retail sales and cooking and started a small leather-work business. She divorced in 1972 and moved back to Arizona in 1994. Patty lived with her father until he died in 1997. She was married for a short time to Sean Cooke.

Patty began to work as a jeweler for the Mummy's Bundle in 1997 and now manages the business. She graduated from massage school in 1999 and is still working at both professions.

Patricia Jo married Tom Hoisch on June 25th, 2005.

LEFT TO RIGHT: RITA & ALAN HOISCH (TOM'S PARENTS), PATTY & TOM HOISCH (BRIDE AND GROOM), DEBBIE & JOHN HOISCH (TOM'S SISTER-IN-LAW AND BROTHER) & THEIR SON MATTHEW HOISCH (IN FRONT)
WEDDING DAY – JUNE 25, 2005

BACK ROW, LEFT TO RIGHT: JACOB LONGWELL, NAOMI PRISER, VALERIE PRISER, TOM & PATTY HOISCH, NANCY PRISER, JANE PRISER, MIKE PRISER, DAVID PRISER; MIDDLE ROW, LEFT TO RIGHT: SARA PRISER, BRADLEY PRISER; FRONT ROW, LEFT TO RIGHT: JASON PRISER, MATTY, THE DOG.

THOMAS DAVID HOISCH & PATRICIA JO PRISER
MARRIAGE CERTIFICATE

Tom was born on February 23rd, 1957 in Los Angeles, California to Alan and Rita Hoisch, who live in Los Angeles, California, where Tom grew up. Tom is a Geology professor at N.A.U and a cellist with the Arizona Opera.

Patty has always enjoyed playing music, hiking, reading, practicing Tai Chi, and beading.

Some of Patty's comments regarding her life:

"I used to take for granted that our parents supported us in our pursuit of the arts. While our parents didn't have a lot of money, they always gave us every opportunity to explore our interests. Mom was very busy driving us to various music lessons and activities. I remember how Dad used to spend long weekend days painting at the kitchen table while listening to classical music. If we started to interrupt, he would give us paper and paints. He would critique our masterpieces, trying to explain that no one can judge another's art. Mom was an avid reader and active in the community. They both encouraged us to think for ourselves about politics and religion. I didn't appreciate how much they had educated themselves by reading and studying on their own until recently.

"My parents supplied me with many musical instruments starting with a banjo when I was seven. They upgraded my cello while I was in high school and I am ever grateful that they also stored it in Mom's clothes closet for many years until I took it up again in 1990. That's around seventeen years of having a cello in one's closet. Now that's love.

"Now that our parents are both gone, it's a comfort to see how we siblings and offspring still get together and keep in touch. It seems we get closer to each other as the years go by. We appreciate and are enriched by our differences."

David Priser – Fifth Generation

David Priser, fifth child of Jacqueline Joan McClelland and John Benjamin Priser, was born on September 17th, 1963 in Flagstaff, Arizona.

David graduated with honors from Coconino High School in Flagstaff, Arizona and attended Northern Arizona University for two years. He met Michelle O'Brian and had one son, Jacob Michael O'Brian, born June 26th, 1990. Jacob was later legally adopted by Bruce Longwell, whom Michelle eventually married. David was invited to remain in Jacob's life, and they have a great relationship.

David moved to Durango, Colorado at age 25 and began working in the building trades. He married Valerie Jean Sterling Tataronis on August 25th, 1996 in Bullhead City, Arizona. They have two boys: Bradley John, born April 19, 1997, and Jason Edward, born March 17, 1999.

DAVID JAMES PRISER AND VALERIE JEAN STERLING
MARRIAGE CERTIFICATE

Valerie Jean Sterling Tataronis was born on June 19th, 1962 in San Diego, California to Richard and Judy Tataronis. Valerie lived near the beach, and her passion for swimming began when she was young. She also enjoyed gymnastics, softball, hiking, and racquetball, and at the age of 18 was a forest fighter. She has worked as a medical transcriptionist for approximately twenty years.

Valerie was married in the 1980s to Terry Sterling and, though she never had children with him, remains in touch with his kids to this day.

She moved to Durango and took a job at the local hospital as the transcription supervisor. This was where she met David.

David and Valerie bought a home on the Blanco River in Pagosa Springs, Colorado in 1998. Dave began his cabinet business.

David and Valerie were divorced in 2000, at which time Valerie, Bradley, and Jason moved to California, where her dad still lived. Dave moved to Camp Verde, Arizona, where his sister Patty lived.

David continues to work as a carpenter in Sedona, Arizona. In 2003, he and Valerie reconciled and the family resides in Camp Verde, Arizona with three dogs—Rocky, Shadow, and Max—and a cat named Sammy.

VALERIE & DAVID PRISER – 1999

DAVID PRISER FAMILY – 2006
LEFT TO RIGHT: JASON, JACOB, DAVID, VALERIE AND BRADLEY

SIXTH GENERATION

Jake Michael Longwell, Bradley John Priser, Jason Edward Priser

Jake Michael Longwell – Sixth Generation

Jake Michael Longwell, son of David Priser and Michelle O'Brian, was born on June 26th, 1990 in Flagstaff, Arizona. He is now 16 and in the 11th grade. He enjoys riding bikes, reading, eating, and sleeping (typical teenager)! His favorite subjects in school are French (which he speaks fluently) and computer classes. He is very generous with his time, whether volunteering for soup kitchens, helping around his church, or working in his church thrift store.

JACOB LONGWELL – 2006

Bradley John Priser – Sixth Generation

Bradley John Priser, first son of David Priser and Valerie Sterling Tataronis, was born on April 19th, 1997 in Durango, Colorado. He is currently in the fourth grade. Bradley enjoys the outdoors—running, biking, and swimming. He also enjoys collecting bugs and lizards and recently caught a snake. He likes playing video games and watching TV, going on the computer, searching the internet, and bidding on eBay. His favorite subjects in school are math, science, and, of course, recess!

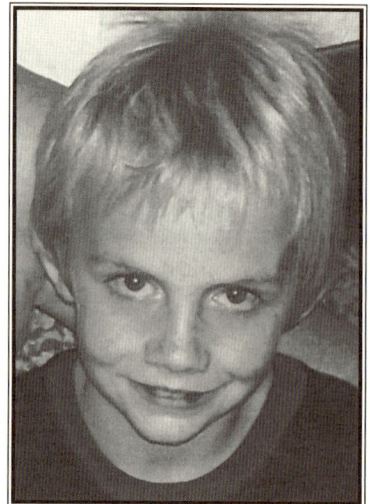

BRADLEY PRISER – 2006

Jason Edward Priser – Sixth Generation

Jason Edward Priser, second son of David Priser and Valerie Tataronis, was born on March 17th, 1999 in Durango, Colorado – St. Partick's Day! He is currently in the second grade. He enjoys playing video games, watching TV, and swimming. He loves to go on the computer, search the internet, and draw. His favorite subjects in school are art, writing, spelling, and math.

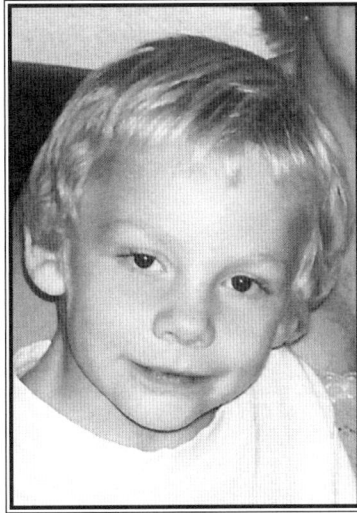

JASON PRISER – 2006

CHAPTER IV
Susan McClelland

SECOND GENERATION

Susan McClelland – Second Generation

Susan McClelland was the fourth child of Thomas McClelland and Susan Henning, born on August 4th, 1841 and baptized August 11th, 1841 at the McClelland family home in the townland of Cloughenramer, close to Newry, County Down, Ireland. Susan was the second daughter in a family of five boys and five girls. The family lived on a farm where, in keeping with the times, a wide range of produce was grown. Some of the produce fed the family, while the rest was transported to the agricultural market in Newry town.

Susan, like her brothers and sisters, grew up with the demands of farming life, and helped as each season brought a different range of tasks.

The family was Presbyterian and members of the 1st Newry Presbyterian Church in Newry.

Susan was in her early twenties in 1864 when her mother died—a major blow to the family, one that they were still coming to terms with in June 1866 when Thomas passed away. Her sister Margaret married in September of the same year, leaving Susan, the eldest girl still at home, with much of the responsibility for the younger members of the family and the running of the household. We can only speculate, but it is possible that this responsibility was the reason Susan did not marry until she was 42.

Susan married James Bradford on September 26th, 1883 in Warrenpoint Presbyterian Church, County Down. Susan's brother David McClelland was a witness at the marriage ceremony.

SUSAN McCLELLAND AND JAMES BRADFORD
MARRIAGE CERTIFICATE

James and Susan set up house on a small holding of eight acres in the townland of Crowreagh, a short distance from Cloughenramer.

SUSAN AND JAMES BRADFORD
RESIDING IN COUNTY DOWN, IRELAND

Below is the cottage (now renovated) in the Townland of Crowreagh, County Down, where Susan McClelland and James Bradford spent the 36 years of their married life. Set amongst the rolling Drumlins of County Down, the cottage and field in this photograph were part of the 8 acres and 35 perches which made up the small holding.

Susan and James Bradford's Cottage
Townland of Crowreagh, County Down

The couple had no children and lived in Crowreagh until Susan's death on April 14th, 1919. James was at her side, and her death certificate records the cause of death as "probably old age."

We know that James, now 71, remarried on March 16th, 1920 in Downshire Road Presbyterian Church. His bride was Jennie Halliday (nee Burns), a widow from the townland of Upper Domolly, close to Newry. This proved to be a short union, as James died on July 11th of the same year.

CHAPTER V
George McClelland

SECOND GENERATION

George McClelland – Second Generation

George McClelland, fifth child of Thomas McClelland and Susan Henning, was born on July 28th, 1846 and baptized December 13th, 1846 in Newry, Ireland.

In his naturalization records, George declared his intention to become a citizen on July 17th, 1876 in New Castle, Pennsylvania.

He married Adeline L. Johnson c1881. Adeline was born on April 19th, 1856 in Johnson, Ohio. They had one child, Alice.

1920 CENSUS, LAWRENCE COUNTY, PENNSYLVANIA
GEORGE, ADELINE, DAUGHTER ALICE AND SON-IN-LAW EUGENE JOHNSON
RESIDING AT 115 EAST FALLS ROAD

George died July 27th, 1927 in New Castle, Pennsylvania.

Obituary – George McClelland

"George McClelland

George McClelland, aged 81 years, one of the best known and highly esteemed men of this city, passed away Wednesday, July 27 at 6:15 p.m. at the family residence, 1417 East Washington Street.

Mr. McClelland's death was due to complications followed by pneumonia which he developed a short time ago.

He was born in Newry, Ireland, July 26, 1846, a son of Thomas and Margaret McClelland. He had been a resident of New Castle for 62 years and had conducted a saddle and harness business on Jefferson Street for 47 years.

Mr. McClelland was a member of the First Presbyterian Church of this city.

Forty-six years ago he was united in married to Adeline L. Johnson, who survives him with one daughter, Mrs. Eugene J. Johnson of this city. He also leaves one sister in Ireland and a niece.

Funeral services will be conducted Saturday, July 30th, at 2 p.m. from his late home with Rev. W.E. McClure of the First Presbyterian Church officiating."

Adeline died July 23rd, 1931 in New Castle, Pennsylvania.

Obituary – Mrs. Adeline L. McClelland

"Mrs. Adeline L. McClelland

Mrs. Adeline Louise McClelland, aged 75, widow of George McClelland, died Thursday at 8 p.m. at the family residence, 1417 East Washington Street, following an illness of five months.

Mrs. McClelland was born in Johnson, Ohio, April 19, 1856, the daughter of William and Alice Johnson and had spent the past fifty-four years of her life in New Castle. She was a member of the First Presbyterian Church.

She is survived by one daughter, Mrs. Eugene J. Johnson.

Funeral services will be held Saturday at 3:30 p.m. from the residence, 1417 East Washington Street, with Dr. W. E. McClure officiating. Interment will be made in Oak Park cemetery."

THIRD GENERATION

Alice McClelland – Third Generation

ADELINE L. JOHNSON AND EUGENE J. JOHNSON
MARRIAGE CERTIFICATE

Alice McClelland, only child of George McClelland and Adeline L. Johnson, was born on May 18th, 1883 in Cortland, Ohio. She married Eugene J. Johnson on June 30th, 1904 in New Castle, Pennsylvania. Eugene was born on September 23rd, 1881.

Alice died September 8th, 1969 in New Castle, Pennsylvania.

Obituary – Mrs. Eugene Johnson

"Mrs. Eugene Johnson

Mrs. Eugene Johnson, 86, the former Alice McClelland of 1417 East Washington St. died at Jameson Memorial Hospital at 3:50 a.m. today after a short illness.

She was born in Cortland, Ohio, May 18, 1883 to George and Louisa Johnson McClelland. She was married June 5, 1904 to Eugene Johnson, who preceded her in death.

She was a member of the First Christian Church.

Surviving is one cousin, Mrs. Bernice Coursen, of Johnston, Ohio.

Friends may call at the Leyde-Tanner Mortuary, 1102 Highland Ave., Tuesday from 2 to 4 and 7 to 9 p.m.

Services will be from the funeral home Wednesday at 3 p.m. Interment will be in the Oak Park Cemetery with Bruce Cooley pastor of First Christian Church presiding."

CHAPTER VI
Alex McClelland

Alex McClelland – Second Generation

Alex McClelland, sixth child of Thomas McClelland and Susan Henning, was born in June 1848 in County Down, Ireland.

Alex became a naturalized United States citizen in May 1874.

He married Mary Virginia Koplin. Mary Virginia was born on July 20th, 1851 in Pennsylvania. Alex and Mary had three children: Mary Eva, born June 30, 1874, Margaret K., born c1877, and Ellie Grace, born c1879.

Alex died November 25th, 1912 in New Castle, Pennsylvania.

Obituary – Alex McClelland

"Alex McClelland, a well known resident of the Eastside, died at his home at 430 County Line Street, Monday morning, November 25th. He had been ill for some weeks past.

Mr. McClelland was 63 years of age, and was born in County Down, Ireland, but had lived in this city for a long time. He was a tinner by occupation. Surviving him are his wife and two children, Mrs. George Park of Youngstown, and Miss Grace McClelland, at home. He leaves also a brother, George McClelland of this city, and two sisters in Ireland. The deceased was a member of the First Christian Church, and was a man of upright character, held in high regard by all who knew him.

Arrangements for the funeral have not been completed, but will be announced later."

Mary Virginia McClelland died January 4th, 1936 in New Castle, Pennsylvania.

Obituary – Mary Virginia McClelland

"Mrs. Mary Virginia McClelland, aged 85 years, an almost lifelong resident of New Castle, and descendant of a pioneer Pennsylvania family, died this morning at 10:20 o'clock in her home, 430 County Line Street.

Mrs. McClelland's death was due to complications which were the result of a fall three years ago in which she broke her hip. She had been confined to her bed since the accident.

She was born at County Down, Ireland, on July 20, 1851, daughter of William and Matilda Koplin. Her father had been born in Reading, Pa. and her mother in New Castle.

Twenty-four years ago Mrs. McClelland was preceded in death by her husband, Alexander McClelland. She is survived by two daughters, Mrs. George Park of Youngstown, O., and Miss Grace McClelland, at home, and two grandchildren.

She was a member of the First Christian Church.

Funeral services will be conducted at 2 p.m., Monday from the residence and internment will be made in Oak Park Cemetery. (Kindly omit flowers)."

THIRD GENERATION

Mary Eva McClelland, Margaret K. McClelland,
Ellie Grace McClelland

Mary Eva McClelland – Third Generation

Mary Eva McClelland, first child of Alex McClelland and Mary Virginia Koplin, was born on June 30th, 1874 in New Castle, Pennsylvania. She married George H. Park c1895. George was born on February 12th, 1872 in Youngstown, Ohio. He worked for B. Brown & Co., and the family lived at 37 Garfield, Youngstown, Ohio.

Mary Eva and George had three children: Paul, born September 19, 1896, Margaret, born December 13, 1898, and Virginia, born August 23, 1906.

Mary Eva McClelland died September 8th, 1946.

Obituary - Mrs. George H. Park

"Mrs. Eva M. Park, aged 72, of 182 Melrose Avenue, died at 7 a.m. Sunday at her home. She had been ill, following a stroke, 14 months ago.

Mrs. Park was born in New Castle, Pa., January 30, 1874, a daughter of Alexander and Virginia Koplin McClelland. She was a member of the Hillman St. Christian church. She was a past president of the American Legion Auxiliary unit 15, the V.F.W. Auxiliary, and the Gold Star Mothers.

She leaves her husband, George H. Park, whom she married 50 years ago; two daughters, Mrs. Margaret Schultz of Youngstown, and Mrs. Marion Swager of Youngstown; a grandson, and a sister, Miss Grace McClelland of New Castle, Pa.

Funeral services will be held at 1:30 P.M. Wednesday in the Hofmeister Memorial Funeral Home, where friends may call Tuesday evening."

George Park died July 20th, 1947.

Obituary - George H. Park

"George H. Park, aged 75, of 182 Melrose Avenue, died at 11 p.m. Sunday at South Side unit of Youngstown Hospital after an illness of five months.

Mr. Park was born in Youngstown February 12, 1872. He was employed by the Republic Steel Corporation for 55 years, retiring in June 1943. He was a member of the Hillman St. Christian Church. His wife, Mary Eva Park died in September 1946.

He leaves two daughters, Mrs. Margaret Schultz and Mrs. Marion Swager, both of Youngstown; a sister, Miss Carrie Park of Poland, and a grandchild.

Funeral services will be held at 4 p.m. Wednesday at the Hofmeister Memorial Funeral Home, where friends may call this evening and Tuesday evening."

FOURTH GENERATION

Paul McClelland Park, Margaret Park, Virginia Park

Paul McClelland Park – Fourth Generation

Paul McClelland Park, first child of George H. Park and Mary Eva McClelland, was born on September 19th, 1896.

Private Paul McClelland Park, Supply Company 136th Field Artillery, 37th Division, died January 30th, 1919 in Commercy, France.

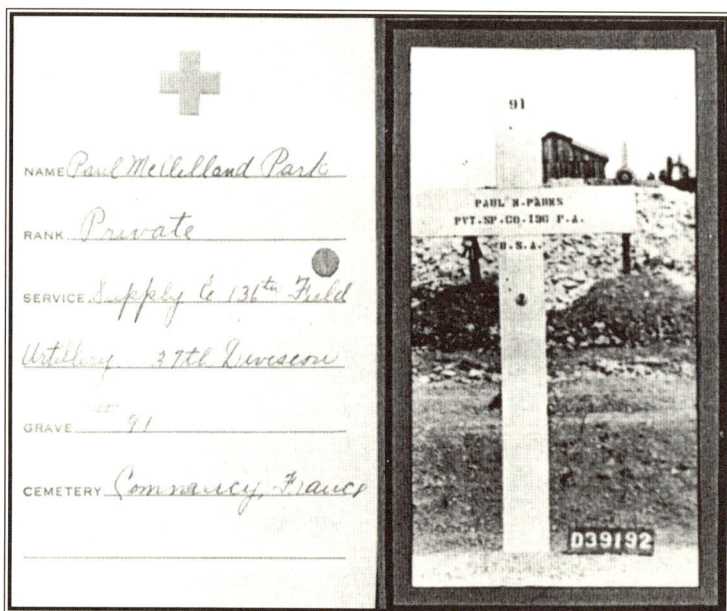

PAUL MCCLELLAND PARK – GRAVESITE,
COMMERCY, FRANCE, JANUARY 30, 1919

PAUL MCCLELLAND PARK

"War Department
The Adjutant General's Office,
Washington

The Enclosed Certificate Is Issued By Direction Of The President, Who Wishes To Express His Deep And Sincere Sympathy."

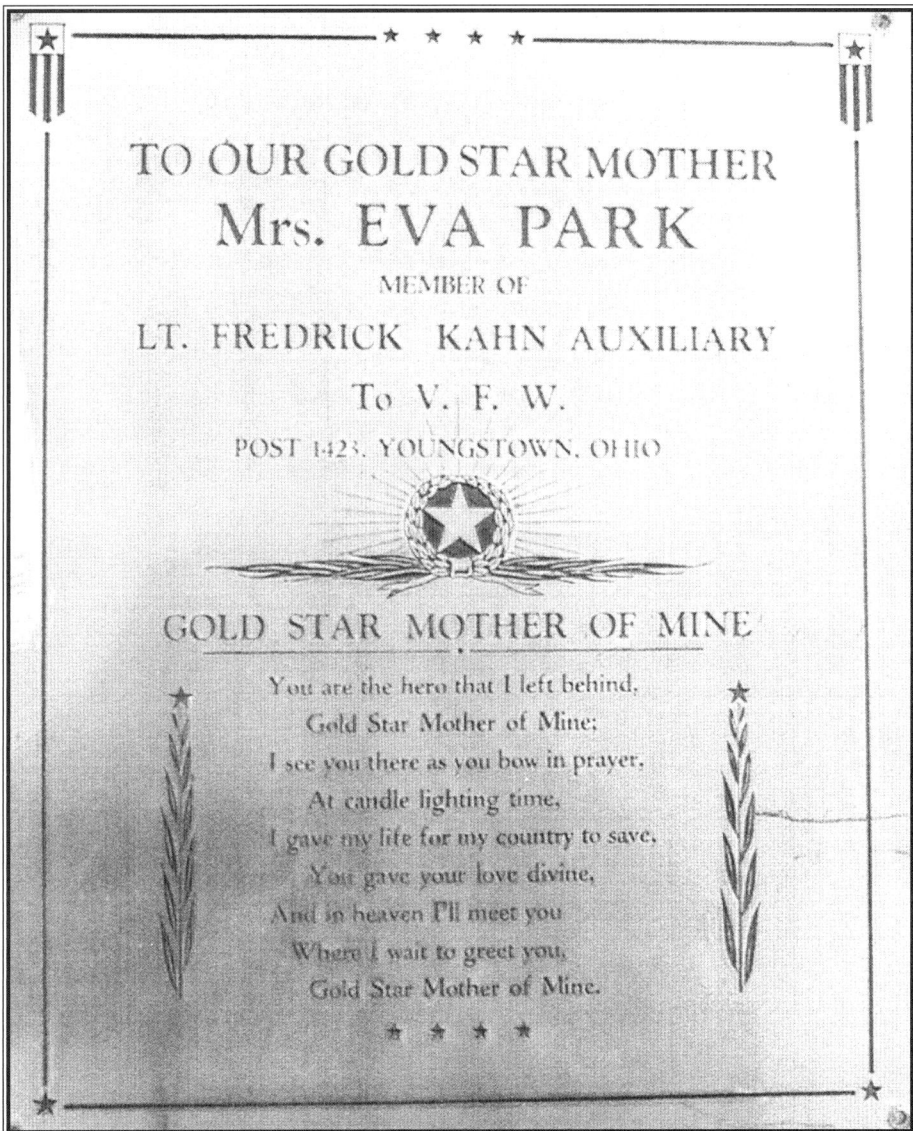

TO OUR GOLD STAR MOTHER
Mrs. EVA PARK
MEMBER OF

LT. FREDRICK KAHN AUXILIARY
To V. F. W.
POST 1423, YOUNGSTOWN, OHIO

GOLD STAR MOTHER OF MINE

You are the hero that I left behind,
Gold Star Mother of Mine;
I see you there as you bow in prayer,
At candle lighting time,
I gave my life for my country to save,
You gave your love divine,
And in heaven I'll meet you
Where I wait to greet you,
Gold Star Mother of Mine.

MRS. EVA PARK – RECOGNITION, "GOLD STAR MOTHER OF MINE"
MEMBER OF LT. FREDERICK KAHN AUXILIARY, V.F.W. POST 1423, YOUNGSTOWN, OHIO

Margaret Park – Fourth Generation

Margaret Park, second child of George H. Park and Mary Eva McClelland, was born on December 13th, 1898.

She married Christian Schultz c1930 in Youngstown, Ohio. Christian was born c1872, in Germany.

MARGARET PARK SCHULTZ

CHRISTIAN AND MARGARET SCHULTZ

They had one son, George Park.

LEFT TO RIGHT: GEORGE, MARGARET, AND
CHRISTIAN

Christian died in 1934.

Margaret died August 2nd, 1959 in Youngstown, Ohio.

Obituary – Margaret Park Schultz

"Mrs. Margaret P. Schultz, 59, of 182 Melrose Avenue died at 4 a.m. in South Side
Hospital. She had been ill several weeks.

Mrs. Schultz was born Dec. 13, 1898, in Youngstown, a daughter of George and Mary E.
McClelland Park. She had lived here all her life. Her husband, Christian, died 25 years ago.

She leaves a son, George, and a sister, Mrs. Marion Swager, of Youngstown.

Private services will be held at 3 p.m. Monday at the Davis Velker Funeral Home, where
friends may call from 2 to 4 and 7 to 9 p.m. Sunday. The family requests that material trib-
utes take the form of contributions to the Arthritis Foundation."

George Park Schultz – Fifth Generation

George Park Schultz, only child of Christian Shultz and Margaret Park, married Althea L. Leonhart, daughter of Mr. and Mrs. W.I. Leonhart, on September 18th, 1954 in the First Presbyterian Church.

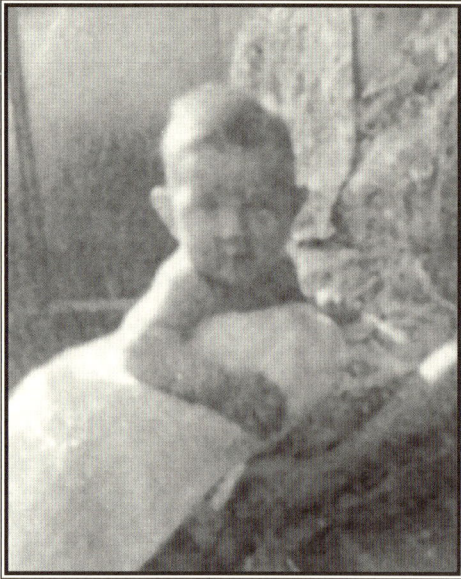

GEORGE PARK SCHULTZ
FOUR MONTHS OLD

GEORGE PARK SCHULTZ
22 YEARS OLD

Leonhart-Schultz Ceremony At First Presbyterian Church

Miss Althea L. Leonhart, daughter of Mr. and Mrs. W. I. Leonhart, 1125 S. Meridian Road, and George P. Schultz, son of Mrs. Margaret Schultz, 182 Melrose Ave. and the late Christian P. Schultz, were united in marriage Saturday afternoon at First Presbyterian Church, with the Rev. W. Frederic Miller performing the double ring ceremony at 1:30 o'clock.

White brocaded taffeta fashioned the ballerina gown worn by the bride, the fitted bodice having a stand-up wing collar and three-quarter length sleeves. Her fingertip veil fell from a little lace cap, and her colonial bouquet of white carnations was centered with a white orchid. She was given in marriage by her father.

Matron of honor for her sister was Mrs. Mason S. Dyer, whose little daughter, Alicia, was flower girl. Their waltz-length frocks were alike, Mrs. Dyer in orchid crystalette and little Miss Dyer in pale gold crystalette. Each carried a colonial bouquet of Talisman roses.

Robert H. Clayton was best man, and Edward Schumm and Mason S. Dyer were the ushers. The reception afterward was held at the bride's home.

When they conclude their wedding trip, Mr. and Mrs. Schultz will reside in Columbus where Mr. Schultz is a senior in the college of architecture at Ohio State University. He also attended Youngstown College. His bride has been secretary to Charles G. Nichols, president and general manager of the G. M. McKelvey Co.

Mrs. George P. Schultz

GEORGE P. SCHULTZ AND ALTHEA L. LEONHART
WEDDING ANNOUNCEMENT – SEPTEMBER 18, 1954

They had one daughter, who died at birth.

Obituary – Infant Schultz

"Funeral services were held this afternoon at the Davis-Velker Funeral Home for the infant daughter of George P. and Althea Leonhart Schultz of 182 Melrose Avenue, who died at birth at 1 a.m. today in North Side Hospital."

Two County Residents Pass State Architect's Examination

2 County Residents Are Among 53 in Ohio to Get Certificates

Two Mahoning County residents are among 53 who passed the recent state examination for certificates of qualification to become architects in Ohio.

They are Mrs. George R. Elwell, 67 W. Dewey Ave., and George P. Schultz, 182 Melrose Ave., Boardman Township.

Mrs. Elwell, the former Mary Lou Fenati, is with the offices of architect P. Arthur D'Orazio here. A native of New Castle, Pa., she is the daughter of Mr. and Mrs. H. M. Fenati of New Castle, where she graduated from high school. She received her bachelor of architecture degree at Carnegie Institute of Technology.

Husband Is Artist

She has lived in Youngstown for a year and a half and is married to George R. Elwell, a local artist.

Schultz is with the offices of architect Donald L. Bostwick in Niles. He is a son of the late Christian Schultz and Mrs. Margaret Schultz. He is a graduate of Boardman High School and received his bachelor of architecture degree last June at Ohio State University.

George Schultz

He is married to the former Althea Leonhart.

Area residents also passing the ba. examinations are Thomas A. Schroth of Niles and George W. Angerson of Ashtabula.

GEORGE SCHULTZ RECEIVES STATE ARCHITECT CERTIFICATE

GEORGE PARK SCHULTZ 1970

Virginia Park – Fourth Generation

Virginia Park, third child of George H. Park and Mary Eva McClelland, was born on August 23rd, 1906 in Youngstown, Ohio.

VIRGINIA PARK

THE VOICE
MID-YEAR SENIORS 1929

VIRGINIA "JINNY" PARK
NATIONAL HONOR SOCIETY
MONITOR 1923 – 1925
"A SILENT WOMAN IS ALWAYS MORE
ADMIRED THAN A NOISY ONE."

Virginia married Marion Herbert Swager on March 16th, 1929 in Youngstown, Ohio. Marion was born on January 21st, 1906 in Trumbull, Ohio.

Virginia was very close to her mother-in-law Julia Manning Swager and enjoyed spending time with her pursuing their mutual interests. Virginia had a passion for weaving and won many medals by her skill.

Virginia and Marion lived on Canfield Road, near Hopkins Road, in Youngstown, Ohio.

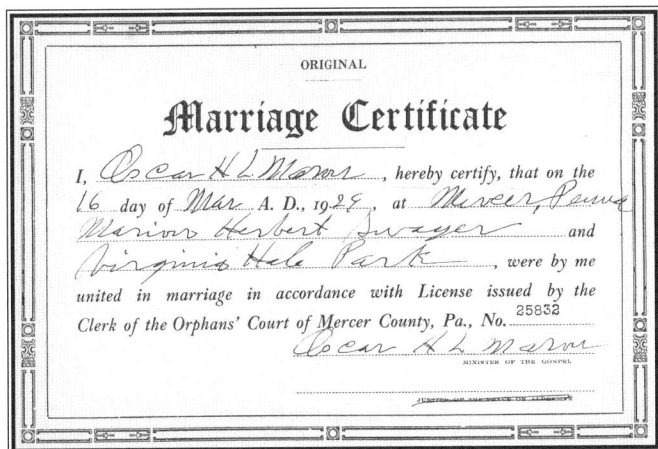

MARION HERBERT SWAGER AND VIRGINIA HALE PARK
MARRIAGE CERTIFICATE – MARCH 16, 1929

MARION HERBERT SWAGER
1935

VIRGINIA & MARION
SWAGER'S HOME
2045 CANFIELD ROAD,
YOUNGSTOWN, OHIO,
1980S

Marion enjoyed writing poetry, and the family has a small book of his poems which they treasure. One of his poems was suggested as the state song, and featured in a composition presented by the First Presbyterian Church choir at the Armistice Day vesper service.

Marion and Virginia had a love for antiques and were the proud owners of The Woodland Antiques, highly respected for both their knowledge and their skill at appraising and estate liquidations.

Virginia died on December 14th, 1997 in Sheridan, Montana. Marion died in 1989.

VIRGINIA & MARION SWAGER
CIRCA 1960

Obituary – Virginia Park Swager

"Virginia Park Swager died Dec. 14 at the Tobacco Root Mountain Care Center in Sheridan, where she had made her home since May. She moved here from her home in Youngstown, Ohio, to be near her niece and nephew, Warren and Carol Lee Swager.

She was born August 23, 1906, at Youngstown, Ohio, the daughter of George and Mary Eva Park. She met Marion Swager at the Dollar Bank where they both worked. They married in March of 1929. She was an accomplished weaver, belonging to the local guild and she won many ribbons at the local fairs. She enjoyed working in the garden, but her love

There will be a gathering of the clan
in honor of the golden wedding anniversaries of
Alice and Warren Swager
and
Virginia and Marion Swager

June 3rd through June 10th, 1979
at the home of Warren M. Swager, Jr.
in Sheridan, Montana

The children of Alice and Warren invite you
to share in the celebration of this special event.

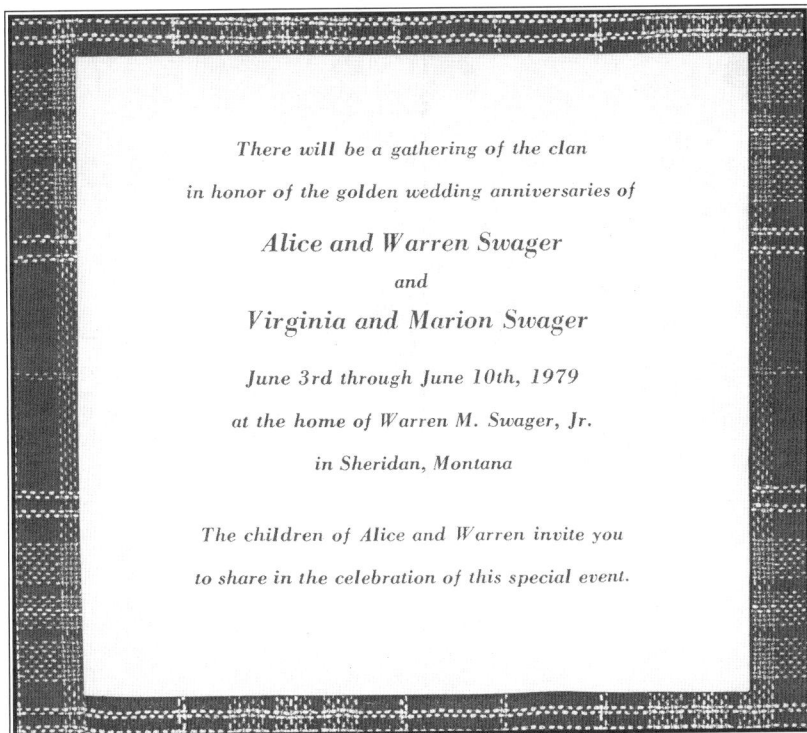

VIRGINIA AND MARION SWAGER/ALICE AND WARREN SWAGER
GOLDEN WEDDING ANNIVERSARIES
JUNE 3 THROUGH JUNE 10, 1979

in later years was antiques. She joined with her husband, Marion, to establish Woodland Antiques, working out of their home on Canfield Road. They were a familiar sight at the local shows around Ohio.

She was preceded in death by her husband, Marion, in 1989, her parents, sister, Margaret Shultz, and brother, Paul Park.

Survivors include nephews, Judson Day, Fred Day, Robert Day, all of Youngstown, Lloyd Day of Lancester, Pennsylvania, Warren Swager of Sheridan, Alan Swager of Jacksonville, Fla., nieces Alison Hopper, Williamsport, Pa., and Julia Swager of Modesto, Ca.

She was a member of the First Presbyterian Church and later of Christ Church Presbyterian on Canfield Road.

At her request, there will be no services.

Memorials may be sent to Christ Church Presbyterian, Youngstown, Tobacco Root Mountain Care Center in Sheridan, or the Rescue Mission Mahoning Valley of Youngstown, Ohio."

Margaret K. McClelland – Third Generation

Margaret McClelland, second child of Alex McClelland and Mary Virginia Koplin, was born c1877, in Pennsylvania.

Margaret died on April 9th, 1902 in New Castle, Pennsylvania.

Obituary – Margaret K. McClelland

"Miss Margaret K. McClelland, daughter of Mr. and Mrs. Alexander McClelland of this city, died at the family home, 14 County Line Street, Wednesday afternoon. The young lady succumbed to typhoid fever with which disease she had been ill less than three weeks.

She was 25 years of age and was born and passed all her life in this city. She was educated in the New Castle public schools and for several years past had been employed in the suit department of Euwers' Store. She was held in high esteem by her employers and was a careful and competent saleswoman. She was courteous and obliging with customers and took great pains to please buyers. Her services were valuable to the firm she worked for and they recognized her ability and the conscientiousness with which she performed her duties.

Miss McClelland was an earnest Christian woman. She united early in life with the Park Christian Church and continued up to her death a prominent worker in its different organizations. She took a special interest in the Christian Endeavor Society and labored assiduously to make the meetings of the organization interesting and helpful.

In her home she was an affectionate and dutiful daughter and there most of all she will be missed though she was a popular young woman and had a large number of acquaintances who will deeply mourn her early death as a personal bereavement.

She was sick about three weeks ago and was very ill from the first. For several days before dissolution, little hope of her recovery was entertained. Her life was such, however, that she was ready for the great change and she passed peacefully into the life beyond.

She leaves her parents and two sisters, Mrs. Eva Park of Youngstown, and Miss Grace, at home.

Funeral Friday afternoon from the family home at 2:30 o'clock. Internment at Oak Park Cemetery at a later hour. Carriages from White's."

Ellie Grace McClelland – Third Generation

Ellie Grace McClelland, third child of Alex McClelland and Mary Virginia Koplin, was born c1879 in Pennsylvania.

Ellie Grace died February 23rd, 1949 in New Castle, Pennsylvania.

Obituary – Grace F. McClelland

"Funeral services for Miss Grace E. McClelland, 430 County Line Street, were conducted Saturday at 2 p.m. from the Cunningham Funeral Home, with Rev. J. Calvin Rose officiating.

Wilfred Diamond, Robert W. Baum, Fred Waldorf, Wilbur Spigler, Phillip and Richard Ferguson served as pallbearers.

Interment took place in Oak Park Cemetery."

CHAPTER VII
Lucy McClelland

Lucy McClelland – Second Generation

Lucy McClelland was the seventh child of Thomas McClelland and Susan Henning. She was born on November 8th, 1850, in Damolly. Her nine brothers and sisters are all recorded as being born in the townland of Cloughenramer.

We know Lucy was a devout girl, as the Communicants Roll in 1st Newry Presbyterian Church shows her a full member of the Church from her early teens. That faith may have been severely tested by the sudden, subsequent deaths of several family members: her mother when Lucy was just twenty years old, her father, two years later, and her eldest sister Margaret, who contracted smallpox during the Ulster outbreak in 1872 and died on April 4th, a day after delivering a stillborn son. Margaret left behind two small children and Lucy, who, as recorded in a memoir written by Minnie McClelland Wright shortly before her death in 1960, "contracted small-pox while nursing her sister, [and] died within a fortnight of her sister's passing." This is borne out by Lucy's death certificate, which records that she died at her home in Cloughenramer on April 22nd, 1872 with her brother-in-law Thomas Tweedie present—a rather significant attendance, as it is unlikely that Thomas Tweedie would have risked leaving his children orphaned had not Lucy selflessly exposed herself to this fatal disease in order to help his wife and children.

The depth of feeling at Lucy's loss and the esteem in which she was held are both suggested by a death notice placed in the *Newry Reporter* on April 23rd, 1872. In the 1870s, this newspaper was given over to more national and international affairs and their local impact. The rise of the "common man" had not yet begun, and as such it was unusual to find death notices for anyone not deemed socially prominent. But Lucy's death was a selfless act to help others and thus considered worthy of a notice – certainly no other family member was accorded this distinction at the time. It was only at the beginning of the 20th century that local newspapers became much more egalitarian and began printing death notices and obituaries for all members of society.

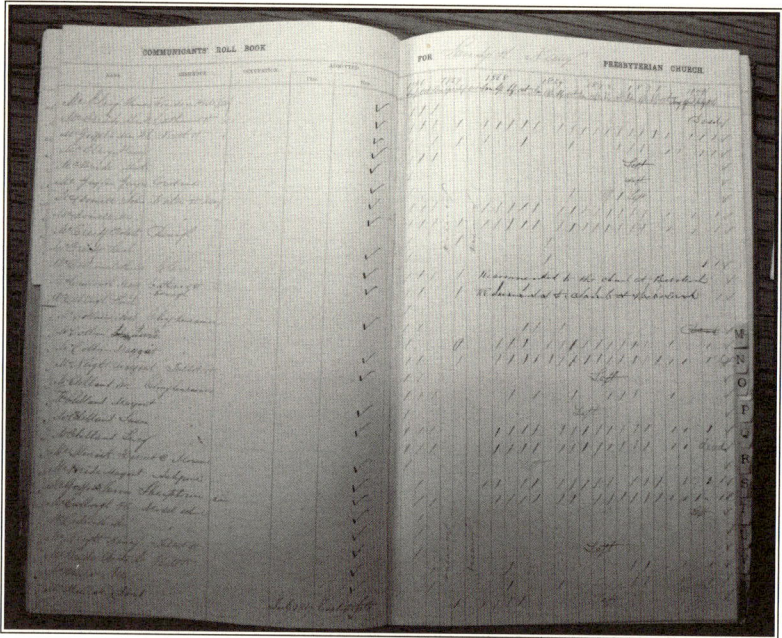

THE COMMUNICANTS ROLL BOOK OF 1ST NEWRY PRESBYTERIAN CHURCH
SHOWING THE NAMES OF WILLIAM, MARGARET, SUSAN, AND LUCY
McCLELLAND (18-21 FROM TOP OF PAGE)

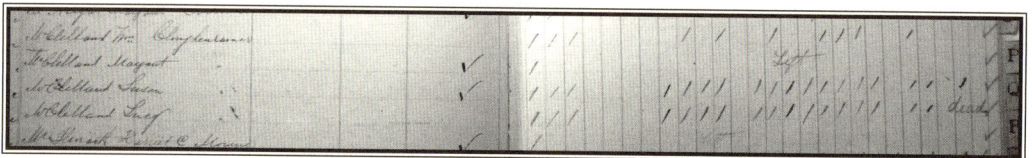

A CLOSE-UP OF THE ABOVE ROLL

Above, Margaret is shown as having left at the time of her marriage in 1866, and the single word "dead" records the untimely passing of Lucy in 1872.

Obituary – Lucy McClelland

"McClelland – April 21, at the residence of her brother, Damolly, Miss McClelland."

CHAPTER VIII
Matilda McClelland

SECOND GENERATION

Matilda McClelland – Second Generation

Matilda McClelland was the eighth child of Thomas McClelland and Susan Henning, born on October 4th, 1852 and baptized on February 20th, 1853. She was brought up in the family home at Cloughenramer outside Newry, County Down.

The family were members of 1st Newry Presbyterian Church, and the young Matilda would have made the two-mile journey from the family home with brothers, sisters, and no doubt neighbors each Sunday to attend both Sunday School and church. Details of Matilda's early life are now lost in the mists of time, but we know that life on small, family-run farms in late 19th-century Ireland was such that all members of the family were required to help out during the busy times of the year such as spring and harvest. Matilda's experience would have been very little different, and the strong bond of family cooperation forged by these early experiences remained with her to the end of her life.

Following the death of her brother William in 1909 and the sale of the family farm, Matilda moved to a small cottage close to her niece Minnie in the townland of Finnard, County Down—a happy move for Matilda, because once again she was close to a working farm and a large family. Minnie married Sam Wright and lived less than one hundred yards away.

Maudie Vallance (nee Hawthorn) remembers coming to Finnard as a small child to spend a ten-week holiday with her Aunt Minnie and seven cousins. The Wright household was a busy place, and the young Maudie and her cousins were always glad to slip away when their prescribed daily chores were completed. Maudie recalls how she and Sam Wright junior loved to visit Matilda, or "Tilly," as she was affectionately known, in her little cottage. An added attraction, Maudie recalls, was, of course, that Matilda always had a penny for her and young Sam, which they would immediately take to a small sweet shop on the nearby Cullion Road.

Tilly's cottage was just a single room, with a small area curtained off in one corner for a bed. It had no running water and no heating other than the open fire.

NORMAN AND BARBARA McCLELLAND
TILLY'S COTTAGE
JUNE 1999

With Minnie close by, Tilly no doubt helped her busy niece with the children, and the bonds of family kinship, particularly strong in those days of nearness and work, were to see Tilly well-companioned as she advanced in years. Indeed, her death certificate records that Sam Wright Sr. was with her when she departed this life on November 3rd, 1929 at 77 years of age. She was buried on Tuesday November 5th in the McClelland family plot at St. Patrick's Parish Church, Newry, County Down.

Obituary – Miss Matilda McClelland
Finnard, Ardarragh

"Miss Matilda McClelland passed away on Sunday, 3rd November, at her residence, Finnard, Ardarragh, at the advanced age of 77 years. She was the only surviving member of a large family of 5 sons and 5 daughters, one of her brothers being the late Wm. McClelland, of Cloughenramer, Newry.

The funeral took place on Tuesday, 5th Inst., to the family burying ground attached to St. Patrick's church.

The chief mourners were Messrs. W. J. Tweedie (nephew), Abel Henning, Jas. Donnell, George Copeland, David Agnew H. Parker, George McCormick, Tom McCormick, R. S. Wright, R. J. Irwin, Masters Bobbie Irwin, Bobbie Wright, and Samuel J. Wright (relatives).

Miss McClelland was of a kindly and cheerful disposition, and was much esteemed by those who had the pleasure of her acquaintance. In religion she was connected with the Brethren, and the services in the house and at the graveside were conducted by Mr. Coolie, Belfast.

The funeral arrangements were carried out in the usual satisfactory manner by Messrs. Gordon & Co., Sugar Island, Newry."

CHAPTER IX
Esther McClelland

SECOND GENERATION

○———————○

Esther McClelland – Second Generation

Esther McClelland was the ninth child of Thomas McClelland and Susan Henning. She is recorded in the Baptismal Book of 1st Newry Presbyterian Church as being born on January 8th, 1855 and baptized on February 10th the following year. This delay in baptism is perhaps an indication that she was a sickly child from birth.

"Espie," as she was affectionately known, was only nine years old when her mother died. Little else is now known of her short life than that the cause of death recorded on her Death Certificate is "Disease of the Heart 3 days certified."

Her father died five months after the passing of this, his youngest daughter.

Esther died on January 20th, 1866, aged 11 years.

CHAPTER X
David McClelland

David McClelland – Second Generation

David McClelland was the tenth child of Thomas McClelland and Susan Henning, born on April 29th, 1858 according to the Baptismal Book of 1st Newry Presbyterian Church, and baptized on October 24th of the same year.

David's mother died when he was six years old, his father less than two years later. David remained unmarried and farmed at Cloughenramer with his brother William until he developed tuberculosis in his late twenties. He died on June 4th, 1887 with his brother William at his side. The cause of death is recorded as "Probably Phthisis" (a 19th-century medical term for tuberculosis no longer in use). David is buried in the McClelland family plot at St. Patrick's Church of Ireland, Newry, County Down.

ACKNOWLEDGEMENTS

The McClelland family genealogy book has been prepared with information from many sources. Uel Wright received and compiled the information for members in Ireland and the U.K., and has carefully produced the story of each family.

McClelland family members in the United States, Australia, and South Africa furnished information to tell their story, which was produced and edited by Norman McClelland and the late Frances McClelland.

Peggy Magee, a genealogist who lives in Prescott, Arizona, researched information about McClelland family members and was particularly helpful with three brothers—John, George, and Alexander McClelland—who came to America in the middle of the nineteenth century.

Many thanks to Uel Wright and my late sister, Frances McClelland, for producing this book. A special thanks to my assistant at Shamrock Foods, Carolyn Lagrand, for her untiring work and help in indexing, filing and inputting all the data into the computer for publishing, and for her careful attention to detail in compiling and reviewing the history data. Thanks also to my granddaughter, Chandra McClelland, for her assistance in the final editing of this volume.

To each McClelland member who contributed his or her family story, pictures, poems, and information on other family members, many, many thanks. It is for each of you, as part of the greater McClelland family, that this book has been written.

APPENDIX
TABLE OF CONTENTS

THE ANCESTORS OF JOHN McCLELLAND OF CLOUGHENRAMER

CHAPTER I

Anna Lucinda Tweedie	Birth Certificate
Anna L. Tweedie & John A. McCormick	Marriage Register
Anna Lucinda Tweedie McCormick	Death Certificate
Anna Lucinda McCormick	Obituary
Anna Lucinda McCormick	Pulpit Reference
Mrs. John McCormack	Memorial Poem by T. McCalden
George McCormick	Birth Certificate
George McCormick & Mary Cartmill	Marriage Certificate
George McCormick	Death Reference
Mary (Minnie) McCormick	Death Reference
Thomas Tweedie McCormick	Birth Certificate
Thomas McCormick & Mary Cartmill	Marriage Reference
Mary Agnes Eileen McCormick	Death Reference
Thomas Tweedie McCormick	Death Reference
John Samuel Wesley McCormick	Birth Certificate
John Samuel Wesley McCormick	Registration of Baptismal Name
John McCormick & Nora Acheson	Marriage Reference
Nora Olivia Acheson	Birth Reference
Eileen Olivia McCormick	Birth Reference
Eileen McCormick & Stephen Wylie	Marriage Reference
Emily Claire Wylie	Birth Reference
Anna Louise Wylie	Birth Reference
Anna Isobel McCormick	Birth Reference
Thomas Winston McCormick	Birth Certificate
Thomas Winston McCormick & Sandra Barron	Marriage Reference
Sandra Barron	Birth Reference
Mary Eileen Allison McCormick	Birth Reference
Geoffrey Thomas Andrew McCormick	Birth Reference
Geoffrey McCormick & Katrina McNaugher	Marriage Reference
James Raymond McCormick	Birth Certificate
James McCormick & Mary Cartmill	Marriage Reference
James Robert Darren McCormick	Birth Reference
James McCormick & Nicola Patterson	Marriage Reference
Thomas Herbert Colin McCormick	Birth Reference
Thomas McCormick & Nicola Richmond	Marriage Reference
Gareth Raymond Edwin McCormick	Birth Reference
John McCormick & Mary (Minnie) Robb	Marriage Reference
John (Jack) McCormick	Birth Reference
Edmond McCormick	Birth Reference
David McCormick	Birth Reference
Robert McCormick	Birth Reference
Robert McCormick & Sarah Barron	Marriage Reference
Sarah (Sadie) Barron	Birth Reference
Robert McCormick	Death Reference

Appendix

Ann (Anna) Barron	Birth Reference
Ann Cartmill (nee Barron) & John McCormick	Marriage Reference
Anna (Annie) McCormick	Death Reference
Sarah Isobel McCormick	Birth Reference
Sally Isobel McCormick & James Freeburn	Marriage Certificate
James Wesley Freeburn	Birth Reference
James Wesley Freeburn & Ruth Louise Lawson	Marriage Certificate
Ruth Louise Lawson	Birth Ref. Not Available
Sarah Louise Freeburn	Birth Reference
Rebecca Freeburn	Birth Reference
Thomas James Freeburn	Birth Reference
Anna Olivia Freeburn	Birth Reference
William George Alan Chambers	Birth Reference
Christopher Alan Chambers	Birth Reference
Sarah Aimee Chambers	Birth Reference
Edith Joan Freeburn	Birth Reference
Robert James Irvine	Birth Reference
James Robert Irvine	Birth Reference
Andrew Thomas Irvine	Birth Reference

CHAPTER II

John McClelland	Ship Manifest, 1859
John McClelland	Census of Pittsburgh, Pennsylvania, 1860
John McClelland to William McClelland	Memorial Deed No. 10-224, 1867
John McClelland	Naturalization Papers No. 11-363, 1868
Elizabeth McCauley	Obituary
John McClelland & Susan Kane	Census of Deadwood, South Dakota, 1900
Mary S. Settlemyer	Listing in City Directory, 1892
Dr. Elmer McClelland & Mary S. Settlemyer	Wedding Announcement
Elmer E. E. McClelland & Mary Settlemyer	Marriage Registration
Elmer McClelland	Census of Box Butte, Nebraska, 1930
Mary S. Settlemyer	Cetification before a Notary Public, 1942
Elmer E. & Mary Salome Settlemyer McClelland	Register of Births in Family Bible
Mary Settlemyer	Family Bible Entries
Dr. Elmer Edward McClelland	Death Certificate
Dr. Elmer Edward McClelland	Obituary
Mary S. McClelland	Obituary
Paul Phillip McClelland	Obituary
Paul Phillip McClelland	*Los Angeles Times* Article, 1938
Ruth Beatrice McClelland Stalder	Death Certificate
Ruth Beatrice McClelland Stalder	Obituary
Lee McClelland	WWI Registration No. 26-1-53-C, 1918

Lee C. McClelland & Lovenia O'Toole	Marriage Certificate
Lee McClelland	*Los Angeles Times* Article, 1956
Lee McClelland	*The Register* Drugstore Article, 1961
Lee Custer McClelland	Obituary
Lovenia McClelland	Obituary
Esther McClelland, Ralph & Maxine Shirey	Census of Yakima County, WA, 1930
Esther M. Shirey & Carl William Howell	Marriage Certificate
Esther Minnie McClelland Howell	Obituary
Esther Minnie Howell	Death Certificate
Elmer E. McClelland & Ruth Tuttle	Marriage Certificate
E.E. McClelland	Letter to Dr. Elmer McClelland, 1927
Lee Custer McClelland	Birth Certificate
Lee Custer McClelland & Carolyn Fay Reif	Marriage Certificate
Michael Lee McClelland	Birth Registration
Joseph Edward McClelland	Birth Certificate
William McClelland & Annetta Wainwright	Marriage Certificate
Janette McClelland & Gregory Newton	Wedding Invitation
Paul Joseph McClelland	Birth Certificate
Paul Daniel McClelland	Birth Certificate
Shawn Patrick McClelland	Birth Certificate
Susan Renee McClelland	Birth Certificate
Elmer McClelland & Stella (Turner) Hardiman	Marriage Certificate
Elmer McClelland	Article, 1946
Elmer McClelland	*Valley News* Article, 1956
Dr. & Mrs. Elmer McClelland	*Valley News* Article, 1961
Elmer Edward Ellsworth McClelland	Death Certificate
Elmer Edward Ellsworth McClelland	Obituary
George & Harriet Reber and Family	Census of Bloomington, CA, 1930
Matilda McClelland & Levi Hastings	Marriage Record
Matilda & Levi Hastings	Census of Polk County, Iowa, 1900
Susan M. McClelland & Sandy Kane	Marriage Record
Susan & Michael Sandy Kane and Family	Census of Deadwood, South Dakota, 1900
Susan M. Kane	Death Certificate
Harriet Hattie McClelland & Ernest Reynolds	Marriage Certificate
Harriet McClelland Reynolds & Ernest Reynolds	Census of King County, WA, 1930
Harriet E. Reynolds	Death Certificate
Minnie M. McClelland & Wm. Turner	Marriage Record
Minnie M. McClelland & William Turner	Wedding Announcement
Minnie May McClelland & William Turner	Marriage Certificate
Minnie McClelland & William Turner	Census of Kewanee, Illinois, 1900
William Turner	Death Certificate
Minnie M. Turner	Obituary
Minnie May Turner	Death Certificate
Harriet Turner	Obituary

Robert M. Turner & Margaret H. Fuller	Marriage Certificate
Robert M. Turner	Obituary
William Turner & Leona Schweer	Wedding Announcement
William Wallace Turner	Obituary
Samuel Francis McClelland	WWI Draft Registration No. 46-1-19C

CHAPTER III

William McClelland & Sarah Donnelly	Marriage Certificate
William McClelland	Memorial No. 46-224, 1886
Sarah McClelland	Death Certificate
Sarah Donnelly McClelland	Obituary
William McClelland	Death Certificate
William McClelland	Obituary
Lucy McClelland	Birth Certificate
Lucy McClelland & Robert Hawthorne	Marriage Certificate
Lucy McClelland	Death Certificate
Mary Minnie McClelland	Birth Certificate
Robert Samuel Little Wright	Birth Certificate
Robert Samuel Wright & Minnie McClelland	Marriage Certificate
Robert Samuel Wright & Minnie McClelland	Spine of Brown's Bible
Robert Samuel Wright & Minnie McClelland	Title Page of Brown's Bible
Robert Wright & Mary Minnie McClelland	Marriage Record, Brown's Bible
Robert Wright & Mary Minnie McClelland	Details, Brown's Bible
Robert Samuel Wright Family	Census of Ireland, 1911
Robert Samuel Wright	Death Certificate
Robert Samuel Wright	Obituary
Mary Minnie Wright	Obituary
Maud Elizabeth Wright	Birth Certificate
Maud Elizabeth Wright & Lewis Alfred Gilpin	Marriage Certificate
Sarah Roberta Wright	Birth Certificate
Sarah R. Wright	King's Scholarship Examination
Bertha Wright	"Fairies in My Room," A Poem, 1943
Mary Lucinda Wright	Birth Certificate
Mary Lucinda Wright & James Alexander Adams	Marriage Certificate
David Alexander Adams	Birth Certificate
Samuel John Adams	Birth Certificate
Maurice James Adams	Birth Certificate
William Brian Adams	Birth Certificate
Dorothy Jean Wright	Birth Certificate
Dorothy Jean Wright & Edward Tighe Brady	Marriage Certificate
Dorothy Jean Brady	Obituary
Edward Tighe Brady	Obituary

Alan Robert Tighe Brady	Birth Certificate
Kenneth Edward Brady	Birth Certificate
Dorothy Wright Brady	Letter from Elizabeth "Cissie" Wright
Rosemary Muriel Brady	Birth Certificate
Samuel Denis Brady	Birth Certificate
Barbara Jean Brady	Birth Certificate
Robert William Wright	Birth Certificate
Robert Wright & Evangeline Dugan	Marriage Certificate
Robert Wright & Evangaline Dugan	Wedding Announcement
John Robert Iain Wright	Birth Certificate
Eleanor Elizabeth Wright	Birth Certificate
Samuel David Wright	Birth Certificate
Samuel Joseph Wright	Birth Certificate
Samuel Wright & Mary Campbell	Marriage Certificate
Helen Anne Wright	Birth Certificate
Roberta Mary Wright	Birth Certificate
Clive Samuel Wright	Birth Certificate
David Wright	Birth Certificate
David Wright & Mary Elizabeth Glenny	Marriage Certificate
Margaret Mary Wright	Birth Certificate
Pauline Elizabeth Wright	Birth Certificate
Brenda Maud Wright	Birth Certificate
Sarah Maud McClelland	Birth Certificate
Sarah Maud McClelland & Albert G. Hawthorn	Marriage Certificate
Sarah Maud McClelland	Death Certificate
William McClelland & Sarah Ann Henning	Marriage Certificate
William & Sarah McClelland Family	Census of Ireland, 1901
William McClelland	Death Certificate
William McClelland	Obituary
Sarah McClelland	Death Certificate
William Thomas McClelland	Birth Certificate
Margaret Copeland	Birth Certificate
Maude McClelland	Birth Certificate
Copeland Family	Census of Ireland, 1911
W.T. McClelland & Sara Winifred Parker	Wedding Announcement
William T. McClelland & Sara Winifred Parker	Marriage Certificate
Sara Winifred Parker	Birth Certificate
Sara Winifred Parker	Ship Manifest, 1920
E. Earl Davis & Elizabeth L. Smith	Marriage Certificate
Andrew & Elizabeth Smith	US Census, 1920
W.T. McClelland	Article, 1919
W.T. McClelland	Article, In Memoriam
Winifred McClelland	Article, "A Tribute to a Great Lady"
Sara Winifred McClelland	Article, In Memoriam

Frances Helen McClelland	Birth Announcement Card
Frances Helen McClelland	Article, In Memoriam
Norman P. McClelland	Biography
Agnes Barbara Dunlop Irwin	Birth Certificate
Barbara Dunlop Irwin & Thomas Gordon Brand	Marriage Certificate
Thomas Gordon Brand	Birth Certificate
Gordon Brand	Invitation to Book Launch
Heather Sarah Margaret Brand	Birth Certificate
Alison Emma Ruth Brand	Birth Certificate
Thomas Henry Clarke	Obituary
Margaret Isobel Clarke	Birth Certificate
Margaret Isobel Clarke & Robert Owen Convery	Marriage Certificate
Robert Owen Convery	Birth Certificate
Robert Owen Convery	Death Certificate
David Andrew Convery	Birth Certificate
Stephen Robert Convery	Birth Certificate
Kathryn Helen Convery	Birth Certificate
Michael Thomas Convery	Birth Certificate
Audrey Jean Irwin	Birth Certificate
David Livingston McClelland	Birth Certificate
David L. McClelland	Honorable Discharge, 1917
David L. McClelland	*The New Chieftain* Article, 1961
David McClelland & Myrtle Haller	Marriage Certificate
Myrtle Wilhelmina Haller	Birth Certificate
David Livingston McClelland	Death Certificate
Myrtle W. McClelland	Death Certificate
Patricia Leah Stephens	Death Certificate
Patricia L. Stephens	Obituary
Ann Elizabeth Stephens	Birth Certificate
Ann Stephens & Richard Willert	Marriage Certificate
Keeley Crystal Willert	Birth Certificate
Kent Christian Willert	Birth Certificate
Alissa Beth Willert	Birth Certificate
David Thomas Lyle Stephens	Birth Certificate
David Thomas Lyle Stephens	Arizona Supreme Court Guardianship
Catalina Nicole Stephens	Birth Certificate
Jacqueline Joan McClelland	Birth Certificate
John Benjamin Priser	Birth Certificate
John Priser Family	*Albuquerque Journal* Article, 1958
Jacqueline Joan Priser	Death Certificate
Jacqueline Joan Priser	Obituary
John Benjamin Priser	Death Certificate
Michael Priser	Article on Eagle Scout Award
Susan Jean Priser	Birth Certificate

Susan Jean Priser & Franciscus Xaverius Prins   Marriage Certificate
Adrian Gonzales   Birth Record
Patricia Jo Priser   Birth Certificate
Patricia Jo Priser & Thomas David Hoisch   Marriage Certificate
David James Priser & Valerie Jean Sterling   Marriage Certificate

CHAPTER IV

Susan McClelland & James Bradford   Marriage Certificate
Susan McClelland & James Bradford   Census of Ireland, 1901
Susan McClelland Bradford   Death Certificate

CHAPTER V

George & Adeline McClelland and Family   Census of Pennsylvania, 1920
George McClelland   Obituary
Adeline L. McClelland   Obituary
Alice J. McClelland & Eugene J. Johnson   Marriage Certificate

CHAPTER VI

Alex McClelland   Obituary
Mary Virginia McClelland   Obituary
Mrs. George H. Park   Obituary
Mr. George H. Park   Obituary
Paul McClelland Park   War Department Death Notice, 1919
Paul McClelland Park   Graveside Memorial, 1919
Eva Park   Goldstar Mother Recognition
Margaret Park Schultz   Obituary
George P. Schultz & Althea L. Leonhart   Wedding Announcement
Infant Schultz   Obituary
George Schultz   Article, State Architect Certificate
Virginia Park   Birth Certificate
Virginia Hale Park & Marion Herbert Swager   Marriage Certificate
Marion Herbert Swager   Birth Certificate
Virginia & Marion, Alice & Warren Swager   Golden Wedding Announcement
Virginia Park Swager   Death Certificate
Virginia Park Swager   Obituary
Margaret K. McClelland   Obituary
Grace F. McClelland   Obituary

Appendix

CHAPTER VII

Lucy McClelland   Obituary
Lucy McClelland   Death Certificate

CHAPTER VIII

Matilda McClelland   Death Certificate
Matilda McClelland   Obituary

CHAPTER IX

Esther McClelland   Death Certificate

CHAPTER X

David McClelland   Death Certificate

THE ANCESTORS OF JOHN MCCLELLAND OF CLOUGHENRAMER

1. Memorial No. 26-65, Thomas McClelland purchasing 18 acres and 34 perches from Mercy Glenny on July 8, 1861, General Registry Office, Dublin, Ireland.

2. Valuation of Tenements, Parish of Newry, McClelland Homestead, 1864, General Registry Office, Dublin, Ireland.

3. Susan McClelland, death certificate, General Registry Office, Dublin, Ireland.

SUSAN MCCLELLAND DEATH CERTIFICATE

4. Thomas McClelland, death certificate, General Registry Office, Dublin, Ireland.

THOMAS MCCLELLAND DEATH CERTIFICATE

5. Thomas McClelland, obituary, June 21, 1866, *Newry Commercial Telegraph*, Newry Library, Newry, Ireland.

CHAPTER I

○━━○

Margaret Peggy McClelland

1. Margaret Peggy McClelland and Thomas Tweedie, marriage certificate, General Registry Office, Oxford House, 49-55 Chichester Street, Belfast, Ireland, BT1 4HL.

2. Letter from Rev. Arthur J. E. Curry to Margaret McGaffin, 1988, from McGaffin family papers.

3. Census of Ireland, 1901, Thomas Tweedie Family, National Archives of Ireland, Dublin, Ireland.

4. Margaret Peggy McClelland Tweedie, death certificate, General Registry Office, Dublin, Ireland.

MARGARET PEGGY MCCLELLAND TWEEDIE DEATH CERTIFICATE

5. Thomas Tweedie, husband of Margaret Peggy McClelland, obituary, December 17, 1907, *Newry Reporter*.

6. William John Tweedie, birth certificate, General Registry Office, Dublin, Ireland.

WILLIAM JOHN TWEEDIE BIRTH CERTIFICATE

7. William John Tweedie and Annie Elizabeth Hooke, marriage certificate, General Registry Office, Dublin, Ireland.

8. William John Tweedie, Certificate of Membership, The Presbyterian Church in Ireland, 1908, from McGaffin family records.

9. Census of Ireland, 1911, William John Tweedie Family, National Archives of Ireland, Dublin, Ireland.

10. Annie Elizabeth Hooke Tweedie, obituary, March 30, 1929, *Newry Reporter*.

11. William John Tweedie, obituary, October 6, 1938, *Newry Reporter*.

12. Margaret Lucy Tweedie, birth certificate, General Registry Office, Dublin, Ireland.

MARGARET LUCY TWEEDIE BIRTH CERTIFICATE

13. Margaret Lucy Tweedie and William Joseph McWilliams, marriage certificate, General Registry Office, Belfast, Northern Ireland.

14. Emigration travel records of Margaret Lucy Tweedie McWilliams 1926 – 1968, from Tweedie family papers.

Appendix

15. Margaret Lucy Tweedie McWilliams, death certificate, General Registry Office, Belfast, Northern Ireland.

MARGARET LUCY TWEEDIE McWILLIAMS DEATH CERTIFICATE

16. Annie Tweedie, birth certificate, General Registry Office, Dublin, Ireland.

ANNIE TWEEDIE BIRTH CERTIFICATE

17. Annie Tweedie and Joseph Enos Dunlop, marriage certificate, General Registry Office, Belfast, Northern Ireland.

533

18. Joseph Enos Dunlop, birth certificate, Vol. 6, Page 970, General Registry Office, Belfast, Ireland.

19. Annie Tweedie Dunlop, death certificate, 1977, Vol. Center 1, Page 465, General Registry Office, Belfast, Northern Ireland.

20. Annie Tweedie Dunlop, crematorium entry, Roselawn Cemetery, Belfast, Northern Ireland.

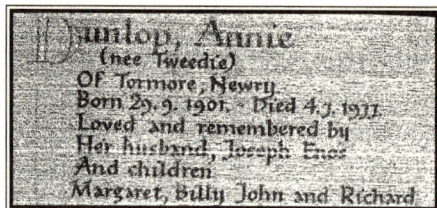

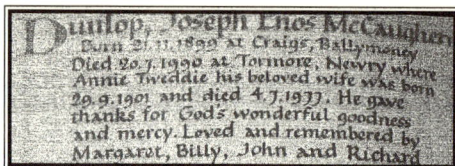

ANNIE TWEEDIE DUNLOP CREMATORIUM ENTRY

21. Joseph Enos Dunlop, death certificate, Vol, Center 1, Page 442, General Registry Office, Belfast, Northern Ireland.

22. Joseph Enos Dunlop, crematorium entry, Roselawn Cemetery, Belfast, Northern Ireland.

JOSEPH ENOS DUNLOP CREMATORIUM ENTRY

23. Margaret Annie Dunlop, birth certificate, General Registry Office, Belfast, Northern Ireland.

MARGARET ANNIE DUNLOP BIRTH CERTIFICATE

Appendix

24. William Tweedie Dunlop, birth certificate, General Registry Office, Belfast, Northern Ireland.

WILLIAM TWEEDIE DUNLOP BIRTH CERTIFICATE

25. Anna Lucinda Tweedie, birth certificate, General Registry Office, Dublin, Ireland.

ANNA LUCINDA TWEEDIE BIRTH CERTIFICATE

26. Anna L. Tweedie and John A. McCormick, marriage register, General Registry Office, Dublin, Ireland.

27. Anna Lucinda Tweedie McCormick, death certificate, General Registry Office, Dublin, Ireland.

ANNA LUCY MCCORMICK DEATH CERTIFICATE

28. Anna Lucinda McCormick, obituary, October 9, 1906, *Newry Reporter*.

29. Anna Lucinda McCormick, pulpit reference, Rev. James Meeke, M.A., Presbyterian, Minister, Kingsmills Presbyterian Church.

30. Poem written by T. McCalden in memory of Mrs. John McCormack, teacher in day school and the Sabbath school of Kingsmills.

31. George McCormick, born August 13th, 1903, Ref: District Newry, Year 1903, Vol. 1, Page 759, Entry 448.

GEORGE McCORMICK BIRTH CERTIFICATE

32. George McCormick and Mary Cartmill, married on October 15, 1947 in Downshire Road Presbyterian Church, Newry, Co. Down.

33. George McCormick, died May 2, 1990 and is buried in Bessbrook Presbyterian Church Graveyard, Co. Armagh, Row 2, Grave 36, under the headstone Cartmill.
Ref: George McCormack (note the incorrect spelling of McCormick on the official document), District Newry and Mourne, Center 1, Page 291, age 87, birth year 1903.

34. Mary (known as Minnie) McCormick, died June 3, 1991 and is buried in Bessbrook Presbyterian Church Graveyard beside husband, George McCormick, in row 2, grave 36 under the headstone Cartmill. Ref: Second Quarter, District Newry and Mourne, Center 1, Page 321, age 80, birth year 1911.

35. Thomas Tweedie McCormick, born September 29th, 1906, Ref: District Newry, Vol. 1, Page 729, Entry 381.

THOMAS TWEEDIE McCORMICK BIRTH CERTIFICATE

Appendix

36. Thomas Tweedie McCormick and Mary Agnes Eileen Cartmill, married on January 12, 1938 in Rostrevor Presbyterian Church, Co. Down, Ref: District Kilkeel, Center 0, Page 777.

37. Mary Agnes Eileen McCormick, died March 14, 1963 and is buried in Kingsmills Presbyterian Church Graveyard beside her husband, Thomas Tweedie McCormick. Ref: Unavailable.

38. Thomas Tweedie McCormick, died November 22, 1993 and is buried in Kingsmills Presbyterian Church Graveyard, Co. Armagh, Ref: Fourth Quarter, District Newry and Mourne, Center 1, Page 689, age 87, birth year 1906.

39. John Samuel Wesley McCormick, born January 4th, 1939, Ref. First Quarter, District Newry, Center: Mullaglass, Page: 711.

JOHN SAMUEL WESLEY McCORMICK BIRTH CERTIFICATE

40. John Samuel Wesley McCormick, certificate of registry of baptismal name, General Registry Office, Belfast, Northern Ireland.

JOHN SAMUEL WESLEY McCORMICK REGISTRATION OF BAPTISMAL NAME

41. John Samuel Wesley McCormick and Nora Olivia Acheson, married on September 5, 1967, in Tullyvallen Presbyterian Church, Co. Armagh, Ref: Third Quarter, District Newry and Mourne, Center 0, Page 2691.

42. Nora Olivia Acheson, born January 21st, 1937, Ref. First Quarter, District Newry, No. 2, Center Null, Page: 703.

43. Eileen Olivia McCormick, born February 3rd, 1969, Ref: First Quarter, District Lurgan, No. 1, Center Null, Page 254.

44. Eileen Olivia McCormick and Stephen Robert Wylie, married on September 7, 1990 in Kingsmills Presbyterian Church, Co. Armagh, Ref: Third Quarter, District Newry and Mourne, Centre 3, Page 2347.

45. Emily Claire Wylie, born Oct. 22nd, 1990, Ref: Fourth Quarter, District Newry and Mourne, Center 1, Page 1546.

46. Anna Louise Wylie, born August 8th, 1994, Ref: Third Quarter, District Armagh, Center 1, Page 334.

47. Anna Isobel McCormick, born February 17th, 1972, Ref: First Quarter, District Lurgan, No. 1, Center Null, Page 420.

48. Thomas Winston McCormick, birth certificate, Ref: Third Quarter, District Mullaglass, Center Null, Page 779.

THOMAS WINSTON MCCORMICK BIRTH CERTIFICATE

49. Thomas Winston McCormick and Sandra Barron, married June 3rd, 1969 in Rostrevor Presbyterian Church, Co. Down, Ref: Second Quarter, District Kilkeel, Center 0, Page 1452.

50. Sandra Barron, born September 1st, 1947, Ref: Third Quarter, District Ballybot, Center Null, Page 810.

51. Mary Eileen Allison McCormick, born September 7th, 1969, Ref: Fourth Quarter, District Lurgan, No. 1, Center Null, Page 40.

52. Geoffrey Thomas Andrew McCormick, born October 25th, 1974, Ref: Fourth Quarter, District Newry and Mourne, Center 1, Page 152.

53. Geoffrey Thomas Andrew McCormick and Katrina McNaugher, married on May 27th, 2005. No reference available.

54. James Raymond McCormick, birth certificate, Ref: Fourth Quarter, District Mullaglass, Center Null, Page 783.

JAMES RAYMOND MCCORMICK BIRTH CERTIFICATE

55. James Raymond McCormick and Mary Elizabeth Cartmill, married on October 28th, 1972 in Kingsmills Presbyterian Church, Co. Armagh, Ref. Null, District Newry, Center 0, Page 1725.

56. James Robert Darren McCormick, born June 20th, 1974, Ref: Second Quarter, District Newry and Mourne, Center 4, Page 25.

57. James Robert Darren McCormick and Nicola Patterson, married on December 17th, 2004 in Kingsmills Presbyterian Church, Co. Armagh, Ref: No reference available.

58. Thomas Herbert Colin McCormick, born March 19th, 1977, Ref: First Quarter, District Newry and Mourne, Center 4, Page 11.

59. Thomas Herbert Colin McCormick and Nicola L. Richmond, married on March 24th, 2001 in Kingsmills Presbyterian Church, Co. Armagh, Ref: First Quarter, District Newry and Mourne, Center Null, Page 601.

60. Gareth Raymond Edwin McCormick, born April 13th, 1982, Ref: Second Quarter, District Newry and Mourne, Center 1, Page 385.

61. John Alexander McCormick and Mary Charlotte Robb (known as Minnie), married on September 25th, 1907 in Kingsmills Presbyterian Church, Co. Armagh, Ref: District Newry, Book 2, Page 47.

62. John (known as Jack) McCormick, born September 27th, 1908, Ref: Fourth Quarter, District Newry, Vol. 1, Page 683, Entry 157.

63. Edmond McCormick, born October 7th, 1911, Ref: Fourth Quarter, District Newry, Vol. 1, Page 691, Entry 29.

64. David McCormick, born June 13th, 1913, Ref: Second Quarter, District Newry, Vol. 1, Page 763, Entry 263.

65. Robert McCormick, born April 20th, 1916, Ref: Second Quarter, District Newry, Vol. 1, Page 689, Entry 85.

66. Robert McCormick and Sarah Barron, married on December 26th, 1945 in Kingsmills Presbyterian Church, Co. Armagh, Ref: Fourth Quarter, District Newry and Mourne, Center 0, Page 1415.

67. Sarah (known as Sadie) Barron, born June 1924, Ref: Second Quarter, District Mullaglass, Center Null, Page 777.

68. Robert McCormick, died April 25th, 1991, Ref: Second Quarter, District Newry and Mourne, Center 1, Page 245, age 75, birth year 1916.

69. Ann (known as Anna) Barron, born August 20th, 1882, Ref: Third Quarter, District Newry, Vol. 1, Page 724.

70. Ann Cartmill (known as Anna) nee Barron and John Alexander McCormick, married on July 5th, 1922 in 1st Newry Presbyterian Church, Co. Down, Ref: Third Quarter, District Newry, Centre 0, Page 1251.

71. Anna (Annie) McCormick (third wife of John Alexander McCormick), died August 6th, 1967, Ref: Third Quarter, District Ballybot, Centre Null, Page 324, age 85, birth year 1882, Note: Anna (Annie) McCormick first married to Samuel Cartmill (maiden name Barron). Her Christian name appears as Ann on her official birth records.

72. Sarah Isobel McCormick, born May 22nd, 1923, Ref: Second Quarter, District Mullaglass, Center Null, Page 900.

73. Sally Isobel McCormick and James Freeburn, marriage certificate, General Registry Office, Belfast, Northern Ireland, Ref: Third Quarter 1959, District Newry and Mourne, Center 0, Page 2274.

74. James Wesley Freeburn, born October 13th, 1960, Ref: Fourth Quarter, District Ballybot, Center Null, Page 486.

75. James Wesley Freeburn and Ruth Louise Lawson, marriage certificate, General Registry Office, Belfast, Northern Ireland, Ref: Third Quarter 1989, District Craigavon, Center 3, Page 2230.

76. Ruth Louise Lawson, born July 6th, 1962, Ref: No records available.

77. Sarah Louise Freeburn, born September 11th, 1993, Ref: Third Quarter, District Dungannon, Center 1, Page 603.

78. Rebecca Freeburn, born February 12th, 1996, Ref: First Quarter, District Dungannon, Center 1, Page 105.

79. Thomas James Freeburn, born April 24th, 1999, Ref: U 1999/52/0222, 24/4/1999, District Dungannon.

80. Anna Olivia Freeburn, born September 8th, 1961, Ref: Third Quarter, District Ballybot, Centre Null, Page 358.

81. William George Alan Chambers, born April 16th, 1956, Ref: Second Quarter, District Kilkeel No. 2, Centre Null, Page 605.

82. Christopher Alan Chambers, born November 18th, 1987, Ref: Fourth Quarter, District Newry and Mourne, Center 1, Page 1834.

83. Sarah Aimee Chambers, born September 15th, 1991, Ref: Second Quarter, District Newry and Mourne, Centre 1, Page 810, Note: Sarah Aimee was clearly born in the Third Quarter but the official record shows the Second Quarter.

84. Edith Joan Freeburn, born September 8th, 1961, Ref: Third Quarter, District Ballybot, Centre Null, Page 359.

85. Robert James Irvine, born 1952, Ref: Fourth Quarter, District Ballybot, Centre Null, Page 757.

86. James Robert Irvine, born September 13th, 1985, Ref: Third Quarter, District Newry and Mourne, Center 1, Page 583.

87. Andrew Thomas Irvine, born July 19th, 1988, Ref: Third Quarter, District Newry and Mourne, Center 1, Page 1249.

CHAPTER II

John McClelland

1. Ship Manifest, John McClelland's arrival September 5, 1859 on steamship *Jason* from Galloway, Ireland.

2. Census of Pittsburgh, Pennsylvania, 1860, John McClelland residing in same home with Samuel McCauley, LDS Family History Library, Salt Lake City, Utah.

3. Memorial Deed No. 10-224, John McClelland to William McClelland, dated February 8, 1867, Registry of Deeds, Dublin, Ireland.

4. John McClelland's Naturalization Papers No. 11-363 dated March 4, 1868, General Registry Office, Dublin, Ireland.

5. Elizabeth McCauley, obituary, October 10, 1899, from Deadwood, South Dakota, Library.

6. Census of Deadwood, South Dakota, 1900, John McClelland and Susan Kane, LDS Family History Library, Salt Lake City, Utah.

7. Mary S. Settlemyer, Physician, listing in City Directory, Des Moines, Iowa, 1892.

8. Dr. Elmer Edward McClelland and Mary S. Settlemyer, wedding announcement, December 5, 1893, *The Daily Iowa Capital*, Des Moines, Iowa, from Lee McClelland family papers.

9. Elmer E. E. McClelland and Mary Salome Settlemyer, marriage registration, December 4, 1893, Polk County, Iowa, LDS Family History Library, Salt Lake City, Utah.

10. Census of Box Butte, Nebraska, 1930, Elmer McClelland, Physician, LDS Family History Library, Salt Lake City, Utah.

11. Mary S. Settlemyer, Certification before a Notary Public, February 7, 1942, from Lee McClelland family papers.

12. Elmer E. and Mary Salome Settlemyer McClelland, register of births in family Bible, from Lee McClelland family papers.

13. Mary Settlemyer's family Bible entries, December 4, 1893, from Lee McClelland family papers.

14. Dr. Elmer Edward McClelland, death certificate, Department of Public Health, Los Angeles, California.

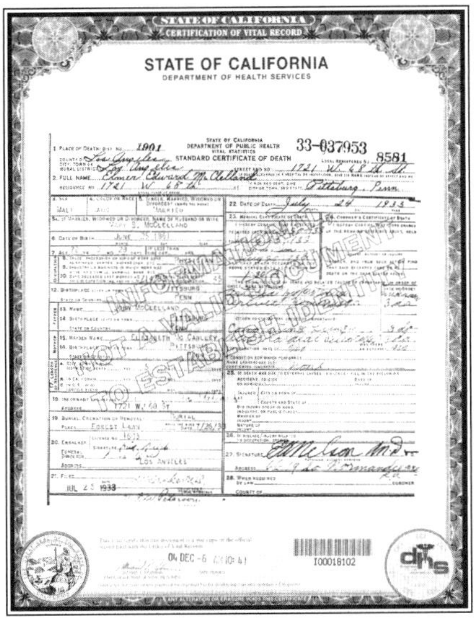

DR. ELMER EDWARD
MCCLELLAND DEATH
CERTIFICATE

15. Dr. Elmer Edward McClelland, obituary, July 24, 1933, *Los Angles Times*, Los Angeles, California.

16. Mary S. McClelland, obituary, Sunday October 6, 1946, *Los Angeles Times*, page 14, part 1, Los Angeles, California.

17. Paul Phillip McClelland, obituary, December 14, 1938, *Los Angeles Times*, Los Angeles, California.

18. Paul Phillip McClelland, article, December 14, 1938, *Los Angeles Times*, Los Angeles, California.

19. Ruth Beatrice McClelland Stalder, death certificate, Department of Public Health, Los Angeles, California.

RUTH BEATRICE
MCCLELLAND
DEATH CERTIFICATE

20. Ruth Beatrice McClelland Stalder, obituary, May 25, 1967, *Los Angeles Times*, Los Angeles, California.

21. Lee McClelland's WWI Registration No. 26-1-53-C, September 12, 1918, Antioch, Nebraska.

22. Lee C. McClelland and Lovenia O'Toole, marriage certificate, Anaheim, California.

23. Lee McClelland, article, November 4, 1956, *Los Angeles Times*, Los Angeles, California, from Lee McClelland family papers.

24. Lee McClelland, drugstore article, November 11, 1961, *The Register*, Santa Ana, California, from Lee McClelland family papers.

25. Lee Custer McClelland, obituary, May 6, 1976, *The Register*, Santa Ana, California.

26. Lovenia McClelland, obituary, January 15, 1979, *Anaheim Bulletin*, Anaheim, California.

27. Census of Yakima County, Washington, 1930, Esther Minnie McClelland, Ralph and Maxine Shirey, LDS Family History Library, Salt Lake City, Utah.

28. Esther M. Shirey and Carl William Howell, marriage certificate, July 26, 1960.

29. Esther Minnie McClelland Howell, obituary, December 1, 1987, *Contra Costa Times*, Contra Costa County, California, from McClelland family papers.

30. Esther Minnie Howell, death certificate, Department of Public Health, Los Angeles, California.

ESTHER MINNIE HOWELL DEATH CERTIFICATE

31. Elmer E. McClelland and Ruth Tuttle, marriage certificate, LDS Family History Library, Salt Lake City, Utah.

32. E. E. McClelland letter to Dr. Elmer McClelland dated November 10, 1927, from Lee McClelland family papers.

33. Lee Custer McClelland, birth certificate, from Lee McClelland family papers.

LEE CUSTER MCCLELLAND BIRTH CERTIFICATE

34. Lee Custer McClelland and Carolyn Fay Reif, marriage certificate, from Lee McClelland family papers.

35. Michael Lee McClelland, birth registration, from Lee McClelland family papers.

MICHAEL LEE MCCLELLAND BIRTH REGISTRATION

36. Joseph Edward McClelland, birth certificate, from Lee McClelland family papers.

JOSEPH EDWARD MCCLELLAND BIRTH CERTIFICATE

37. William Dennis McClelland and Annetta L. Wainwright, marriage certificate, from William Dennis McClelland family papers.

38. Janette Marie McClelland and Gregory Dean Newton, wedding invitation, from William Dennis McClelland family papers.

39. Paul Joseph McClelland, birth certificate, from Lee McClelland family papers.

PAUL JOSEPH MCCLELLAND BIRTH CERTIFICATE

40. Paul Daniel McClelland, birth certificate, from Lee McClelland family papers.

PAUL DANIEL MCCLELLAND BIRTH CERTIFICATE

41. Shawn Patrick McClelland, birth certificate, from Lee McClelland family papers.

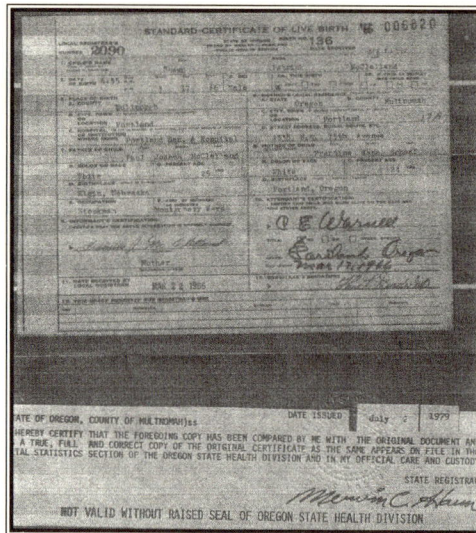

SHAWN PATRICK MCCLELLAND BIRTH CERTIFICATE

42. Susan Renee McClelland, birth certificate, from Lee McClelland family papers.

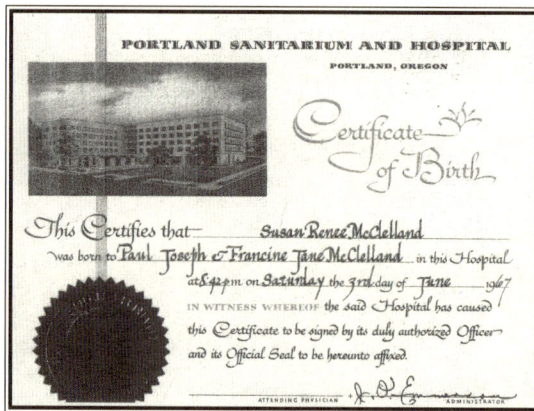

SUSAN RENEE MCCLELLAND BIRTH CERTIFICATE

43. Elmer Edward McClelland and Stella St. Clair (Turner) Hardiman, marriage certificate, General Register Office, Somerset House, London, England.

44. Elmer McClelland, article, July 6, 1946, Germany, from Stella McClelland family.

45. Elmer McClelland, *Valley News* article, Panorama City Chamber, February 16, 1956.

46. Dr. and Mrs. Elmer McClelland, article, August 27, 1961, *Valley News*, Van Nuys, California, from Lee McClelland family papers.

47. Elmer Edward Ellsworth McClelland, death certificate, Department of Public Health, Los Angeles, California.

ELMER EDWARD ELLSWORTH MCCLELLAND
DEATH CERTIFICATE

48. Elmer Edward Ellsworth McClelland, obituary, October 4, 1963, *Valley News*, Van Nuys, California.

49. Census of San Bernardino County, Bloomington, California, 1930, George and Harriet Reber and family, LDS Family History Library, Salt Lake City, Utah.

50. Matilda McClelland and Levi Hastings, marriage record, Polk County, Iowa.

51. Census of Polk County, Iowa, 1900, Matilda and Levi Hastings, LDS Family History Library, Salt Lake City, Utah.

52. Susan M. McClelland and Sandy Kane, marriage record, Polk County, Iowa.

53. Census of Deadwood, South Dakota, 1900, Susan and Michael Sandy Kane and family, LDS Family History Library, Salt Lake City, Utah.

54. Susan M. Kane, death certificate, State of Washington, Department of Health, Tacoma, Washington.

SUSAN M. KANE DEATH CERTIFICATE

55. Harriet Hattie McClelland and Ernest Reynolds, marriage certificate, Director of Records, King County, State of Washington.

56. Census of King County, Washington, 1930, Harriet McClelland Reynolds and Ernest Reynolds, LDS Family History Library, Salt Lake City, Utah.

57. Harriet E. Reynolds, death certificate, State of Washington, Department of Health, Tacoma, Washington.

HARRIET E. REYNOLDS DEATH CERTIFICATE

58. Minnie M. McClelland and Wm. Turner, marriage record, Polk County, Iowa.

59. Minnie M. McClelland and William Turner, wedding announcement, *The Daily Iowa Capital*.

60. Minnie May McClelland and William Turner, marriage certificate, Polk County, Iowa.

61. Census of Kewanee, Illinois, 1900, Minnie McClelland and William Turner, LDS Family History Library, Salt Lake City, Utah.

62. William Turner, death certificate, State of Illinois, Department of Health, Kewanee, Illinois.

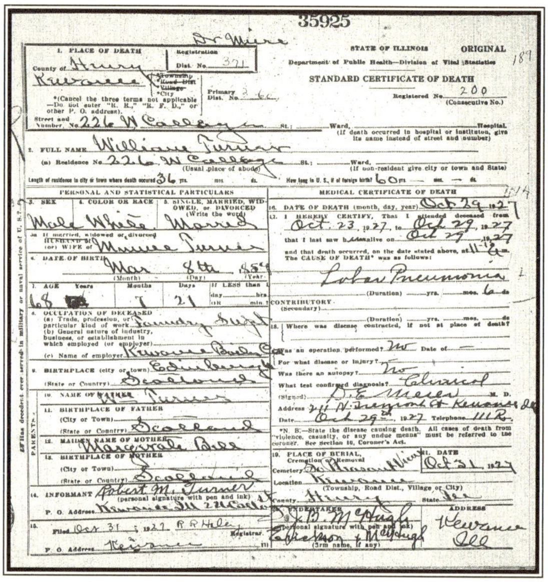
35925
STATE OF ILLINOIS — ORIGINAL
Department of Public Health—Division of Vital Statistics
STANDARD CERTIFICATE OF DEATH
Registered No. 200 (Consecutive No.)
1. PLACE OF DEATH
County of Henry
Registration Dist. No. 371
Primary Dist. No. 366
Kewanee City
*(Cancel the three terms not applicable—Do not enter "R. R.," "R. F. D.," or other P. O. address).
Street and Number, No. 226 W College St.; Ward, Hospital.
(If death occurred in hospital or institution, give its name instead of street and number)
2. FULL NAME William Turner
(a) Residence No. 226 W College St.; Ward,
(Usual place of abode) (If non-resident give city or town and State)
Length of residence in city or town where death occurred 36 yrs. mos. ds. How long in U. S., if of foreign birth? 60 yrs. mos. ds.
PERSONAL AND STATISTICAL PARTICULARS
3. SEX Male
4. COLOR OR RACE White
5. SINGLE, MARRIED, WIDOWED, or DIVORCED (Write the word) Married
5a. If married, widowed or divorced HUSBAND of (or) WIFE of Minnie Turner
6. DATE OF BIRTH Mar 8th (Month) (Day) (Year)
7. AGE Years 68 Months 7 Days 21 If LESS than 1 day hrs. or min.
8. OCCUPATION OF DECEASED
(a) Trade, profession, or particular kind of work Foundry Supt
(b) General nature of industry, business, or establishment in which employed (or employer)
(c) Name of employer Kewanee Boiler Co
9. BIRTHPLACE (city or town) Edinburgh
(State or Country) Scotland
10. NAME OF FATHER Wm Turner
11. BIRTHPLACE OF FATHER (City or Town)
(State or Country) Scotland
12. MAIDEN NAME OF MOTHER Margaret Bell
13. BIRTHPLACE OF MOTHER (City or Town)
(State or Country) Scotland
14. INFORMANT Robert M. Turner (personal signature with pen and ink)
P. O. Address Kewanee Ill 226 W College St
15. Filed Oct 31, 1927 R R Hale, Registrar.
P. O. Address Kewanee Ill
MEDICAL CERTIFICATE OF DEATH
16. DATE OF DEATH (month, day, year) Oct 29 1927
17. I HEREBY CERTIFY, That I attended deceased from Oct. 23, 1927, to Oct 29, 1927
that I last saw him alive on Oct 29, 1927
and that death occurred, on the date stated above, at 11-12 a.m.
The CAUSE OF DEATH* was as follows:
Lobar Pneumonia
(Duration) yrs. mos. 6 ds.
CONTRIBUTORY (Secondary)
(Duration) yrs. mos. ds.
18. Where was disease contracted, if not at place of death?
Was an operation performed? No Date of —
For what disease or injury?
Was there an autopsy? No
What test confirmed diagnosis? Clinical
(Signed) D. E. Meier M. D.
Address 211 N. Tremont St Kewanee Ill
Date Oct 29th, 1927 Telephone 111R
*N. B.—State the disease causing death. All cases of death from "violence, casualty, or any undue means" must be referred to the coroner. See Section 10, Coroner's Act.
19. PLACE OF BURIAL, Cremation or Removal
Cemetery Pleasant View
20. DATE Oct 31, 1927
Location Kewanee (Township, Road Dist., Village or City)
County Henry State Ill
21. UNDERTAKER J. B. McHugh (personal signature with pen and ink)
ADDRESS Kewanee Ill
Erickson & McHugh (firm name, if any)

WILLIAM TURNER DEATH CERTIFICATE

63. Minnie M. Turner, obituary, *Kewanee Star Courier*, October 15, 1947, Kewanee, Illinois.

64. Minnie May Turner, death certificate, State of Illinois, Department of Health, Kewanee Illinois.

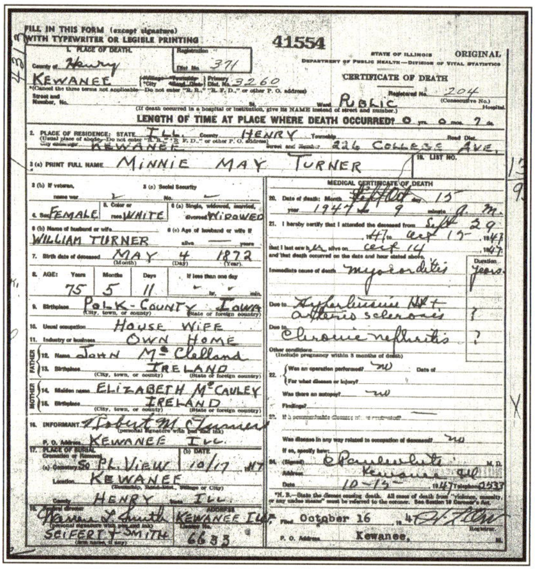
FILL IN THIS FORM (except signature) WITH TYPEWRITER OR LEGIBLE PRINTING
41554
STATE OF ILLINOIS — ORIGINAL
DEPARTMENT OF PUBLIC HEALTH—DIVISION OF VITAL STATISTICS
CERTIFICATE OF DEATH
Registered No. 204 (Consecutive No.)
1. PLACE OF DEATH
County of Henry
Registration Dist. No. 371
Kewanee City
Primary Dist. No. 3260
*(Cancel the three terms not applicable—Do not enter "R. R.," "R. F. D.," or other P. O. address)
Street and Number, No. St. Ward Public Hospital.
(If death occurred in a hospital or institution, give its NAME instead of street and number.)
LENGTH OF TIME AT PLACE WHERE DEATH OCCURRED? 0 yrs. 0 mos. 7 ds.
2. PLACE OF RESIDENCE: STATE Ill. County Henry Township Road Dist.
City Kewanee Street and Number 226 College Ave.
3 (a) PRINT FULL NAME MINNIE MAY TURNER
3 (b) If veteran, name war —
3 (c) Social Security No. —
4. Sex FEMALE
5. Color or race WHITE
6 (a) Single, widowed, married, divorced WIDOWED
6 (b) Name of husband or wife WILLIAM TURNER
6 (c) Age of husband or wife if alive — years
7. Birth date of deceased MAY 4 1872 (Month) (Day) (Year).
8. AGE: Years 75 Months 5 Days 11 If less than one day — hr. — min.
9. Birthplace POLK-COUNTY IOWA (City, town, or county) (State or foreign country)
10. Usual occupation HOUSE WIFE
11. Industry or business OWN HOME
FATHER 12. Name JOHN McClelland
13. Birthplace IRELAND (City, town, or county) (State or foreign country)
MOTHER 14. Maiden name ELIZABETH McCAULEY
15. Birthplace IRELAND (City, town, or county) (State or foreign country)
16. INFORMANT Robert M Turner (personal signature with pen and ink)
P. O. Address KEWANEE ILL.
17. PLACE OF BURIAL, Cremation or Removal
(a) Cemetery So Pl. View
(b) DATE 10/17 /47
Location KEWANEE (Township, Road District, Village or City)
County HENRY State ILL.
18. Funeral director Warren L. Smith (personal signature with pen and ink)
ADDRESS KEWANEE ILL.
SEIFERT & SMITH (firm name, if any)
License No. 6633
MEDICAL CERTIFICATE OF DEATH
20. Date of death: Month Oct day 15 year 1947 hour 9 minute a. m.
21. I hereby certify that I attended the deceased from Sept 29, 1947, to Oct 15, 1947
that I last saw her alive on Oct 14, 1947
and that death occurred on the date and hour stated above.
Immediate cause of death myocarditis — Duration years
Due to hypertension HD & arterio sclerosis ?
Due to Chronic nephritis ?
Other conditions (Include pregnancy within 3 months of death)
22. Was an operation performed? no Date of
For what disease or injury?
Was there an autopsy? no
Findings?
Was disease in any way related to occupation of deceased? no
If so, specify how.
24. (Signed) M. D.
Address Kewanee Ill
Date 10-15, 1947 Telephone 1537
*N. B.—State the disease causing death. All cases of death from "violence, casualty, or any undue means" must be referred to the coroner. See Section 10 Coroner's Act.
Filed October 16, 1947 Registrar.
P. O. Address Kewanee,

MINNIE MAY McCELLAND DEATH CERTIFICATE

65. Harriet Turner, obituary, December 12, 1964, *Kewanee Star Courier*, Kewanee, Illinois.

66. Robert M. Turner and Margaret H. Fuller, marriage certificate, Henry County, Illinois.

67. Robert M. Turner, obituary, May 31, 1976, *Kewanee Star Courier*, Kewanee, Illinois.

68. William Wallace Turner and Leona Dorothy Schweer, wedding announcement, *Kewanee Star Courier*, Kewanee, Illinois.

69. William Wallace Turner, obituary, *Kewanee Star Courier*, Kewanee, Illinois.

70. Samuel Francis McClelland, WWI draft registration No. 46-1-19C, Seattle, Washington.

SAMUEL FRANCIS MCCLELLAND WWI DRAFT REGISTRATION

CHAPTER III

William McClelland

1. William McClelland and Sarah Donnelly, marriage certificate, General Registry Office, Dublin, Ireland.

2. Memorial No. 46-224, William McClelland purchasing 6 acres from Mercy Glenny, dated November 12, 1886, General Registry Office, Dublin, Ireland.

3. Sarah McClelland, death certificate, General Registry Office, Dublin, Ireland.

SARAH MCCLELLAND DEATH CERTIFICATE

4. Sarah Donnelly McClelland, obituary, September 22, 1885, *Newry Reporter*, Newry, Co. Down, Ireland.

5. William McClelland, death certificate, General Registry Office, Dublin, Ireland.

WILLIAM MCCLELLAND DEATH CERTIFICATE

6. William McClelland, obituary, March 25, 1909, *Newry Reporter*, Newry, Co. Down, Ireland.

7. Lucy McClelland, birth certificate, General Registry Office, Dublin, Ireland.

LUCY MCCLELLAND BIRTH CERTIFICATE

8. Lucy McClelland and Robert Hawthorne, marriage certificate, General Registry Office, Dublin, Ireland.

9. Lucy McClelland, death certificate, General Register Office, New Register House, Edinburgh, Scotland.

LUCY MCCLELLAND DEATH CERTIFICATE

10. Mary Minnie McClelland, birth certificate, General Registry Office, Dublin, Ireland.

MARY MINNIE MCCLELLAND BIRTH CERTIFICATE

11. Robert Samuel Little Wright, birth certificate, General Registry Office, Dublin, Ireland.

ROBERT SAMUEL LITTLE WRIGHT BIRTH CERTIFICATE

12. Robert Samuel Wright and Minnie McClelland, marriage certificate, General Registry Office, Dublin, Ireland.

13. Photo of the Spine of Brown's Bible, from the Uel Wright family records.

14. Copy of the Title Page of Brown's Bible, from the Uel Wright family records.

15. Details in Brown's Bible – Robert Wright marriage to Mary Minnie McClelland, from the Uel Wright family records.

16. Details as found in Brown's Bible, from the Uel Wright family records.

17. Census of Ireland, 1911, Robert Samuel Wright Family, National Archives of Ireland, Dublin, Ireland.

18. Robert Samuel Wright, death certificate, General Registry Office, Belfast, Northern Ireland.

ROBERT SAMUEL WRIGHT DEATH CERTIFICATE

19. Robert Samuel Wright, obituary, October 5, 1956, *Outlook Newspaper*, Rathfriland, Co. Down, Northern Ireland.

ROBERT SAMUEL WRIGHT OBITUARY

20. Mary Minnie Wright, obituary, April 8, 1960, *Outlook Newspaper*, Rathfriland, Co. Down, Northern Ireland.

MARY MINNIE MCCLELLAND OBITUARY

21. Maud Elizabeth Wright, birth certificate, General Registry Office, Dublin, Ireland.

MAUD ELIZABETH WRIGHT BIRTH CERTIFICATE

22. Maud Elizabeth Wright and Lewis Alfred Gilpin, marriage certificate, General Registry Office, Dublin, Northern Ireland.

23. Sarah Roberta Wright, birth certificate, General Registry Office, Dublin, Ireland.

SARAH ROBERTA WRIGHT BIRTH CERTIFICATE

24. Sarah R. Wright, King's Scholarship Examination, 1928, Ministry of Education for Northern Ireland.

25. Bertha Wright, "Fairies In My Room," a poem written by Bertha in 1943, from the Uel Wright personal family papers.

26. Mary Lucinda Wright, birth certificate, General Registry Office, Dublin, Ireland.

MARY LUCINDA WRIGHT BIRTH CERTIFICATE

27. Mary Lucinda Wright and James Alexander Adams, marriage certificate, General Registry Office, Dublin, Northern Ireland.

28. David Alexander Adams, birth certificate, General Registry Office, Belfast, Northern Ireland.

DAVID ALEXANDER ADAMS BIRTH CERTIFICATE

29. Samuel John Adams, birth certificate, General Registry Office, Belfast, Northern Ireland.

SAMUEL JOHN ADAMS BIRTH CERTIFICATE

30. Maurice James Adams, birth certificate, General Registry Office, Belfast, Northern Ireland.

MAURICE JAMES ADAMS BIRTH CERTIFICATE

31. William Brian Adams, birth certificate, General Registry Office, Belfast, Northern Ireland.

WILLIAM BRIAN ADAMS BIRTH CERTIFICATE

32. Dorothy Jean Wright, birth certificate, General Registry Office, Dublin, Ireland.

DOROTHY JEAN WRIGHT BIRTH CERTIFICATE

33. Dorothy Jean Wright and Edward Tighe Brady, marriage certificate, General Registry Office, Belfast, Northern Ireland.

34. Dorothy Jean Brady, obituary, *Belfast Telegraph Newspaper*, April 9, 1979, Belfast, Northern Ireland.

DOROTHY JEAN
WRIGHT OBITUARY

Appendix

35. Edward Tighe Brady, obituary, *Belfast Telegraph Newspaper*, January 18, 1986, Belfast, Northern Ireland.

BRADY — January 17, 1986 (suddenly), at his residence, Hebron, 4 Robin Hill, Dundrum, Edward Tighe (Founder and Editor of the Outlook Press), dearly-loved husband of the late Dorothy J. and dear father of Alan, Kenneth, Rosemary, Denis and Barbara. Funeral from his home, to-morrow (Sunday), at 2 p.m., to Ryans Presbyterian Church for service at 3 p.m. Interment immediately afterwards in adjoining graveyard. House private. Family flowers only, please. Donations in lieu of flowers, if desired, to J. G. Bullick, Funeral Directors, 15 Main Street, Rathfriland, for Arthritis Rheumatoid Council. Very deeply regretted by his sorrowing Sons, Daughters, Sons-in-law, Daughters-in-law, Grandchildren and all the Family Circle.

EDWARD TIGHE BRADY OBITUARY

36. Alan Robert Tighe Brady, birth certificate, General Registry Office, Belfast, Northern Ireland.

ALAN ROBERT TIGHE BRADY BIRTH CERTIFICATE

37. Kenneth Edward Brady, birth certificate, General Registry Office, Belfast, Northern Ireland.

KENNETH EDWARD BRADY BIRTH CERTIFICATE

39. Letter to Dorothy Wright Brady, from Great-Aunt Elizabeth "Cissie" Wright, on the birth of her second son, Kenneth.

40. Rosemary Muriel Brady, birth certificate, General Registry Office, Belfast, Northern Ireland.

ROSEMARY MURIEL BRADY BIRTH CERTIFICATE

41. Samuel Denis Brady, birth certificate, General Registry Office, Belfast, Northern Ireland.

SAMUEL DENIS BRADY BIRTH CERTIFICATE

42. Barbara Jean Brady, birth certificate, General Registry Office, Belfast, Northern Ireland.

BARBARA JEAN BRADY BIRTH CERTIFICATE

Appendix

43. Robert William Wright, birth certificate, General Registry Office, Dublin, Ireland.

ROBERT WILLIAM WRIGHT BIRTH CERTIFICATE

44. Robert William Wright and Evangeline Margaret Dugan, marriage certificate, General Registry Office, Belfast, Northern Ireland.

45. Robert Wright and Evangeline Margaret Dugan, wedding announcement, *Outlook Newspaper*, May 30, 1944, Rathfriland, Co. Down, Northern Ireland.

46. John Robert Iain Wright, birth certificate, General Registry Office, Belfast, Northern Ireland.

JOHN ROBERT IAIN WRIGHT BIRTH CERTIFICATE

47. Eleanor Elizabeth Wright, birth certificate, General Registry Office, Belfast, Northern Ireland.

ELEANOR ELIZABETH WRIGHT BIRTH CERTIFICATE

THE MCCLELLANDS OF CLOUGHENRAMER

48. Samuel David Wright, birth certificate, General Registry Office, Belfast, Northern Ireland.

SAMUEL DAVID WRIGHT BIRTH CERTIFICATE

49. Samuel Joseph Wright, birth certificate, General Registry Office, Belfast, Northern Ireland.

SAMUEL JOSEPH WRIGHT BIRTH CERTIFICATE

50. Samuel Joseph Wright and Mary Elizabeth Campbell, marriage certificate, General Registry Office, Dublin, Ireland.

51. Helen Anne Wright, birth certificate, General Registry Office, Belfast, Northern Ireland.

HELEN ANNE WRIGHT BIRTH CERTIFICATE

52. Roberta Mary Wright, birth certificate, General Registry Office, Belfast, Northern Ireland.

ROBERTA MARY WRIGHT BIRTH CERTIFICATE

53. Clive Samuel Wright, birth certificate, General Registry Office, Belfast, Northern Ireland.

CLIVE SAMUEL WRIGHT BIRTH CERTIFICATE

54. David Wright, birth certificate, General Registry Office, Dublin, Northern Ireland.

DAVID WRIGHT BIRTH CERTIFICATE

55. David Wright and Mary Elizabeth Glenny, marriage certificate, General Registry Office, Belfast, Northern Ireland.

56. Margaret Mary Wright, birth certificate, General Registry Office, Belfast, Northern Ireland.

MARGARET MARY WRIGHT BIRTH CERTIFICATE

57. Pauline Elizabeth Wright, birth certificate, General Registry Office, Belfast, Northern Ireland.

PAULINE ELIZABETH WRIGHT BIRTH CERTIFICATE

58. Brenda Maud Wright, birth certificate, General Registry Office, Belfast, Northern Ireland.

BRENDA MAUD WRIGHT BIRTH CERTIFICATE

59. Sarah Maud McClelland, birth certificate, General Registry Office, Dublin, Ireland.

SARAH MAUD MCCLELLAND BIRTH CERTIFICATE

60. Sarah Maud McClelland and Albert G. Hawthorn, marriage certificate, July 2, 1906.

61. Sarah Maud McClelland, death certificate, General Register Office, New Register House, Edinburg, Scotland.

SARAH MAUD MCCLELLAND DEATH CERTIFICATE

62. William McClelland and Sarah Ann Henning, marriage certificate, General Registry Office, Dublin, Ireland.

63. Census of Ireland, 1901, William & Sarah McClelland family, National Archives of Ireland, Dublin, Ireland.

64. William McClelland, death certificate, General Registry Office, Dublin, Ireland.

WILLIAM McCLELLAND DEATH CERTIFICATE

65. William McClelland, obituary, March 25, 1909, *Newry Reporter*, Newry, Co. Down, Northern Ireland.

66. Sarah McClelland, death certificate, General Registry Office, Dublin, Ireland.

SARAH McCLELLAND DEATH CERTIFICATE

67. William Thomas McClelland, birth certificate, General Registry Office, Dublin, Ireland.

WILLIAM THOMAS McCLELLAND BIRTH CERTIFICATE

68. Margaret Copeland, birth certificate, General Registry Office, Belfast, Ireland.

MARGARET COPELAND BIRTH CERTIFICATE

69. Maude McClelland, birth certificate, General Registry Office, Dublin, Ireland.

MAUDE MCCLELLAND BIRTH CERTIFICATE

70. Census of Ireland, 1911, Copeland family, National Archives of Ireland, Dublin, Ireland

71. W. T. McClelland and Sara Winifred Parker, wedding announcement, August 10, 1919, Tucson, Arizona.

72. William T. McClelland and Sara Winifred Parker, marriage certificate, General Registry Office, Dublin, Ireland.

73. Sara Winifred Parker, birth certificate, General Registry Office, Dublin, Ireland.

SARA WINIFRED PARKER BIRTH CERTIFICATE

74. Sara Winifred Parker, passenger on the *Baltic*, Ship Manifest dated December 19, 1920, The Statue of Liberty - Ellis Island Foundation, Inc.

BALTIC SHIP MANIFEST, SHOWING SARA WINIFRED PARKER AS A PASSENGER, ARRIVING IN NEW YORK DECEMBER 19, 1920

75. E. Earl Davis and Elizabeth L. Smith, marriage certificate, Arizona State Archives, Phoenix, Arizona.

76. US Census, 1920, Andrew and Elizabeth Smith, National Archives, Washington, D.C.

THE 1920 CENSUS ABOVE SHOWS ANDREW AND ELIZABETH
RESIDING AT 141 EAST ALAMEDA STREET, TUCSON, ARIZONA.

77. W. T. McClelland, article, Tucson, Arizona, 10 August 1919, Shamrock Foods Company Library, Phoenix, Arizona.

78. Mr. W. T. McClelland, In Memoriam, Shamrock Foods Company Library, Phoenix, Arizona.

79. Winifred McClelland, "A Tribute to a Great Lady," Special Memorial Issue, *Shamrock News*, December 1977, Shamrock Foods Company Library.

80. Memoriam for Sara Winifred McClelland, Shamrock Foods Company Library, Phoenix, Arizona.

81. Frances Helen McClelland, birth announcement card, Shamrock Foods Company Library, Phoenix, Arizona.

82. In Memoriam: Frances Helen McClelland, Shamrock Foods Company Library, Phoenix, Arizona.

83. Norman P. McClelland, biography, Shamrock Foods Company Library, Phoenix, Arizona.

84. Agnes Barbara Dunlop Irwin, birth certificate, General Registry Office, Belfast, Northern Ireland.

AGNES BARBARA DUNLOP IRWIN
BIRTH CERTIFICATE

85. Barbara Dunlop Irwin and Thomas Gordon Brand, marriage certificate, General Registry Office, Belfast, Northern Ireland.

86. Thomas Gordon Brand, birth certificate, General Registry Office, Belfast, Northern Ireland.

THOMAS GORDON BRAND
BIRTH CERTIFICATE

87. Invitation to the launch of the new book on the Irish writer William Caleton, edited by Gordon Brand.

88. Heather Sarah Margaret Brand, birth certificate, General Registry Office, Belfast, Northern Ireland.

HEATHER SARAH MARGARET BRAND
BIRTH CERTIFICATE

89. Alison Emma Ruth Brand, birth certificate, District Registry, Bulawayo, Zimbabwe, Africa.

ALISON EMMA RUTH BRAND BIRTH CERTIFICATE

90. Thomas Henry Clarke, obituary, *Newry Reporter*, Newry, Co. Down, Northern Ireland.

91. Margaret Isobel Clarke, birth certificate, General Registry Office, Belfast, Northern Ireland.

MARGARET ISOBEL CLARKE BIRTH CERTIFICATE

92. Margaret Isobel Clarke and Robert Owen Convery, marriage certificate, General Registry Office, Belfast, Northern Ireland.

93. Robert Owen Convery, birth certificate, General Registry Office, Belfast, Northern Ireland.

ROBERT OWEN CONVERY
BIRTH CERTIFICATE

94. Robert Owen Convery, death certificate, General Registry Office, Belfast, Northern Ireland.

ROBERT OWEN CONVERY
DEATH CERTIFICATE

95. David Andrew Convery, birth certificate, General Registry Office, Belfast, Northern Ireland.

DAVID ANDREW CONVERY BIRTH CERTIFICATE

96. Stephen Robert Convery, birth certificate, General Registry Office, Belfast, Northern Ireland.

STEPHEN ROBERT CONVERY BIRTH CERTIFICATE

97. Kathryn Helen Convery, birth certificate, General Registry Office, Belfast, Northern Ireland.

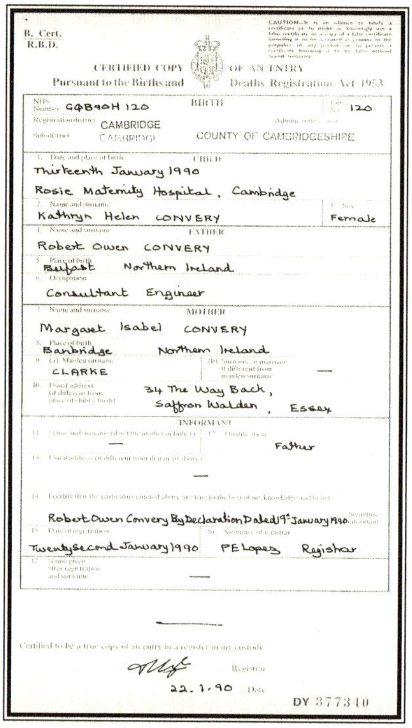

B. Cert.
R.B.D.

CAUTION—It is an offence to falsify a certificate or to make or knowingly use a false certificate or a copy of a false certificate intending it to be accepted as genuine to the prejudice of any person, or to possess a certificate knowing it to be false without lawful authority

CERTIFIED COPY OF AN ENTRY
Pursuant to the Births and Deaths Registration Act 1953

NHS Number: G4B90H 120 — BIRTH — Entry No. 120
Registration district: CAMBRIDGE
Sub-district: CAMBRIDGE
Administrative area: COUNTY OF CAMBRIDGESHIRE

CHILD
1. Date and place of birth: Thirteenth January 1990, Rosie Maternity Hospital, Cambridge
2. Name and surname: Kathryn Helen CONVERY
3. Sex: Female

FATHER
4. Name and surname: Robert Owen CONVERY
5. Place of birth: Belfast Northern Ireland
6. Occupation: Consultant Engineer

MOTHER
7. Name and surname: Margaret Isabel CONVERY
8. Place of birth: Banbridge Northern Ireland
9. (a) Maiden surname: CLARKE
9. (b) Surname at marriage if different from maiden surname: —
10. Usual address (if different from place of child's birth): 34 The Way Back, Saffron Walden, Essex

INFORMANT
11. Name and surname (if not the mother or father): —
12. Qualification: Father
13. Usual address (if different from that in 10 above): —
14. I certify that the particulars entered above are true to the best of my knowledge and belief
Robert Owen Convery By Declaration Dated 19th January 1990 — Signature of informant
15. Date of registration: Twenty Second January 1990
16. Signature of registrar: PE Lopes Registrar
17. Name given after registration and surname: —

Certified to be a true copy of an entry in a register in my custody
Registrar
22.1.90 Date
DY 377340

Kathryn Helen Convery Birth Certificate

98. Michael Thomas Convery, birth certificate, General Registry Office, Belfast, Northern Ireland.

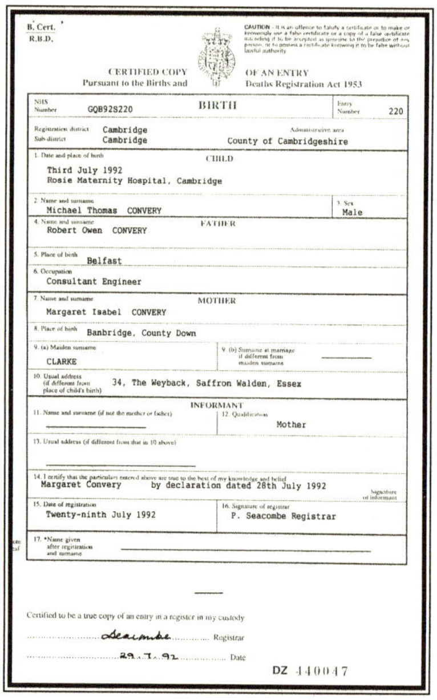

B. Cert.
R.B.D.

CAUTION - It is an offence to falsify a certificate or to make or knowingly use a false certificate or a copy of a false certificate intending it to be accepted as genuine to the prejudice of any person, or to possess a certificate knowing it to be false without lawful authority

CERTIFIED COPY OF AN ENTRY
Pursuant to the Births and Deaths Registration Act 1953

NHS Number: GQB92S220 — BIRTH — Entry Number: 220
Registration district: Cambridge
Sub-district: Cambridge
Administrative area: County of Cambridgeshire

CHILD
1. Date and place of birth: Third July 1992, Rosie Maternity Hospital, Cambridge
2. Name and surname: Michael Thomas CONVERY
3. Sex: Male

FATHER
4. Name and surname: Robert Owen CONVERY
5. Place of birth: Belfast
6. Occupation: Consultant Engineer

MOTHER
7. Name and surname: Margaret Isabel CONVERY
8. Place of birth: Banbridge, County Down
9. (a) Maiden surname: CLARKE
9. (b) Surname at marriage if different from maiden surname: ——
10. Usual address (if different from place of child's birth): 34, The Weyback, Saffron Walden, Essex

INFORMANT
11. Name and surname (if not the mother or father): ——
12. Qualification: Mother
13. Usual address (if different from that in 10 above): ——
14. I certify that the particulars entered above are true to the best of my knowledge and belief
Margaret Convery by declaration dated 28th July 1992 — Signature of informant
15. Date of registration: Twenty-ninth July 1992
16. Signature of registrar: P. Seacombe Registrar
17. *Name given after registration and surname: ——

Certified to be a true copy of an entry in a register in my custody
Seacombe Registrar
29.7.92 Date
DZ 440047

Michael Thomas Convery Birth Certificate

99. Audrey Jean Irwin, birth certificate, General Registry Office, Dublin, Northern Ireland.

AUDREY JEAN IRWIN BIRTH CERTIFICATE

100. David Livingston McClelland, birth certificate, General Registry Office, Dublin, Ireland.

DAVID LIVINGSTON McCLELLAND BIRTH CERTIFICATE

101. David L. McClelland, Honorable Discharge, United States Army, September 22, 1917.

102. Article, November 17, 1961, *The New Chieftain*, Alburqueque, New Mexico, David L. McClelland receiving letter of appreciation.

103. David Livingston McClelland and Myrtle Wilhelmina Haller, marriage certificate, County of San Diego, State of California.

104. Myrtle Wilhelmina Haller, birth certificate, County of Ellis, State of Texas.

MYRTLE WILHELMINA HALLER
BIRTH CERTIFICATE

105. David Livingston McClelland, death certificate, New Mexico Registrar, Albuquerque, New Mexico.

DAVID LIVINGSTON McCLELLAND
DEATH CERTIFICATE

106. Myrtle W. McClelland, death certificate, Pima County, Department of Vital Records, Tucson, Arizona.

MYRTLE W. McCLELLAND DEATH CERTIFICATE

107. Patricia Leah Stephens, death certificate, Pima County, Department of Vital Records, Tucson, Arizona.

PATRICIA LEAH STEPHENS DEATH CERTIFICATE

108. Patricia L. Stephens, obituary, April 21, 2002, Tucson, Arizona.

109. Ann Elizabeth Stephens, birth certificate, Registrar, Arizona Department of Health Services.

ANN ELIZABETH STEPHENS BIRTH CERTIFICATE

110. Ann Elizabeth Stephens and Richard Raymond Willert, marriage certificate, Arizona Department of Health Services.

111. Keeley Crystal Willert, birth certificate, Registrar, Arizona Department of Health Services.

KEELEY CRYSTAL WILLERT BIRTH CERTIFICATE

112. Kent Christian Willert, birth certificate, Registrar, Arizona Department of Health Services.

KENT CHRISTIAN WILLERT BIRTH CERTIFICATE

113. Alissa Beth Willert, birth certificate, Registrar, Arizona Department of Health Services.

ALISSA BETH WILLERT BIRTH CERTIFICATE

114. David Thomas Lyle Stephens, birth certificate, Registrar, Colorado Department of Public Health.

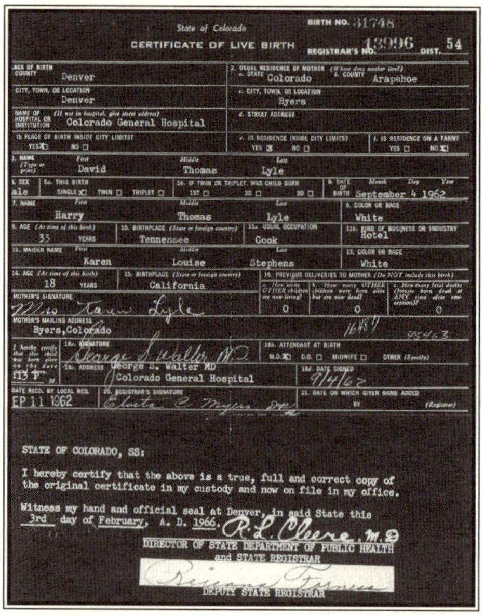

State of Colorado
CERTIFICATE OF LIVE BIRTH
BIRTH NO. 31748
REGISTRAR'S NO. 13996 DIST. 54

PLACE OF BIRTH COUNTY: Denver
CITY, TOWN, OR LOCATION: Denver
NAME OF HOSPITAL OR INSTITUTION (If not in hospital, give street address): Colorado General Hospital
IS PLACE OF BIRTH INSIDE CITY LIMITS? YES ☒ NO ☐
2. USUAL RESIDENCE OF MOTHER (Where does mother live?) a. STATE: Colorado b. COUNTY: Arapahoe
c. CITY, TOWN, OR LOCATION: Byers
d. STREET ADDRESS
e. IS RESIDENCE INSIDE CITY LIMITS? YES ☒ NO ☐
f. IS RESIDENCE ON A FARM? YES ☐ NO ☒
3. NAME (Type or print) First: David Middle: Thomas Last: Lyle
4. SEX: Male
5a. THIS BIRTH: SINGLE ☒ TWIN ☐ TRIPLET ☐
5b. IF TWIN OR TRIPLET, WAS CHILD BORN 1ST ☐ 2D ☐ 3D ☐
6. DATE OF BIRTH (Month Day Year): September 4 1962
7. NAME First: Harry Middle: Thomas Last: Lyle
8. COLOR OR RACE: White
9. AGE (At time of this birth): 33 YEARS
10. BIRTHPLACE (State or foreign country): Tennessee
11a. USUAL OCCUPATION: Cook
11b. KIND OF BUSINESS OR INDUSTRY: Hotel
12. MAIDEN NAME First: Karen Middle: Louise Last: Stephens
13. COLOR OR RACE: White
14. AGE (At time of this birth): 18 YEARS
15. BIRTHPLACE (State or foreign country): California
16. PREVIOUS DELIVERIES TO MOTHER (Do NOT include this birth)
a. How many OTHER children are now living? 0
b. How many OTHER children were born alive but are now dead? 0
c. How many fetal deaths (fetuses born dead at ANY time after conception)? 0
MOTHER'S SIGNATURE: Mrs Karen Lyle
MOTHER'S MAILING ADDRESS: Byers, Colorado
16487
95463
I hereby certify that this child was born alive on the date stated above. 1:13 P M.
18a. SIGNATURE: George S. Walter M.D.
18b. ATTENDANT AT BIRTH: M.D. ☒ D.O. ☐ MIDWIFE ☐ OTHER (Specify)
18c. ADDRESS: George S. Walter MD, Colorado General Hospital
18d. DATE SIGNED: 9/4/62
DATE RECD. BY LOCAL REG.: SEP 11 1962
20. REGISTRAR'S SIGNATURE: Electa C. Myers Dep.
21. DATE ON WHICH GIVEN NAME ADDED BY (Registrar)

STATE OF COLORADO, SS:

I hereby certify that the above is a true, full and correct copy of the original certificate in my custody and now on file in my office.

Witness my hand and official seal at Denver, in said State this 3rd day of February, A. D. 1966.

R. L. Cleere, M.D.
DIRECTOR OF STATE DEPARTMENT OF PUBLIC HEALTH and STATE REGISTRAR

DEPUTY STATE REGISTRAR

DAVID THOMAS LYLE STEPHENS BIRTH CERTIFICATE

115. David Thomas Lyle Stephens, guardianship, State of Arizona Supreme Court.

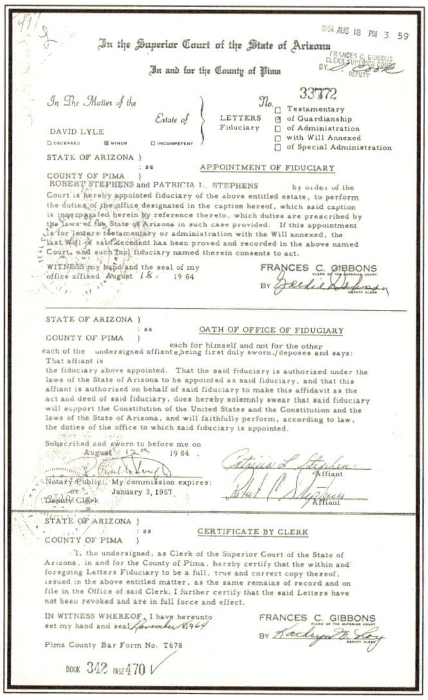

1964 AUG 18 PM 3 59

In the Superior Court of the State of Arizona
In and for the County of Pima

FRANCES C. GIBBONS CLERK SUPERIOR COURT BY DEPUTY

In The Matter of the Estate of DAVID LYLE
☐ DECEASED ☒ MINOR ☐ INCOMPETENT

No. 33772
LETTERS Fiduciary
☐ Testamentary
☒ of Guardianship
☐ of Administration
☐ with Will Annexed
☐ of Special Administration

STATE OF ARIZONA)
: ss APPOINTMENT OF FIDUCIARY
COUNTY OF PIMA)

ROBERT STEPHENS and PATRICIA L. STEPHENS by order of the Court is hereby appointed fiduciary of the above entitled estate, to perform the duties of the office designated in the caption hereof, which said caption is incorporated herein by reference thereto, which duties are prescribed by the laws of the State of Arizona in such case provided. If this appointment is for letters testamentary or administration with the Will annexed, the last Will of said decedent has been proved and recorded in the above named Court, and such (no) fiduciary named therein consents to act.

WITNESS my hand and the seal of my office affixed August 18, 1964

FRANCES C. GIBBONS CLERK OF THE SUPERIOR COURT
BY DEPUTY CLERK

STATE OF ARIZONA)
: ss OATH OF OFFICE OF FIDUCIARY
COUNTY OF PIMA)

each of the undersigned affiants, each for himself and not for the other being first duly sworn, deposes and says: That affiant is the fiduciary above appointed. That the said fiduciary is authorized under the laws of the State of Arizona to be appointed as said fiduciary, and that this affiant is authorized on behalf of said fiduciary to make this affidavit as the act and deed of said fiduciary, does hereby solemnly swear that said fiduciary will support the Constitution of the United States and the Constitution and the laws of the State of Arizona, and will faithfully perform, according to law, the duties of the office to which said fiduciary is appointed.

Subscribed and sworn to before me on August 12th 1964.

Notary Public, or Deputy Clerk. My commission expires: January 3, 1967

Patricia L. Stephens, Affiant
Robert C. Stephens, Affiant

STATE OF ARIZONA)
: ss CERTIFICATE BY CLERK
COUNTY OF PIMA)

I, the undersigned, as Clerk of the Superior Court of the State of Arizona, in and for the County of Pima, hereby certify that the within and foregoing Letters Fiduciary to be a full, true and correct copy thereof, issued in the above entitled matter, as the same remains of record and on file in the Office of said Clerk; I further certify that the said Letters have not been revoked and are in full force and effect.

IN WITNESS WHEREOF, I have hereunto set my hand and seal November 1964

FRANCES C. GIBBONS CLERK OF THE SUPERIOR COURT
BY DEPUTY CLERK

Pima County Bar Form No. T678

BOOK 342 PAGE 470

DAVID THOMAS LYLE STEPHENS GUARDIANSHIP

116. Catalina Nicole Stephens, birth certificate, Registrar, Arizona Department of Health Services.

CATALINA NICOLE STEPHENS
BIRTH CERTIFICATE

117. Jacqueline Joan McClelland, birth certificate, Registrar, California Department of Public Health, San Diego, California.

JACQUELINE JOAN McCLELLAND BIRTH CERTIFICATE

118. John Benjamin Priser, birth certificate, Registrar, Colorado Bureau of Vital Statistics.

JOHN BENJAMIN PRISER BIRTH CERTIFICATE

119. Article, August 27, 1958, *Albuquerque Journal*, John Priser family bound for Argentina.

120. Jacqueline Joan Priser, death certificate, Registrar, Arizona Department of Health Services.

JACQUELINE JOAN PRISER DEATH CERTIFICATE

Appendix

121. Jacqueline Joan Priser, obituary, January 18, 1987, Flagstaff newspaper.

122. John Benjamin Priser, death certificate, Registrar, Arizona Department of Health Services.

JOHN BENJAMIN PRISER DEATH CERTIFICATE

123. Article, Flagstaff newspaper, Michael Priser receiving Eagle Scout Award.

124. Susan Jean Priser, birth certificate, Registrar, Arizona Department of Health Services.

SUSAN JEAN PRISER BIRTH CERTIFICATE

125. Susan Jean Priser and Franciscus Xaverius Prins, marriage certificate, Magistrate, Stellenbosch, Republic of South Africa.

126. Adrian Gonzales, birth record, Arizona Department of Health Services.

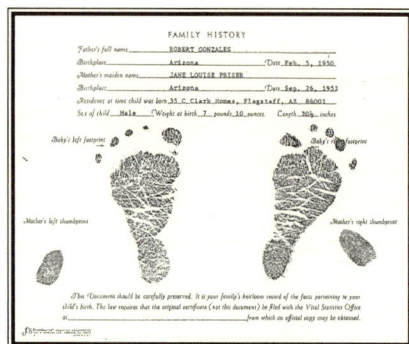

ADRIAN GONZALES BIRTH RECORD

127. Patricia Jo Priser, birth certificate, Good Samaritan Hospital, Dayton, Ohio.

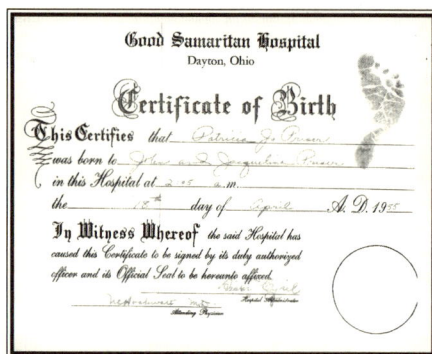

PATRICIA JO PRISER BIRTH CERTIFICATE

128. Patricia Jo Priser and Thomas David Hoisch, marriage certificate, Clerk of the Court, Yavapai County, Arizona.

129. David James Priser and Valerie Jean Sterling, marriage certificate, Clerk of the Court, Mohave County, Arizona.

CHAPTER IV

Susan McClelland

1. Susan McClelland and James Bradford, marriage certificate, General Registry Office, Dublin, Ireland.

2. Census of Ireland, 1901, Susan McClelland and James Bradford, National Archives of Ireland, Dublin, Ireland.

3. Susan McClelland Bradford, death certificate, General Registry Office, Belfast, Northern Ireland.

SUSAN McCLELLAND BRADFORD DEATH CERTIFICATE

CHAPTER V

George McClelland

1. Census of Lawrence County, Pennsylvania, 1920, George and Adeline McClelland, daughter, Alice and son-in-law Eugene Johnson residing.

2. George McClelland, obituary, July 28, 1927, *New Castle News*, New Castle, Pennsylvania.

3. Adeline L. McClelland, obituary, July 24, 1931, *New Castle News*, New Castle, Pennsylvania.

4. Alice J. McClelland and Eugene J. Johnson, marriage certificate, LDS Family History Library, Salt Lake City, Utah.

CHAPTER VI

Alex McClelland

1. Alex McClelland, obituary, November 25, 1912, *New Castle News*, New Castle, Pennsylvania.

2. Mary Virginia McClelland, obituary, January 4, 1936, *New Castle News*, New Castle, Pennsylvania.

3. Mrs. George H. Park, obituary, September 1946, newspaper, Youngstown, Ohio.

4. Mr. George H. Park, obituary, newspaper, Youngstown, Ohio.

5. Notice from War Department, January 30, 1919, Adjutant General's Office, Washington, D.C., death of Paul McClelland Park.

6. Graveside Memorial, Commercy, France, January 30, 1919, death of Paul McClelland Park.

7. Goldstar Mother Recognition to Eva Park from Lt. Frederick Kahn Auxillary, V.F.W. Post 1423, Youngstown, Ohio.

8. Margaret Park Schultz, obituary, August 2, 1959, *Vindicator*, Youngstown, Ohio.

9. George P. Schultz and Althea L. Leonhart, wedding announcement, newspaper, Youngstown, Ohio.

10. Infant Schultz, obituary, newspaper, Youngstown, Ohio.

11. Article, newspaper, Youngstown, Ohio, George Schultz receives State Architect Certificate.

12. Virginia Park, birth certificate, Clerk of Probate Court, Mahoning County, State of Ohio.

CERTIFIED COPY OF BIRTH RECORD

THE STATE OF OHIO, Mahoning County, ss: PROBATE COURT
Date of Record July 7 1907 No. 75
Name in Full Virginia Park
Date of Birth—Year, 1906, Month August, Day 23
Place of Birth
State Ohio, County Mahoning
City Youngstown, Town
Township
Sex Female Color White
Name of Father Geo. H. Park
Maiden Name of Mother Eva M. McClelland
Residence of Parents 135 Williamson

VIRGINIA PARK BIRTH CERTIFICATE

13. Virginia Hale Park and Marion Herbert Swager, marriage certificate, Clerk of Orphan's Court, Mercer County, Pennsylvania.

14. Marion Herbert Swager, birth certificate, Clerk of Probate Court, Trumbull County, State of Ohio.

CERTIFICATION OF BIRTH

The State of Ohio, Trumbull County. Probate Court
Date of Record June 18 A.D. 1956
No. 5541
Name in Full Marion Herbert Swager
Date of Birth—Year 1906, Month January, Day 21st
Place of Birth—State Ohio, County Trumbull
City, Town or Township Warren
Sex male

MARION HERBERT SWAGER BIRTH CERTIFICATE

15. Virginia and Marion Swager/Alice and Warren Swager, Golden Wedding Anniversary announcement.

589

16. Virginia Park Swager, death certificate, Deputy Registrar, Sheridan, Montana.

VIRGINIA PARK SWAGER
DEATH CERTIFICATE

17. Virginia Park Swager, obituary, December 25, 1997, *The Madisonian*.

18. Margaret K. McClelland, obituary, April 10, 1902, *New Castle News*, New Castle, Pennsylvania.

19. Grace F. McClelland, obituary, February 28, 1949, *New Castle News*, New Castle, Pennsylvania.

CHAPTER VII

Lucy McClelland

1. Lucy McClelland, obituary, April 23, 1872, *Newry Reporter*, Newry, Co. Down, Ireland.

2. Lucy McClelland, death certificate, General Registry Office, Belfast, Ireland.

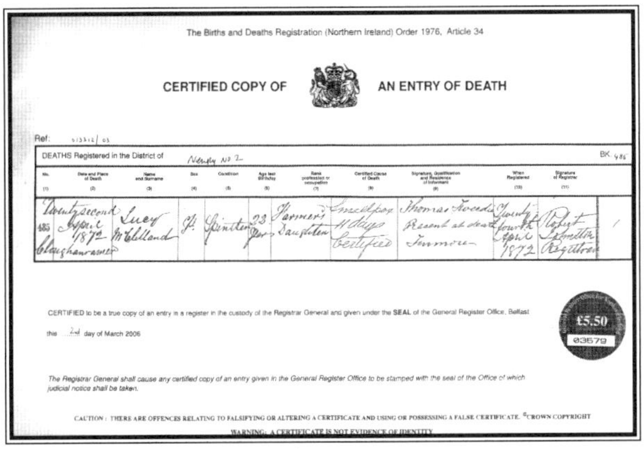

The Births and Deaths Registration (Northern Ireland) Order 1976, Article 34

CERTIFIED COPY OF AN ENTRY OF DEATH

Ref: 013312/03

DEATHS Registered in the District of Newry No 2 BK. 485

No. (1)	Date and Place of Death (2)	Name and Surname (3)	Sex (4)	Condition (5)	Age last Birthday (6)	Rank profession or occupation (7)	Certified Cause of Death (8)	Signature, Qualification and Residence of Informant (9)	When Registered (10)	Signature of Registrar (11)
485	Twentysecond April 1872 Cloghanramer	Lucy McClelland	F.	Spinster	23 Years	Farmer's Daughter	Smallpox 11 days Certified	Thomas [illegible] Present at death [illegible]	Twenty fourth April 1872	Robert [illegible] Registrar

CERTIFIED to be a true copy of an entry in a register in the custody of the Registrar General and given under the SEAL of the General Register Office, Belfast

this 2nd day of March 2006

£5.50 03579

The Registrar General shall cause any certified copy of an entry given in the General Register Office to be stamped with the seal of the Office of which judicial notice shall be taken.

CAUTION: THERE ARE OFFENCES RELATING TO FALSIFYING OR ALTERING A CERTIFICATE AND USING OR POSSESSING A FALSE CERTIFICATE. ©CROWN COPYRIGHT

WARNING: A CERTIFICATE IS NOT EVIDENCE OF IDENTITY

Lucy McClelland Death Certificate

CHAPTER VIII

Matilda McClelland

1. Matilda McClelland, death certificate, General Registry Office, Belfast, Ireland.

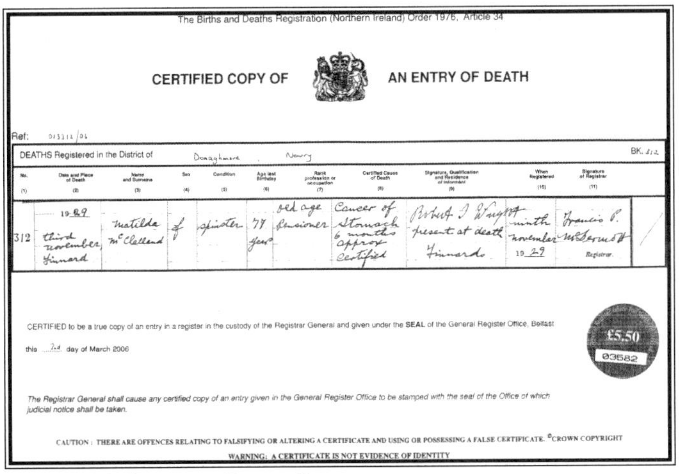

The Births and Deaths Registration (Northern Ireland) Order 1976, Article 34

CERTIFIED COPY OF AN ENTRY OF DEATH

Ref: 013311/06

DEATHS Registered in the District of Donaghmore, Newry BK. 312

No. (1)	Date and Place of Death (2)	Name and Surname (3)	Sex (4)	Condition (5)	Age last Birthday (6)	Rank profession or occupation (7)	Certified Cause of Death (8)	Signature, Qualification and Residence of Informant (9)	When Registered (10)	Signature of Registrar (11)
312	1929 third november, Finnard	Matilda McClelland	F	spinster	77 years	old age pensioner	Cancer of Stomach 6 months approx certified	Robert J Wright present at death Finnards	ninth november 1929	Francis P. McDermott Registrar

CERTIFIED to be a true copy of an entry in a register in the custody of the Registrar General and given under the SEAL of the General Register Office, Belfast

this 2nd day of March 2006

£5.50 03582

The Registrar General shall cause any certified copy of an entry given in the General Register Office to be stamped with the seal of the Office of which judicial notice shall be taken.

CAUTION: THERE ARE OFFENCES RELATING TO FALSIFYING OR ALTERING A CERTIFICATE AND USING OR POSSESSING A FALSE CERTIFICATE. ©CROWN COPYRIGHT

WARNING: A CERTIFICATE IS NOT EVIDENCE OF IDENTITY

Matilda McClelland Death Certificate

2. Matilda McClelland, obituary, November 7, 1929, *Newry Reporter*, Newry, Co. Down, Northern Ireland.

CHAPTER IX

Esther McClelland

1. Esther McClelland, death certificate, General Registry Office, Belfast, Northern Ireland.

ESTHER McCLELLAND DEATH CERTIFICATE

CHAPTER X

David McClelland

1. David McClelland, death certificate, General Registry Office, Belfast, Northern Ireland.

DAVID McCLELLAND DEATH CERTIFICATE

ILLUSTRATIⵙNS

Illustrations

THE McCLELLANDS OF CLOUGHENRAMER INDEX

Note: *italic* page numbers indicate pictures or illustrations.

and Kenneth Brady, 201

and Robert Samuel (Sam) Wright, , 163, 166, 170

and Robert W. Wright, 230, 231

S

Schaaf, Francine Jane. *See* McClelland, Francine Jane Schaaf

Schuerman, Jean Parker, *333*

Schultz, Althea L. Leonhart, 500–501, *501*

death of baby, 501

Schultz, Christian, 498–499, *498*, *499*

Schultz, George Park, 499, *499*, 500–501, *500*, *502*

death of baby, 501

state architect certificate, *502*

Schultz, Margaret Park, 494, 495, 498–499, *498*, *499*, 505

obituary, 499

Schweer, Carol. *See* Anderson, Carol Schweer

Schweer, Leona Cook. *See* Turner, Leona Cook Schweer

Schweer, Otto, 148

Searle, David, *264*, 265–266

Searle, Emily Louise, *264*, 266, 267

Searle, Jane Elizabeth Wright, 247, *249*, *261*, 264–266, *264*, 267

Searle, Lydia Catherine, *264*, 266, 267

Settlemyer, Mary Salome. *See* McClelland, Mary Salome Settlemyer

Shamrock Dairy, 325–326, 339

and Frances McClelland, 32

and Kathe McClelland, 347

and Kent McClelland, 353

and Norman McClelland, 339, *340–341*

and Sara Winifred Parker, 322

and University of Arizona, 328

Shear, Keeley Crystal Willert, 443, 444–446

birth certificate, *580*

photos, *437*, *440*, *443*, *444*, *445*, *446*, *448*

Shear, Marta and Richard, 446

Shear, William Scovel (Billy), 443, 445–446, *445*, *446*, *448*

Shirey, Maxine. *See* Bacon, Maxine Shirey Underwood

Shirey, Ralph, 86

Short, Patricia Jacqueline. *See* McClelland, Patricia Jacqueline Short

Sikora, Barbara, *307*

Singleton, Margaret. *See* Irwin, Margaret Singleton

Sloan, R., 162

Smith, A.W., 320, 324, *324*

census record, *571*

Smith, Bessie. *See* Davis, Elizabeth L. Smith (Bessie)

Smith, Brent, 353

Smith, Elizabeth (Smithy), 320, 323, 324, *324*

census record, *571*

Smith, Michelle, 353

Smith, Rawlen T., 353

Smith, Sarah Ann, 324

Somauroo, Adam, *273*, 276, *277*, 278

Somauroo, Kahlil, *273*, 276, *277*, 278

Somauroo, Margaret Mary Wright, 272,

at Matilda McClelland's cottage, *246*

at McClelland homestead, *158*

memories of Matilda McClelland, 511

Vallance, Pauline Mary. *See* McElhill, Pauline Mary Vallance

Vallance, Robert Climie, 293, 297, *298*

Von Kleinschmidt, President, 432

W

Waddell, Bob, *327*

Waddell, Frances, *327*

Waddell, Jim, *327*

Waddell, Kathleen, *327*

Wainwright, Anne. *See* McClelland, Anne Wainwright

Wainwright, Ruth Strain, *102*

Waldorf, Fred, 507

Warren, Nicola. *See* Worthington, Nicola Warren

Watson, Brian David, 198–199

Watson, Emma Victoria, 199, *199*

Watson, Jennifer Lynn Brady, 197, 198–199, *198*

Watson, Sophie Alexandra, 199, *199*

Webb, Alison Grace Brady, 202, 207–208, *207, 208, 209*

Webb, Holly Rebekah, 207, 209, *209*

Webb, Lucinda Joanne. *See* Browne, Lucinda Joanne Webb

Webb, Max Daniel, 207, 209, *209*

Webb, Stephen, 207–208, *208, 209*

White, Sarah (Sadie). *See* Adams, Sarah White (Sadie)

Whiteside, Peter, *184*

Widdows, Claire Alexandra McConville, 250, *255, 257–258, 258*

Widdows, Nick John, 258, *258*

Willert, Alissa Beth, 443, 449–450

birth certificate, *581*

photos, *437, 443, 444, 446, 447, 448, 450*

Willert, Ann Elizabeth Stephens, 436, 442–443, 450, 451

birth certificate, *580*

marriage certificate, *442*

photos, *437, 442, 443, 444, 446, 448*

Willert, Cecilia, 442

Willert, Emily Mae Ingham, 447–448, *448*

Willert, Keeley Crystal. *See* Shear, Keeley Crystal Willert

Willert, Kent Christian, 443, 447–448

birth certificate, *581*

photos, *441, 443, 444, 446, 447, 448*

Willert, Richard Raymond, 442–443, 451

marriage certificate, *442*

photos, *442, 443, 444, 445, 446, 447, 448*

Willert, Will, 442

Willis, Edna Rosemary. *See* Dunlop, Rosemary

Wilson, Allan, *33, 34, 34*

Wilson, Angus, 212, *213,* 214

Wilson, Annabel Emily Rose, 212, *213,* 214, *216*

Wilson, Carla Tighe, 214–215, *215*

Wilson, Ellie Rose, *213,* 219, *219,* 220

Wilson, Euan, *33, 34, 34,* 35

Wilson, Isaac Michael, 219, *219,* 220

Wilson, Jennifer Ruth, *33, 34, 34,* 35